The Complete Wales FC 1876-2020

Dirk Karsdorp

British Library Cataloguing in Publication Data
A catalogue record for this book is available from the British Library

ISBN 978-1-86223-443-7

Copyright © 2020, SOCCER BOOKS LIMITED. (01472 696226)
72 St. Peter's Avenue, Cleethorpes, N.E. Lincolnshire, DN35 8HU, England

All rights are reserved. No part of this publication may be reproduced, stored in a retrieval system or transmitted, in any form or by any means, electronic, mechanical, photocopying, recording, or otherwise, without the prior written permission of Soccer Books Limited.

Printed in the UK by Severn

FOREWORD

Three years ago we published a book covering the international games played by Wales from their very first international match against Scotland in 1876 through to 2017. This new edition brings these statistics right up to date to the end of 2020 and, as before, lists full team line-ups and goalscorers for both Wales and their opponents.

Only officially-recognised full international games are included in this book and other titles updated to 2020 in this series are also available for England, Scotland, Northern Ireland and the Republic of Ireland. We have also published new books containing complete statistics for the international matches of Belgium, Italy and the Netherlands.

Although we have endeavoured to include statistics which are as complete as possible, inevitably there are omissions with one or two small pieces of information missing for a handful of games. Most notably, the times at which goals were scored were not recorded for a number of the earliest games although the goalscorers themselves are known. In such cases, the following symbol has been used to indicate that the time of the goal is not known: "#".

1. 25.03.1876
SCOTLAND v WALES 4-0 (1-0)

Hamilton Crescent, Partick

Referee: Robert Gardner (Scotland)   Attendance: 17,000

SCOTLAND: Alexander McGeoch, Joseph Taylor, Robert W. Neill, Alexander Kennedy, Charles Campbell (Cap), Thomas Cochrane Highet, John Ferguson, James Lang, William MacKinnon, Moses McLay McNeil, Henry McNeil

WALES: David Thomson, William Addams Williams Evans, Samuel Llewelyn Kenrick (Cap), Edwin Alfred Cross, William Williams, Dr. Daniel Grey, William Henry Davies, George Frederick Thomson, John Hawley Edwards, John Jones, Alfred Davies.

Goals: John Ferguson (40), James Lang (48), William MacKinnon (53), Henry McNeil (70)

2. 05.03.1877
WALES v SCOTLAND 0-2 (0-0)

The Racecourse, Wrexham

Referee: William Dick (Scotland)   Attendance: 4,000

WALES: Thomas Blundell Burnett, William Evans, Samuel Llewelyn Kenrick (Cap), John Richard Morgan, Edwin Alfred Cross, William Henry Davies, Alfred Davies, John Henry Price, Alexander Fletcher Jones, John Hughes, George Frederick Thomson.

SCOTLAND: Alexander McGeoch, Robert Neill, Thomas Vallance, James Phillips, Charles Campbell (Cap), John Smith, John McGregor, John Ferguson, John McDougall, Henry McNeil, John Hunter.

Goals: Charles Campbell (55), William Evans (75 own goal)

3. 23.03.1878
SCOTLAND v WALES 9-0 (6-0)

1st Hampden Park, Glasgow

Referee: Robert Gardner (Scotland)   Attendance: 6,000

SCOTLAND: Robert Parlane, James Duncan, Robert Neill (Cap), James Phillips, David Davidson, John Ferguson, John Campbell Baird, James Lang, James Begg Weir, James A.K. Watson, Peter Campbell.

WALES: Edward Phennah, George Garnet Higham (Cap), John Powell, Henry Valentine Edwards, William Williams, George Foulkes Savin, James Davies, Daniel Grey, Thomas Johnson Britten, John Henry Price, Charles Edwards.

Goals: Peter Campbell (4, 18), James Begg Weir (15, 42), John Campbell Baird (37), John Ferguson (38, 50), James A.K. Watson (60), James Lang (70)

4. 18.01.1879
ENGLAND v WALES 2-1 (2-0)

Kennington Oval, London

Referee: Richard Segal Bastard (England)   Att: 2000

ENGLAND: Rupert Darnley Anderson, Lindsay Bury, Claude William Wilson, Norman Coles Bailey, William Edwin Clegg, Edward Hagarty Parry, Thomas Heathcote Sorby, Arthur William Cursham (Cap), Henry Wace, William Mosforth, Herbert Whitfeld.

WALES: George William Glascodine, Samuel Llewelyn Kenrick (Cap), George Garnet Higham, William Williams, Thomas Owen, William Henry Davies, Watkin William Shone, Dennis Heywood, John Henry Price, William Digby Owen, William Roberts.

Goals: Herbert Whitfeld (8), Thomas Heathcote Sorby (20) / William Henry Davies (45)

This was was played as two halves of 30 minutes each due to the very bad weather conditions.

5. 07.04.1879
WALES v SCOTLAND 0-3 (0-1)

The Racecourse, Wrexham

Referee: John W.A. Cooper (Wales)   Attendance: 2,000

WALES: John Davies, Samuel Llewelyn Kenrick (Cap), John Richard Morgan, Knyvett Crosse, William Williams, James William Lloyd, George Woosnam, John Hughes, John Roberts, William Roberts, John Vaughan.

SCOTLAND: Robert Parlane, Thomas Vallance, William Somers, John Campbell McLeod McPherson, David Davidson, Henry McNeil, John McDougall (Cap), Peter Campbell, Robert Paton, William Wightman Beveridge, Dr. John Smith.

Goals: Peter Campbell (34), John Smith 2 (60, 70)

6. 15.03.1880
WALES v ENGLAND 2-3 (0-0)

The Racecourse, Wrexham

Referee: Robert Lythgoe (England)   Attendance: 3,000

WALES: Harold Hibbott, John Richard Morgan (Cap), John Powell, Henry Valentine Edwards, William Williams, William Pierce Owen, William Henry Davies, Thomas Boden, John Henry Price, John Roberts, William Roberts.

ENGLAND: John Sands, Edwin Luntley, Thomas Brindle, John Hunter, Frederick William Hargreaves, Thomas Marshall, Henry Alfred Cursham, Francis John Sparks (Cap), Clement Mitchell, Edward Johnson, William Mosforth.

Goals: John Roberts (74), William Roberts (85) / Francis John Sparks (50, 70), Thomas Brindle (55)

7. 27.03.1880
SCOTLAND v WALES 5-1 (2-0)

1st Hampden Park, Glasgow

Referee: Alexander Stuart (Scotland)   Attendance: 2,000

SCOTLAND: George Gillespie, William Somers, Archibald Lang, David Davidson (Cap), Hugh McIntyre, James Douglas, James McAdam, Malcolm James Eadie Fraser, Joseph Lindsay, John Campbell, William Wightman Beveridge

WALES: Harold Hibbott, John Richard Morgan (Cap), John Powell, Edward Bowen, Henry Valentine Edwards, William Pierce Owen, William Roberts, John Roberts, John Henry Price, Thomas Johnson Britten, John Vaughan.

Goals: David Davidson (38), William Beveridge (40), Joseph Lindsay (50), James McAdam (55), John Campbell (60) / William Roberts (85)

8. 26.02.1881
ENGLAND v WALES 0-1 (0-0)

Alexandra Meadows, Blackburn

Referee: Richard Segal Bastard (England)   Att: 3000

ENGLAND: John Purvis Hawtrey, Alfred Harvey, Arthur Leopold Bambridge, John Hunter (Cap), Frederick William Hargreaves, Thomas Marshall, Tot Rostron, James Brown, George Tait, John Hargreaves, William Mosforth.

WALES: Robert McMillan, John Richard Morgan (Cap), Samuel Llewelyn Kenrick, William Stafford Bell, William Williams, William Pierce Owen, Thomas Lewis, Knyvett Crosse, John Henry Price, Uriah Goodwin, John Vaughan.

Goal: John Vaughan (34)

9. 14.03.1881
WALES v SCOTLAND 1-5 (1-4)

The Racecourse, Wrexham

Referee: Samuel Llewelyn Kenrick (Wales)   Att: 1,500

WALES: Robert McMillan, John Richard Morgan (Cap), John Roberts, William Stafford Bell, William Williams, William Pierce Owen, Thomas Lewis, Knyvett Crosse, John Henry Price, William Roberts, John Vaughan.

SCOTLAND: George Gillespie, Andrew Watson, Thomas C. Vallance, John Campbell McLeod McPherson, David Davidson (Cap), William McGuire, David Hill, George Ker, Joseph Lindsay, Henry McNeil, John Smith

Goals: Knyvett Crosse (5) / George Ker (7, 44), Henry McNeil (9), William Stafford Bell (10 own goal), John Richard Morgan (52 own goal)

10. 25.02.1882
WALES v IRELAND 7-1 (4-1)

The Racecourse, Wrexham

Referee: Robert Lythgoe (England)   Attendance: 2,000

WALES: Harry Adams, John Richard Morgan (Cap), John Powell, Frederick William Hughes, William Williams, William Pierce Owen, Edward Gough Shaw, Charles Frederick Ketley, John Henry Price, John Roberts, John Vaughan.

IRELAND: James Hamilton, William Crone, John McAlery (Cap), Donald Martin, John Hastings, John Robert Davison, William McWha, John Condy, John Sinclair, Alex Dill, Samuel Johnston.

Goals: John Richard Morgan (10), John Price (#, #, #, #), William Pierce Owen (#, #) / Samuel Johnston (20)

11. 13.03.1882
WALES v ENGLAND 5-3 (1-3)

The Racecourse, Wrexham

Referee: Morgan Roberts (England)   Attendance: 5,000

WALES: Harry Adams, John Richard Morgan (Cap), John Powell, Henry Valentine Edwards, Frederick William Hughes, William Williams, William Pierce Owen, Walter Hugh Roberts, John Henry Price, John Roberts, John Vaughan.

ENGLAND: Harry Albemarle Swepstone, John Hunter, Alfred Jones, Norman Coles Bailey (Cap), Edward Charles Bambridge, Edward Hagarty Parry, Henry Alfred Cursham, Percival Chase Parr, Arthur Brown, Oliver Howard Vaughton, William Mosforth.

Goals: William Pierce Owen (32, 87), John Morgan (50), Alfred Jones (60 own goal), John Vaughan (89) / William Mosforth (30), Edward Hagarty Parry (35), Henry Alfred Cursham (48)

12. 25.03.1882
SCOTLAND v WALES 5-0 (1-0)

First Hampden Park, Glasgow

Referee: Donald Hamilton (Scotland)   Attendance: 5,000

SCOTLAND: Archibald Rowan (Cap), Andrew Hair Holm, James Duncan, Charles Campbell, Alexander Kennedy, Malcolm James Eadie Fraser, David Hill, George Ker, James McAulay, John Leck Kay, James Tassie Richmond

WALES: Henry Phoenix, John Richard Morgan (Cap), John Powell, Henry Valentine Edwards, William Williams, John Roberts, William Pierce Owen, Walter Hugh Roberts, John Henry Price, John Roberts, John Vaughan.

Goals: John Leck Kay (25), George Ker (50), Malcolm James Eadie Fraser (60, 70), James McAulay (88)

13. 03.02.1883
ENGLAND v WALES 5-0 (2-0)

Kennington Oval, London

Referee: Donald Hamilton (Scotland)   Attendance: 2,000

ENGLAND: Harry Albemarle Swepstone, Percy John de Paravincini, Bruce Bremner Russell, Norman Coles Bailey (Cap), Stuart Macrae, Arthur William Cursham, Arthur Leopold Bambridge, Clement Mitchell, Harry Chester Goodhart, Henry Alfred Cursham, Edward Charles Bambridge.

WALES: Harry Adams, John Richard Morgan, John Powell (Cap), Thomas Burke, Frederick William Hughes, Walter Hugh Roberts, William Pierce Owen, John Price Davies, William Roberts, John Roberts, John Vaughan.

Goals: Clement Mitchell (16, 70, 86), Edward Bambridge (43), Arthur William Cursham (65)

14. 12.03.1883
WALES v SCOTLAND 0-3 (0-2)

The Racecourse, Wrexham

Referee: Robert Lythgoe (England)   Attendance: 2,000

WALES: Richard Thomas Gough, Frederick William Hughes, John Powell (Cap), Edward Bowen, Henry Valentine Edwards, John Jones, William Pierce Owen, Walter Hugh Roberts, John Henry Price, William Roberts, John Vaughan.

SCOTLAND: James McAulay, Andrew Hair Holm (Cap), Walter Arnott, Peter Miller, John Campbell McLeod McPherson, Malcolm James Eadie Fraser, William Anderson, John Smith, John Inglis, John Leck Kay, William Neilson McKinnon.

Goals: John Smith (35), Malcolm James Eadie Fraser (38), William Anderson (60)

15. 17.03.1883
IRELAND v WALES 1-1 (0-0)

Ulster Cricket Ground, Ballynafeigh, Belfast

Referee: John McDowell (Scotland)   Attendance: 1,000

IRELAND: James Rankin, James Watson, David Rattray, Thomas Molyneux, John Hastings, William Morrow, Renwick Potts, William McWha, John Robert Davison (Cap), Ned Spiller, Alex Dill.

WALES: Harry Adams, Frederick William Hughes, John Powell (Cap), John Price Davies, William Williams, John Jones I, Robert Davies, Walter Hugh Roberts, John Henry Price, John Arthur Eyton-Jones, John Vaughan

Goals: William Morrow (67) / Walter Hugh Roberts (50)

16. 09.02.1884   British Championship
WALES v IRELAND 6-0 (1-0)

The Racecourse, Wrexham

Referee: Robert Sloan (England)   Attendance: 2,000

WALES: Elias Owen, Charles Conde, Walter Davies, William Tanat Foulkes, Peter Griffiths, Henry Valentine Edwards, William Pierce Owen (Cap), Robert Davies, Edward Gough Shaw, John Arthur Eyton-Jones, Robert Albert Jones.

IRELAND: Robert John Hunter, Matt Wilson, William Crone, Thomas Molyneux, Henry Lockhart, Robert Redmond, John Robert Davison (Cap), John Gibb, John Reid, Ned Spiller, Alex Dill.

Goals: Edward Shaw (20, 68), William Pierce Owen (55, 70), Robert Albert Jones (59), John Arthur Eyton-Jones (82)

17. 17.03.1884   British Championship
WALES v ENGLAND 0-4 (0-1)

The Racecourse, Wrexham

Referee: Sydney Broadfoot (Scotland)   Attendance: 4,500

WALES: Elias Owen, John Powell (Cap), Charles Conde, Maurice John Evans, Peter Griffiths, Joseph Henry Williams, William Pierce Owen, John Arthur Eyton-Jones, William Owen, John Vaughan, Robert Albert Jones.

ENGLAND: William Crispin Rose, Alfred Thomas Carrick Dobson, Joseph Beverley, Norman Coles Bailey (Cap), James Henry Forrest, Charles Plumpton Wilson, George Holden, Oliver Howard Vaughton, William Bromley-Davenport, William Gunn, Edward Charles Bambridge.

Goals: William Bromley-Davenport (7, 85), Norman Coles Bailey (75), William Gunn (90)

18. 29.03.1884
SCOTLAND v WALES 4-1 (1-1)

Cathkin Park, Glasgow

Referee: Robert Sloan (England)   Attendance: 5,000

SCOTLAND: Thomas Turner, Michael Paton (Cap), John Forbes, Alexander Kennedy, James McIntyre, Robert Brown, Francis Watson Shaw, Samuel Thomson, Joseph Lindsay, John Leck Kay, William Neilson McKinnon

WALES: Elias Owen, Robert Roberts, Charles Conde, Frederick William Hughes, Thomas Burke, John Jones, William Pierce Owen (Cap), Walter Hugh Roberts, Edward Gough Shaw, John Arthur Eyton-Jones, Robert Albert Jones.

Goals: Joseph Lindsay (22), Francis Watson Shaw (49), John Leck Kay (65, 87) / Robert Roberts (15)

19. 14.03.1885   British Championship
ENGLAND v WALES 1-1 (1-1)
Leamington Road, Blackburn

Referee: Alexander Stuart (Scotland)   Attendance: 7,500

ENGLAND: William John Herbert Arthur, Henry Thomas Moore, James Thomas Ward, Norman Coles Bailey (Cap), James Henry Forrest, Joseph Morris Lofthouse, James Kenneth Davenport, James Brown, Clement Mitchell, John Augur Dixon, Edward Charles Bambridge.

WALES: Robert Herbert Mills-Roberts, Frederick Robert Jones, George Thomas, Robert Davies, Humphrey Jones (Cap), Thomas Burke, John Edward Davies, Thomas Vaughan, George Farmer, William Lewis, Job Wilding.

Goal: Clement Mitchell (35) / Job Wilding (37)

20. 23.03.1885
WALES v SCOTLAND 1-8 (0-3)
The Racecourse, Wrexham

Referee: Robert Sloan (England)   Attendance: 2,000

WALES: Dr. Robert Herbert Mills-Roberts, George Thomas, Seth Powell, Thomas Burke, William Tanat Foulkes, Humphrey Jones (Cap), James William Lloyd, Job Wilding, Harold Hibbott, George Farmer, Robert Albert Jones.

SCOTLAND: James McAulay, Walter Arnott, Michael Paton (Cap), Robert Robinson Kelso, Leitch Keir, Alexander Hamilton, William Anderson, Joseph Lindsay, Robert Calderwood, Robert Brown, David Steel Allan

Goals: Robert Albert Jones (50) / Robert Calderwood (8, 80), William Anderson (20, 76), David Steel Allan (30), Joseph Lindsay (56, 84, 88)

21. 11.04.1885.   British Championship
IRELAND v WALES 2-8 (2-0)
Ulster Cricket Ground, Ballynafeigh, Belfast

Referee: John McDowell (Scotland)   Attendance: 1,500

IRELAND: Anthony Henderson, William Johnston, William Eames (Cap), Thomas Molyneux, Robert Muir, William McWha, William James Hamilton, William Drummond Hamilton, John Gibb, George McGee, Alex Dill.

WALES: Robert Herbert Mills-Roberts, Frederick Robert Jones, Alfred Owen Davies, Thomas Burke, John Owen Vaughan, Humphrey Jones (Cap), Robert Davies, William Owen, Job Wilding, Herbert Sisson, John Roach

Goals: Thomas Molyneux (23), Alex Dill (40) / William Owen (50), Thomas Burke (52), Herbert Sisson (55, 59, 60), John Roach (64, 89), Humphrey Jones (69)

22. 27.02.1886   British Championship
WALES v IRELAND 5-0 (1-0)
The Racecourse, Wrexham

Referee: Richard Gregson (England)   Attendance: 700

WALES: Albert Malcolm Hersee, Robert Roberts, Seth Powell, John Owen Vaughan, William Stafford Bell, Humphrey Jones (Cap), William Roberts, Job Wilding, Richard Hersee, Herbert Sisson, Thomas Bryan.

IRELAND: Shaw Gillespie, Edward R.Whitfield, James Watson (Cap), Thomas Molyneux, William Crone, Alexander McArthur, John McClatchey, James Williams, Richard Henry Smyth, John Lemon, Edward Roper.

Goals: William Roberts (#), Job Wilding (#), Richard Hersee (#), Thomas Bryan (#), Herbert Sisson (#)

23. 29.03.1886   British Championship
WALES v ENGLAND 1-3 (1-0)
The Racecourse, Wrexham

Referee: Stewart Lawrie (Scotland)   Attendance: 5,000

WALES: Dr.Robert Herbert Mills-Roberts, Dr. Alfred Owen Davies, Seth Powell, John Owen Vaughan, William Stafford Bell, Humphrey Jones (Cap), Job Wilding, William Roberts, Thomas Davies, Thomas Bryan, William Lewis.

ENGLAND: William John Herbert Arthur, Ralph Tyndall Squire, Percy Melmoth Walters, Norman Coles Bailey (Cap), Andrew Amos, James Henry Forrest, Frederick Dewhurst, George Brann, Tinsley Lindley, William Nevill Cobbold, Edward Charles Bambridge.

Goals: William Lewis (43) / Frederick Dewhurst (70), Tinsley Lindley (74), Edward Charles Bambridge (#)

24. 10.04.1886   British Championship
SCOTLAND v WALES 4-1 (1-0)
First Hampden Park, Glasgow

Referee: John Sinclair (Ireland)   Attendance: 35500

SCOTLAND: George Gillespie, James Lundie, William Semple (Cap), Robert Robinson Kelso, Andrew Jackson, John Marshall, Robert McCormick, James McGhee, William Harrower, David Steel Allan, James McCall.

WALES: Albert Malcolm Hersee, Dr. Alfred Owen Davies, Frederick Robert Jones, John Owen Vaughan, William Stafford Bell, Humphrey Jones (Cap), Richard Parry Williams, William Roberts, John Doughty, Herbert Sisson, William Lewis.

Goals: Robert McCormick (30), James McCall (47), David Steel Allan (53), William Harrower (56) / John Owen Vaughan (88)

25. 26.02.1887   British Championship
ENGLAND v WALES 4-0 (1-0)
Kennington Oval, London
Referee: Thomas Devlin (Scotland)   Attendance: 4,500
ENGLAND: William John Herbert Arthur, Percy Melmoth Walters, Arthur Melmoth Walters, George Haworth, Norman Coles Bailey (Cap), James Henry Forrest, Joseph Morris Lofthouse, Frederick Dewhurst, Tinsley Lindley, William Nevill Cobbold, Edward Charles Bambridge.
WALES: Dr.Robert Herbert Mills-Roberts, Dr. Alfred Owen Davies, John Powell, Thomas Burke, Humphrey Jones (Cap), Edward Clement Evelyn, William Owen, John Bonamy Challen, Job Wilding, William Haighton Turner, William Lewis.
Goals: William Cobbold (14, 75), Tinsley Lindley (55, 80)

26. 12.03.1887   British Championship
IRELAND v WALES 4-1 (2-0)
Oldpark Avenue, Belfast
Referee: James McKillop (Scotland)   Attendance: 4,000
IRELAND: Shaw Gillespie (Cap), Frederick Browne, James Watson, Joseph Sherrard, Archibald Rosbotham, Oliver Devine, Robert Moore, Robert Baxter, John Gibb, Olphert Stanfield, John Peden.
WALES: Robert Roberts, Alfred William Townsend, Samuel Jones, Henry Valentine Edwards (Cap), Alexander Hunter, Ernest Percival Whitley Hughes, Henry Wilmshurst Sabine, William Roberts, John Doughty, George Griffiths, William Haighton Turner.
Goals: Olphert Stanfield (20), Frederick Browne (44), John Peden (65), Joseph Sherrard (70) / Henry Wilmshurst Sabine (55)

27. 21.03.1887   British Championship
WALES v SCOTLAND 0-2 (0-1)
The Racecourse, Wrexham
Referee: Alfred Bertram Hall (England)   Attendance: 2,000
WALES: James Trainer, Dr. Alfred Owen Davies, John Powell (Cap), Robert Roberts, James Morris, Thomas Burke, John Bonamy Challen, Richard Owen Jones, William Ernest Pryce-Jones, William Lewis, John Doughty.
SCOTLAND: James McAulay (Cap), Walter Arnott, John Forbes, Robert Robinson Kelso, John Robertson Auld, Leitch Keir, John Marshall, William Robertson, William Sellar, James McCall, James Allan.
Goals: William Robertson (40), James Allan (80)

28. 04.02.1888   British Championship
ENGLAND v WALES 5-1 (1-1)
Nantwich Road, Crewe
Referee: John Sinclair (Ireland)   Attendance: 6,000
ENGLAND: William Robert Moon, Robert Henry Howarth, Charles Mason, Frank Etheridge Saunders, Henry Allen, Charles Henry Holden-White, George Woodhall, John Goodall, Tinsley Lindley (Cap), Frederick Dewhurst, Dennis Hodgetts.
WALES: Dr. Robert Herbert Mills-Roberts, Dr. Alfred Owen Davies (Cap), John Powell, Robert Roberts, Peter Griffiths, Joseph Davies, William Ernest Pryce-Jones, John Bonamy Challen, John Doughty, William Lewis, William Owen.
Goals: Frederick Dewhurst (15, 65, 88), George Woodhall (70), Tinsley Lindley (75) / John Doughty (17)

29. 03.03.1888   British Championship
WALES v IRELAND 11-0 (5-0)
The Racecourse, Wrexham
Referee: Thomas Hindle (England)   Attendance: 2,000
WALES: Robert Herbert Mills-Roberts, Dr. Alfred Owen Davies (Cap), John Powell, Reuben Humphreys, Joseph Davies, David Jones, William Ernest Pryce-Jones, Job Wilding, John Doughty, Edmund Gwynne Howell, Roger Doughty.
IRELAND: John Clugston, George Forbes, William Crone, Joseph Sherrard, Archibald Rosbotham, Oliver Devine, Arthur Gaussen, Olphert Stanfield (Cap), John Barry, James Wilton, John Peden.
Goals: John Doughty (#, #, #), Roger Doughty (#, #), Edmund Gwynne Howell (#, #), Job Wilding (#, #, #, #)

30. 10.03.1888   British Championship
SCOTLAND v WALES 5-1 (3-1)
Easter Road Park, Edinburgh
Referee: John Charles Clegg (England)   Attendance: 8,000
SCOTLAND: James Wilson, Andrew Hannah, Robert Smellie (Cap), James Johnstone, James McCrory Gourlay, James McLaren, Alexander Latta, William Groves, William Paul, John "Kitey" McPherson, Neil Munro.
WALES: James Trainer, David Jones, John Powell (Cap), Thomas Burke, Joseph Davies, Robert Roberts, William Ernest Pryce-Jones, Job Wilding, John Doughty, George Alfred Owen, Roger Doughty.
Goals: William Paul (6), Neil Munro (30), Alexander Latta (33, 75), William Groves (65) / John Doughty (41)

31. 23.02.1889   British Championship
ENGLAND v WALES 4-1 (1-1)
Victoria Ground, Stoke-on-Trent

Referee: John Campbell (Scotland)   Attendance: 6,000

ENGLAND: William Robert Moon, Arthur Melmoth Walters (Cap), Percy Melmoth Walters, Albert Thomas Fletcher, Arthur Lowder, William Betts, William Isaiah Bassett, John Goodall, John Southworth, Frederick Dewhurst, William John Townley.

WALES: James Trainer, William Jones, David Jones, Ernest Percival Whitley Hughes, Humphrey Jones (Cap), Robert Roberts, John Hallam, Richard Owen Jones, William Lewis, Arthur Lea, William Owen.

Goals: John Goodall (#), William Isaiah Bassett (65), Frederick Dewhurst (#), John Southworth (#) / William Owen (14)

32. 15.04.1899   British Championship
WALES v SCOTLAND 0-0
The Racecourse, Wrexham

Referee: John Sinclair (Ireland)   Attendance: 6,000

WALES: Allen Pugh (30 Samuel Gladstone Gillam), Dr. Alfred Owen Davies (Cap), David Jones, Robert Roberts, Joseph Davies, Humphrey Jones, Joseph Davies, William Owen, John Doughty, George Alfred Owen, William Lewis.

SCOTLAND: John McLeod, Andrew Thomson (Cap), James Rae, Allan Stewart, Alexander Lochhead, John Robertson Auld, Francis Watt, Henry Campbell, William Paul, William Johnstone, James Hannah.

33. 27.04.1889   British Championship
IRELAND v WALES 1-3 (1-2)
Ulster Cricket Ground, Ballynafeigh, Belfast

Referee: Thomas Park (Scotland)   Attendance: 1,500

IRELAND: John Clugston, Allan Elleman, James Watson, Alexander Crawford, Lionel Vaughan Bennett, John Reid, Arthur Gaussen, Olphert Stanfield (Cap), James Percy, John Lemon, John Gillespie.

WALES: Samuel Gladstone Gillam, William Jones, David Jones, Ernest Percival Whitley Hughes, Thomas Patrick McCarthy, Patrick Leary, Joseph Davies, William Owen (Cap), George Alfred Owen, Richard Henry Jarrett, William Lewis

Goals: Olphert Stanfield (10) / Richard Jarrett (20, 44, 60)

34. 08.02.1890   British Championship
WALES v IRELAND 5-2 (2-2)
Old Racecourse, Shrewsbury

Referee: James McKillop (Scotland)   Attendance: 3,000

WALES: Samuel Gladstone Gillam, Robert Lee Roberts, William Jones, Peter Griffiths, Abel Hayes, Humphrey Jones (Cap), David Morral Lewis, William Ernest Pryce-Jones, William Owen, Albert Richard Wilcock, John Charles Henry Bowdler.

IRELAND: William Gailbraith, Robert Crone, Robert Stewart, William Crone, John Reynolds, John Reid, William Dalton, George Gaffikin, Samuel Johnston, Samuel Torrans, John Peden.

Goals: William Owen (6), Albert Wilcock (27), David Morral Lewis (#), William Ernest Pryce-Jones (56, 90) / William Dalton (11, 44)

35. 15.03.1890   British Championship
WALES v ENGLAND 1-3 (1-0)
The Racecourse, Wrexham

Referee: James Walker (Scotland)   Attendance: 5,000

WALES: Samuel Gladstone Gillam, Dr. Alfred Owen Davies (Cap), David Jones, Joseph Davies, Humphrey Jones, Walter Gwynne Evans, John Bonamy Challen, Richard Owen Jones, John Doughty, Edmund Gwynne Howell, William Lewis.

ENGLAND: William Robert Moon, Arthur Melmoth Walters (Cap), Percy Melmoth Walters, Albert Thomas Fletcher, John Holt, Alfred Shelton, William Isaiah Bassett, Edward Samuel Currey, Tinsley Lindley, Henry Butler Daft, Harry Wood.

Goals: William Lewis (38) / Edward Samuel Currey (#, 49), Tinsley Lindley (#)

36. 22.03.1890   British Championship
SCOTLAND v WALES 5-0 (3-0)
Underwood Park, Paisley

Referee: William Finlay (Ireland)   Attendance: 7,500

SCOTLAND: George Gillespie (Cap), Andrew Whitelaw, John Winning Murray, Matthew McQueen, Andrew Brown, Hugh Wilson, J. Brown, Francis Watt, William Paul, James Dunlop, Daniel Bruce

WALES: James Trainer, William P. Jones, Samuel Jones, Peter Griffiths, Humphrey Jones (Cap), Robert Roberts, David Morral Lewis, Oswald Davies, William Owen, Richard Henry Jarrett, William Haighton Turner.

Goals: Hugh Wilson (20), William Paul (36, 43, 60, 70)

37. 07.02.1891 British Championship
IRELAND v WALES 7-2 (4-2)
Ulsterville, Belfast
Referee: Robert Harrison (Scotland)   Attendance: 6,000
IRELAND: John Clugston, Manliffe Fraser Goodbody, Robert Morrison, Alexander Crawford (Cap), John Reynolds, Richard Moore, William Dalton, George Gaffikin, Olphert Stanfield, Samuel Torrans, John Peden.
WALES: Richard E. Turner, Robert Roberts, Robert Arthur Lloyd, Peter Griffiths, John Mates, Arthur Lea, Joseph Davies, William Owen (Cap), Albert Thomas Davies, Benjamin Lewis, John Charles Henry Bowdler.
Goals: William Dalton (19), Olphert Stanfield (22, 34, 42, 80), George Gaffikin (60), Samuel Torrans (63) / Robert Roberts (10), Albert Thomas Davies (37)

38. 07.03.1891 British Championship
ENGLAND v WALES 4-1 (4-0)
Newcastle Road, Sunderland
Referee: Thomas Park (Scotland)   Attendance: 15,000
ENGLAND: Leonard Rodwell Wilkinson, Thomas Stoddard Porteous, Elphinstone Jackson, Albert Smith, John Holt, Alfred Shelton, George Brann, John Goodall (Cap), John Southworth, Alfred Weatherell Milward, Edgar Wallace Chadwick.
WALES: Richard Turner, Walter Gwynne Evans, Seth Powell, William Hughes, Humphrey Jones (Cap), Charles Frederick Parry, Joseph Davies, William Owen, William Haighton Turner, Edmund Gwynne Howell, William Lewis.
Goals: John Goodall (7), John Southworth (30), Edgar Wallace Chadwick (40), Alfred Weatherell Milward (43) / Edmund Gwynne Howell (84)

39. 21.03.1891 British Championship
WALES v SCOTLAND 3-4 (2-1)
The Racecourse, Wrexham
Referee: Charles Crump (England)   Attendance: 4,000
WALES: James Trainer, Seth Powell, David Jones, Arthur Lea, Humphrey Jones (Cap), Charles Frederick Parry, Joseph Davies, William Owen, William Haighton Turner, John Charles Henry Bowdler, William Lewis.
SCOTLAND: John McCorkindale, Archibald Ritchie, James Hepburn, Matthew McQueen, Andrew Brown, Thomas Robertson (Cap), William Gulliland, Robert Buchanan, James Logan, Robert Boyd, Alexander Lowson Keillor.
Goals: John Charles Henry Bowdler 2, William Owen (48) / Robert Boyd (15, 51), James Logan (59), Robert Buchanan (75)

40. 27.02.1892 British Championship
WALES v IRELAND 1-1 (1-0)
Penrhyn Park, Bangor
Referee: James Campbell (Scotland)   Attendance: 4,000
WALES: James Trainer (Cap), Smart Arridge, David Jones, William Hughes, Caesar August Llewelyn Jenkyns, Robert Roberts, Robert DaviesI, Archibald Middleship Bastock, William Lewis, John Charles Henry Bowdler, Benjamin Lewis.
IRELAND: John Clugston, William Gordon, Robert Stewart, Nathaniel McKeown, Samuel Spencer (Cap), William Cunningham, William Dalton, George Gaffikin, Olphert Stanfield, Samuel Torrans, John Peden.
Goals: Benjamin Lewis (15) / Olphert Stanfield (87)

41. 05.03.1892 British Championship
WALES v ENGLAND 0-2 (0-1)
The Racecourse, Wrexham
Referee: James Robertson (Scotland)   Attendance: 4,500
WALES: Dr.Robert Herbert Mills-Roberts, Walter Gwynne Evans, Seth Powell, Joseph Davies, Caesar August Llewelyn Jenkyns, John Owen, William Owen (Cap), Joseph Hudson Turner, Benjamin Lewis, Robert Davies, William Lewis.
ENGLAND: George Toone, Arthur Tempest Blakiston Dunn (Cap), Harry Edward Lilley, Anthony Henry Hossack, William Norman Winckworth, George Kinsey, Robert Cunliffe Gosling, George Huth Cotterill, Arthur George Henfrey, Joseph Alfred Schofield, Rupert Renorden Sandilands.
Goals: Arthur Henfrey (15), Rupert Sandilands (87)

42. 26.03.1892 British Championship
SCOTLAND v WALES 6-1 (4-0)
Tynecastle Park, Edinburgh
Referee: John Reid (Ireland)   Attendance: 600
SCOTLAND: Robert Downie, James Adams, James Orr, Isaac Begbie, James Campbell, John Hill (Cap), John Daniel Taylor, William Thomson, James Hamilton, John "Kitey" McPherson, David Baird.
WALES: James Trainer, Smart Arridge, Seth Powell, William Hughes, Caesar August Llewelyn Jenkyns, Robert Roberts (Cap), Job Wilding, William Owen, William Lewis, Thomas William Egan, Benjamin Lewis.
Goals: William Thomson (1), James Hamilton (6, 65), John "Kitey" McPherson (15, 44), David Baird (55) / Benjamin Lewis (87)

11

43.   13.03.1893   British Championship
ENGLAND v WALES 6-0 (2-0)
Victoria Ground, Stoke-on-Trent
Referee: John Campbell (Scotland)   Attendance: 10,000
ENGLAND: John William Sutcliffe, Thomas Clare, Robert Holmes (Cap), John Reynolds, Charles Perry, James Albert Turner, William Isaiah Bassett, James Whitehead, John Goodall, Joseph Alfred Schofield, Frederick Spiksley.
WALES: James Trainer (Cap), David Jones, Charles Frederick Parry, Edwin Hugh Williams, Joseph Davies, Edward Morris, John Butler, James Vaughan, Edwin James, Benjamin Lewis, Robert Roberts.
Goals: Frederick Spiksley (25, 43), William Bassett (47), John Goodall (49), John Reynolds (75), Joseph Schofield (88)

44.   18.03.1893   British Championship
WALES v SCOTLAND 0-8 (0-5)
The Racecourse, Wrexham
Referee: William Stacey (England)   Attendance: 4,500
WALES: Samuel Jones, Oliver David Shepston Taylor, Frederick William Jones, George Williams, Edwin Hugh Williams, Edward Morris, William Owen (Cap), James Vaughan, John Butler, Benjamin Lewis, Harold Ernest Bowdler.
SCOTLAND: John McLeod, Daniel Doyle, Robert Foyers, Donald Currie Sillars (Cap), Andrew McCreadie, David Stewart, John Daniel Taylor, William Thomson, John Madden, John Barker, William Allan Lambie.
Goals: John Madden (4, 20, 47, 89), John Barker (25, 30, 40), William Allan Lambie (65)

45.   08.04.1893   British Championship
IRELAND v WALES 4-3 (2-1)
Solitude, Belfast
Referee: James Campbell (Scotland)   Attendance: 3,000
IRELAND: John Clugston, William Gordon, Robert Stewart, Alexander Crawford, Nathaniel McKeown, Samuel Johnston, James Small (Cap), George Gaffikin, Olphert Stanfield, James Wilton, John Peden.
WALES: Samuel Jones, Alfred William Townsend, Oliver David Shepston Taylor, Arthur Lea (Cap), John Evans, Edward Morris, James Vaughan, William Owen, John Butler, George Alfred Owen, Edwin James.
Goals: John Peden (5, 50, 58), James Wilton (82) / William Owen (8), George Alfred Owen (34, 80)

46.   24.02.1894   British Championship
WALES v IRELAND 4-1 (1-0)
St Helen's Rugby Ground, Swansea
Referee: James Campbell (Scotland)   Attendance: 7,000
WALES: James Trainer (Cap), Smart Arridge, Oliver David Shepston Taylor, Robert Samuel Jones, Thomas Chapman, Abel Hayes, John Evans, Benjamin Lewis, William Lewis, John Charles Rea, Edwin James.
IRELAND: Thomas Gordon, Robert Stewart, Samuel Torrans (Cap), Nathaniel McKeown, John Burnett, Robert Milne, William Dalton, George Gaffikin, Olphert Stanfield, William Kennedy Gibson, James Barron.
Goals: William Lewis (55, 82), Edwin James (65, 75) / Olphert Stanfield (20)

47.   12.03.1894   British Championship
WALES v ENGLAND 1-5 (1-2)
The Racecourse, Wrexham
Referee: Thomas Park (Scotland)   Attendance: 5,500
WALES: James Trainer (Cap), Charles Frederick Parry, David Jones, John Evans, Thomas Chapman, Abel Hughes, Edwin James, Benjamin Lewis, William Lewis, John Charles Rea, John Charles Henry Bowdler.
ENGLAND: Leslie Hewitt Gay, Lewis Vaughn Lodge, Frederick Raymond Pelly, Anthony Henry Hossack, Charles Wreford-Brown (Cap), Arthur George Topham, Robert Topham, Robert Cunliffe Gosling, Gilbert Oswald Smith, John Gould Veitch, Rupert Renorden Sandilands.
Goals: John Charles Henry Bowdler (10) / John Gould Veitch (30, 55, 80), Charlie Parry (44 own goal), Robert Cunliffe Gosling (85)

48.   24.03.1894   British Championship
SCOTLAND v WALES 5-2 (2-2)
Rugby Park, Kilmarnock
Referee: Joseph McBride (Ireland)   Attendance: 10,000
SCOTLAND: Andrew Baird, David Crawford, Robert Foyers, Edward McBain, James Kelly (Cap), John Johnstone, Andrew Stewart, Thomas Chambers, David Alexander, Davidson Berry, John Barker.
WALES: Samuel Gladstone Gillam, Oliver David Shepston Taylor (Cap), Abel Hughes, George Williams, Thomas Chapman, Thomas Worthington, Hugh Morris, Benjamin Lewis, William Lewis, John Charles Rea, Edwin James.
Goals: Davidson Berry (42), John Barker (44), Thomas Chambers (70), David Alexander (75), John Johnstone (85) / Hugh Morris (15, 40)

39. 16.03.1895   British Championship
IRELAND v WALES 2-2 (1-0)
Solitude, Belfast
Referee: William Jope (England)   Attendance: 6,000
IRELAND: Thomas Scott, Hugh Gordon, Lewis Irwin Scott, Hymie McKie, Robert Milne, John Burnett, Thomas Morrison, William Sherrard, Thomas Jordan (Cap), George Warrington Gaukrodger, George Gaffikin.
WALES: James Trainer (Cap), Smart Arridge, James Alfred Edwards, George Williams, Thomas Chapman, John Leonard Jones, William Henry Meredith, Joseph Davies, Harry Trainer, William Parry, William Lewis.
Goals: George Gaukrodger (32), Thomas Jordan (42) / Harry Trainer (10, 85)

50. 18.03.1895   British Championship
ENGLAND v WALES 1-1 (0-0)
Queen's Club, London
Referee: Thomas Park (Scotland)   Attendance: 13,000
ENGLAND: George Berkeley Raikes, Lewis Vaughn Lodge, William John Oakley, Arthur George Henfrey, Charles Wreford-Brown (Cap), Robert Raine Barker, Morris Hugh Stanbrough, Gerald Powys Dewhurst, Gilbert Oswald Smith, Robert Cunliffe Gosling, Rupert Renorden Sandilands.
WALES: James Trainer (Cap), Charles Frederick Parry, David Jones, George Williams, Caesar August Llewelyn Jenkyns, John Leonard Jones, William Henry Meredith, Joseph Davies, Harry Trainer, Albert Westhead Pryce-Jones, William Lewis.
Goal: Gilbert Oswald Smith (74) / William Lewis (69)

51. 23.03.1895   British Championship
WALES v SCOTLAND 2-2 (1-2)
The Racecourse, Wrexham
Referee: William Jope (England)   Attendance: 4,000
WALES: Samuel Jones, Robert Arthur Lloyd, Charles Frederick Parry (Cap), George Williams, Thomas Chapman, John Leonard Jones, Joseph Davies, Benjamin Lewis, Harry Trainer, William Lewis, John Charles Rea.
SCOTLAND: Francis Barrett, Donald Currie Sillars (Cap), Robert Glen, James Simpson, William McColl, Alexander Lowson Keillor, John H. Fyfe, John Murray, John Madden, William Sawers, John Divers.
Goals: William Lewis (10), Thomas Chapman (60) / John Madden (15), John Divers (20)

52. 29.02.1896   British Championship
WALES v IRELAND 6-1 (4-0)
The Racecourse, Wrexham
Referee: James Cooper (England)   Attendance: 3,000
WALES: Samuel Jones I, Charles Frederick Parry (Cap), John Samuel Matthias, Joseph Rogers, Price Foulkes White, John Leonard Jones, William Henry Meredith, David Henry Pugh, Arthur Grenville Morris, John Charles Rea, William Lewis.
IRELAND: Thomas Scott, Joseph Ponsonby, Samuel Torrans, Sam McCoy, Robert Milne, John Campbell, Edward Turner, Giddy Baird, Olphert Stanfield (Cap), James McCashin, John Peden.
Goals: William Lewis (9, 20), William Meredith (22, 84), Arthur Grenville Morris (34), David Henry Pugh (60) / Edward Turner (70)

53. 16.03.1896   British Championship
WALES v ENGLAND 1-9 (0-5)
The Arms Park, Cardiff
Referee: Thomas Robertson (Scotland)   Attendance: 10,000
WALES: Samuel Jones, Charles Frederick Parry (Cap), Smart Arridge, Joseph Rogers, Thomas Chapman, John Leonard Jones, William Henry Meredith, Joseph Davies, Arthur Grenville Morris, Hugh Morris, William Lewis.
ENGLAND: George Berkeley Raikes, William John Oakley, James William Crabtree, Arthur George Henfrey, Thomas Henry Crawshaw, George Kinsey, William Isaiah Bassett, Stephen Bloomer, Gilbert Oswald Smith (Cap), John Goodall, Rupert Renorden Sandilands.
Goals: Thomas Chapman (65 pen) / Gilbert O. Smith (15, 44), Stephen Bloomer (25, 40, 60, 83, 89), William Bassett (33), John Goodall (80)

54. 21.03.1896   British Championship
SCOTLAND v WALES 4-0 (2-0)
Carolina Port, Dundee
Referee: Joseph McBride (Ireland)   Attendance: 11,700
SCOTLAND: Robert MacFarlane, Duncan McLean, Robert Glen, John Gillespie (Cap), Robert Neil, William Blair, William Thomson, Daniel John Ferguson Paton, Robert Smyth McColl, Alexander King, Alexander Lowson Keillor
WALES: James Trainer (Cap), Charles Frederick Parry, John Samuel Matthias, Joseph Rogers, Caesar August Llewelyn Jenkyns, John Leonard Jones, David Henry Pugh, John Garner, Arthur Grenville Morris, John Charles Rea, William Lewis.
Goals: Robert Neil (19, 71), Alexander Lowson Keillor (30), Daniel John Ferguson Paton (59)

55. 06.03.1897   British Championship
IRELAND v WALES 4-3 (1-3)
Solitude, Belfast

Referee: Thomas Robertson (Scotland)   Attendance: 10,000

IRELAND: Thomas Scott, William Kennedy Gibson, Samuel Torrans, John Pyper, Joseph Ponsonby (Cap), George McMaster, James Campbell, Olphert Stanfield, James Pyper, John Peden, James Barron.

WALES: James Trainer (Cap), James Alfred Edwards, Charles Frederick Parry, Sydney Darvell, Caesar August Llewelyn Jenkyns, John Leonard Jones, William Henry Meredith, David Henry Pugh, Morgan Maddox Morgan-Owen, William Nock, John Charles Rea.

Goals: James Barron (7), Olphert Stanfield (62), John Pyper (66), John Peden (68) / William Meredith (19, 36), Caesar August Llewelyn Jenkyns (27)

56. 20.03.1897   British Championship
WALES v SCOTLAND 2-2 (1-1)
The Racecourse, Wrexham

Referee: Thomas Armitt (England)   Attendance: 5,000

WALES: James Trainer (Cap), William Roberts Jones, John Samuel Matthias, Sydney Darvell, John Mates, John Leonard Jones, William Henry Meredith, David Henry Pugh, Morgan Maddox Morgan-Owen, John Charles Rea, William Lewis.

SCOTLAND: John Patrick, John Ritchie (Cap), David Richmond Gardner, Bernard Breslin, David Kennedy Russell, Alexander Lowson Keillor, John Kennedy, Patrick Murray, James Oswald, James McMillan, John Walker

Goals: Morgan Maddox Morgan-Owen (40), David Pugh (#) / John L. Ritchie (11 pen), John Walker (61)

57. 29.03.1897   British Championship
ENGLAND v WALES 4-0 (2-0)
Bramall Lane, Sheffield

Referee: Thomas Robertson (Scotland)   Attendance: 5,000

ENGLAND: William Foulke, William John Oakley, Howard Spencer, John Reynolds, Thomas Henry Crawshaw, Ernest Needham, William Charles Athersmith, Stephen Bloomer, Gilbert Oswald Smith (Cap), Francis Becton, Alfred Weatherell Milward.

WALES: James Trainer (Cap), John Samuel Matthias, James Alfred Edwards, Thomas Chapman, John Mates, John Leonard Jones, William Henry Meredith, Joseph Davies, Arthur Grenville Morris, Hugh Morris, William Lewis.

Goals: Ernest Needham (23), Stephen Bloomer (44), Alfred Weatherell Milward (62, 64)

58. 19.02.1898   British Championship
WALES v IRELAND 0-1 (0-0)
The Oval, Llandudno

Referee: Thomas Robertson (Scotland)   Attendance: 6,000

WALES: John Morris, Charles Frederick Parry (Cap), Smart Arridge, George Williams, John Henry Edwards, John Leonard Jones, William Henry Meredith, Thomas John Thomas, William Lewis, Albert Lockley, John Charles Rea.

IRELAND: Thomas Scott, William Kennedy Gibson (Cap), Michael Cochrane, William Anderson, Robert Milne, John Lytle, James Campbell, John Thompson Mercer, James Pyper, James McCashin, John Peden.

Goal: John Peden (85)

59. 19.03.1898   British Championship
SCOTLAND v WALES 5-2 (4-1)
Fir Park, Motherwell

Referee: William H. Stacey (England)   Attendance: 3,500

SCOTLAND: W. Watson, Nicol Smith, Matthew McLintock Scott (Cap), William Thomson, Alexander John Christie, Peter Campbell, James Gillespie, James Millar, James McKie, Hugh Morgan, Robert Findlay.

WALES: James Trainer (Cap), Charles Frederick Parry, David Jones, Richard Jones, Caesar August Llewelyn Jenkyns, John Leonard Jones, Edwin James, Thomas John Thomas, Morgan Maddox Morgan-Owen, Arthur Grenville Morris, Alfred Ernest Watkins.

Goals: James Gillespie (12, 20, 61), James McKie (29, 40) / Thomas John Thomas (44), Morgan Morgan-Owen (#)

60. 28.03.1898   British Championship
WALES v ENGLAND 0-3 (0-1)
The Racecourse, Wrexham

Referee: Thomas Robertson (Scotland)   Attendance: 4,000

WALES: James Trainer, Charles Frederick Parry, Smart Arridge, John Taylor, Caesar August Llewelyn Jenkyns (Cap), John Leonard Jones, William Henry Meredith, Thomas Bartley, Morgan Maddox Morgan-Owen, Alfred Ernest Watkins, Edwin James.

ENGLAND: John William Robinson, William John Oakley, William Williams, Thomas Perry, Thomas Edward Booth, Ernest Needham, William Charles Athersmith, John Goodall, Gilbert Oswald Smith (Cap), George Frederick Wheldon, Frederick Spiksley.

Goals: George Wheldon (9, 75), Gilbert Oswald Smith (88)

61. 04.03.1899   British Championship
IRELAND v WALES 1-0 (0-0)
Grosvenor Park, Belfast
Referee: Charles Sutcliffe (England)   Attendance: 10,000
IRELAND: James Lewis, John Pyper, Samuel Torrans, Archibald Goodall, Robert Milne, John Taggart, Thomas Morrison, James Meldon, John Daniel Hanna, Joseph McAllen (Cap), John Peden.
WALES: James Trainer, Charles Edward Thomas, Horace Elford Blew, George Richards, John Leonard Jones (Cap), Edward Hughes, Frederick Charles Kelly, Robert Atherton, Edwin James, David Charles Davies, William James Jackson.
Goal: James Meldon (60)

62. 18.03.1899   British Championship
WALES v SCOTLAND 0-6 (0-1)
The Racecourse, Wrexham
Referee: Charles Sutcliffe (England)   Attendance: 12,000
WALES: James Trainer, John Samuel Matthias, Horace Elford Blew, George Richards, John Leonard Jones (Cap), Edward Hughes, Frederick Charles Kelly, Trevor Owen, Morgan Maddox Morgan-Owen, Ralph Stanley Jones, Arthur Grenville Morris.
SCOTLAND: Daniel McArthur, Nicol Smith (Cap), David Storrier, Neil Gibson, Henry James Hall Marshall, Alexander King, John Campbell, Robert Cumming Hamilton, Robert Smyth McColl, John Bell, Davidson Berry.
Goals: John Campbell (22, 55), Robert McColl (50, 75, 85), Henry James Hall Marshall (70)

63. 20.03.1899   British Championship
ENGLAND v WALES 4-0 (2-0)
Ashton Gate, Bristol
Referee: Thomas Robertson (Scotland)   Attendance: 10,000
ENGLAND: John William Robinson, Henry Thickett, William Williams, Ernest Needham, James William Crabtree, Frank Forman, William Charles Athersmith, Stephen Bloomer, Gilbert Oswald Smith (Cap), James Settle, Frederick Ralph Forman.
WALES: Samuel Jones, Horace Elford Blew, Smart Arridge (Cap), George Richards, Thomas John Buckland, William Clare Harrison, James Vaughan, William Henry Meredith, Trevor Owen, Arthur Grenville Morris, Robert Atherton.
Goals: Ernest Needham (30), Stephen Bloomer (44, 86), Frederick Ralph Forman (60)

64. 03.02.1900   British Championship
SCOTLAND v WALES 5-2 (4-1)
Pittodrie Park, Aberdeen
Referee: Charles Sutcliffe (England)   Attendance: 12,500
SCOTLAND: Matthew Dickie, Nicol Smith, David Crawford, James Hay Irons, Robert G. Neil, John Tait Robertson, John Bell, David Wilson, Robert Smyth McColl, Robert Cumming Hamilton (Cap), Alexander Smith
WALES: Frederick John Griffiths, Charles Edward Thomas, Charles Richard Morris, Samuel Meredith, John Leonard Jones (Cap), William Clare Harrison, David Henry Pugh, William Thomas Butler, Richard Jones, Thomas David Parry, Alfred Ernest Watkins.
Goals: John Bell (2), David Wilson (7, 35), Robert Cumming Hamilton (40), Alexander Smith (60) / Thomas David Parry (44), William Thomas Butler (60)

65. 24.02.1900   British Championship
WALES v IRELAND 2-0 (0-0)
The Oval, Llandudno
Referee: Charles Sutcliffe (England)   Attendance: 6,000
WALES: Leigh Richmond Roose, David Jones (Cap), Charles Richard Morris, Samuel James Brookes, Robert Morris, William Clare Harrison, William Henry Meredith, William Thomas Butler, Richard Jones, Thomas David Parry, David Charles Davies.
IRELAND: Thomas Scott, John Pyper, Michael Cochrane, John McShane, Archibald Goodall, Hugh Maginnis, George Sheehan (Cap), Thomas Morrison, John Henry Kirwan, Alfred Kearns, Joseph McAllen.
Goals: Thomas Parry (73), William Henry Meredith (87 pen)

66. 26.03.1900   British Championship
WALES v ENGLAND 1-1 (0-1)
The Arms Park, Cardiff
Referee: Thomas Robertson (Scotland)   Attendance: 20,000
WALES: Frederick John Griffiths, David Jones (Cap), Charles Richard Morris, Samuel James Brookes, Robert Morris, William Clare Harrison, William Henry Meredith, Joseph Davies, Hugh Morgan-Owen, Alfred Ernest Watkins, Thomas David Parry.
ENGLAND: John William Robinson, Howard Spencer, William John Oakley, William Harold Johnson, Arthur Chadwick, James William Crabtree, William Charles Athersmith, Reginald Erskine Foster, Gilbert Oswald Smith (Cap), George Plumpton Wilson, William Alfred Spouncer.
Goals: William Meredith (55) / George Plumpton Wilson (3)

67. 02.03.1901   British Championship
WALES v SCOTLAND 1-1 (0-0)
The Racecourse, Wrexham

Referee: Charles Sutcliffe (England)   Attendance: 5,000

WALES: Leigh Richmond Roose, Samuel Meredith, Charles Richard Morris (Cap), Maurice Pryce Parry, William James Jones, Edward Hughes, David Henry Pugh, John Owen Jones, Morgan Maddox Morgan-Owen, Thomas David Parry, Ephrahim Williams.

SCOTLAND: George Chappell McWattie, Nicol Smith, Bernard Battles, Neil Gibson, David Kennedy Russell, John Tait Robertson (Cap), Mark Dickson Bell, Robert Walker, Robert Smyth McColl, John Campbell, Alexander Smith.

Goal: Thomas David Parry (78) / John Tait Robertson (74)

68. 18.03.1901   British Championship
ENGLAND v WALES 6-0 (1-0)
St.JamesPark, Newcastle

Referee: Thomas Robertson (Scotland)   Attendance: 11,000

ENGLAND: Matthew Kingsley, James William Crabtree, William John Oakley, Albert Wilkes, William Bannister, Ernest Needham (Cap), Walter Bennett, Stephen Bloomer, William Edwin Beats, Reginald Erskine Foster, Bertram Oswald Corbett.

WALES: Leigh Richmond Roose, Samuel Meredith, Charles Richard Morris (Cap), Maurice Pryce Parry, William James Jones, Edward Hughes, William Henry Meredith, David Henry Pugh, Morgan Maddox Morgan-Owen, Thomas David Parry, Ephrahim Williams.

Goals: Stephen Bloomer (38, 60, 71, 74), Ernest Needham (51 pen), Reginald Erskine Foster (72)

69. 23.03.1901   British Championship
IRELAND v WALES 0-1 (0-1)
Solitude, Belfast

Referee: Charles Sutcliffe (England)   Attendance: 7,000

IRELAND: James Nolan-Whelan, William Kennedy Gibson (Cap), Samuel Torrans, Patrick Farrell, Robert Milne, Joseph Burnison, James Campbell, James Smith, H. McKelvie, Harry O'Reilly, Joseph McAllen.

WALES: Leigh Richmond Roose, Samuel Meredith, Charles Richard Morris (Cap), Maurice Pryce Parry, Robert Morris, William Clare Harrison, William Henry Meredith, John Owen Jones, Arthur William Green, Thomas David Parry, Ephrahim Williams.

Goal: John Owen Jones (55)

70. 22.02.1902   British Championship
WALES v IRELAND 0-3 (0-1)
The Arms Park, Cardiff

Referee: Arthur Kingscott (England)   Attendance: 7,000

WALES: Robert Owen Evans, Horace Elford Blew, Hugh Jones, Maurice Pryce Parry, Edward Hughes, John Leonard Jones (Cap), Frederick Charles Kelly, Thomas Jenkins, Roger Evans, Ephraim Williams, Richard Morris.

IRELAND: James Nolan-Whelan, William Kennedy Gibson (Cap), William McCracken, John Darling, Robert Milne, Harold Nicholl, John Thompson Mercer, James Maxwell, Andrew Gara, Alfred Kearns, John Henry Kirwan.

Goals: Andrew Gara (40, 60, 75)

71. 03.03.1902   British Championship
WALES v ENGLAND 0-0
The Racecourse, Wrexham

Referee: Thomas Robertson (Scotland)   Attendance: 8,000

WALES: Leigh Richmond Roose, Samuel Meredith, Charles Richard Morris, Maurice Pryce Parry, John Leonard Jones (Cap), William James Jones, William Henry Meredith, Walter Martin Watkins, Thomas David Parry, Ephrahim Williams, Richard Morris.

ENGLAND: William George, Robert Crompton, James William Crabtree, Albert Wilkes, Walter Abbott, Ernest Needham, William Hogg, Stephen Bloomer, Charles Sagar, Reginald Erskine Foster (Cap), Herbert Broughall Lipsham.

72. 15.03.1902   British Championship
SCOTLAND v WALES 5-1 (1-0)
Cappielow Park, Greenock

Referee: Joseph McBride (Ireland)   Attendance: 5,284

SCOTLAND: Henry George Rennie, Henry Allan, John Drummond, Hugh Wilson, Albert Thoroughgood Buick, John Tait Robertson, John Campbell (Cap), Robert Walker, Robert Cumming Hamilton, Alexander McMahon, Alexander Smith.

WALES: Leigh Richmond Roose, Horace Elford Blew, Robert Morris, Maurice Pryce Parry, John Leonard Jones (Cap), William James Jones, William Henry Meredith, Llewelyn Griffiths, Hugh Morgan-Owen, Richard Morris, Joseph Owens.

Goals: John Tait Robertson (38), Albert Buick (47), Alexander Smith (50), Robert Walker (55), John Campbell (88) / Hugh Morgan-Owen (#)

73. 02.03.1903   British Championship
ENGLAND v WALES 2-1 (1-0)
Fratton Park, Portsmouth
Referee: Thomas Robertson (Scotland)   Attendance: 4,000
ENGLAND: John William Sutcliffe, Robert Crompton (Cap), George Molyneux, William Harold Johnson, Frank Forman, Albert Edward Houlker, Harry Davis, William Garraty, Vivian John Woodward, Joseph William Bache, Reginald Corbett.
WALES: Robert Owen Evans, Horace Elford Blew, Charles Richard Morris (Cap), Maurice Pryce Parry, Robert Morris, Thomas Davies, William Henry Meredith, Walter Martin Watkins, Arthur William Green, Arthur Grenville Morris, Robert Atherton.
Goals: Joseph William Bache (12), Vivian Woodward (78) / Walter Martin Watkins (54)

73. 09.03.1903   British Championship
WALES v SCOTLAND 0-1 (0-1)
The Arms Park, Cardiff
Referee: Frederick Thomas Kirkham (England)   Att: 11,000
WALES: Robert Owen Evans, Horace Elford Blew, Charles Richard Morris (Cap), Maurice Pryce Parry, Morgan Maddox Morgan-Owen, Thomas Davies, William Henry Meredith, Walter Martin Watkins, Arthur Grenville Morris, Richard Morris, Robert Atherton.
SCOTLAND: Henry George Rennie, Andrew McCombie, James Watson, Andrew Aitken, Alexander Galloway Raisbeck (Cap), John Tait Robertson, Robert Bryson Templeton, Robert Walker, John Campbell, Finlay Ballantyne Speedie, Alexander Smith.
Goal: Finlay Ballantyne Speedie (25)

75. 28.03.1903   British Championship
IRELAND v WALES 2 0 (0-0)
Solitude, Belfast
Referee: Frederick Thomas Kirkham (England)   Att: 14,000
IRELAND: William Scott, Alexander McCartney, Peter Boyle (Cap), John Darling, Archibald Goodall, Hugh Maginnis, John Thompson Mercer, James Maxwell, Maurice Joseph Connor, James Sheridan, John Henry Kirwan.
WALES: Robert Owen Evans, Samuel Meredith, Charles Richard Morris (Cap), George Richards, Robert Morris, Thomas Davies, William Henry Meredith, William Wynn, William Davies, Richard Morris, Robert Atherton.
Goals: Archibald Goodall (#), James Sheridan (#)

76. 29.02.1904   British Championship
WALES v ENGLAND 2-2 (1-0)
The Racecourse, Wrexham
Referee: Thomas Robertson (Scotland)   Attendance: 9,000
WALES: Leigh Richmond Roose, Samuel Meredith, Horace Elford Blew, Richard Morris, Maurice Pryce Parry, Edward Hughes, John Leonard Jones (Cap), William Henry Meredith, Walter Martin Watkins, Lloyd Davies, Robert Atherton.
ENGLAND: Thomas Baddeley, Robert Crompton (Cap), Herbert Burgess, Ernest Albert Lee, Thomas Henry Crawshaw, Herod Ruddlesdin, William Frederick Brawn, Alfred Common, Arthur Samuel Brown, Joseph William Bache, George Henry Davis.
Goals: Walter Martin Watkins (15), Lloyd Davies (85) / George Henry Davis (68), Joseph William Bache (77)

77. 12.03.1904   British Championship
SCOTLAND v WALES 1-1 (1-0)
Dens Park, Dundee
Referee: Frederick Thomas Kirkham (England)   Att: 12,000
SCOTLAND: Dr.Leslie Henderson Skene, Thomas Alexander Skinner Jackson, James Sharp (Cap), William Orr, Thomas Parker Sloan, John Tait Robertson, John Walker, Robert Walker, Alexander Bennett, Alexander MacFarlane, George Wilson.
WALES: David Davies, Horace Elford Blew, Thomas Davies, George Richards, Edward Hughes, John Leonard Jones (Cap), Arthur Davies, Walter Martin Watkins, Arthur William Green, Richard Morris, Robert Atherton.
Goals: Robert Walker (5) / Robert Atherton (65)

78. 21.03.1904   British Championship
WALES v IRELAND 0-1 (0-0)
The Cricket Ground, Bangor
Referee: Frederick Thomas Kirkham (England)   Att: 10,000
WALES: David Davies, Horace Elford Blew, Charles Richard Morris, Maurice Pryce Parry, Edward Hughes, John Leonard Jones (Cap), Alfred Ernest Watkins, Walter Martin Watkins, Arthur William Green, Richard Morris, Robert Atherton.
IRELAND: William Scott, William McCracken, Alexander McCartney, James English McConnell, Robert Milne, Hugh Maginnis, John Thompson Mercer, Thomas Shanks, Archibald Goodall (Cap), Hugh Kirkwood, John Henry Kirwan.
Goal: William McCracken (77 pen)

79. 06.03.1905   British Championship
WALES v SCOTLAND 3-1 (1-0)

The Racecourse, Wrexham

Referee: Frederick Thomas Kirkham (England)   Att: 6,000

WALES: Leigh Richmond Roose, Horace Elford Blew, Charles Richard Morris (Cap), George Latham, Edward Hughes, John Hughes, William Henry Meredith, Arthur Davies, Walter Martin Watkins, Arthur Grenville Morris, Alfred Oliver.

SCOTLAND: Henry George Rennie, Andrew McCombie, Thomas Jackson (Cap), Andrew Aitken, Charles Bellany Thomson, John Tait Robertson, Robert Bryson Templeton, Robert Walker, Samuel Watson Kennedy, Thomas Tindal Fitchie, Alexander Smith.

Goals: Walter Watkins (30), Arthur Grenville Morris (47), William Henry Meredith (76) / John Tait Robertson (86)

80. 27.03.1905   British Championship
ENGLAND v WALES 3-1 (0-0)

Anfield Road, Liverpool

Referee: Thomas Robertson (Scotland)   Attendance: 16,100

ENGLAND: James Henry Linacre, Howard Spencer (Cap), Herbert Smith, Samuel Wolstenholme, Charles Roberts, Alexander Leake, Richard Bond, Stephen Bloomer, Vivian John Woodward, Stanley Schute Harris, Harold Payne Hardman.

WALES: Leigh Richmond Roose, Albert Thomas Jones, Charles Richard Morris, George Latham, Edward Hughes, John Hughes, William Henry Meredith (Cap), William Jones, Walter Martin Watkins, Arthur Grenville Morris, Alfred Oliver.

Goals: Vivian Woodward (55, 88), Stanley Schute Harris (80) / Arthur Grenville Morris (75)

81. 08.04.1905   British Championship
IRELAND v WALES 2-2 (2-2)

Solitude, Belfast

Referee: Frederick Thomas Kirkham (England)   Att: 15,000

IRELAND: Robert Reynolds, William McCracken, George McMillan, John Darling, James Connor, Samuel Johnston, Andrew Hunter, James Maxwell, Neill Murphy, Charles O'Hagan, John Henry Kirwan (Cap).

WALES: John Tracey Morgan, Horace Elford Blew, Charles Richard Morris, George Richards, Edward Hughes (Cap), John Hughes, William Henry Matthews, Walter Martin Watkins, William Davies, William Jones, Robert Atherton.

Goals: Neill Murphy (25), Charles O'Hagan (45) / Walter Martin Watkins (20), Robert Atherton (#)

82. 03.03.1906   British Championship
SCOTLAND v WALES 0-2 (0-0)

Tynecastle Park, Edinburgh

Referee: John Lewis (England)   Attendance: 25,000

SCOTLAND: James Smith Raeside, Donald McLeod, Andrew Richmond, Alexander McNair, Charles Bellany Thomson (Cap), John May, George Stewart, Alexander MacFarlane, James Quinn, Thomas Tindal Fitchie, George Wilson.

WALES: Leigh Richmond Roose, Horace Elford Blew, Charles Richard Morris (Cap), Edwin Hughes, Morgan Maddox Morgan-Owen, George Latham, William Jones, Richard Morris, John "Love" Jones, Richard Jones, Robert Ernest Evans.

Goals: William Jones (50), John "Love" Jones (65)

83. 19.03.1906   British Championship
WALES v ENGLAND 0-1 (0-0)

The Arms Park, Cardiff

Referee: Robert Murray (Scotland)   Attendance: 15,000

WALES: Leigh Richmond Roose, Albert Thomas Jones, Horace Elford Blew, Maurice Pryce Parry (Cap), Morgan Maddox Morgan-Owen, Edward Hughes, William Jones, Hugh Morgan-Owen, Arthur William Green, John Richard Lewis, Robert Ernest Evans.

ENGLAND: James Ashcroft, Robert Crompton, Herbert Smith, Benjamin Warren, Colin Campbell McKechnie Veitch, Albert Edward Houlker, Richard Bond, Samuel Hulme Day, Alfred Common, Stanley Schute Harris (Cap), Edward Gordon Dundas Wright.

Goal: Samuel Hulme Day (86)

84. 02.04.1906   British Championship
WALES v IRELAND 4-4 (3-2)

The Racecourse, Wrexham

Referee: Frederick Thomas Kirkham (England)   Att: 5,000

WALES: Leigh Richmond Roose, James Roberts, Horace Elford Blew (Cap), Edwin Hughes, Morgan Maddox Morgan-Owen, Edward Hughes, William Jones, Hugh Morgan-Owen, Arthur William Green, Richard Jones II, Robert Ernest Evans.

IRELAND: Frederick McKee, George Willis, John Darling, John Wright, Robert Milne, Joseph Ledwige, Andrew Hunter, James Maxwell, Charles O'Hagan, Harold Alexander Sloan, John Henry Kirwan (Cap).

Goals: Arthur Green (#, #, #), Hugh Morgan-Owen (#) / James Maxwell (72), Harold Alexander Sloan (10, 25, 74)

18

85. 23.02.1907   British Championship
IRELAND v WALES 2-3 (1-1)
Solitude, Belfast
Referee: Frederick Thomas Kirkham (England)   Att: 12,000
IRELAND: James Sherry, John Seymour, Alexander McCartney, John Wright (Cap), Charles Crothers, George McClure, John Blair, Valentine Harris, Harold Alexander Sloan, Charles O'Hagan, John Henry Kirwan.
WALES: Leigh Richmond Roose, James Roberts, Lloyd Davies, George Latham, George Owen Williams, Llewelyn Davies, William Henry Meredith (Cap), William Jones, Arthur Howell Hughes, Richard Morris, Gordon Peace Jones.
Goals: Charles O'Hagan (10), Harold Alexander Sloan (80) / Richard Morris (12), William Meredith (#), William Jones (#)

86. 04.03.1907   British Championship
WALES v SCOTLAND 1-0 (0-0)
The Racecourse, Wrexham
Referee: James Mason (England)   Attendance: 7,715
WALES: Leigh Richmond Roose (Cap), Horace Elford Blew, Charles Richard Morris, George Latham, Lloyd Davies, Ioan Haydn Price, William Henry Meredith, William Jones, Hugh Morgan-Owen, Arthur Grenville Morris, Gordon Peace Jones.
SCOTLAND: Peter McBride, Thomas Alexander Skinner Jackson, James Sharp, Andrew Aitken, Charles Bellany Thomson (Cap), Peter McWilliam, George Stewart, George Turner Livingstone, Alexander Simpson Young, Thomas Tindal Fitchie, Alexander Smith.
Goal: Arthur Grenville Morris (50)

87. 18.03.1907   British Championship
ENGLAND v WALES 1-1 (0-1)
Craven Cottage, London
Referee: Robert Murray (Scotland)   Attendance: 25,000
ENGLAND: Samuel Hardy, Robert Crompton (Cap), Jesse Pennington, Benjamin Warren, William John Wedlock, Colin Campbell McKechnie Veitch, John Rutherford, Stephen Bloomer, Irvine Thornley, James Stewart, George Wall.
WALES: Leigh Richmond Roose, Lloyd Davies, Samuel Meredith, George Latham, Morgan Maddox Morgan-Owen, Edward Hughes, William Henry Meredith (Cap), William Jones, Arthur William Green, Arthur Grenville Morris, Robert Ernest Evans.
Goal: James Stewart (62) / William Jones (25)

88. 07.03.1908   British Championship
SCOTLAND v WALES 2-1 (0-1)
Dens Park, Dundee
Referee: James Mason (England)   Attendance: 18,000
SCOTLAND: Henry George Rennie, William Barbour Agnew, George Duncan Chaplin, Alexander McNair, Charles Bellany Thomson (Cap), James Hill Galt, Alexander Bennett, Robert Walker, James Hamilton Speirs, Alexander MacFarlane, William Lennie.
WALES: Leigh Richmond Roose, Horace Elford Blew (Cap), Charles Richard Morris, Maurice Pryce Parry, Edwin Hughes, Lloyd Davies, William Charles Davies, William Jones, William Davies, Arthur William Green, Robert Ernest Evans.
Goals: Alexander Bennett (60), William Lennie (87) / William Jones (30)

89. 16.03.1908   British Championship
WALES v ENGLAND 1-7 (0-4)
The Racecourse, Wrexham
Referee: David Phillips (Scotland)   Attendance: 8,000
WALES: Leigh Richmond Roose (46 David Davies), Charles Richard Morris, Horace Elford Blew, Maurice Pryce Parry, Edwin Hughes, George Latham, William Henry Meredith (Cap), William Henry Matthews, William Davies, Arthur Grenville Morris, Robert Ernest Evans.
ENGLAND: Horace Peter Bailey, Robert Crompton, Jesse Pennington, Benjamin Warren, William John Wedlock, Evelyn Henry Lintott, John Rutherford, Vivian John Woodward (Cap), George Richard Hilsdon, James Edward Windridge, Harold Payne Hardman.
Goals: William Davies (90) / Vivian Woodward (18, 70, 80), James Edward Windridge (25), William John Wedlock (30), George Richard Hilsdon (40, 63)

Roose left the field due to injury after just 15 minutes following a shoulder-charge by Vivian Woodward. Davies was the first substitute in any England match, eventually coming on as a replacement in the 46th minute.

90. 11.04.1908   British Championship
WALES v IRELAND 0-1 (0-1)
Athletic Ground, Aberdare
Referee: James Ibbotson (England)   Attendance: 6,000
WALES: Robert Owen Evans, Horace Elford Blew, Jeffrey Woodward Jones, Ernest Peake, Maurice Pryce Parry, Ioan Haydn Price, William Henry Meredith, Richard Morris, Walter Martin Watkins (Cap), Albert Victor Hodgkinson, Thomas Daniel Jones.
IRELAND: William Scott, Alexander Craig (Cap), Alexander McCartney, John Darling, James English McConnell, Valentine Harris, Andrew Hunter, William Hamilton, Harold Alexander Sloan, Charles O'Hagan, Henry Redmond Buckle.
Goal: Harold Alexander Sloan (28)

91. 01.03.1909   British Championship
WALES v SCOTLAND 3-2 (3-0)

The Racecourse, Wrexham

Referee: Thomas Campbell (England)   Attendance: 6,000

WALES: Leigh Richmond Roose, Horace Elford Blew, Charles Richard Morris, Maurice Pryce Parry, Ernest Peake, Ioan Haydn Price, William Henry Meredith (Cap), George Arthur Wynn, William Davies, William Jones, Robert Ernest Evans.

SCOTLAND: Peter McBride, Thomas Collins, James Sharp, John May, Charles Bellany Thomson (Cap), Peter McWilliam, Alexander Bennett, John Bryson Hunter, Robert Walker, Peter Somers, Harold McDonald Paul.

Goals: William Davies (25, 39), William Jones (29) / Robert Walker (70), Harold McDonald Paul (73)

92. 15.03.1909   British Championship
ENGLAND v WALES 2-0 (2-0)

City Ground, Nottingham

Referee: David Phillips (Scotland)   Attendance: 11,500

ENGLAND: Samuel Hardy, Robert Crompton (Cap), Jesse Pennington, Benjamin Warren, William John Wedlock, Colin Campbell McKechnie Veitch, Frederick Beaconsfield Pentland, Vivian John Woodward (Cap), Bertram Clewley Freeman, George Henry Holley, George Arthur Bridgett.

WALES: Leigh Richmond Roose, Charles Richard Morris (Cap), Horace Elford Blew, Maurice Pryce Parry, Ernest Peake, Ioan Haydn Price, William Henry Meredith, George Arthur Wynn, William Davies, William Jones, William Charles Davies.

Goals: George Holley (15), Bertram Clewley Freeman (42)

93. 20.03.1909   British Championship
IRELAND v WALES 2-3 (1-1)

Grosvenor Park, Belfast

Referee: James Stark (Scotland)   Attendance: 8,000

IRELAND: William Scott, John Seymour, Alexander McCartney, Valentine Harris (Cap), James Connor, James English McConnell, Andrew Hunter, William Lacey, William Greer, Charles Webb, Jack Slemin.

WALES: Leigh Richmond Roose, Charles Richard Morris (Cap), Jeffrey Woodward Jones, George Latham, Ernest Peake, Lloyd Davies, William Henry Meredith, George Arthur Wynn, William Davies, William Jones, Ioan Haydn Price.

Goals: William Lacey (30), Andrew Hunter (75) / William Jones (#), George Arthur Wynn (#), William Henry Meredith (#)

94. 05.03.1910   British Championship
SCOTLAND v WALES 1-0 (0-0)

Rugby Park, Kilmarnock

Referee: Herbert Bamlett (England)   Attendance: 22,000

SCOTLAND: James Brownlie, George Law, James Mitchell, Alexander McNair, William Loney, James Hay (Cap), Alexander Bennett, James McMenemy, James Quinn, Andrew Devine, George Robertson.

WALES: Leigh Richmond Roose, Jeffrey Woodward Jones, Charles Richard Morris (Cap), Edwin Hughes, Ernest Peake, Llewelyn Davies, William Henry Meredith, William Charles Davies, Evan Jones, Arthur Grenville Morris, Robert Ernest Evans.

Goal: Andrew Devine (75)

95. 14.03.1910   British Championship
WALES v ENGLAND 0-1 (0-0)

The Arms Park, Cardiff

Referee: James Stark (Scotland)   Attendance: 20,000

WALES: Leigh Richmond Roose, Horace Elford Blew, Charles Richard Morris, Edwin Hughes, George Latham, Llewelyn Davies, William Henry Meredith (Cap), George Arthur Wynn, William Jones, Arthur Grenville Morris, Robert Ernest Evans.

ENGLAND: Samuel Hardy, Robert Crompton (Cap), Jesse Pennington, Andrew Ducat, William John Wedlock, William Bradshaw, Richard Bond, Harold John Fleming, John Parkinson, George Henry Holley, George Wall.

Goal: Andrew Ducat (66)

96. 11.04.1910   British Championship
WALES v IRELAND 4-1 (3-0)

The Racecourse, Wrexham

Referee: James Mason (England)   Attendance: 8,000

WALES: Leigh Richmond Roose, Lloyd Davies, Charles Richard Morris (Cap), Edwin Hughes, Ernest Peake, Llewelyn Davies, William Henry Meredith, John "Love" Jones, Evan Jones, Arthur Grenville Morris, Robert Ernest Evans.

IRELAND: John O'Hehir, James Balfe, Patrick McCann, Valentine Harris, James English McConnell (Cap), John Darling, William Thomas James Renneville, William Lacey, James Murray, John Murphy, Frank Thompson. Trainer: William Crone

Goals: Robert Evans (#, #), Arthur Grenville Morris (#, #) / John Darling (47 pen)

97. 28.01.1911   British Championship
IRELAND v WALES 1-2 (0-0)
Windsor Park, Belfast
Referee: Thomas Rowbotham (England)   Att: 15,000

IRELAND: William Scott (Cap), Samuel Burnison, P.J. Thunder, Valentine Harris, James Connor, Henry Vernon Hampton, William Thomas James Renneville, William Lacey, William Halligan, James Lowry Macauley, Frank Thompson.

WALES: Robert Owen Evans, Thomas John Hewitt, Charles Richard Morris (Cap), Edwin Hughes, Ernest Peake, Llewelyn Davies, William Henry Meredith, George Arthur Wynn, William Davies, Arthur Grenville Morris, Edward Thomas Vizard.

Goal: William Halligan (#) /
William Davies (50), Arthur Grenville Morris (75)

98. 06.03.1911   British Championship
WALES v SCOTLAND 2-2 (1-1)
Ninian Park, Cardiff
Referee: James Mason (England)   Attendance: 14,000

WALES: Leigh Richmond Roose, Thomas John Hewitt, Charles Richard Morris (Cap), Edwin Hughes, Lloyd Davies, Llewelyn Davies, William Henry Meredith, Evan Jones, William Davies, Arthur Grenville Morris, Edward Thomas Vizard.

SCOTLAND: James Brownlie, Donald Cameron Colman, John Walker, Thomas Somerville Tait, Wilfrid Lawson Low, Peter McWilliam (Cap), Alexander Bennett, James McMenemy, William Reid, Alexander MacFarlane, Robert Cumming Hamilton.

Goals: Arthur Grenville Morris (20, 67) /
Robert Cumming Hamilton (35, 89)

99. 13.03.1911   British Championship
ENGLAND v WALES 3-0 (0-0)
The Den, Millwall, London
Referee: James Stark (Scotland)   Attendance: 22,000

ENGLAND: Reginald Garnet Williamson, Robert Crompton, Jesse Pennington, Benjamin Warren, William John Wedlock, Kenneth Reginald Gunnery Hunt, John Simpson, Harold John Fleming, George William Webb, Vivian John Woodward (Cap), Robert Ernest Evans.

WALES: Robert Owen Evans, Charles Richard Morris, Thomas John Hewitt, Edwin Hughes, Lloyd Davies, William Jones, William Henry Meredith, Evan Jones, William Davies (Cap), Arthur Grenville Morris, Edward Thomas Vizard.

Goals: Vivian Woodward (65, 83), George William Webb (67)

100. 02.03.1912   British Championship
SCOTLAND v WALES 1-0 (0-0)
Tynecastle Park, Edinburgh
Referee: James Mason (England)   Attendance: 32,000

SCOTLAND: James Brownlie, Alexander McNair, John Walker, Robert Mercer, Charles Bellany Thomson (Cap), James Hay, George William Llyod Sinclair, James McMenemy, James Quinn, Robert Walker, George Robertson.

WALES: Robert Owen Evans, Llewelyn Davies, Lloyd Davies (Cap), Joseph Thomas Jones, Edwin Hughes, Moses Richard Russell, William Henry Meredith, George Arthur Wynn, Evan Jones, James William Williams, Edward Thomas Vizard.

Goal: James Quinn (87)

101. 11.03.1912   British Championship
WALES v ENGLAND 0-2 (0-2)
The Racecourse, Wrexham
Referee: Thomas Dougray (Scotland)   Attendance: 14,000

WALES: Robert Owen Evans, Llewelyn Davies, Lloyd Davies, Edwin Hughes, Ernest Peake, Joseph Thomas Jones, William Henry Meredith (Cap), George Arthur Wynn, Evan Jones, Arthur Grenville Morris, Edward Thomas Vizard.

ENGLAND: Reginald Garnet Williamson, Robert Crompton (Cap), Jesse Pennington, James Thomas Brittleton, William John Wedlock, Joseph William Harry Makepeace, John Simpson, Frank Jefferis, Bertram Clewley Freeman, George Henry Holley, Robert Ernest Evans.

Goals: George Holley (2), Bertram Clewley Freeman (41)

102. 13.04.1912   British Championship
WALES v IRELAND 2-3 (1-0)
Ninian Park, Cardiff
Referee: Herbert Bamlett (England)   Attendance: 10,000

WALES: Robert Owen Evans, Llewelyn Davies, Moses Richard Russell, Edwin Hughes, Leonard Francis Newton, Joseph Thomas Jones, William Henry Meredith (Cap), James William Williams, William Davies, David Walter Davies, John Hugh Evans.

IRELAND: John Hanna, Alexander Craig, William George McConnell, Henry Vernon Hampton, B. Brennan, David Rollo, John Houston, Denis Hannon, John McDonnell, John McCandless, Frank Thompson.

Goals: William Davies (30), David Walter Davies (53) /
John McCandless (#), B. Brennan (#), John McCandless (#)

103. 18.01.1913   British Championship
IRELAND v WALES   0-1 (0-1)
Grosvenor Park, Belfast
Referee: John Hargreaves Pearson (England)   Att: 8,000
IRELAND: William Scott (Cap), Samuel Burnison, Patrick McCann, David Rollo, Leo Donnelly, Henry Vernon Hampton, John Houston, William Lacey, John McDonnell, John McCandless, Frank Thompson.
WALES: William Ellis Bailiff, Thomas John Hewitt, Llewelyn Davies (Cap), George Latham, Ernest Peake, Joseph Thomas Jones, William Henry Meredith, David Walter Davies, Walter Otto Davis, James Roberts, John Hugh Evans.
Goal: James Roberts (15)

104. 03.03.1913   British Championship
WALES v SCOTLAND   0-0
The Racecourse, Wrexham
Referee: Isaac Baker (England)   Attendance: 8,000
WALES: William Ellis Bailiff, Thomas John Hewitt, Llewelyn Davies, Edwin Hughes (Cap), Lloyd Davies, William Jones, William Henry Meredith, George Arthur Wynn, Walter Otto Davis, James Roberts, Edward Thomas Vizard.
SCOTLAND: James Brownlie, Robert Abbie Orrock, John Walker, James Eadie Gordon, Charles Bellany Thomson (Cap), James Campbell, Andrew McAtee, Robert Walker, William Reid, Andrew Wilson, Robert Bryson Templeton.

105. 17.03.1913   British Championship
ENGLAND v WALES   4-3 (3-1)
Ashton Gate, Bristol
Referee: Alexander Jackson (Scotland)   Attendance: 8,000
ENGLAND: Ernald Oak Scattergood, Robert Crompton (Cap), Jesse Pennington, Hugh Moffat, Joseph McCall, William Bradshaw, Charles William Wallace, Harold John Fleming, Joseph Harold Hampton, Edwin Gladstone Latheron, Joseph Charles Hodkinson.
WALES: William Ellis Bailiff, Llewelyn Davies, Lloyd Davies, Thomas John Hewitt, Edwin Hughes, Ernest Peake, Joseph Thomas Jones, William Henry Meredith, George Arthur Wynn, Walter Otto Davis (Cap), William Jones.
Goals: Harold Fleming (28), Edwin Gladstone Latheron (35), Joseph McCall (40), Joseph Harold Hampton (63) /
Walter Otto Davis (10), William Henry Meredith (52), Ernest Peake (70)

106. 19.01.1914   British Championship
WALES v IRELAND   1-2 (1-2)
The Racecourse, Wrexham
Referee: Isaac Baker (England)   Attendance: 5,000
WALES: Edward John Peers, Llewelyn Davies, Lloyd Davies (Cap), Edwin Hughes, Ernest Peake, Joseph Thomas Jones, William Henry Meredith, Evan Jones, Walter Otto Davis, William Jones, Edward Thomas Vizard.
IRELAND: Frederick McKee, William George McConnell, Alexander Craig, Valentine Harris (Cap), Patrick O'Connell, David Rollo, H. Seymour, Samuel Young, William Gillespie, William Lacey, Louis Bookman.
Goals: Evan Jones (60 pen) /
Samuel Young (#), William Gillespie (#)

107. 28.02.1914   British Championship
SCOTLAND v WALES   0-0
Celtic Park, Glasgow
Referee: Harold Taylor (England)   Attendance: 10,000
SCOTLAND: James Brownlie, Thomas Kelso, Joseph Dodds, Peter Nellies (Cap), Peter Pursell, Harold Anderson, Alexander Pollock Donaldson, James McMenemy, James Greig Reid, James Anderson Croal, J. Browning.
WALES: Edward John Peers, Thomas John Hewitt, William Jennings, Thomas James Matthias, Lloyd Davies (Cap), Joseph Thomas Jones, William Henry Meredith, George Arthur Wynn, Walter Otto Davis, William Jones, John Hugh Evans.

108. 16.03.1914   British Championship
WALES v ENGLAND   0-2 (0-0)
Ninian Park, Cardiff
Referee: James Mason (England)   Attendance: 17,000
WALES: Edward John Peers, Moses Richard Russell, Thomas James Matthias, Thomas John Hewitt, Lloyd Davies, William Jennings, William Henry Meredith, George Arthur Wynn, Alfred Stanley Rowlands, William Charles Davies, Edward Thomas Vizard (Cap).
ENGLAND: Samuel Hardy, Robert Crompton (Cap), Henry Colclough, James Thomas Brittleton, William John Wedlock, Robert McNeal, John Simpson, Daniel Shea, Joseph Harold Hampton, Joseph Smith, Edwin Mosscrop.
Goals: Joseph Smith (50), William John Wedlock (70)

109. 14.02.1920   British Championship
IRELAND v WALES 2-2 (1-0)
The Oval, Belfast

Referee: Isaac Baker (England)   Attendance: 30,000

IRELAND: William O'Hagan, Robert Manderson, David Rollo, William McCandless, Michael Hamill, William Emerson (Cap), David Lyner, William Lacey, William Gillespie, James Ferris, John McCandless.

WALES: William Ellis Bailiff, Harold Millership, Moses Richard Russell (Cap), Thomas James Matthias, Joseph Thomas Jones, Frederick Charles Keenor, William Henry Meredith, William Jones, Stanley Charles Davies, Ivor Jones, John Hugh Evans.

Goals: William McCandless (#), William Emerson (#) / Stanley Charles Davies (#, #)

110. 26.02.1920   British Championship
WALES v SCOTLAND 1-1 (1-0)
Ninian Park, Cardiff

Referee: James Mason (England)   Attendance: 16,000

WALES: Edward John Peers, Harold Millership, Moses Richard Russell, Thomas James Matthias, Joseph Thomas Jones, William Jennings, William Henry Meredith (Cap), Ivor Jones, Stanley Charles Davies, Richard William Richards, John Hugh Evans.

SCOTLAND: Kenneth Campbell, Alexander McNair, David Thomson, James Eadie Gordon, William Cringan (Cap), James McMullan, James Greig Reid, John Anderson Crosbie, Andrew Nesbit Wilson, Thomas Cairns, Alan Lauder Morton.

Goals: John Hugh Evans (5) / Thomas Cairns (78)

111. 15.03.1920   British Championship
ENGLAND v WALES 1-2 (1-2)
Highbury, London

Referee: Alexander Jackson (Scotland)   Attendance: 21,110

ENGLAND: Samuel Hardy, Thomas Clay, Jesse Pennington (Cap), Andrew Ducat, Frank Barson, Arthur Grimsdell, Samuel Chedgzoy, Charles Murray Buchan, George Washington Elliott, Joseph Smith, Alfred Edward Quantrill.

WALES: Edward John Peers, Harold Millership, Moses Richard Russell, Thomas James Matthias, Joseph Thomas Jones, Frederick Charles Keenor, William Henry Meredith (Cap), William Jones, Stanley Charles Davies, Richard William Richards, Edward Thomas Vizard.

Goal: Charles Murray Buchan (7) / Stanley Davies (11 pen), Richard William Richards (35)

112. 12.02.1921   British Championship
SCOTLAND v WALES 2-1 (1-1)
Pittodrie, Aberdeen

Referee: James Mason (England)   Attendance: 20,824

SCOTLAND: Kenneth Campbell (Cap), John Marshall, William McStay, Joseph Harris, Charles Ross Pringle, James McMullan, Alexander Archibald, Andrew Cunningham, Andrew Nesbit Wilson, Joseph Cassidy, Alexander Troup.

WALES: Edward John Peers, Harold Millership, Moses Richard Russell, Frederick Charles Keenor, Joseph Thomas Jones, Thomas James Matthias, David Rees Williams, David Collier, Francis Thomas Hoddinott, Stanley Charles Davies, Edward Thomas Vizard.

Goals: Andrew Nesbit Wilson (10, 46) / David Collier (30)

113. 14.03.1921   British Championship
WALES v ENGLAND 0-0
Ninian Park, Cardiff

Referee: Alexander Jackson (Scotland)   Attendance: 12,000

WALES: Edward John Peers, Harold Millership, Moses Richard Russell, Frederick Charles Keenor, Joseph Thomas Jones, Thomas James Matthias, David Rees Williams, Ivor Jones, Francis Thomas Hoddinott, Stanley Charles Davies, Edward Thomas Vizard.

ENGLAND: Ernest Herbert Coleman, Warneford Cresswell, John Silcock, John Bamber, George Wilson, Thomas George Bromilow, Samuel Chedgzoy, Robert Kelly, Charles Murray Buchan (Cap), Henry Chambers, Alfred Edward Quantrill.

114. 09.04.1921   British Championship
WALES v NORTHERN IRELAND 2-1
Vetch Field, Swansea

Referee: John Thomas Howcroft (England)   Att: 12,000

WALES: Edward John Peers, Moses Richard Russell, Harold Millership, Frederick Charles Keenor, Robert William Matthews, Thomas James Matthias, William James Hole, Ivor Jones, Stanley Charles Davies, Richard William Richards, Edward Thomas Vizard.

NORTHERN IRELAND: Elisha Scott, David Rollo, William McCandless, William Lacey, Michael Scraggs, John Harris, Patrick Robinson, John Brown, Robert James Chambers, Allan Mathieson, Louis Bookman.

Goals: William James Hole (#), Stanley Charles Davies (#) / Robert James Chambers (#)

23

115. 04.02.1922   British Championship
WALES v SCOTLAND 2-1 (2-0)
The Racecourse, Wrexham
Referee: Arthur Ward (England)   Attendance: 8,000
WALES: Edward John Peers, Edward Parry, James Henry Evans, Herbert Price Evans, Joseph Thomas Jones, Thomas James Matthias, Stanley Charles Davies, Ivor Jones, Leonard Stephen Davies, Richard William Richards, Edward Thomas Vizard.
SCOTLAND: Kenneth Campbell, John Marshall (Cap), Donald McKinlay, David Ditchburn Meiklejohn, Michael Gilhooley, William Collier, Alexander Archibald, John White, Andrew Nesbit Wilson, Frank Walker, Alan Lauder Morton.
Goals: Leonard Davies (7), Stanley Charles Davies (25) / Alexander Archibald (65)

116. 13.03.1922   British Championship
ENGLAND v WALES 1-0 (1-0)
Anfield Road, Liverpool
Referee: Forshaw (England)   Attendance: 30,000
ENGLAND: John Edward Davison, Thomas Clay, Frederick Titmuss, Bertram Smith, Maxwell Woosnam (Cap), Thomas George Bromilow, Frederick Ingram Walden, Robert Kelly, William Ernest Rawlings, William Henry Walker, William Henry Smith.
WALES: Edward John Peers, Moses Richard Russell, James Henry Evans, Herbert Price Evans, Joseph Thomas Jones, Thomas James Matthias, William James Hole, Stanley Charles Davies, Leonard Stephen Davies, Richard William Richards, Edward Thomas Vizard.
Goal: Robert Kelly (3)

117. 01.04.1922   British Championship
NORTHERN IRELAND v WALES 1-1
Windsor Park, Belfast
Referee: Arthur Ward (England)   Attendance: 20,000
NORTHERN IRELAND: Joseph Alexander Cuthbert Mehaffy, William McCracken, John Joseph Curran, Robert McCracken, Michael Terence O'Brien, William Emerson, David Lyner, William Crooks, John Francis Doran, William Gillespie, Joseph Toner.
WALES: Edward John Peers, Moses Richard Russell, James Henry Evans, Herbert Price Evans, Joseph Thomas Jones, Thomas James Matthias, Stanley Charles Davies, Frederick Charles Keenor, Leonard Stephen Davies, Ivor Jones, John Hugh Evans.
Goals: William Gillespie (#) / Leonard Stephen Davies (#)

118. 05.03.1923   British Championship
ENGLAND v WALES 2-2 (1-1)
Ninian Park, Cardiff
Referee: Bryan (England)   Attendance: 15,000
ENGLAND: Edward Hallows Taylor, Ephraim Longworth, Frederick Titmuss, Thomas Patrick Magee, George Wilson, Arthur Grimsdell (Cap), Jack Carr, James Marshall Seed, Victor Martin Watson, Henry Chambers, Owen Williams.
WALES: Edward John Peers, Edward Parry, Moses Richard Russell, Frederick Charles Keenor, Robert William Matthews, William Jennings, William James Hole, Ivor Jones, Leonard Stephen Davies, Edward Thomas Vizard, John Hugh Evans.
Goals: Henry Chambers (36), Victor Martin Watson (48) / Frederick Charles Keenor (17), Ivor Jones (86)

119. 17.03.1923   British Championship
SCOTLAND v WALES 2-0 (1-0)
Love Street, St.Mirren Park, Paisley
Referee: Isaac Baker (England)   Attendance: 25,000
SCOTLAND: William Harper, John Hutton, James Blair, John McNab, William Cringan (Cap), David Morton Steele, Henry McGill Ritchie, Andrew Cunningham, Andrew Nesbit Wilson, Thomas Cairns, Alan Lauder Morton.
WALES: George Alfred Godding, Moses Richard Russell, James Henry Evans, Thomas James Matthias, Frederick Charles Keenor, Robert Frederick John, David Rees Williams, Robert Idwal Davies, Stanley Charles Davies, Leonard Stephen Davies, David Sidney Nicholas.
Goals: Andrew Nesbit Wilson (7, 55)

120. 14.04.1923   British Championship
WALES v NORTHERN IRELAND 0-3
The Racecourse, Wrexham
Referee: George Nunnerley (England)   Attendance: 12,222
WALES: George Alfred Godding, Moses Richard Russell, Edward Parry, Robert Frederick John, Frederick Charles Keenor, William Jennings, William James Hole, Ivor Jones, Leonard Stephen Davies, Edward Thomas Vizard, John Hugh Evans.
NORTHERN IRELAND: Thomas Farquharson, John Alexander Mackie, Andrew Kennedy, Samuel Johnstone Irving, Ernest Edwin Smith, William Emerson, David Lyner, Patrick Gallagher, Robert William Irvine, William Gillespie, Joseph Toner.
Goals: Robert William Irvine (#, #), William Gillespie (#)

121. 16.02.1924   British Championship
WALES v SCOTLAND 2-0 (0-0)
Ninian Park, Cardiff
Referee: H.W. Andrews (England)   Attendance: 26,000
WALES: Albert Gray, Moses Richard Russell, John Jenkins, Herbert Price Evans, Frederick Charles Keenor, William Jennings, William Davies, Ivor Jones, Leonard Stephen Davies, Richard William Richards, Edward Thomas Vizard.
SCOTLAND: William Harper, John Marshall, James Blair (Cap), David Ditchburn Meiklejohn, Neil McBain, Thomas Allan Muirhead, Alexander Archibald, William Fraser Russell, Joseph Cassidy, John McKay, Alan Lauder Morton.
Goals: William Davies (61), Leonard Stephen Davies (72)

122. 03.03.1924   British Championship
ENGLAND v WALES 1-2 (0-0)
Ewood Park, Blackburn
Referee: George Noel Watson (England)   Att: 30,000
ENGLAND: William Ronald Sewell, Thomas Smart, Thomas Mort, Frederick William Kean, George Wilson (Cap), Percival Henry Barton, Samuel Chedgzoy, David Bone Nightingale Jack, William Thomas Roberts, Clement Stephenson, Frederick Edward Tunstall.
WALES: Albert Gray, Moses Richard Russell, John Jenkins, Herbert Price Evans, Frederick Charles Keenor, William Jennings, William Davies, John Barry Nicholls, Leonard Stephen Davies, Richard William Richards, Edward Thomas Vizard.
Goal: William Thomas Roberts (55) / William Davies (59), Edward Thomas Vizard (62)

123. 15.03.1924   British Championship
NORTHERN IRELAND v WALES 0-1
Windsor Park, Belfast
Referee: Arthur Kingscott (England)   Attendance: 40,000
NORTHERN IRELAND: Thomas Farquharson, David Rollo, William McCandless, Joseph Gowdy, Michael Terence O'Brien, Samuel Johnstone Irving, John Brown, Patrick Gallagher, Patrick McIlvenny, William Gillespie, Joseph Toner.
WALES: Albert Gray, Moses Richard Russell, John Jenkins, Herbert Price Evans, Frederick Charles Keenor, William Jennings, William Davies, John Barry Nicholls, Leonard Stephen Davies, Richard William Richards, Edward Thomas Vizard.
Goal: Moses Richard Russell (# penalty)

124. 14.02.1925   British Championship
SCOTLAND v WALES 3-1 (2-1)
Tynecastle Park, Edinburgh
Referee: Arthur Ward (England)   Attendance: 25,000
SCOTLAND: William Harper, James Nelson, William McStay, David Ditchburn Meiklejohn, David Morris (Cap), Robert Hunter Brown Bennie, Alexander Skinner Jackson, James Dunn, Hugh Kilpatrick Gallacher, Thomas Cairns, Alan Lauder Morton.
WALES: Albert Gray, Moses Richard Russell, John Jenkins, Stanley Charles Davies, Frederick Charles Keenor, William Williams, William Davies, John Barry Nicholls, Leonard Stephen Davies, George Beadles, Frederick Cook.
Goals: David Ditchburn Meiklejohn (9), Hugh Kilpatrick Gallacher (20, 61) / William Williams II (43)

125. 28.02.1925   British Championship
WALES v ENGLAND 1-2 (1-2)
Vetch Field, Swansea
Referee: J. Cahill (Northern Ireland)   Attendance: 8,000
WALES: Albert Gray, Ernest James Morley, Moses Richard Russell, Edwin Samuel Jenkins, Frederick Charles Keenor, Daniel Edgar Thomas, William Davies, John Barry Nicholls, John Fowler, George Beadles, Frederick Cook.
ENGLAND: Richard Henry Pym, William Ashurst, Alfred George Bower (Cap), John Henry Hill, Charles William Spencer, Leonard Graham, Robert Kelly, Frank Roberts, Thomas Edwin Reed Cook, William Henry Walker, Arthur Reginald Dorrell.
Goals: Frederick Keenor (35) / Frank Roberts (11, 15)

126. 18.04.1925   British Championship
WALES v NORTHERN IRELAND 0-0
The Racecourse, Wrexham
Referee: Ernest Pinkston (England)   Attendance: 10,000
WALES: Albert Gray, Edward Parry, John Jenkins, John Reginald Blacknall Moulsdale, Frederick Charles Keenor, Robert Frederick John, William Davies, Stanley Charles Davies, James Jones, Leonard Stephen Davies, Jesse Thomas Williams.
NORTHERN IRELAND: Elisha Scott, David Rollo, William Henry McConnell, John Garrett, Michael Terence O'Brien, Samuel Johnstone Irving, Tom Cowan, Patrick Gallagher, Andrew Sloan, Hugh Leonard Meek, Henry Wilson.

127. 31.10.1925 British Championship
WALES v SCOTLAND 0-3 (0-0)
Ninian Park, Cardiff

Referee: Ernest Pinkstone (England) Attendance: 18,000

WALES: Albert Gray, Moses Richard Russell, John Jenkins, Samuel Bennion, Frederick Charles Keenor, James John Lewis, David Rees Williams, William Davies, Stanley Charles Davies, Richard William Richards, Edward Thomas Vizard.

SCOTLAND: William Robb, John Hutton, William McStay, William Clunas, Thomas Townsley (Cap), James McMullan, Alexander Skinner Jackson, John Duncan, Hugh Kilpatrick Gallacher, Alexander Wilson James, Adam McLean.

Goals: John Duncan (70), Adam McLean (80), William Clunas (82)

128. 13.02.1926 British Championship
NORTHERN IRELAND v WALES 3-0
Windsor Park, Belfast

Referee: Peter Craigmyle (Scotland) Attendance: 25,000

NORTHERN IRELAND: Elisha Scott, Walter Brown, William Henry McConnell, Samuel Johnstone Irving, Michael Terence O'Brien, Thomas Sloan, Andrew Bothwell, Alexander Steele, Samuel Curran, William Gillespie, David McMullan.

WALES: Arthur Ivor Brown, Edward Parry, Thomas Jones, John Newnes, Robert William Matthews, David Evans, William Davies, Leonard Stephen Davies, John Fowler, Stanley Charles Davies, Ivor Jones.

Goals: William Gillespie (#), Samuel Curran (#, #)

129. 01.03.1926 British Championship
ENGLAND v WALES 1-3 (0-1)
Selhurst Park, London

Referee: William Russell (England) Attendance: 23,000

ENGLAND: Richard Henry Pym, Warneford Cresswell, Samuel John Wadsworth (Cap), Willis Edwards, John Edward Townrow, George Henry Green, Thomas Urwin, Robert Kelly, Norman Bullock, William Henry Walker, James Henry Dimmock.

WALES: Albert Gray, Moses Richard Russell, John Jenkins, Stanley Charles Davies, William John Pullen, Robert Frederick John, William Davies, Leonard Stephen Davies, John Fowler, Charles Jones, Edward Thomas Vizard.

Goal: William Henry Walker (54) /
John Fowler (43, 57), William Davies (56)

130. 30.10.1926 British Championship
SCOTLAND v WALES 3-0 (2-0)
Ibrox Park, Glasgow

Referee: John Forshaw (England) Attendance: 41,000

SCOTLAND: Allan McClory, William McStay (Cap), William Wiseman, James Davidson Gibson, Robert Gillespie, James McMullan, Alexander Skinner Jackson, Andrew Cunningham, Hugh Kilpatrick Gallacher, Thomas Bruce McInally, Adam McLean.

WALES: Albert Gray, Thomas John Evans, John Jenkins, Samuel Bennion, Frederick Charles Keenor, William Jennings, William Davies, Stanley Charles Davies, John Fowler, Charles Jones, Edward Thomas Vizard.

Goals: Hugh Kilpatrick Gallacher (20), Alexander Skinner Jackson (33, 73)

131. 12.02.1927 British Championship
WALES v ENGLAND 3-3 (2-2)
The Racecourse, Wrexham

Referee: Albert Edward Fogg (England) Att: 16,101

WALES: Daniel Lewis, Thomas Jones, Robert Frederick John, Frederick Charles Keenor, Thomas Percival Griffiths, David Evans, David Rees Williams, Wilfred Leslie Lewis, Leonard Stephen Davies, David Sidney Nicholas, Henry Thomas.

ENGLAND: John Henry Brown, Alfred George Bower (Cap), George Smith Waterfield, Willis Edwards, James Seddon, George Henry Green, William Harold Pease, George Brown, William Ralph Dean, William Henry Walker, Louis Antonia Page.

Goals: Leonard Stephen Davies (13, 36 pen), Wilfred Leslie Lewis (60) /
William Ralph Dean (11, 63), William Henry Walker (17)

132. 09.04.1927 British Championship
WALES v NORTHERN IRELAND 2-2 (2-0)
Ninian Park, Cardiff

Referee: Ernest Pinkston (England) Attendance: 10,000

WALES: Sidney John Vivian Leonard Evans, Thomas Jones, William Jennings, Frederick Charles Keenor, Thomas Percival Griffiths, David Evans, David Rees Williams, Wilfred Leslie Lewis, Leonard Stephen Davies, Charles Jones, David Sidney Nicholas.

NORTHERN IRELAND: Elisha Scott, Andrew McCluggage, William Henry McConnell, Samuel Johnstone Irving, Thomas Sloan, Michael Terence O'Brien, Andrew Bothwell, Robert William Irvine, Harold Johnston, William Gillespie, Harold McCaw.

Goals: David Rees Williams (#, #) / Harold Johnston (#, #)

133. 29.10.1927   British Championship
WALES v SCOTLAND 2-2 (1-2)
The Racecourse, Wrexham

Referee: Arthur Kingscott (England)   Attendance: 16,000

WALES: Albert Gray, Moses Richard Russell, Thomas John Evans, Samuel Bennion, Frederick Charles Keenor, Stanley Charles Davies, William James Hole, Leonard Stephen Davies, John Fowler, Ernest Robert Curtis, Frederick Cook.

SCOTLAND: William Robb, John Hutton, William McStay, David Ditchburn Meiklejohn, James Davidson Gibson, James McMullan (Cap), Alexander Skinner Jackson, Robert McKay, Hugh Kilpatrick Gallacher, George Stevenson, Alan Lauder Morton.

Goals: Ernest Robert Curtis (44), James Gibson (76 own goal) / Hugh Kilpatrick Gallacher (14), John Hutton (16 pen)

134. 28.11.1927   British Championship
ENGLAND v WALES 1-2 (0-2)
Turf Moor, Burnley

Referee: Bell (Scotland)   Attendance: 32,089

ENGLAND: Richard Daniel Tremelling, Frederick Roy Goodall, Reginald Osborne, Alfred Baker, John Henry Hill (Cap), Henry Nuttall, Joseph Harold Anthony Hulme, George Brown, William Ralph Dean, Arthur Rigby, Louis Antonia Page.

WALES: Albert Gray, Benjamin David Williams, Thomas John Evans, Samuel Bennion, Frederick Charles Keenor, Robert Frederick John, William James Hole, Leonard Stephen Davies, Wilfred Leslie Lewis, Charles Jones, Frederick Cook.

Goal: Albert Gray (79 own goal) / Wilfred Leslie Lewis (22), John Henry Hill (40 own goal)

135. 04.02.1928   British Championship
NORTHERN IRELAND v WALES 1-2
Windsor Park, Belfast

Referee: H. Hopkinson (England)   Attendance: 27,563

NORTHERN IRELAND: Elisha Scott, Andrew McCluggage, William Henry McConnell, Samuel Johnstone Irving, Francis Gerald Morgan, Thomas Sloan, Robert James Chambers, James Dunne, Hugh Davey, Patrick McConnell, John Mahood.

WALES: Daniel Lewis, Benjamin David Williams, Thomas John Evans, Samuel Bennion, Frederick Charles Keenor, Robert Frederick John, William James Hole, William Davies, Wilfred Leslie Lewis, Leonard Stephen Davies, Rev. Hywel Davies.

Goal: Robert James Chambers (#) / William Davies (#), Wilfred Leslie Lewis (#)

136. 27.10.1928   British Championship
SCOTLAND v WALES 4-2 (2-1)
Ibrox Park, Glasgow

Referee: Arthur Kingscott (England)   Attendance: 55,000

SCOTLAND: John Diamond Harkness, Douglas Herbert Gray, Daniel Blair, Thomas Allan Muirhead, William King, James McMullan (Cap), Alexander Skinner Jackson, James Dunn, Hugh Kilpatrick Gallacher, Robert Low McPhail, Alan Lauder Morton.

WALES: Albert Gray, Ernest James Morley, William Jennings, Samuel Bennion, Frederick Charles Keenor, David Evans, William James Hole, William Davies, Wilfred Leslie Lewis, Leonard Stephen Davies, David Rees Williams.

Goals: Hugh Gallacher (25, 42, 49), James Dunn (56) / William Davies (12, 75)

137. 17.11.1928   British Championship
WALES v ENGLAND 2-3 (0-2)
Vetch Field, Swansea

Referee: Bell (Scotland)   Attendance: 22,000

WALES: Albert Gray, Ernest James Morley, Moses Richard Russell, Thomas Percival Griffiths, Frederick Charles Keenor, Samuel Bennion, William James Hole, William Davies, John Fowler, Leonard Stephen Davies, David Rees Williams.

ENGLAND: John Hacking, Thomas Cooper, Ernest Blenkinsop, Willis Edwards (Cap), Ernest Arthur Hart, Austin Fenwick Campbell, Joseph Harold Anthony Hulme, Ernest William Hine, William Ralph Dean, Joseph Bradford, James William Ruffel.

Goals: John Fowler (55), Frederick Charles Keenor (88) / Joseph Harold Anthony Hulme (11, 25), Ernest Hine (86)

138. 02.02.1929   British Championship
WALES v NORTHERN IRELAND 2-2
The Racecourse, Wrexham

Referee: James Victor Pennington (England)   Att. 12,000

WALES: Albert Gray, Ernest James Morley, Arthur Albert Lumberg, Samuel Bennion, Frederick Charles Keenor, Stanley James Bowsher, William Davies, Eugene O'Callaghan, Albert William Mays, Leonard Stephen Davies, Frederick Windsor Warren.

NORTHERN IRELAND: Elisha Scott, Andrew McCluggage, William McCandless, Joseph Miller, James H. Elwood, Alexander Steele, Robert James Chambers, Richard William Morris Rowley, Joseph Bambrick, Lawrence Cumming, John Mahood.

Goals: Albert William Mays (#), Frederick Warren (#) / John Mahood (#), Andrew McCluggage (# penalty)

139. 26.10.1929   British Championship
WALES v SCOTLAND 2-4 (0-2)
Ninian Park, Cardiff
Referee: William McLean (Northern Ireland)   Att: 25,000
WALES: Albert Gray, Benjamin David Williams, Arthur Albert Lumberg, Samuel Bennion, Frederick Charles Keenor, Robert Frederick John, William Davies, Eugene O'Callaghan, Leonard Stephen Davies, Charles Jones, Frederick Cook.
SCOTLAND: John Diamond Harkness, Douglas Herbert Gray, Joseph Nibloe, James Davidson Gibson, John Ainslie Johnstone, Thomas Craig, Alexander Skinner Jackson, Thomas Allan Muirhead (Cap), Hugh Kilpatrick Gallacher, Alexander Wilson James, Alan Lauder Morton.
Goals: Eugene O'Callaghan (55), Leonard Davies (63) / Hugh Gallacher (7, 20), Alexander Wilson James (74), James Davidson Gibson (77)

140. 20.11.1929   British Championship
ENGLAND v WALES 6-0 (2-0)
Stamford Bridge, London
Referee: William McLean (Northern Ireland)   Att: 32,945
ENGLAND: Henry Edward Hibbs, Thomas Smart, Ernest Blenkinsop, Willis Edwards (Cap), Ernest Arthur Hart, William Marsden, Hugh Adcock, Ernest William Hine, George Henry Camsell, Thomas Clark Fisher Johnson, James William Ruffel.
WALES: Daniel Lewis, Benjamin David Williams, Arthur Albert Lumberg, Frederick Charles Keenor, Thomas Percival Griffiths, Robert Frederick John, William Davies, Leonard Stephen Davies, Wilfred Leslie Lewis, Charles Jones, Frederick Cook.
Goals: Thomas Clark Fisher Johnson (12, 65), George Henry Camsell (16, 61, 75), Hugh Adcock (70)

141. 01.02.1930   British Championship
NORTHERN IRELAND v WALES 7-0 (2-0)
Celtic Park, Belfast
Referee: Thomas Crewe (England)   Attendance: 25,000
NORTHERN IRELAND: Alfred Gardiner, Andrew McCluggage, Robert Fulton, William McCleery, John Jones, Thomas Sloan, Robert James Chambers, Richard William Morris Rowley, Joseph Bambrick, James McCambridge, John Mahood.
WALES: Richard Prytherch Finnegan, Arthur Ronald Hugh, Thomas Jones, Edward Lawrence, Frederick Charles Keenor, John Pugsley, William Davies, Bertie Williams, Tudor James Martin, Stanley Charles Davies, Frederick Cook.
Goals: Joseph Bambrick (6 goals), Andrew McCluggage (#)

142. 25.10.1930   British Championship
SCOTLAND v WALES 1-1 (1-1)
Ibrox Park, Glasgow
Referee: C.E. Lines (England)   Attendance: 23,106
SCOTLAND: John Thomson, Douglas Herbert Gray, John Rooney Gilmour, Colin Duncan McNab, Robert Gillespie (Cap), Frank Robert Hill, Daniel McRorie, George Clark Phillips Brown, Bernard Joseph Battles, George Stevenson, Alan Lauder Morton.
WALES: Sidney John Vivian Leonard Evans, Frederick Dewey, Wynne Crompton, William Rogers, Frederick Charles Keenor, Emrys Ellis, William Collins, John Edward Neal, Thomas Bamford, Walter William Robbins, William Rees Thomas.
Goals: Bernard Joseph Battles (37) / Thomas Bamford (6)

143. 22.11.1930   British Championship
WALES v ENGLAND 0-4 (0-2)
The Racecourse, Wrexham
Referee: Hugh Watson (Scotland)   Attendance: 11,282
WALES: Sidney John Vivian Leonard Evans, Frederick Dewey, Wynne Crompton, William Rogers, Frederick Charles Keenor, Emrys Ellis, Albert Leslie Williams, John Edward Neal, Thomas Bamford, Walter William Robbins, William Rees Thomas.
ENGLAND: Henry Edward Hibbs, Frederick Roy Goodall (Cap), Ernest Blenkinsop, Alfred Henry Strange, Thomes Leach, Austin Fenwick Campbell, Samuel Dickinson Crooks, Gordon Hodgson, James Hampson, Joseph Bradford, William Eric Houghton.
Goals: James Hampson (12, 70), Gordon Hodgson (35), Joseph Bradford (72)

144. 22.04.1931   British Championship
WALES v NORTHERN IRELAND 3-2
The Racecourse, Wrexham
Referee: William Percy Harper (England)   Att: 11,000
WALES: William Ronald John, Benjamin David Williams, Wynne Crompton, Frederick Charles Keenor, Thomas Percival Griffiths, David Thomas Richards, Cuthbert Phillips, David Astley, Thomas Bamford, Wilfred Bernard James, Frederick Windsor Warren.
NORTHERN IRELAND: John Diffin, Andrew McCluggage, Robert Fulton, Samuel Johnstone Irving, John Jones, William McCleery, Harold Anthony Duggan, Richard William Morris Rowley, James Dunne, James McCambridge, Harold McCaw.
Goals: Cuthbert Phillips (#), Thomas Percival Griffiths (#), Frederick Windsor Warren (#) / James Dunne (#), Richard William Morris Rowley (#)

28

145. 31.10.1931   British Championship
WALES v SCOTLAND 2-3 (1-2)

The Racecourse, Wrexham

Referee: Isaac Caswell (England)   Attendance: 10,860

WALES: Albert Gray, Aneurin Glyndwr Richards, Arthur Albert Lumberg, Thomas Edwards, Thomas Percival Griffiths, Edward Lawrence, Philip Henry, Eugene O'Callaghan, Ernest Matthew Glover, Walter William Robbins, Ernest Robert Curtis.

SCOTLAND: John Diamond Harkness, Daniel Blair, Robert McAulay, Alexander Massie, David Ditchburn Meiklejohn (Cap), George Clark Phillips Brown, Robert Austin Thomson, George Stevenson, James Edward McGrory, Robert Low McPhail, Alan Lauder Morton.

Goals: Ernest Curtis (15 pen), Eugene O'Callaghan (78) / George Stevenson (25), Robert Austin Thomson (31), James Edward McGrory (55)

146. 18.11.1931   British Championship
ENGLAND v WALES 3-1 (1-1)

Anfield Road, Liverpool

Referee: Bunnell (England)   Attendance: 15,000

ENGLAND: Henry Edward Hibbs, Thomas Cooper, Ernest Blenkinsop, Alfred Henry Strange (Cap), Charles William Gee, Austin Fenwick Campbell, Samuel Dickinson Crooks, John William Smith, Thomas Waring, Ernest William Hine, Clifford Sydney Bastin.

WALES: Albert Gray, Benjamin David Williams, Benjamin Ellis, Charles Jones, Thomas Percival Griffiths, Robert Frederick John, Cuthbert Phillips, Eugene O'Callaghan, David Astley, Walter William Robbins, Frederick Cook.

Goals: John Smith (38), Samuel Dickinson Crooks (50), Ernest William Hine (65) / Walter William Robbins (30)

147. 05.12.1931   British Championship
NORTHERN IRELAND v WALES 4-0

Windsor Park, Belfast

Referee: Peter Snape (England)   Attendance: 10,000

NORTHERN IRELAND: Elisha Scott, John McNinch, Robert Fulton, William McCleery, Maurice Pyper, William Mitchell, Robert James Chambers, Robert William Irvine, Joseph Bambrick, William Millar, James Kelly.

WALES: Albert Gray, Sidney Wilfred Lawrence, Hugh Edward Foulkes, Samuel Bennion, Thomas Percival Griffiths, Emrys Ellis, Thomas John Jones, Wilfred Bernard James, Thomas Bamford, Walter William Robbins, John Edward Parris.

Goals: James Kelly (#, #), William Millar (#), Joseph Bambrick (#)

148. 26.10.1932   British Championship
SCOTLAND v WALES 2-5 (0-4)

Tynecastle Park, Edinburgh

Referee: William Harper (England)   Attendance: 31,000

SCOTLAND: Alexander McLaren, Douglas Herbert Gray, Daniel Blair, Hugh Morrison Wales, John Ainslie Johnstone (Cap), John Ross Thomson, James Crawford, Alexander Thomson, Neil Hamilton Dewar, Alexander Wilson James, Douglas Duncan.

WALES: William Ronald John, Benjamin David Williams, Benjamin Ellis, Frederick Charles Keenor, Thomas Percival Griffiths, David Thomas Richards, Cuthbert Phillips, Eugene O'Callaghan, David Astley, Walter William Robbins, David Jenkin Lewis.

Goals: Neil Hamilton Dewar (63), Douglas Duncan (70) / John Ross Thomson (9 own goal), Thomas Griffiths (20), Eugene O'Callaghan (25, 46), David Astley (43)

149. 16.11.1932   British Championship
WALES v ENGLAND 0-0

The Racecourse, Wrexham

Referee: Samuel Thompson (Northern Ireland)   Att: 25,250

WALES: William Ronald John, Benjamin David Williams, Benjamin Ellis, James Patrick Murphy, Thomas Percival Griffiths, David Thomas Richards, Frederick Windsor Warren, Eugene O'Callaghan, David Astley, Walter William Robbins, David Jenkin Lewis.

ENGLAND: Henry Edward Hibbs, Frederick Roy Goodall, Ernest Blenkinsop, Lewis Stoker, Alfred Young, Joseph Thomas Tate, Samuel Dickinson Crooks, David Bone Nightingale Jack (Cap), George Brown, Edward Sandford, Arthur Cunliffe.

150. 07.12.1932   British Championship
WALES v NORTHERN IRELAND 4-1

The Racecourse, Wrexham

Referee: George Hewitt (England)   Attendance: 8,500

WALES: William Ronald John, Benjamin David Williams, Robert Frederick John, James Patrick Murphy, Thomas Percival Griffiths, David Thomas Richards, William Edward Richards, Eugene O'Callaghan, David Astley, Walter William Robbins, William Evans.

NORTHERN IRELAND: Elisha Scott, William Cook, Thomas Willighan, William Mitchell, John Jones, William McCleery, William Houston, Samuel English, James Dunne, James Doherty, James Kelly.

Goals: David Astley (#, #), Walter William Robbins (#, #) / Samuel English (#)

151. 25.05.1933
FRANCE v WALES 1-1 (0-0)
Yves du Manoir, Colombes, Paris
Referee: Raphaël Van Praag (Belgium)   Attendance: 25,000
FRANCE: Robert Défossé, Jules Vandooren, Étienne Mattler, Célestine Delmer, Georges Verriest, Edmond Delfour, Albert Polge, Noël Liétaer, Jean Nicolas, Roger Rio, Marcel Langiller (Cap).
WALES: William Ronald John, Robert Frederick John, Sidney Wilfred Lawrence, James Patrick Murphy, Thomas Percival Griffiths, Charles Jones, Thomas John Jones, Leslie Jenkin Jones, Thomas Bamford, Walter William Robbins, Frederick Windsor Warren.
Goals: Jean Nicolas (78) / Thomas Percival Griffiths (57)

152. 04.10.1933   British Championship
WALES v SCOTLAND 3-2 (2-0)
Ninian Park, Cardiff
Referee: Edward Wood (England)   Attendance: 40,000
WALES: William Ronald John, Sidney Wilfred Lawrence, Benjamin Ellis, James Patrick Murphy, Thomas Percival Griffiths, David Thomas Richards, Cuthbert Phillips, Eugene O'Callaghan, David Astley, Walter William Robbins, William Evans.
SCOTLAND: John Diamond Harkness, Andrew Anderson (Cap), Duncan Urquhart, Matthew Busby, John Blair, James Sime McLuckie, Francis Reynolds McGurk, John McMenemy, William McFadyen, James Ferrier Easson, Douglas Duncan.
Goals: William Evans (25), Walter William Robbins (35), David Astley (56) /
William McFadyen (76), Douglas Duncan (81)

153. 04.11.1933   British Championship
NORTHERN IRELAND v WALES 1-1
Windsor Park, Belfast
Referee: Mungo Charles Hutton (Scotland)   Att: 20,000
NORTHERN IRELAND: Elisha Scott, Sydney Edward Reid, Robert Fulton, William Mitchell, John Jones, Samuel Jones, E.J.Mitchell, Alexander Ernest Stevenson, David Kirker Martin, John Coulter, James Kelly.
WALES: Sidney John Vivian Leonard Evans, Sidney Wilfred Lawrence, David Owen Jones, Alfred Day, Harry Hanford, David Thomas Richards, Cuthbert Phillips, Eugene O'Callaghan, Ernest Matthew Glover, Thomas James Mills, Ernest Robert Curtis.
Goal: Samuel Jones (#) / Ernest Matthew Glover (#)

154. 15.11.1933   British Championship
ENGLAND v WALES 1-2 (0-1)
St.James' Park, Newcastle
Referee: Samuel Thompson (Northern Ireland)   Att: 15,000
ENGLAND: Henry Edward Hibbs, Frederick Roy Goodall (Cap), Edris Albert Hapgood, Alfred Henry Strange, James Phillips Allen, Wilfred Copping, Samuel Dickinson Crooks, Albert Thomas Grosvenor, John William Anslow Bowers, Clifford Sydney Bastin, Eric Frederick George Brook.
WALES: William Ronald John, Sidney Wilfred Lawrence, David Owen Jones, James Patrick Murphy, Thomas Percival Griffiths, David Thomas Richards, Cuthbert Phillips, Eugene O'Callaghan, David Astley, Thomas James Mills, William Evans.
Goal: Eric Frederick George Brook (59) /
Thomas James Mills (22), David Astley (82)

155. 29.09.1934   British Championship
WALES v ENGLAND 0-4 (0-2)
Ninian Park, Cardiff
Referee: Samuel Thompson (Northern Ireland)   Att: 51,000
WALES: William Ronald John, Sidney Wilfred Lawrence, David Owen Jones, James Patrick Murphy, Thomas Percival Griffiths, David Thomas Richards, Cuthbert Phillips, Eugene O'Callaghan, Ronald Williams, Thomas James Mills, William Evans.
ENGLAND: Henry Edward Hibbs, Thomas Cooper (Cap), Edris Albert Hapgood, Clifford Samuel Britton, John William Barker, John Bray, Stanley Matthews, Edwin Raymond Bowden, Samuel Frederick Tilson, Raymond William Westwood, Eric Frederick George Brook.
Goals: Samuel Frederick Tilson (10, 85), Eric Frederick George Brook (30), Stanley Matthews (84)

156. 21.11.1934   British Championship
SCOTLAND v WALES 3-2 (1-0)
Pittodrie Park, Aberdeen
Referee: Samuel Thompson (Northern Ireland)   Att: 26,334
SCOTLAND: Allan McClory, Andrew Anderson, Peter McGonagle, Alexander Massie, James McMillan Simpson (Cap), George Clark Phillips Brown, William Lawrence Cook, Thomas Walker, David McCulloch, Charles Edward Napier, Douglas Duncan.
WALES: William Ronald John, Sidney Wilfred Lawrence, David Owen Jones, James Patrick Murphy, Harry Hanford, David Thomas Richards, Idris Morgan Hopkins, Ronald Williams, David Astley, Thomas James Mills, Cuthbert Phillips.
Goals: Douglas Duncan (23), Charles Edward Napier (46, 85) / Cuthbert Phillips (73), David Astley (88)

157. 27.03.1935   British Championship
WALES v NORTHERN IRELAND 3-1

The Racecourse, Wrexham

Referee: Peco Bauwens (Germany)   Attendance: 16,000

WALES: John Iorweth Hughes, Benjamin David Williams, Robert Frederick John, James Patrick Murphy, Thomas Percival Griffiths, David Thomas Richards, Idris Morgan Hopkins, Leslie Jenkin Jones, Charles Wilson Jones, Brynmor Jones, Cuthbert Phillips.

NORTHERN IRELAND: Thomas Breen, John Alexander Mackie, Robert Fulton, Keiller McCullough, John Jones, William Alexander Gowdy, Harold Anthony Duggan, John Brown I, Joseph Bambrick, Peter Dermont Doherty, John Coulter.

Goals: Charles Wilson Jones (#), Cuthbert Phillips (#), Idris Morgan Hopkins (#) / Joseph Bambrick (#)

158. 05.10.1935   British Championship
WALES v SCOTLAND 1-1 (1-1)

Ninian Park, Cardiff

Referee: Isaac Caswell (England)   Attendance: 35,004

WALES: William Ronald John, Sidney Wilfred Lawrence, Robert Frederick John, James Patrick Murphy, Thomas Percival Griffiths, David Thomas Richards, Cuthbert Phillips, Brynmor Jones, Ernest Matthew Glover, Leslie Jenkin Jones, Walter William Robbins.

SCOTLAND: John Jackson, Andrew Anderson, George Wilfred Cummings, Alexander Massie, James McMillan Simpson (Cap), George Clark Phillips Brown, James Delaney, Thomas Walker, Matthew Armstrong, William Mills, Douglas Duncan.

Goals: Cuthbert Phillips (42) / Douglas Duncan (35)

159. 05.02.1936   British Championship
ENGLAND v WALES 1-2 (1-0)

Molineux, Wolverhampton

Referee: Willie Webb (Scotland)   Attendance: 22,613

ENGLAND: Henry Edward Hibbs, Charles George Male, Edris Albert Hapgood (Cap), William John Crayston, John William Barker, John Bray, Samuel Dickinson Crooks, Edwin Raymond Bowden, Edward Joseph Drake, Clifford Sydney Bastin, Eric Frederick George Brook.

WALES: William Ronald John, David Owen Jones, Benjamin Ellis, James Patrick Murphy, Harry Hanford, David Thomas Richards, Idris Morgan Hopkins, Cuthbert Phillips, David Astley, Brynmor Jones, William Evans.

Goal: Edwin Raymond Bowden (38) / David Astley (47), Brynmor Jones (66)

160. 11.03.1936   British Championship
NORTHERN IRELAND v WALES 3-2 (1-2)

Celtic Park, Belfast

Referee: Henry Nattrass (England)   Attendance: 20,000

NORTHERN IRELAND: Elisha Scott, William Cook, Robert Fulton, William Alexander Gowdy, John Jones, Robert James Browne, Noel Kernaghan, James Gibb, David Kirker Martin, Alexander Ernest Stevenson, James Kelly.

WALES: William Ronald John, Thomas Percival Griffiths, David Owen Jones, James Patrick Murphy, Harry Hanford, David Thomas Richards, Idris Morgan Hopkins, Cuthbert Phillips, David Astley, Brynmor Jones, William Evans.

Goals: James Gibb (#), Alexander Ernest Stevenson (#), Noel Kernaghan (#) / David Astley (#), Cuthbert Phillips (#)

161. 17.10.1936   British Championship
WALES v ENGLAND 2-1 (0-1)

Ninian Park, Cardiff

Referee: William McLean (Northern Ireland)   Att: 44,729

WALES: Albert Gray, Herbert Gwyn Turner, Robert Frederick John, John Warner, Thomas Percival Griffiths, David Thomas Richards, Idris Morgan Hopkins, Brynmor Jones, Ernest Matthew Glover, Leslie Jenkin Jones, Seymour Morris.

ENGLAND: George Henry Holdcroft, Bert Sproston, Arthur Edward Catlin, Tom Smalley, John William Barker (Cap), Errington Ridley Liddell Keen, Samuel Dickinson Crooks, William Reed Scott, Frederick Charles Steele, Raymond William Westwood, Clifford Sydney Bastin.

Goal: Seymour Morris (64), Ernest Matthew Glover (66) / Clifford Sydney Bastin (44)

162. 02.12.1936   British Championship
SCOTLAND v WALES 1-2 (0-1)

Dens Park, Dundee

Referee: Dr. Arthur Barton (England)   Attendance: 23,858

SCOTLAND: James Dawson, Andrew Anderson, Robert Francis Dudgeon Ancell, Alexander Massie, James McMillan Simpson (Cap), George Clark Phillips Brown, Alexander Dewar Munro, Thomas Walker, David McCulloch, William Mills, Douglas Duncan.

WALES: Albert Gray, Herbert Gwyn Turner, Benjamin Ellis, James Patrick Murphy, Thomas Percival Griffiths, David Thomas Richards, Idris Morgan Hopkins, Brynmor Jones, Ernest Matthew Glover, Leslie Jenkin Jones, Seymour Morris.

Goals: Thomas Walker (59) / Ernest Matthew Glover (22, 47)

163. 17.03.1937   British Championship
WALES v NORTHERN IRELAND 4-1

The Racecourse, Wrexham

Referee: Arthur James Jewell (England)   Attendance: 19,000

WALES: Albert Gray, Herbert Gwyn Turner, David Owen Jones, James Patrick Murphy, Thomas Percival Griffiths, David Thomas Richards, Idris Morgan Hopkins, Brynmor Jones, Ernest Matthew Glover, Leslie Jenkin Jones, Frederick Windsor Warren.

NORTHERN IRELAND: Thomas Breen, William Cook, Robert Fulton, Thomas Henry Brolly, John Jones, William Mitchell, John Brown I, Peter Dermont Doherty, S.J. Banks, Alexander Ernest Stevenson, John Coulter.

Goals: Ernest Glover (#, #), Frederick Windsor Warren (#), Brynmor Jones (#) / Alexander Ernest Stevenson (#)

164. 30.10.1937   British Championship
WALES v SCOTLAND 2-1 (1-0)

Ninian Park, Cardiff

Referee: Charles Argent (England)   Attendance: 41,800

WALES: Albert Gray, Herbert Gwyn Turner, William Marshall Hughes, James Patrick Murphy, Harry Hanford, David Thomas Richards, Cuthbert Phillips, Brynmor Jones, Edwin Perry, Leslie Jenkin Jones, Seymour Morris.

SCOTLAND: James Dawson, Andrew Anderson, George Wilfred Cummings, Alexander Massie, James McMillan Simpson (Cap), George Clark Phillips Brown, Robert Frame Main, Thomas Walker, Francis O'Donnell, Robert Low McPhail, Douglas Duncan.

Goals: Brynmor Jones (26), Seymour Morris (51) / Alexander Massie (72)

165. 17.11.1937   British Championship
ENGLAND v WALES 2-1 (1-1)

Ayresome Park, Middlesbrough

Referee: Willie Webb (Scotland)   Attendance: 30,608

ENGLAND: Victor Robert Woodley, Bert Sproston, Samuel Barkas (Cap), William John Crayston, Stanley Cullis, Wilfred Copping, Stanley Matthews, George William Hall, George Robert Mills, Leonard Arthur Goulden, Eric Frederick George Brook.

WALES: Albert Gray, Herbert Gwyn Turner, William Marshall Hughes, James Patrick Murphy, Harry Hanford, David Thomas Richards, Idris Morgan Hopkins, Leslie Jenkin Jones, Edwin Perry, Brynmor Jones, Seymour Morris.

Goals: Stanley Matthews (28), George William Hall (59) / Edwin Perry (18)

166. 16.03.1938   British Championship
NORTHERN IRELAND v WALES 1-0

Windsor Park, Belfast

Referee: Herbert Reginald Mortimer (England)   Att: 15,000

NORTHERN IRELAND: James Franus Twoomey, William Cook, Robert Fulton, Thomas Henry Brolly, Walter McMillen, Robert James Browne, John Brown I, Paddy Farrell, Joseph Bambrick, Alexander Ernest Stevenson, John Coulter.

WALES: Albert Gray, Herbert Gwyn Turner, William Marshall Hughes, George Henry Green, Thomas George Jones, David Thomas Richards, Idris Morgan Hopkins, Leslie Jenkin Jones, Edwin Perry, Brynmor Jones, Frederick Windsor Warren.

Goal: Joseph Bambrick (#)

167. 22.10.1938   British Championship
WALES v ENGLAND 4-2 (2-2)

Ninian Park, Cardiff

Referee: William Hamilton (Northern Ireland)   Att: 55,000

WALES: William Ronald John, William John Whatley, William Marshall Hughes, George Henry Green, Thomas George Jones, David Thomas Richards, Idris Morgan Hopkins, Leslie Jenkin Jones, David Astley, Brynmor Jones, Reginald Horace Cumner.

ENGLAND: Victor Robert Woodley, Bert Sproston, Edris Albert Hapgood (Cap), Charles Kenneth Willingham, Alfred Young, Wilfred Copping, Stanley Matthews, John Robinson, Thomas Lawton, Leonard Arthur Goulden, Walter Edward Boyes.

Goals: David Astley (#, 5), Idris Morgan Hopkins (33), Brynmor Jones (61) / Thomas Lawton (27 pen), Stanley Matthews (35)

168. 09.11.1938   British Championship
SCOTLAND v WALES 3-2 (1-1)

Tynecastle Park, Edinburgh

Referee: Thomas Thompson (England)   Attendance: 34,810

SCOTLAND: John Bell Brown, Andrew Anderson (Cap), Andrew Beattie, William Shankly, Robert Denholm Baxter, Archibald Miller, James Delaney, Thomas Walker, David McCulloch, Robert Beattie, Torance Gillick.

WALES: William Ronald John, William John Whatley, William Marshall Hughes, Donald John Dearson, Thomas George Jones, David Thomas Richards, Idris Morgan Hopkins, Leslie Jenkin Jones, David Astley, Brynmor Jones, Reginald Horace Cumner.

Goals: Torance Gillick (38), Thomas Walker (83, 84) / David Astley (20), Leslie Jenkin Jones (86)

169. 15.03.1939   British Championship
WALES v NORTHERN IRELAND 3-1

The Racecourse, Wrexham

Referee: Arthur Barton (England)   Attendance: 22,997

WALES: George Poland, Herbert Gwyn Turner, William Marshall Hughes, George Henry Green, Thomas George Jones, Donald John Dearson, Idris Morgan Hopkins, Leslie Mervyn Boulter, Ernest Matthew Glover, Brynmor Jones, Reginald Horace Cumner.

NORTHERN IRELAND: Thomas Breen, William Cook, Malcolm Partridge Butler, Thomas Henry Brolly, Johnny Leatham, Ned Weir, David Cochrane, Alexander Ernest Stevenson, Dudley Milligan, Peter Dermont Doherty, John Brown I.

Goals: Leslie Mervyn Boulter (#), Ernest Matthew Glover (#), Reginald Horace Cumner (#) / Dudley Milligan (#)

170. 21.05.1939   British Championship
FRANCE v WALES 2-1 (2-0)

Yves du Manoir, Colombes, Paris

Referee: Laurent Franken (Belgium)   Attendance: 23,000

FRANCE: Julien Darui, Jules Vandooren, Étienne Mattler (Cap), François Bourbotte, Auguste Jordan, Raoul Diagne, Jules Bigot, Oscar Heisserer, Désiré Korányi, Emile Veinante, Jules Mathé.

WALES: George Poland, Herbert Gwyn Turner, William Marshall Hughes, George Henry Green, Harry Hanford, John Warner, John James Williams, David Astley, Charles Wilson Jones, Donald John Dearson, Seymour Morris.

Goals: Jules Bigot (10), Désiré Korányi (13) / David Astley (53)

171. 19.10.1946   British Championship
WALES v SCOTLAND 3-1 (0-0)

The Racecourse, Wrexham

Referee: W.H.E. Evans (England)   Attendance: 29,568

WALES: Cyril Sidlow, Raymond Lambert, William Marshall Hughes, Douglas Frederick Witcomb, Thomas George Jones, William Arthur Ronald Burgess, William Ernest Arthur Jones, Aubrey Powell, Trevor Ford, Brynmor Jones, George Edwards.

SCOTLAND: William Miller, James Findlay Stephen (Cap), David Shaw, Hugh Brown, Francis Brennan, John Husband, William Waddell, Cornelius Dougall, William Thornton, James Alfred Blair, William Beveridge Liddell.

Goals: Brynmor Jones (52), Trevor Ford (78), James Stephen (87 own goal) / William Waddell (49 pen)

172. 13.11.1946   British Championship
ENGLAND v WALES 3-0 (2-0)

Maine Road, Manchester

Referee: Willie Webb (Scotland)   Attendance: 59,121

ENGLAND: Frank Victor Swift, Lawrence Scott, George Francis Moutry Hardwick (Cap), William Ambrose Wright, Cornelius "Neil" Franklin, Henry Cockburn, Thomas Finney, Horatio Stratton Carter, Thomas Lawton, Wilfred Mannion, Robert Langton.   Manager: Walter Winterbottom

WALES: Cyril Sidlow, Alfred Thomas Sherwood, William Marshall Hughes, Douglas Frederick Witcomb, Thomas George Jones, William Arthur Ronald Burgess, William Ernest Arthur Jones, Aubrey Powell, Stanley Verdun Richards, Ivor Verdun Powell, George Edwards.

Goals: Wilfred Mannion (8, 16), Thomas Lawton (40)

173. 16.04.1947   British Championship
NORTHERN IRELAND v WALES 2-1 (1-1)

Windsor Park, Belfast

Referee: Not recorded   Attendance: 41,000

NORTHERN IRELAND: Edward Hinton, William Charles Gorman, John James Carey, Josiah Walter Sloan, John Joseph Vernon, Peter Desmond Farrell, David Cochrane, Alexander Ernest Stevenson, David John Walsh, Peter Dermont Doherty, Thomas Joseph Eglington.

WALES: William Warren Shortt, Alfred Thomas Sherwood, William Marshall Hughes, Douglas Frederick Witcomb, John Vaughan Humphreys, William Arthur Ronald Burgess, William Maldwyn Griffiths, William Morris, Trevor Ford, Brynmor Jones, George Edwards.

Goals: Alexander Stevenson (#), Peter Dermont Doherty (#) / Trevor Ford (#)

174. 18.10.1947   British Championship
WALES v ENGLAND 0-3 (0-3)

Ninian Park, Cardiff

Referee: James Martin (Scotland)   Attendance: 55,000

WALES: Cyril Sidlow, Raymond Lambert, Walley Barnes, Ivor Verdun Powell, Thomas George Jones, William Arthur Ronald Burgess, David Sidney Thomas, Aubrey Powell, George Lowrie, Brynmor Jones, George Edwards.

ENGLAND: Frank Victor Swift, Lawrence Scott, George Francis Moutry Hardwick (Cap), Philip Henry Taylor, Cornelius "Neil" Franklin, William Ambrose Wright, Stanley Matthews, Stanley Harding Mortensen, Thomas Lawton, Wilfred Mannion, Thomas Finney.
Manager: Walter Winterbottom

Goals: Thomas Finney (6), Stanley Harding Mortensen (11), Thomas Lawton (15)

33

175. 12.11.1947   British Championship
SCOTLAND v WALES 1-2 (1-2)
Hampden Park, Glasgow
Referee: Arthur Edward Ellis (England)   Att: 88,000
SCOTLAND: William Miller, John Govan, James Findlay Stephen, Archibald Renwick MacAuley, William Alexander Woodburn (Cap), Alexander Rooney Forbes, Gordon Smith, Andrew McLaren, James Delaney, William Steel, William Beveridge Liddell.
WALES: Cyril Sidlow, Alfred Thomas Sherwood, Walley Barnes, Ivor Verdun Powell, Thomas George Jones, William Arthur Ronald Burgess, David Sidney Thomas, Aubrey Powell, Trevor Ford, George Lowrie, George Edwards.
Goals: Andrew McLaren (10) /
Trevor Ford (35), George Lowrie (42)

176. 10.03.1948   British Championship
WALES v NORTHERN IRELAND 2-0 (1-0)
The Racecourse, Wrexham
Referee: Not recorded   Attendance: 33,160
WALES: Cyril Sidlow, Alfred Thomas Sherwood, Walley Barnes, Ivor Verdun Powell, Thomas George Jones, William George Baker, David Sidney Thomas, Aubrey Powell, Trevor Ford, George Lowrie, George Edwards.
NORTHERN IRELAND: Edward Hinton, Cornelius Joseph Martin, William Charles Gorman, William Walsh, John Joseph Vernon, Peter Desmond Farrell, David Cochrane, Samuel Smyth, David John Walsh, Peter Dermont Doherty, Thomas Joseph Eglington.
Goals: George Lowrie (#), George Edwards (#)

177. 23.10.1948   British Championship
WALES v SCOTLAND 1-3 (1-3)
Ninian Park, Cardiff
Referee: David Maxwell (Northern Ireland)   Att: 59,911
WALES: Cyril Sidlow, Alfred Thomas Sherwood, Walley Barnes, Roy Paul, Frederick Stansfield, William Arthur Ronald Burgess, David Sidney Thomas, William Henry Lucas, Trevor Ford, Brynmor Jones, William Ernest Arthur Jones.
SCOTLAND: James Clews Cowan, Hugh Howie, David Shaw, Robert Evans, George Lewis Young (Cap), William Yates Redpath, William Waddell, James Mason, Lawrence Reilly, William Steel, John Carmichael Kelly.
Goal: Brynmor Jones (22) /
Hugh Howie (15), William Waddell (20, 30)

178. 10.11.1948   British Championship
ENGLAND v WALES 1-0 (1-0)
Villa Park, Birmingham
Referee: John Alexander Mowatt (Scotland)   Att: 67,770
ENGLAND: Frank Victor Swift, Lawrence Scott, John Aston, Timothy Victor Ward, Cornelius "Neil" Franklin, William Ambrose Wright (Cap), Stanley Matthews, Stanley Harding Mortensen, John Edward Thompson Milburn, Leonard Francis Shackleton, Thomas Finney.   Manager: Walter Winterbottom
WALES: William Arthur Hughes, Alfred Thomas Sherwood, Walley Barnes, Roy Paul, Thomas George Jones, William Arthur Ronald Burgess, William Ernest Arthur Jones, Aubrey Powell, Trevor Ford, William Morris, Royston James Clarke.
Goal: Thomas Finney (39)

179. 09.03.1949   British Championship
NORTHERN IRELAND v WALES 0-2 (/0-1)
Windsor Park, Belfast
Referee: Not recorded   Attendance: 22,880
NORTHERN IRELAND: Cecil Moore, John James Carey, Thomas Aherne, James Joseph McCabe, John Joseph Vernon, Peter Desmond Farrell, David Cochrane, Samuel Smyth, David John Walsh, Robert Anderson Brennan, John Francis O'Driscoll.
WALES: William Arthur Hughes, Walley Barnes, Alfred Thomas Sherwood, Roy Paul, Thomas George Jones, William Arthur Ronald Burgess, Harold Williams, William Rees, Trevor Ford, William Henry Lucas, George Edwards.
Goals: George Edwards (#), Trevor Ford (#)

180. 15.05.1949
PORTUGAL v WALES 3-2 (1-2)
Nacional, Lisboa
Referee: Generoso Dattilo (Italy)   Attendance: 51,000
PORTUGAL: Frederico Barrigana, VIRGÍLIO Marques Mendes, SERAFIM das Neves, Carlos Augusto Ribeiro Canário, FÉLIX Assunção Antunes, Francisco Ferreira, Armando Félix Ferreira (Cap), Manuel Vasques, Domingos Carrilho Demétrio "Patalino" (40 José Mota), José António Barreto Travaços, ROGÉRIO Lantres de Carvalho.
Trainer: Armando Sampaio
WALES: William Arthur Hughes, Alfred Thomas Sherwood, Raymond Lambert, Roy Paul, Thomas George Jones, William Arthur Ronald Burgess, William Maldwyn Griffiths, William Henry Lucas, Trevor Ford, George Lowrie, George Edwards.
Goals: Domingos Carrilho Demétrio "Patalino" (39), José Mota (65), Manuel Vasques (79) / Trevor Ford (11, 40)

181. 22.05.1949
BELGIUM v WALES 3-1 (3-0)
Sclessin, Liège
Referee: Boes (France)   Attendance: 19,079

BELGIUM: Henri Meert, Léon Aernaudts, René Gillard, Henri Coppens, Louis Carré, Jan Van der Auwera, Victor Lemberechts, Henri Govard, Joseph Mermans, Frédéric Chavès D'Aguilar (Cap), Albert De Hert.
Trainer: William Gormlie

WALES: William Arthur Hughes, Hopkin John Roberts, Raymond Lambert, Ivor Verdun Powell, Thomas George Jones, William Arthur Ronald Burgess, William Maldwyn Griffiths, William Rees, Trevor Ford, William Henry Lucas, George Edwards.

Goals: Henri Govard (13, 35), Albert De Hert (43) / Trevor Ford (60)

182. 26.05.1949
SWITZERLAND v WALES 4-0 (1-0)
Wankdorf, Bern
Referee: Not recorded

SWITZERLAND: Eugenio Corrodi, André Neury, Roger Quinche, Bernard Lanz, Robert Hasler, Roger Bocquet, Robert Ballaman, Charles Antenen, Jean Tamini, Lucien Pasteur, Jacques Fatton.   Trainer: Karl Rappan

WALES: William Arthur Hughes, Alfred Thomas Sherwood, Raymond Lambert, Roy Paul, Thomas George Jones, William Arthur Ronald Burgess, Harold Williams, William Rees, Trevor Ford, William Henry Lucas, George Edwards.

Goals: Jacques Fatton (#, #), Lucien Pasteur (#), Robert Ballaman (#)

183. 15.10.1949   British Championship, 4th World Cup Qualifiers
WALES v ENGLAND 1-4 (0-3)
Ninian Park, Cardiff
Referee: John Mowatt (Scotland)   Attendance: 61,079

WALES: Cyril Sidlow, Walley Barnes, Alfred Thomas Sherwood, Roy Paul, Thomas George Jones, William Arthur Ronald Burgess, William Maldwyn Griffiths, William Henry Lucas, Trevor Ford, Francis Henry Scrine, George Edwards.

ENGLAND: Bert Frederick Williams, Bertram Mozley, John Aston, William Ambrose Wright (Cap), Cornelius "Neil" Franklin, James William Dickinson, Thomas Finney, Stanley Harding Mortensen, John Edward Thompson Milburn, Leonard Francis Shackleton, John Hancocks.   Manager: Walter Winterbottom

Goals: William Maldwyn Griffiths (80) / Stanley Harding Mortensen (22), John Milburn (29, 34, 66)

184. 09.11.1949   British Championship, 4th World Cup Qualifiers
SCOTLAND v WALES 2-0 (1-0)
Hampden Park, Glasgow
Referee: S E. Law (England)   Attendance: 73,781

SCOTLAND: James Clews Cowan, George Lewis Young (Cap), Samuel Richmond Cox, Robert Evans, William Alexander Woodburn, George Graham Aitken, William Beveridge Liddell, John McPhail, Alexander Bryce Linwood, William Steel, Lawrence Reilly.

WALES: Keith B. Jones, Walley Barnes, Alfred Thomas Sherwood, Ivor Verdun Powell, Thomas George Jones, William Arthur Ronald Burgess, William Maldwyn Griffiths, Roy Paul, Trevor Ford, Royston James Clarke, George Edwards.

Goals: John McPhail (25), Alexander Bryce Linwood (78)

185. 23.11.1949
WALES v BELGIUM 5-1 (4-0)
Ninian Park, Cardiff
Referee: W. Pearce (England)   Attendance: 27,998

WALES: William Warren Shortt, Walley Barnes, Alfred Thomas Sherwood, Ivor Verdun Powell, Thomas George Jones, William Arthur Ronald Burgess, William Maldwyn Griffiths, Roy Paul, Trevor Ford, Aubrey Powell, Royston James Clarke.

BELGIUM: Henri Meert, Léon Aernaudts, René Gillard, Jan Van der Auwera, Louis Carré, Victor Mees, Théo Lacroix, Rik Coppens, Joseph Mermans (Cap), Albert De Hert, Léopold Anoul.   Trainer: William Gormlie

Goals: Roy Paul (18), Trevor Ford (24, 37, 49), Royston James Clarke (30) / Rik Coppens (90)

186. 08.03.1950   British Championship, 4th World Cup Qualifiers
WALES v NORTHERN IRELAND 0-0
The Racecourse, Wrexham
Referee: Reginald Leafe (England)   Attendance: 30,000

WALES: William Warren Shortt, Walley Barnes, Alfred Thomas Sherwood, Roy Paul, William John Charles, William Arthur Ronald Burgess, Harold Williams, William Rees, Trevor Ford, Francis Henry Scrine, Royston James Clarke.

NORTHERN IRELAND: Hugh Redmond Kelly, Gerard Columba Bowler, Thomas Aherne, Robert Denis Blanchflower, Cornelius Joseph Martin, Reginald Alphonso Ryan, John McKenna, Samuel Smyth, David John Walsh, Robert Anderson Brennan, Norman Lockhart.

187. 21.10.1950   British Championship
WALES v SCOTLAND 1-3 (0-1)
Ninian Park, Cardiff
Referee: Arthur Edward Ellis (England)   Att: 50,000
WALES: Brynley John Parry, Walley Barnes, Alfred Thomas Sherwood, Ivor Verdun Powell, Roy Paul, William Arthur Ronald Burgess, Harold Williams, Brynley William Allen, Trevor Ford, Aubrey Powell, Royston James Clarke.
SCOTLAND: James Clews Cowan, George Lewis Young (Cap), Samuel Richmond Cox, Robert Evans, William Alexander Woodburn, Alexander Rooney Forbes, Robert Inglis Campbell, Allan Duncan Brown, William Russell Logan Bauld, William Steel, William Beveridge Liddell.
Goal: Aubrey Powell (68) /
William Russell Logan Bauld (20), Allan Duncan Brown (23)

188. 15.11.1950   British Championship
ENGLAND v WALES 4-2 (2-0)
Roker Park, Sunderland
Referee: John Alexander Mowatt (Scotland)   Att: 59,137
ENGLAND: Bert Frederick Williams, Alfred Ernest Ramsey (Cap), Lionel Smith, William Watson, Leslie Harry Compton, James William Dickinson, Thomas Finney, Wilfred Mannion, John Edward Thompson Milburn, Edward Francis Baily, Leslie Dennis Medley.   Manager: Walter Winterbottom
WALES: Iorwerth Hughes, Walley Barnes, Alfred Thomas Sherwood, Roy Paul, William Raymond Daniel, William Henry Lucas, William Maldwyn Griffiths, Brynley William Allen, Trevor Ford, Ivor John Allchurch, Royston James Clarke.
Goals: Edward Francis Baily (31, 40), Wilfred Mannion (66), John Edward Thompson Milburn (89) / Trevor Ford (59, 74)

189. 07.03.1951   British Championship
NORTHERN IRELAND v WALES 1-2 (0-1)
Windsor Park, Belfast
Referee: Not recorded   Attendance: 12,000
NORTHERN IRELAND: Edward Hinton, William George Leonard Graham, William Edward Cunningham, James Joseph McCabe, John Joseph Vernon, William Dickson, William Hughes, Edward James McMorran, William Simpson, J. Kevin McGarry, Norman Lockhart.
WALES: Iorwerth Hughes, Walley Barnes, Alfred Thomas Sherwood, Roy Paul, William Raymond Daniel, William Arthur Ronald Burgess, William Maldwyn Griffiths, Noel Kinsey, Trevor Ford, Ivor John Allchurch, Royston James Clarke.
Goal: William Simpson (#) / Royston James Clarke (#, #)

190. 12.05.1951
WALES v PORTUGAL 2-1 (1-0)
Ninian Park, Cardiff
Referee: William Ling (England)   Attendance: Not recorded
WALES: Iorwerth Hughes, Walley Barnes, Alfred Thomas Sherwood, Roy Paul, William Raymond Daniel, William Arthur Ronald Burgess, William Maldwyn Griffiths, Noel Kinsey, Trevor Ford, Ivor John Allchurch, Royston James Clarke.
PORTUGAL: ERNESTO Nogueira de Oliveira, VIRGÍLIO Marques Mendes, SERAFIM das Neves, Carlos Augusto Ribeiro Canário, FÉLIX Assunção Antunes, Francisco Ferreira (Cap), Carlos MARTINHO Gomes, José António Barreto Travaços, Henrique Ben David, Fernando Augusto Amoral Caiado, ALBANO Narciso Pereira.   Trainer: Tavares da Silva
Goals: William Maldwyn Griffiths (36), Trevor Ford (73) / Henrique Ben David (78)

191. 16.05.1951
WALES v SWITZERLAND 3-2 (1-0)
The Racecourse, Wrexham
Referee: Not known
WALES: Iorwerth Hughes, Glyndwr James John Williams, Alfred Thomas Sherwood, Roy Paul, William John Charles, William Arthur Ronald Burgess, William Maldwyn Griffiths, Noel Kinsey, Trevor Ford, Ivor John Allchurch, Royston James Clarke.
SWITZERLAND: Walter Eich, Willy Steffen, Roger Bocquet, André Neury, Gerhard Lusenti, Roger Quinche, Robert Ballaman, Charles Antenen, Alfred Bickel, Roger Vonlanthen, Jacques Fatton.   Selection Commitee: William Baumgartner, Gaston Tschirren & Leopold Kielholz
Goals: Trevor Ford (#, #), William Arthur Ronald Burgess (#) / Robert Ballaman (#), Charles Antenen (#)

192. 20.10.1951   British Championship
WALES v ENGLAND 1-1 (1-1)
Ninian Park, Cardiff
Referee: G. Gerrard (Scotland)   Attendance: 60,000
WALES: William Warren Shortt, Walley Barnes, Alfred Thomas Sherwood, Roy Paul, William Raymond Daniel, William Arthur Ronald Burgess, William Isaiah Foulkes, Noel Kinsey, Trevor Ford, Ivor John Allchurch, Royston James Clarke.
ENGLAND: Bert Frederick Williams, Alfred Ernest Ramsey, Lionel Smith, William Ambrose Wright (Cap), Malcolm Williamson Barrass, James William Dickinson, Thomas Finney, Thomas Thompson, Nathaniel Lofthouse, Edward Francis Baily, Leslie Dennis Medley.
Manager: Walter Winterbottom
Goal: William Isaiah Foulkes (3) / Edward Francis Baily (6)

193. 14.11.1951   British Championship
SCOTLAND v WALES 0-1 (0-0)
Hampden Park, Glasgow
Referee: Patrick Morris (Northern Ireland)   Att: 71,272
SCOTLAND: James Clews Cowan, George Lewis Young (Cap), Samuel Richmond Cox, Thomas Henderson Docherty, William Alexander Woodburn, Alexander Rooney Forbes, William Waddell, Thomas Bingham Orr, Lawrence Reilly, William Steel, William Beveridge Liddell.
WALES: William Warren Shortt, Walley Barnes, Alfred Thomas Sherwood, Roy Paul, William Raymond Daniel, William Arthur Ronald Burgess, William Isaiah Foulkes, William Morris, Trevor Ford, Ivor John Allchurch, Royston James Clarke.
Goal: Ivor John Allchurch (89)

194. 08.12.1951
WALES v REST OF UNITED KINGDOM 3-2 (2-0)
Ninian Park, Cardiff
Referee: Not recorded   Attendance: 26,454
WALES: William Warren Shortt, Walley Barnes, Alfred Thomas Sherwood, Roy Paul, William Raymond Daniel, William Arthur Ronald Burgess, William Isaiah Foulkes, William Morris, Trevor Ford, Ivor John Allchurch, Royston James Clarke.
REST OF THE UNITED KINGDOM: James Cowan, George Young, Alfred McMichael, Thomas Docherty, John Vernon, William Wright, Gordon Smith, Charles Fleming, Nathaniel Lofthouse, Edward Baily, Leslie Medley.
Goals: Ivor John Allchurch (15, 62), Trevor Ford (23) / Charles Fleming (62), Leslie Medley (83)

195. 19.03.1952   British Championship
WALES v NORTHERN IRELAND 3-0 (1-0)
Vetch Field, Swansea
Referee: Not recorded   Attendance: 30,000
WALES: William Warren Shortt, Walley Barnes, Alfred Thomas Sherwood, Roy Paul, William Raymond Daniel, William Arthur Ronald Burgess, William Isaiah Foulkes, William Morris, Trevor Ford, Ivor John Allchurch, Royston James Clarke.
NORTHERN IRELAND: William Uprichard, William George Leonard Graham, Alfred McMichael, Robert Denis Blanchflower, William Dickson, Francis Joseph McCourt, William Bingham, Samuel Donal D'Arcy, Edward James McMorran, James McIlroy, Norman Lockhart.
Goals: Walley Barnes (# penalty), Ivor John Allchurch (#), Royston James Clarke (#)

196. 18.10.1952   British Championship
WALES v SCOTLAND 1-2 (1-1)
Ninian Park, Cardiff
Referee: Alfred Bond (England)   Attendance: 60,261
WALES: William Warren Shortt, Arthur Richard Lever, Alfred Thomas Sherwood, Roy Paul, William Raymond Daniel, William Arthur Ronald Burgess, William Isaiah Foulkes, Ellis Reginald Davies, Trevor Ford, Ivor John Allchurch, Royston James Clarke.
SCOTLAND: George Neil Farm, George Lewis Young (Cap), Samuel Richmond Cox, James Scoular, Francis Brennan, George Graham Aitken, Thomas Wright, Allan Duncan Brown, Lawrence Reilly, William Steel, William Beveridge Liddell.
Goal: Trevor Ford (23) /
Allan Duncan Brown (32), William Beveridge Liddell (69)

197. 12.11.1952   British Championship
ENGLAND v WALES 5-2 (2-1)
Wembley, London
Referee: D. Gerrard (Scotland)   Attendance: 94,094
ENGLAND: Gilbert Harold Merrick, Alfred Ernest Ramsey, Lionel Smith, William Ambrose Wright (Cap), Jack Froggatt, James William Dickinson, Thomas Finney, Redfern Froggatt, Nathaniel Lofthouse, Roy Thomas Frank Bentley, William Henry Elliott.   Manager: Walter Winterbottom
WALES: William Warren Shortt, Roland Frederick Stitfall, Alfred Thomas Sherwood, Roy Paul, William Raymond Daniel, William Arthur Ronald Burgess, William Isaiah Foulkes, Ellis Reginald Davies, Trevor Ford, Ivor John Allchurch, Royston James Clarke.
Goals: Thomas Finney (8), Nathaniel Lofthouse (10, 75), Jack Froggatt (44), Roy Thomas Frank Bentley (47) /
Trevor Ford (15, 49)

198. 15.04.1953   British Championship
NORTHERN IRELAND v WALES 2-3 (1-3)
Windsor Park, Belfast
Referee: Not recorded   Attendance: 33,000
NORTHERN IRELAND: William Uprichard, James Joseph McCabe, Alfred McMichael, Robert Denis Blanchflower, William Dickson, Francis Joseph McCourt, William Bingham, James McIlroy, Edward James McMorran, Samuel Donal D'Arcy, Charles Tully.
WALES: William Warren Shortt, Derrick Sullivan, Alfred Thomas Sherwood, Roy Paul, William Raymond Daniel, William Arthur Ronald Burgess, Terence Cameron Medwin, William John Charles, Trevor Ford, Ivor John Allchurch, James Henry Griffiths.
Goals: Edward James McMorran (#, #) /
William John Charles (#, #), Trevor Ford (#)

199. 14.05.1953
FRANCE v WALES 6-1 (4-1)
Yves du Manoir, Colombes, Paris
Referee: José Viera Da Costa (Portugal)   Attendance: 33,020
FRANCE: Jean Ruminski, Lazare Gianessi, Robert Jonquet, Roger Marche (Cap), Antoine Bonifaci, Jean-Jacques Marcel, Edouard Kargu, Roger Piantoni, Joseph Ujlaki, Raymond Kopa, René Gardien.
WALES: William Warren Shortt, Derrick Sullivan, Alfred Thomas Sherwood, Roy Paul, William Raymond Daniel, William Arthur Ronald Burgess, Terence Cameron Medwin, William John Charles, Trevor Ford, Ivor John Allchurch, William Isaiah Foulkes.
Goals: René Gardien (10, 33), Raymond Kopa (14, 37), Antoine Bonifaci (73), Joseph Ujlaki (88) / Ivor John Allchurch (2)

200. 21.05.1953
YUGOSLAVIA v WALES 5-2 (4-1)
JNA, Beograd
Referee: John Best (United States)   Attendance: 50,000
YUGOSLAVIA: Vladimir Beara, Branko Stanković, Tomislav Crnković, Zlatko Čajkovski (Cap), Ivan Horvat, Vujadin Boškov, Zdravko Rajkov, Rajko Mitić, Miloš Milutinović, Bernard Vukas, Branko Zebec.
Selection committee: Milorad Arsenijević, Aleksandar Tirnanić & Leo Lemešić
WALES: William Warren Shortt, Derrick Sullivan, Alfred Thomas Sherwood, Roy Paul, William Raymond Daniel, William Arthur Ronald Burgess, Terence Cameron Medwin, William John Charles, Trevor Ford, Ivor John Allchurch, William Isaiah Foulkes.
Goals: Rajko Mitić (10, 14, 24), Bernard Vukas (15), Zdravko Rajkov (55) / Trevor Ford (36, 52)

201. 10.10.1953   British Championship,
5th World Cup Qualifiers
WALES v ENGLAND 1-4 (1-1)
Ninian Park, Cardiff
Referee: Charles Edward Faultless (Scotland)   Att: 61,000
WALES: Ronald Gilbert Howells, Walley Barnes, Alfred Thomas Sherwood, Roy Paul, William Raymond Daniel, William Arthur Ronald Burgess, William Isaiah Foulkes, Ellis Reginald Davies, William John Charles, Ivor John Allchurch, Royston James Clarke.
ENGLAND: Gilbert Harold Merrick, Thomas Garrett, William Eckersley, William Ambrose Wright (Cap), Harry Johnstonon, James William Dickinson, Thomas Finney, Albert Quixall, Nathaniel Lofthouse, Dennis James Wilshaw, James Mullen.   Manager: Walter Winterbottom
Goals: Ivor John Allchurch (22) / Dennis James Wilshaw (45, 48), Nathaniel Lofthouse (50, 51)

202. 04.11.1953   British Championship,
5th World Cup Qualifiers
SCOTLAND v WALES 3-3 (2-0)
Hampden Park, Glasgow
Referee: Thomas Mitchell (Northern Ireland)   Att: 71,387
SCOTLAND: George Neil Farm, George Lewis Young (Cap), Samuel Richmond Cox, Robert Evans, William Douglas Telfer, Douglas Cowie, John Archibald MacKenzie, Robert Johnstone, Lawrence Reilly, Allan Duncan Brown, William Beveridge Liddell.
WALES: Ronald Gilbert Howells, Walley Barnes, Alfred Thomas Sherwood, Roy Paul, William Raymond Daniel, William Arthur Ronald Burgess, William Isaiah Foulkes, Ellis Reginald Davies, William John Charles, Ivor John Allchurch, Royston James Clarke.
Goals: Allan Duncan Brown (19), Robert Johnstone (42), Lawrence Reilly (58) / William John Charles (49, 88), Ivor John Allchurch (73)

203. 31.03.1954   British Championship,
5th World Cup Qualifiers
WALES v NORTHERN IRELAND 1-2 (0-1)
The Racecourse, Wrexham
Referee: Charles Faultless (Scotland)   Attendance: 32,817
WALES: Alfred John Kelsey, Derrick Sullivan, Alfred Thomas Sherwood, Roy Paul, William Raymond Daniel, William Arthur Ronald Burgess, William Isaiah Foulkes, Noel Kinsey, William John Charles, Ivor John Allchurch, Royston James Clarke.
NORTHERN IRELAND: Harry Gregg, William George Leonard Graham, Alfred McMichael, Robert Denis Blanchflower, William Dickson, Robert Peacock, William Bingham, John Blanchflower, William John McAdams, James McIlroy, Peter James McParland.
Goals: William John Charles (80) / Peter McParland (1, 52)

204. 09.05.1954
AUSTRIA v WALES 2-0 (0-0)
Prater, Wien
Referee: Louis Fauquembergue (France)   Att: 58,000
AUSTRALIA: Franz Pelikan (46 Kurt Schmied), Karl Stotz, Gerhard Hanappi, Ernst Ocwirk, Ernst Happel, Leopold Barschandt, Paul Halla, Robert Körner, Robert Dienst, Erich Probst, Dr. Walter Schleger (46 Alfred Körner II).
Trainer: Walter Nausch
WALES: Alfred John Kelsey, Stuart Grenville Williams, Alfred Thomas Sherwood, William Charles Harris, William John Charles, William Arthur Ronald Burgess, William Maldwyn Griffiths, Derek Robert Tapscott, Trevor Ford, Ivor John Allchurch, Clifford William Jones.
Goals: Robert Dienst (50), Paul Halla (81)

38

205. 22.09.1954
WALES v YUGOSLAVIA 1-3 (0-0)
Ninian Park, Cardiff
Referee: Leopold Sylvain Horn (Holland)   Att: 45,000
WALES: Alfred John Kelsey, Walley Barnes, Alfred Thomas Sherwood, Roy Paul, William John Charles, David Lloyd Bowen, William George Reed, Derek Robert Tapscott, Trevor Ford, Ivor John Allchurch, Royston James Clarke.
YUGOSLAVIA: Vladimir Beara, Branko Stanković, Milan Zeković, Lav Mantula, Ivan Horvat, Vujadin Boškov, Aleksandar Petaković, Stanoje Jocić, Stjepan Bobek (Cap), Bernard Vukas, Dionizie Dvornić (46 Todor Veselinović). Selection committee: Branko Pešić, Aleksandar Tirnanić, Leo Lemešić, Franjo Völfl & Milovan Ćirić
Goal: Ivor Allchurch (56) / Todor Veselinović (62 pen, 77, 89)

206. 16.10.1954   British Championship
WALES v SCOTLAND 0-1 (0-0)
Ninian Park, Cardiff
Referee: William Ling (England)   Attendance: 53,000
WALES: Alfred John Kelsey, Walley Barnes, Alfred Thomas Sherwood, Roy Paul, William John Charles, David Lloyd Bowen, William George Reed, Derek Robert Tapscott, Trevor Ford, Ivor John Allchurch, Royston James Clarke.
SCOTLAND: William Alexander Fraser, George Lewis Young (Cap), William Carruthers Cunningham, Thomas Henderson Docherty, James Anderson Davidson, Douglas Cowie, William Waddell, Henry Yorston, Patrick McCabe Buckley, William Fernie, Thomas Ring.
Goal: Patrick McCabe Buckley (70)

207. 10.11.1954   British Championship
ENGLAND v WALES 3-2 (0-1)
Wembley, London
Referee: Charles Edward Faultless (Scotland)   Att: 89,789
ENGLAND: Raymond Ernest Wood, Ronald Staniforth, Roger William Byrne, Leonard Horace Phillips, William Ambrose Wright (Cap), William John Slater, Stanley Matthews, Roy Thomas Frank Bentley, Ronald Allen, Leonard Francis Shackleton, Frank Blunstone.
Manager: Walter Winterbottom
WALES: John King, Stuart Grenville Williams, Alfred Thomas Sherwood, Roy Paul, William Raymond Daniel, Derrick Sullivan, Derek Robert Tapscott, Trevor Ford, William John Charles, Ivor John Allchurch, Royston James Clarke.
Goals: Roy Thomas Frank Bentley (70, 74, 81) / William John Charles (36, 74)

208. 20.04.1955   British Championship
NORTHERN IRELAND v WALES 2-3 (2-2)
Windsor Park, Belfast
Referee: Not recorded   Attendance: 30,000
NORTHERN IRELAND: William Uprichard, William George Leonard Graham, Alfred McMichael, Robert Denis Blanchflower, Ernie McCleary, Thomas Casey, William Bingham, Edward Crossan, James Walker, James McIlroy, Norman Lockhart.
WALES: Alfred John Kelsey, Stuart Grenville Williams, Alfred Thomas Sherwood, Melvyn Charles, William Raymond Daniel, Derrick Sullivan, Derek Robert Tapscott, Trevor Ford, William John Charles, Ivor John Allchurch, Leonard Allchurch.
Manager: Walley Barnes
Goals: Edward Crossan (#), James Walker (#) / William John Charles (#, #, #)

209. 22.10.1955   British Championship
WALES v ENGLAND 2-1 (2-0)
Ninian Park, Cardiff
Referee: Thomas Mitchell (Northern Ireland)   Att: 60,000
WALES: Alfred John Kelsey, Stuart Grenville Williams, Alfred Thomas Sherwood, Melvyn Charles, William John Charles, Roy Paul, Derek Robert Tapscott, Noel Kinsey, Trevor Ford, Ivor John Allchurch, Clifford William Jones.
Manager: Walley Barnes
ENGLAND: Bert Frederick Williams, Jeffrey James Hall, Roger William Byrne, William Harry McGarry, William Ambrose Wright (Cap), James William Dickinson, Stanley Matthews, Donald George Revie, Nathaniel Lofthouse, Dennis James Wilshaw, Thomas Finney.
Manager: Walter Winterbottom
Goal: Derek Robert Tapscott (41), Clifford William Jones (43) / William John Charles (51 own goal)

210. 09.11.1955   British Championship
SCOTLAND v WALES 2-0 (2-0)
Hampden Park, Glasgow
Referee: Reginald Leafe (England)   Attendance: 53,887
SCOTLAND: Thomas Younger, Alexander Hershaw Parker, Joseph McDonald, Robert Evans, George Lewis Young (Cap), Douglas Cowie, Gordon Smith, Robert Johnstone, Lawrence Reilly, Robert Young Collins, John Gillespie Henderson.
WALES: Alfred John Kelsey, Stuart Grenville Williams, Alfred Thomas Sherwood, Melvyn Charles, William John Charles, Roy Paul, Derek Robert Tapscott, Noel Kinsey, Trevor Ford, Ivor John Allchurch, Clifford William Jones.
Manager: Walley Barnes
Goals: Robert Johnstone (14, 25)

211. 23.11.1955
WALES v AUSTRIA 1-2 (1-2)
The Racecourse, Wrexham
Referee: Louis Fauquembergue (France)   Att: 30,000
WALES: Alfred John Kelsey, Stuart Grenville Williams, Alfred Thomas Sherwood, Melvyn Charles, William John Charles, Roy Paul, Leonard Allchurch, Derek Robert Tapscott, Trevor Ford, Ivor John Allchurch, Clifford William Jones. Manager: Walley Barnes
AUSTRALIA: Bruno Engelmeier, Paul Halla, Franz Swoboda, Ernst Ocwirk, Karl Stotz, Karl Koller, Herbert Grohs, Theodor Wagner (26 Richard Brousek), Gerhard Hanappi, Alfred Körner, Dr.Walter Schleger.   Trainer: Karl Geyer
Goal: Derek Robert Tapscott (35) /
Theodor Wagner (5), Gerhard Hanappi (20)

212. 11.04.1956   British Championship
WALES v NORTHERN IRELAND 1-1 (1-0)
Ninian Park, Cardiff
Referee: Not recorded   Attendance: 37,510
WALES: Alfred John Kelsey, Alfred Thomas Sherwood, Melvyn Hopkins, Alan Charles Harrington, William John Charles, Roy Paul, Clifford William Jones, Derek Robert Tapscott, Trevor Ford, Ivor John Allchurch, Royston James Clarke.   Manager: James Patrick Murphy
NORTHERN IRELAND: William Uprichard, William Edward Cunningham, Alfred McMichael, Robert Denis Blanchflower, John Blanchflower, Thomas Casey, William Bingham, James McIlroy, James Jones I, Edward James McMorran, Norman Lockhart.
Goals: Royston James Clarke (#) / James Jones (#)

213. 20.10.1956   British Championship
WALES v SCOTLAND 2-2 (2-2)
Ninian Park, Cardiff
Referee: Robert Mann (England)   Attendance: 60,000
WALES: Alfred John Kelsey, Alfred Thomas Sherwood, Melvyn Hopkins, Alan Charles Harrington, William Raymond Daniel, Derrick Sullivan, Terence Cameron Medwin, William John Charles, Trevor Ford, Ivor John Allchurch, Clifford William Jones.   Manager: James Patrick Murphy
SCOTLAND: Thomas Younger, Alexander Hershaw Parker, John Davidson Hewie, John Miller McColl, George Lewis Young (Cap), Douglas Cowie, Graham Leggat, John Knight Mudie, Lawrence Reilly, Robert Young Collins, William Fernie.
Goals: Trevor Ford (7), Terence Cameron Medwin (32) / William Fernie (22), Lawrence Reilly (36)

214. 14.11.1956   British Championship
ENGLAND v WALES 3-1 (0-1)
Wembley, London
Referee: Hugh Phillips (Scotland)   Attendance: 93,796
ENGLAND: Edwin George Ditchburn, Jeffrey James Hall, Roger William Byrne, Ronald Clayton, William Ambrose Wright (Cap), James William Dickinson, Stanley Matthews, John Brooks, Thomas Finney, John Norman Haynes, Colin Grainger.   Manager: Walter Winterbottom
WALES: Alfred John Kelsey, Alfred Thomas Sherwood, Melvyn Hopkins, Alan Charles Harrington, William Raymond Daniel, Melvyn Charles, Derrick Sullivan, Terence Cameron Medwin, William John Charles, Ivor John Allchurch, Clifford William Jones.   Manager: James Patrick Murphy
Goals: John Norman Haynes (52), John Brooks (54), Thomas Finney (75) / William John Charles (8)

215. 10.04.1957   British Championship
NORTHERN IRELAND v WALES 0-0
Windsor Park, Belfast
Referee: Not recorded   Attendance: 30,000
NORTHERN IRELAND: Harry Gregg, William Edward Cunningham, Alfred McMichael, Robert Denis Blanchflower, Wilbur Cush, Robert Peacock, William Bingham, James McIlroy, James Jones, Thomas Casey, Peter James McParland.
WALES: Alfred John Kelsey, Leonard Trevor Edwards, Melvyn Hopkins, Melvyn Charles, William Raymond Daniel, David Lloyd Bowen, Terence Cameron Medwin, Derek Robert Tapscott, William John Charles, Thomas Royston Vernon, Clifford William Jones.   Manager: James Patrick Murphy

216. 01.05.1957   6th World Cup Qualifiers
WALES v CZECHOSLOVAKIA 1-0 (0-0)
Ninian Park, Cardiff
Referee: Just Bronkhorst (Holland)   Attendance: 45,000
WALES: Alfred John Kelsey, Roland Frederick Stitfall, Melvyn Hopkins, Melvyn Charles, William John Charles, David Lloyd Bowen, Terence Cameron Medwin, Derek Robert Tapscott, Colin Webster, Thomas Royston Vernon, Clifford William Jones.   Manager: James Patrick Murphy
CZECHOSLOVAKIA: Břetislav Dolejši, Jan Hertl, Jiří Čadek, Ladislav Novák (Cap), Svatopluk Pluskal, Josef Masopust, Arnošt Pazdera, Emil Svoboda, Vlastimil Bubník, Jaroslav Borovička, Tadeáš Kraus.   Trainer: Antonín Rýgr
Goal: Thomas Royston Vernon (72)

217. 19.05.1957 6th World Cup Qualifiers
EAST GERMANY v WALES 2-1 (1-1)
Zentral, Leipzig
Referee: Nikolay Latyshev (Soviet Union)   Att: 110,000
EAST GERMANY: Karl-Heinz Spickenagel, Georg Buschner, Herbert Schoen (Cap), Brinfried Müller, Karl Wolf, Siegfried Wolf, Lothar Meyer, Günter Schröter, Willy Tröger, Manfred Kaiser, Günther Wirth.   Trainer: János Gyarmati
WALES: Alfred John Kelsey, Leonard Trevor Edwards, Melvyn Hopkins, William Charles Harris, Melvyn Charles, William John Charles, David Lloyd Bowen, Terence Cameron Medwin, Derek Robert Tapscott, Thomas Royston Vernon, Clifford William Jones.   Manager: James Patrick Murphy
Goals: Günther Wirth (21), Willy Tröger (61) / Melvyn Charles (6)

218. 26.05.1957 6th World Cup Qualifiers
CZECHOSLOVAKIA v WALES 2-0 (1-0)
Stahov, Praha
Referee: Paul Wyssling (Switzerland)   Attendance: 45,000
CZECHOSLOVAKIA: Imrich Stacho, Jan Hertl, Jiří Hledík, Ladislav Novák (Cap), Svatopluk Pluskal, Josef Masopust, Kazimír Gajdoš, Anton Moravčík, Jaroslav Borovička, Pavol Molnár, Tadeáš Kraus.   Trainer: Antonín Rýgr
WALES: Alfred John Kelsey, David Thomas, Melvyn Hopkins, Melvyn Charles, William Raymond Daniel, William Charles Harris, Terence Cameron Medwin, Desmond Frederick Palmer, William John Charles, Thomas Royston Vernon, Clifford William Jones.   Manager: James Patrick Murphy
Goals: William Raymond Daniel (22 own goal), Tadeáš Kraus (65)

219. 25.09.1957 6th World Cup Qualifiers
WALES v EAST GERMANY 4-1 (3-0)
Ninian Park, Cardiff
Referee: Reginald Leafe (England)   Attendance: 17,000
WALES: Graham Vearncombe, David Thomas, Melvyn Hopkins, Melvyn Charles, William Charles Harris, David Lloyd Bowen, Leonard Allchurch, Ellis Reginald Davies, Desmond Frederick Palmer, Thomas Royston Vernon, Clifford William Jones.   Manager: James Patrick Murphy
EAST GERMANY: Günther Busch, Brinfried Müller, Herbert Schoen (Cap), Georg Buschner, Karl Wolf, Siegfried Wolf, Lothar Meyer, Günter Schröter, Willy Tröger, Manfred Kaiser, Günther Wirth.   Trainer: János Gyarmati
Goals: Desmond Frederick Palmer (38, 44, 73), Clifford William Jones (42) / Manfred Kaiser (57)

220. 19.10.1957 British Championship
WALES v ENGLAND 0-4 (0-2)
Ninian Park, Cardiff
Referee: Thomas Mitchell (Northern Ireland)   Att: 58,000
WALES: Alfred John Kelsey, Stuart Grenville Williams, Melvyn Hopkins, William Charles Harris, Melvyn Charles, David Lloyd Bowen, Terence Cameron Medwin, Ellis Reginald Davies, Desmond Frederick Palmer, Thomas Royston Vernon, Clifford William Jones.   Manager: James Patrick Murphy
ENGLAND: Edward Hopkinson, Donald Howe, Roger William Byrne, Ronald Clayton, William Ambrose Wright (Cap), Duncan Edwards, Bryan Douglas, Derek Tennyson Kevan, Thomas Taylor, John Norman Haynes, Thomas Finney.   Manager: Walter Winterbottom
Goals: Melvyn Hopkins (2 own goals), John Haynes (44, 67), Thomas Finney (64)

221. 13.11.1957 British Championship
SCOTLAND v WALES 1-1 (1-0)
Hampden Park, Glasgow
Referee: John Harold Clough (England)   Att: 42,918
SCOTLAND: Thomas Younger, Alexander Hershaw Parker, Eric Caldow, Thomas Henderson Docherty (Cap), Robert Evans, William Fernie, Alexander Silcock Scott, Robert Young Collins, James Ian Gardiner, John Knight Mudie, Thomas Ewing.
WALES: Alfred John Kelsey, Stuart Grenville Williams, Melvyn Hopkins, Alan Charles Harrington, Melvyn Charles, David Lloyd Bowen, Leonard Allchurch, William Charles Harris, Terence Cameron Medwin, Thomas Royston Vernon, Clifford William Jones.   Manager: James Patrick Murphy
Goal: Terence Cameron Medwin (76)

222. 15.01.1958 6th World Cup Qualifier Play-Off
ISRAEL v WALES 0-2 (0-1)
National, Ramat Gan, Tel Aviv
Referee: Maurice Guigue (France)   Attendance: 55,000
ISRAEL: Yaacov Hodorov, Amatsia Levkovich, Noah Reznik, Gidon Tish, Hanoch Mordechovich, Aharon Amar, Yosef Goldstein, Itzhak Nahmias, Nahum Stelmach, Yehosua Glazer, Zecharia Ratzabi.   Trainer: Moshe Varon
WALES: Alfred John Kelsey, Stuart Grenville Williams, Melvyn Hopkins, Alan Charles Harrington, Melvyn Charles, David Lloyd Bowen, Leonard Allchurch, William John Charles, Terence Cameron Medwin, Ivor John Allchurch, Clifford William Jones.   Manager: James Patrick Murphy
Goals: Ivor John Allchurch (38), David Lloyd Bowen (65)

223. 05.02.1958   6th World Cup Qualifier Play-Off
WALES v ISRAEL 2-0 (0-0)
Ninian Park, Cardiff
Referee: Klas Schipper (Holland)   Attendance: 38,000
WALES: Alfred John Kelsey, Stuart Grenville Williams, Melvyn Hopkins, Alan Charles Harrington, Melvyn Charles, David Lloyd Bowen, Terence Cameron Medwin, Ronald Hewitt, William John Charles, Ivor John Allchurch, Clifford William Jones.   Manager: James Patrick Murphy
ISRAEL: Yaacov Hodorov, Amatsia Levkovich, Noah Reznik, Gidon Tish, Hanoch Mordechovich, Aharon Amar, Yosef Goldstein, Itzhak Nahmias, Nahum Stelmach, Bohos Jojosian, Yehosua Glazer.   Trainer: Moshe Varon
Goals: Ivor John Allchurch (76), Clifford William Jones (80)

224. 16.04.1958   British Championship
WALES v NORTHERN IRELAND 1-1 (0-0)
Ninian Park, Cardiff
Referee: Not recorded   Attendance: 25,677
WALES: Alfred John Kelsey, Stuart Grenville Williams, Melvyn Hopkins, Alan Charles Harrington, Derrick Sullivan, David Lloyd Bowen, Leonard Allchurch, Ronald Hewitt, Terence Cameron Medwin, Ivor John Allchurch, Clifford William Jones.   Manager: James Patrick Murphy
NORTHERN IRELAND: Harry Gregg, William Edward Cunningham, Alfred McMichael, Robert Denis Blanchflower, Richard Matthewson Keith, Robert Peacock, William Bingham, Wilbur Cush, William Simpson, James McIlroy, Peter James McParland.
Goals: Richard Matthewson Keith (# own goal) / William Simpson (#)

225. 08.06.1958   6th World Cup, 1st Round
WALES v HUNGARY 1-1 (1-1)
Jernvallen, Sandviken
Referee: José Maria Codesal (Uruguay)   Attendance: 15,343
WALES: Alfred John Kelsey, Stuart Grenville Williams, Melvyn Hopkins, Derrick Sullivan, Melvyn Charles, David Lloyd Bowen, Colin Webster, Terence Cameron Medwin, William John Charles, Ivor John Allchurch, Clifford William Jones.   Manager: James Patrick Murphy
HUNGARY: Gyula Grosics, Sándor Mátrai, Ferenc Sipos, László Sárosi, József Bozsik, Pál Berendi, Károly Sándor, Nándor Hidegkuti (Cap), Lajos Tichy, Dezső Bundzsák, Máté Fenyvesi.   Trainer: Lajos Baróti
Goals: William John Charles (26) / József Bozsik (5)

226. 11.06.1958   6th World Cup, 1st Round
MEXICO v WALES 1-1 (1-1)
Råsunda, Stockholm
Referee: Leo Lemešić (Yugoslavia)   Attendance: 15,150
MEXICO: Antonio Carbajal, Jesús del Muro, Jorge Romo, Miguel Gutiérrez, Raúl Cárdenas (Cap), Francisco Flores, Jaime Belmonte, Salvador Reyes, Carlos Blanco, Carlos González, Enrique Sesma.   Trainer: Antonio López Herranz
WALES: Alfred John Kelsey, Stuart Grenville Williams, Melvyn Hopkins, Colin Walter Baker, Melvyn Charles, David Lloyd Bowen, Colin Webster, Terence Cameron Medwin, William John Charles, Ivor John Allchurch, Clifford William Jones.   Manager: James Patrick Murphy
Goals: Jaime Belmonte (89) / Ivor John Allchurch (32)

227. 15.06.1958   First Round, 6th World Cup
SWEDEN v WALES 0-0
Råsunda, Stockholm
Referee: Lucien Van Nuffel (Belgium)   Attendance: 29,800
SWEDEN: Karl Svensson, Orvar Bergmark, Sven Axbom, Reino Börjesson, Bengt Gustavsson (Cap), Sigvard Parling, Bengt Berndtsson, Gösta Löfgren, Henry Källgren, Arne Selmosson, Lennart Skoglund.   Trainer: George Raynor
WALES: Alfred John Kelsey, Stuart Grenville Williams, Melvyn Hopkins, Derrick Sullivan, Melvyn Charles, David Lloyd Bowen, Thomas Royston Vernon, Ronald Hewitt, William John Charles, Ivor John Allchurch, Clifford William Jones.   Manager: James Patrick Murphy

228. 17.06.1958   6th World Cup, 1st Round Play-Off
WALES v HUNGARY 2-1 (0-1)
Råsunda, Stockholm
Referee: Nikolay Latyshev (Soviet Union)   Att: 2,823
WALES: Alfred John Kelsey, Stuart Grenville Williams, Melvyn Hopkins, Derrick Sullivan, Melvyn Charles, David Lloyd Bowen, Terence Cameron Medwin, Ronald Hewitt, William John Charles, Ivor John Allchurch, Clifford William Jones.   Manager: James Patrick Murphy
HUNGARY: Gyula Grosics (Cap), Sándor Mátrai, Ferenc Sipos, László Sárosi, József Bozsik, Antal Kotász, László Budai, József Bencsics, Dezső Bundzsák, Lajos Tichy, Máté Fenyvesi.   Trainer: Lajos Baróti
Sent off: Ferenc Sipos (85)
Goals: Ivor Allchurch (55), Terence Cameron Medwin (76) / Lajos Tichy (33)

229. 19.06.1958   6th World Cup, Quarter-Final
BRAZIL v WALES 1-0 (0-0)
Ullevi, Göteborg

Referee: Friedrich Seipelt (Austria)   Attendance: 25,923

BRAZIL: GILMAR dos Santos Neves, Nílton de Sordi, Hideraldo Luiz Bellini (Cap), ORLANDO Peçanha de Carvalho, NÍLTON Reís dos SANTOS, José Eli de Miranda "Zito", Waldir Pereira "Didi", Manoel Francisco dos Santos "Garrincha", José João Altafini "Mazzola", Édson Arantes do Nascimento "Pelé", Mário Jorge Lobo Zagallo.
Trainer: Vicente Feola

WALES: Alfred John Kelsey, Stuart Grenville Williams, Melvyn Hopkins, Derrick Sullivan, Melvyn Charles, David Lloyd Bowen, Terence Cameron Medwin, Ronald Hewitt, Colin Webster, Ivor John Allchurch, Clifford William Jones.   Manager: James Patrick Murphy

Goal: Édson Arantes do Nascimento "Pelé" (65)

230. 18.10.1958   British Championship
WALES v SCOTLAND 0-3 (0-1)
Ninian Park, Cardiff

Referee: Reginald Leafe (England)   Attendance: 59,162

WALES: Alfred John Kelsey, Stuart Grenville Williams, Melvyn Hopkins, Derrick Sullivan, Melvyn Charles, David Lloyd Bowen, Leonard Allchurch, Thomas Royston Vernon, Terence Cameron Medwin, Ivor John Allchurch, Philip Abraham Woosnam.   Manager: James Patrick Murphy

SCOTLAND: William Dallas Fyfe Brown, John Grant, Eric Caldow, David Craig MacKay (Cap), William Toner, Thomas Henderson Docherty, Graham Leggat, Robert Young Collins, David George Herd, Denis Law, John Gillespie Henderson.
Manager: Matthew Busby

Goals: Graham Leggat (30), Denis Law (70), Robert Young Collins (82)

231. 26.11.1958   British Championship
ENGLAND v WALES 2-2 (1-1)
Villa Park, Birmingham

Referee: Albert Dusch (West Germany)   Attendance: 41,581

ENGLAND: Colin Agnew McDonald, Donald Howe, Graham Laurence Shaw, Ronald Clayton, William Ambrose Wright (Cap), Ronald Flowers, Daniel Robert Clapton, Peter Frank Broadbent, Nathaniel Lofthouse, John Norman Haynes, Alan A'Court.   Manager: Walter Winterbottom

WALES: Alfred John Kelsey, Stuart Grenville Williams, Melvyn Hopkins, Victor Herbert Crowe, Melvyn Charles, David Lloyd Bowen, Terence Cameron Medwin, David Ward, Derek Robert Tapscott, Ivor John Allchurch, Philip Abraham Woosnam.   Manager: James Patrick Murphy

Goals: Peter Frank Broadbent (42, 75) / Derek Robert Tapscott (15), Ivor John Allchurch (70)

232. 22.04.1959   British Championship
NORTHERN IRELAND v WALES 4-1 (3-0)
Windsor Park, Belfast

Referee: Not recorded   Attendance: 45,000

NORTHERN IRELAND: Harry Gregg, Richard Matthewson Keith, Alfred McMichael, Robert Denis Blanchflower, William Edward Cunningham, Robert Peacock, William Bingham, James McIlroy, Wilbur Cush, Matthew James Hill, Peter James McParland.

WALES: Raymond Victor Rouse, Stuart Grenville Williams, Melvyn Hopkins, Victor Herbert Crowe, Derrick Sullivan, David Lloyd Bowen, Terence Cameron Medwin, Derek Robert Tapscott, Antonio Camilio Rowley, Ivor John Allchurch, Clifford William Jones.   Manager: James Patrick Murphy

Goals: Peter James McParland (#), Robert Peacock (#), James McIlroy (#), Wilbur Cush (#) / Derek Robert Tapscott (#)

233. 17.10.1959   British Championship
WALES v ENGLAND 1-1 (0-1)
Ninian Park, Cardiff

Referee: Thomas Mitchell (Northern Ireland)   Att: 62,000

WALES: Alfred John Kelsey, Stuart Grenville Williams, Melvyn Hopkins, Victor Herbert Crowe, Melvyn Tudor George Nurse, Derrick Sullivan, Terence Cameron Medwin, Philip Abraham Woosnam, Graham Moore, Ivor John Allchurch, Clifford William Jones.   Manager: James Patrick Murphy

ENGLAND: Edward Hopkinson, Donald Howe, Anthony Allen, Ronald Clayton (Cap), Trevor Smith, Ronald Flowers, John Michael Connelly, James Peter Greaves, Brian Howard Clough, Robert Charlton, Edwin Holliday.
Manager: Walter Winterbottom

Goal: Graham Moore (89) / James Peter Greaves (25)

234. 04.11.1959   British Championship
SCOTLAND v WALES 1-1 (0-1)
Hampden Park, Cardiff

Referee: Kevin Howley (England)   Attendance: 55,813

SCOTLAND: William Dallas Fyfe Brown, Eric Caldow, John Davidson Hewie, David Craig MacKay, Robert Evans (Cap), Robert Johnston McCann, Graham Leggat, John Anderson White, Ian St. John, Denis Law, Robert Auld.
Manager: Andrew Beattie

WALES: Alfred John Kelsey, Stuart Grenville Williams, Melvyn Hopkins, Derrick Sullivan, William John Charles, Colin Walter Baker, Terence Cameron Medwin, Philip Abraham Woosnam, Graham Moore, Ivor John Allchurch, Clifford William Jones.   Manager: James Patrick Murphy

Goals: Graham Leggat (46) / William John Charles (8)

235. 06.04.1960   British Championship
WALES v NORTHERN IRELAND 3-2 (1-0)
The Racecourse, Wrexham
Referee: Not recorded   Attendance: 16,979
WALES: Alfred John Kelsey, Stuart Grenville Williams, Graham Evan Williams, Victor Herbert Crowe, Melvyn Tudor George Nurse, Colin Walter Baker, Terence Cameron Medwin, Philip Abraham Woosnam, Graham Moore, Thomas Royston Vernon, Clifford William Jones.
Manager: James Patrick Murphy
NORTHERN IRELAND: Harry Gregg, Alexander Russell Elder, Alfred McMichael, Robert Denis Blanchflower, William Edward Cunningham, Wilbur Cush, William Bingham, James McIlroy, William Ian Lawther, Matthew James Hill, Peter James McParland.
Goals: Terence Medwin (#, #), Philip Woosnam (# penalty) / Robert Denis Blanchflower (# penalty), William Bingham (#)

236. 28.09.1960
REPUBLIC OF IRELAND v WALES 2-3 (1-1)
Dalymount Park, Dublin
Referee: Best (United States)   Attendance: 20,000
IRELAND: Noel Michael Dwyer, James Philip Vincent Kelly, John O'Neill, Michael McGrath, Charles John Hurley, Patrick Saward (Cap), Fionan Fagan, John Michael Giles, Peter Joseph Fitzgerald, Noel Peyton, Joseph Haverty.
WALES: Graham Vearncombe, Stuart Grenville Williams, Graham Evan Williams, Victor Herbert Crowe, Melvyn Tudor George Nurse, Colin Walter Baker, Terence Cameron Medwin, Philip Abraham Woosnam, Graham Moore, Thomas Royston Vernon, Clifford William Jones.
Manager: James Patrick Murphy
Goals: Fionan Fagan (#, # penalty) / Clifford William Jones (#, #), Philip Abraham Woosnam (#)

237. 22.10.1960   British Championship
WALES v SCOTLAND 2-0 (1-0)
Ninian Park, Cardiff
Referee: Arthur Holland (England)   Attendance: 55,000
WALES: Alfred John Kelsey, Alan Charles Harrington, Graham Evan Williams, Victor Herbert Crowe, Melvyn Tudor George Nurse, Colin Walter Baker, Terence Cameron Medwin, Philip Abraham Woosnam, Kenneth Leek, Thomas Royston Vernon, Clifford William Jones.
Manager: James Patrick Murphy
SCOTLAND: Lawrence Grant Leslie, Duncan Mackay, Eric Caldow (Cap), James Gabriel, John Martis, David Craig MacKay, George Herd, John Anderson White, Alexander Young, William Hunter, David Wilson.
Goals: Clifford Jones (43), Thomas Royston Vernon (72)

238. 23.11.1960   British Championship
ENGLAND v WALES 5-1 (3-0)
Wembley, London
Referee: Robert Holley Davidson (Scotland)   Att: 65,000
ENGLAND: Alan Hodgkinson, James Christopher Armfield, Michael McNeil, Robert William Robson, Peter Swan, Ronald Flowers, Bryan Douglas, James Peter Greaves, Robert Alfred Smith, John Norman Haynes (Cap), Robert Charlton.
Manager: Walter Winterbottom
WALES: Alfred John Kelsey, Alan Charles Harrington, Graham Evan Williams, Victor Herbert Crowe, Melvyn Tudor George Nurse, Colin Walter Baker, Terence Cameron Medwin, Philip Abraham Woosnam, Kenneth Leek, Thomas Royston Vernon, Clifford William Jones.
Manager: James Patrick Murphy
Goals: James Peter Greaves (2, 69), Robert Charlton (22), Robert Alfred Smith (34), John Norman Haynes (61) / Kenneth Leek (75)

239. 12.04.1961   British Championship
NORTHERN IRELAND v WALES 1-5 (0-3)
Windsor Park, Belfast
Referee: Not recorded   Attendance: 30,000
NORTHERN IRELAND: John McClelland, Richard Matthewson Keith, Alexander Russell Elder, Robert Denis Blanchflower, William Edward Cunningham, James Joseph Nicholson, Thomas C. Stewart, Alexander Derek Dougan, William John McAdams, James McIlroy, Peter James McParland.
WALES: Alfred John Kelsey, Stuart Grenville Williams, Melvyn Hopkins, Melvyn Charles, Melvyn Tudor George Nurse, Victor Herbert Crowe, Clifford William Jones, Philip Abraham Woosnam, Kenneth Leek, Ivor John Allchurch, George Graham Williams.   Manager: James Patrick Murphy
Goal: Alexander Derek Dougan (#) / Melvyn Charles (#), Kenneth Leek (#), Ivor John Allchurch (#), Clifford William Jones (#, #)

240. 19.04.1961   7th World Cup Qualifiers
WALES v SPAIN 1-2 (1-1)
Ninian Park, Cardiff
Referee: Marcel Raeymaeckers (Belgium)   Att: 45,000
WALES: Alfred John Kelsey, Stuart Grenville Williams, Melvyn Hopkins, Melvyn Charles, Melvyn Tudor George Nurse, Victor Herbert Crowe, Terence Cameron Medwin, Philip Abraham Woosnam, Kenneth Leek, Ivor John Allchurch, George Graham Williams.
Manager: James Patrick Murphy

SPAIN: Antonio Ramallets (Cap), Alfonso María Rodríguez "Foncho", José Emilio Santamaría, Isacio Calleja, Ignacio Zoco, Enrique Gensana, Luis María "Koldo" Aguirre, Luis Del Sol, Alfredo Di Stéfano, Luis Suárez, Francisco Gento. Trainer: Pedro Escartín

Goals: Ivor John Allchurch (7) / Alfonso María Rodríguez "Foncho" (21), Alfredo Di Stéfano (78)

241. 18.05.1961   7th World Cup Qualifiers
SPAIN v WALES 1-1 (0-0)
Santiago Bernabéu, Madrid

Referee: Leopold Sylvain Horn (Holland)

SPAIN: Antonio Ramallets (Cap), Alfonso María Rodríguez "Foncho", José Emilio Santamaría, Isacio Calleja, Ignacio Zoco, Enrique Gensana, Luis María "Koldo" Aguirre, Luis Del Sol, Alfredo Di Stéfano, Joaquín Peiró, Francisco Gento. Trainer: Pedro Escartín

WALES: Alfred John Kelsey, Stuart Grenville Williams, Melvyn Hopkins, Melvyn Charles, Melvyn Tudor George Nurse, Victor Herbert Crowe, Clifford William Jones, Graham Moore, Kenneth Leek, Ivor John Allchurch, George Graham Williams.   Manager: James Patrick Murphy

Goals: Joaquín Peiró (55) / Ivor John Allchurch (69)

242. 28.05.1961
HUNGARY v WALES 3-2 (2-1)
Népstadion, Budapest

Referee: Cesare Jonni (Italy)   Attendance: 40,000

HUNGARY: Gyula Grosics, Sándor Mátrai, Ferenc Sipos, Jenő Dalnoki, Ernő Solymosi, Antal Kotász, Károly Sándor, János Göröcs, Flórián Albert, Lajos Tichy, Máté Fenyvesi dr. Trainer: Lajos Baróti

WALES: Alfred John Kelsey, Stuart Grenville Williams, Melvyn Hopkins, Melvyn Charles, Melvyn Tudor George Nurse, Victor Herbert Crowe, Clifford William Jones, Philip Abraham Woosnam, Kenneth Leek, Ivor John Allchurch, George Graham Williams.   Manager: James Patrick Murphy

Goals: Ernő Solymosi (1), Lajos Tichy (7, 88 pen) / Clifford William Jones (18)

243. 14.10.1961   British Championship
WALES v ENGLAND 1-1 (1-1)
Ninian Park, Cardiff

Referee: Hugh Phillips (Scotland)   Attendance: 61,566

WALES: Alfred John Kelsey, Alan Charles Harrington, Stuart Grenville Williams, Melvyn Charles, William John Charles, Victor Herbert Crowe, Clifford William Jones, Philip Abraham Woosnam, David Ward, Ivor John Allchurch, George Graham Williams.   Manager: James Patrick Murphy

ENGLAND: Ronald Derrick Springettt, James Christopher Armfield, Ramon Wilson, Robert William Robson, Peter Swan, Ronald Flowers, John Michael Connelly, Bryan Douglas, Raymond Pointer, John Norman Haynes (Cap), Robert Charlton.   Manager: Walter Winterbottom

Goal: George Graham Williams (30) / Bryan Douglas (44)

244. 08.11.1961   British Championship
SCOTLAND v WALES 2-0 (1-0)
Hampden Park, Glasgow

Referee: Arthur Holland (England)   Attendance: 74,329

SCOTLAND: William Dallas Fyfe Brown, Alexander William Hamilton, Eric Caldow (Cap), Patrick Timothy Crerand, John Francombe Ure, James Curran Baxter, Alexander Silcock Scott, John Anderson White, Ian St. John, Ralph Laidlaw Brand, David Wilson.   Manager: John Miller McColl

WALES: Alfred John Kelsey, Alan Charles Harrington, Stuart Grenville Williams, Victor Herbert Crowe, Melvyn Charles, Colin Walter Baker, Leonard Allchurch, Philip Abraham Woosnam, Kenneth Leek, Ivor John Allchurch, Clifford William Jones.   Manager: James Patrick Murphy

Goals: Ian St. John (22, 50)

245. 11.04.1962   British Championship
WALES v NORTHERN IRELAND 4-0 (2-0)
Ninian Park, Cardiff

Referee: Not recorded   Attendance: 13,250

WALES: Alfred John Kelsey, Stuart Grenville Williams, Melvyn Hopkins, Peter Malcolm Lucas, Harold Michael England, William Terence Hennessey, Leonard Allchurch, Philip Abraham Woosnam, Melvyn Charles, Thomas Royston Vernon, Clifford William Jones.
Manager: James Patrick Murphy

NORTHERN IRELAND: William Ronald Briggs, Richard Matthewson Keith, William Edward Cunningham, Robert Denis Blanchflower, William John Terence Neill, James Joseph Nicholson, William Humphries, William Cecil Johnston, James O'Neill, James Christopher McLaughlin, Robert Munn Braithwaite.

Goals: Melvyn Charles (4 goals)

246. 12.05.1962
BRAZIL v WALES 3-1 (2-0)
Maracanã, Rio de Janeiro
Referee: Sérgio Bustamante (Chile)   Attendance: 100,000
BRAZIL: GILMAR dos Santos Neves, JAIR MARINHO de Oliveira, MAURO Ramos de Oliveira (DJALMA Pereira DIAS Júnior), ZÓZIMO Alves Calazans, NÍLTON Reís dos SANTOS, José Márcio Pereira da Silva "Zequinha", MENGÁLVIO Pedro Figueiró, Manoel Francisco dos Santos "Garrincha", Antônio Wilson Honório "Coutinho", Édson Arantes do Nascimento "Pelé", José Macia "Pepe".   Trainer: Aymoré Moreira
WALES: Alfred John Kelsey, Stuart Grenville Williams, Melvyn Hopkins, William Terence Hennessey, William John Charles, Victor Herbert Crowe, Leonard Allchurch, Thomas Royston Vernon, Melvyn Charles, Ivor John Allchurch, Clifford William Jones.   Manager: James Patrick Murphy
Goals: Manoel Francisco dos Santos "Garrincha" (#), Antônio Wilson Honório "Coutinho" (#), Édson Arantes do Nascimento "Pelé" / Ivor John Allchurch (#)

247. 16.05.1962
BRAZIL v WALES 3-1 (1-1)
Morumbi, São Paulo
Referee: Sérgio Bustamante (Chile)   Attendance: 60,000
BRAZIL: GILMAR dos Santos Neves, Djalma Santos, MAURO Ramos de Oliveira, JURANDIR de Freiras, NÍLTON Reís dos SANTOS, José Márcio Pereira da Silva "Zequinha", Waldir Pereira "Didi", Jair da Costa (Manoel Francisco dos Santos "Garrincha"), Antônio Wilson Honório "Coutinho" (Edvaldo Izídio Neto "Vavá"), Édson Arantes do Nascimento "Pelé", Mário Jorge Lobo Zagallo.   Trainer: Aymoré Moreira
WALES: Alfred John Kelsey (David Michael Hollins), Stuart Grenville Williams, William John Charles, Harold Michael England, William Terence Hennessey, Melvyn Hopkins, Philip Abraham Woosnam, Thomas Royston Vernon, Graham Moore (Kenneth Leek), Ivor John Allchurch, Clifford William Jones.   Manager: James Patrick Murphy
Goals: Edvaldo Izídio Neto "Vavá" (17), Édson Arantes do Nascimento "Pelé" (80, 82) / Kenneth Leek (62)

248. 22.05.1962
MEXICO v WALES 2-1 (2-0)
Olímpico Universitário, Ciudad de México
Referee: Diego de Leo (Mexico)   Attendance: 75,000
MEXICO: Jaime Gómez, Jesús del Muro, Guillermo Sepúlveda, José Villegas, Raúl Cárdenas, Pedro Nájera, Alfredo del Aguila, Salvador Reyes, Héctor Hernández, Antonio Jasso, Isidoro Díaz.   Trainer: Ignacio Tréllez

WALES: David Michael Hollins, Stuart Grenville Williams, Melvyn Hopkins, Peter Malcolm Lucas, Harold Michael England, Victor Herbert Crowe, Thomas Royston Vernon, William John Charles, Kenneth Leek, Ivor John Allchurch, Clifford William Jones.   Manager: James Patrick Murphy
Sent off: Clifford William Jones (65)
Goals: Antonio Jasso (26, 55) / William John Charles (78)

249. 20.10.1962   British Championship
WALES v SCOTLAND 2-3 (1-1)
Ninian Park, Cardiff
Referee: Kenneth Dagnall (England)   Attendance: 58,000
WALES: Anthony Horace Millington, Stuart Grenville Williams, Melvyn Hopkins, William Terence Hennessey, William John Charles, Peter Malcolm Lucas, Barrie Spencer Jones, Ivor John Allchurch, Melvyn Charles, Thomas Royston Vernon, Clifford William Jones.
Manager: James Patrick Murphy
SCOTLAND: William Dallas Fyfe Brown, Alexander William Hamilton, Eric Caldow (Cap), Patrick Timothy Crerand, John Francombe Ure, James Curran Baxter, William Henderson, John Anderson White, Ian St. John, Denis Law, David Wilson.
Manager: John Miller McColl
Goals: Ivor John Allchurch (40), William John Charles (88) / Eric Caldow (19 pen), Denis Law (63), W. Henderson (79)

250. 07.11.1962   2nd European Champs, 1st Round
HUNGARY v WALES 3-1 (2-1)
Népstadion, Budapest
Referee: Jozef Kowál (Poland)   Attendance: 40,000
HUNGARY: Antal Szentmihályi, Sándor Mátrai, Kálmán Mészöly, Kálmán Sóvári, Ernő Solymosi, Ferenc Sipos, Károly Sándor, János Göröcs, Flórián Albert, Lajos Tichy, Máté Fenyvesi dr.   Trainer: Lajos Baróti
WALES: Anthony Horace Millington, Stuart Grenville Williams, Melvyn Hopkins, William Terence Hennessey, Melvyn Tudor George Nurse, Victor Herbert Crowe, Terence Cameron Medwin, Ivor John Allchurch, Melvyn Charles, Thomas Royston Vernon, Barrie Spencer Jones.
Manager: James Patrick Murphy
Goals: Flórián Albert (6), Lajos Tichy (35), Károly Sándor (48) / Terence Cameron Medwin (18)

251. 21.11.1962   British Championship
ENGLAND v WALES 4-0 (2-0)
Wembley, London
Referee: Samuel Carswell (Ireland)   Attendance: 27,500
ENGLAND: Ronald Derrick Springettt, James Christopher Armfield (Cap), Graham Laurence Shaw, Robert Frederick Moore, Brian Leslie Labone, Ronald Flowers, John Michael Connelly, Frederick Hill, Alan Peacock, James Peter Greaves, Robert Victor Tambling.   Manager: Walter Winterbottom
WALES: Anthony Horace Millington, Stuart Grenville Williams, Reginald Clifford Sear, William Terence Hennessey, Melvyn Tudor George Nurse, Peter Malcolm Lucas, Barrie Spencer Jones, Ivor John Allchurch, Kenneth Leek, Thomas Royston Vernon, Terence Cameron Medwin.
Manager: James Patrick Murphy
Goals: John Michael Connelly (10), Alan Peacock (35, 60), James Peter Greaves (88)

252. 20.03.1963   2nd European Champs, 1st Round
WALES v HUNGARY 1-1 (1-0)
Ninian Park, Cardiff
Referee: John Spillane (Republic of Ireland)   Att: 30,413
WALES: David Michael Hollins, Stuart Grenville Williams, Graham Evan Williams, William Terence Hennessey, Harold Michael England, Alwyn Derek Burton, Barrie Spencer Jones, Philip Abraham Woosnam, Graham Moore, Ivor John Allchurch, Clifford William Jones.
Manager: James Patrick Murphy
HUNGARY: Antal Szentmihályi, Sándor Mátrai, Kálmán Mészöly, László Sárosi, Ernő Solymosi, Ferenc Sipos, Károly Sándor, János Göröcs, Flórián Albert, Lajos Tichy, Máté Fenyvesi dr.   Trainer: Lajos Baróti
Goals: Clifford William Jones (25 pen) / Lajos Tichy (73 pen)

253. 03.04.1963   British Championship
NORTHERN IRELAND v WALES 1-4 (1-2)
Windsor Park, Belfast
Referee: Not recorded   Attendance: 25,000
NORTHERN IRELAND: Robert James Irvine, Edward James Magill, Alexander Russell Elder, Martin Harvey, Albert Campbell, William John Terence Neill, William Humphries, John Andrew Crossan, William John Irvine, James McIlroy, James Christopher McLaughlin.
WALES: David Michael Hollins, Melvyn Hopkins, Graham Evan Williams, Alwyn Derek Burton, Harold Michael England, Barrington Gerard Hole, Barrie Spencer Jones, Philip Abraham Woosnam, Graham Moore, Ivor John Allchurch, Clifford William Jones.   Manager: James Patrick Murphy
Goals: Martin Harvey (#) /
Clifford William Jones (#, #, #), Philip Abraham Woosnam (#)

254. 12.10.1963   British Championship
WALES v ENGLAND 0-4 (0-1)
Ninian Park, Cardiff
Referee: W. Brittle (Scotland)   Attendance: 48,350
WALES: David Michael Hollins, Stuart Grenville Williams, Graham Evan Williams, William Terence Hennessey, Harold Michael England, Alwyn Derek Burton, Leonard Allchurch, Thomas Royston Vernon, Ronald Wyn Davies, Ivor John Allchurch, Clifford William Jones.
Manager: James Patrick Murphy
ENGLAND: Gordon Banks, James Christopher Armfield (Cap), Ramon Wilson, Gordon Milne, Maurice Norman, Robert Frederick Moore, Terence Lionel Paine, James Peter Greaves, Robert Alfred Smith, George Edward Eastham, Robert Charlton.   Manager: Alfred Ramsey
Goals: Robert Alfred Smith (5, 67), James Peter Greaves (65), Robert Charlton (86)

255. 20.11.1963   British Championship
SCOTLAND v WALES 2-1 (1-0)
Hampden Park, Glasgow
Referee: William Clements (England)   Attendance: 51,167
SCOTLAND: William Dallas Fyfe Brown, Alexander William Hamilton, James Kennedy, David Craig MacKay (Cap), William McNeill, James Curran Baxter, William Henderson, John Anderson White, Alan John Gilzean, Denis Law, Alexander Silcock Scott.   Manager: John Miller McColl
WALES: Gareth Sprake, Stuart Grenville Williams, Graham Evan Williams, William Terence Hennessey, Harold Michael England, Melvyn Tudor George Nurse, Barrie Spencer Jones, Graham Moore, William John Charles, Thomas Royston Vernon, Clifford William Jones.
Manager: James Patrick Murphy
Goals: John Anderson White (44), Denis Law (47) /
Barrie Spencer Jones (57)

256. 15.04.1964   British Championship
WALES v NORTHERN IRELAND 2-3 (1-3)
Vetch Field, Swansea
Referee: Not recorded   Attendance: 10,343
WALES: Gareth Sprake, Royston Sidney Evans, Graham Evan Williams, Michael George Johnson, Harold Michael England, Barrington Gerard Hole, Barrie Spencer Jones, Graham Moore, Ronald Tudor Davies, Brian Cameron Godfrey, Clifford William Jones.   Trainer: David Bowen
NORTHERN IRELAND: Patrick Anthony Jennings, Edward James Magill, Alexander Russell Elder, Martin Harvey, William John Terence Neill, William James McCullough, George Best, John Andrew Crossan, Samuel Wilson, James Christopher McLaughlin, Robert Munn Braithwaite.
Goals: Brian Godfrey (#), Ronald Tudor Davies (#) /
James McLaughlin (#), Samuel Wilson (#), Martin Harvey (#)

47

257. 03.10.1964   British Championship
WALES v SCOTLAND 3-2 (1-2)
Ninian Park, Cardiff
Referee: Kevin Howley (England)   Attendance: 37,093
WALES: Gareth Sprake, Stuart Grenville Williams, Graham Evan Williams, Barrington Gerard Hole, William John Charles, William Terence Hennessey, Clifford William Jones, Kenneth Leek, Ronald Wyn Davies, Ivor John Allchurch, Ronald Raymond Rees.   Trainer: David Bowen
SCOTLAND: Robert Campbell Forsyth, Alexander William Hamilton, James Kennedy, John Greig, Ronald Yeats, James Curran Baxter, James Connolly Johnstone, David Wedderburn Gibson, Stephen Chalmers, Denis Law (Cap), James Gillen Robertson.   Manager: John Miller McColl
Goals: Ronald Wyn Davies (6), Kenneth Leek (87, 89) / Stephen Chalmers (28), David Wedderburn Gibson (29)

258. 21.10.1964   8th World Cup Qualifiers
DENMARK v WALES 1-0 (0-0)
Idraetsparken, København
Referee: Ottmar Huber (Switzerland)   Attendance: 22,473
DENMARK: Leif Nielsen, Leif Hartwig, Bent Wolmar, Bent Hansen, Birger Larsen, Jens Petersen, Palle Kähler, Ole Fritsen, Ole Madsen (Cap), Ole Sørensen, Tom Søndergaard.   Trainer: Poul Petersen
WALES: Gareth Sprake, Stuart Grenville Williams, Graham Evan Williams, William Terence Hennessey, Harold Michael England, Barrington Gerard Hole, Barrie Spencer Jones, Brian Cameron Godfrey, Ronald Wyn Davies, Clifford William Jones, Ronald Raymond Rees.   Trainer: David Bowen
Goal: Ole Madsen (48)

259. 18.11.1964   British Championship
ENGLAND v WALES 2-1 (1-0)
Wembley, London
Referee: Thomas Mitchell (Northern Ireland)   Att: 40,000
ENGLAND: Anthony Keith Waiters, George Reginald Cohen, Robert Anthony Thomson, Michael Alfred Bailey, Ronald Flowers (Cap), Gerald Morton Young, Peter Thompson, Roger Hunt, Frank Wignall, John Joseph Byrne, Alan Thomas Hinton.   Manager: Alfred Ramsey
WALES: Anthony Horace Millington, Stuart Grenville Williams, Graham Evan Williams, William Terence Hennessey, Harold Michael England, Barrington Gerard Hole, Ronald Raymond Rees, Ronald Tudor Davies, Ronald Wyn Davies, Ivor John Allchurch, Clifford William Jones.   Trainer: David Bowen
Goals: Frank Wignall (18, 60) / Clifford William Jones (75)

260. 09.12.1964   8th World Cup Qualifiers
GREECE v WALES 2-0 (1-0)
Panathinaikos, Athína
Referee: Wacław Majdan (Poland)   Attendance: 20,663
GREECE: Konstantinos Valianos, Aristeídis Kamaras, Panagiótis Papoulidis, Giórgos Andreou, Stélios Skevofylax, Neotákis Loukanidis, Pavlos Vasiliou, Giánnis Komianidis, Dimítris Domazos, Dimítris Papaïoánnou (Cap), Andréas Papaemmanouil.
Trainers: Lakis Petropoulos & Giórgos Mageiras
WALES: Gareth Sprake, Peter Joseph Rodrigues, Graham Evan Williams, William Terence Hennessey, Harold Michael England, Barrington Gerard Hole, Ronald Raymond Rees, Kenneth Leek, Ronald Wyn Davies, Herbert John Williams, Clifford William Jones.   Trainer: David Bowen
Goals: Dimítris Papaïoánnou (4), A. Papaemmanouil (47)

261. 17.03.1965   8th World Cup Qualifiers
WALES v GREECE 4-1 (1-1)
Ninian Park, Cardiff
Referee: Pieter Paulus Roomer (Holland)   Att: 11,159
WALES: David Michael Hollins, Peter Joseph Rodrigues, Graham Evan Williams, Herbert John Williams, Harold Michael England, Barrington Gerard Hole, Clifford William Jones, Ivor John Allchurch, Kenneth Leek, Thomas Royston Vernon, Ronald Raymond Rees.   Trainer: David Bowen
GREECE: Konstantinos Valianos, Aristeídis Kamaras, Panagiótis Papoulidis, Giórgos Andreou, Neotákis Loukanidis, Stélios Skevofylax, Pavlos Vasiliou, Giórgos Sideris, Dimítris Domazos, Dimítris Papaïoánnou (Cap), Andréas Papaemmanouil.
Trainers: Lakis Petropoulos & Giórgos Mageiras
Goals: Ivor Allchurch (26, 74), Harold Michael England (51), Thomas Royston Vernon (65) / Dimítris Papaïoánnou (3)

262. 31.03.1965   British Championship
NORTHERN IRELAND v WALES 0-5 (0-2)
Windsor Park, Belfast
Referee: Not recorded   Attendance: 15,000
NORTHERN IRELAND: Robert James Irvine, John Parke, Alexander Russell Elder, Martin Harvey, William John Terence Neill, James Joseph Nicholson, William Humphries, John Andrew Crossan, William John Irvine, James Christopher McLaughlin, David Clements.
WALES: David Michael Hollins, Peter Joseph Rodrigues, Graham Evan Williams, Cyril Lea, Harold Michael England, Barrington Gerard Hole, Clifford William Jones, Ivor John Allchurch, Ronald Wyn Davies, Thomas Royston Vernon, Ronald Raymond Rees.   Trainer: David Bowen
Goals: Thomas Royston Vernon (#, #), Clifford Jones (#), Graham Evan Williams (#), Ivor John Allchurch (#)

263. 01.05.1965
ITALY v WALES 4-1 (1-0)
Comunale, Firenze
Referee: Michel Kitabdjian (France)   Attendance: 43,000
ITALY: Enrico Albertosi, Enzo Robotti, Romano Micelli, Giancarlo Bercellino, Sandro Salvadore (Cap), Romano Fogli, Bruno Mora, Giovanni Lodetti, Alberto Orlando (46 Cosimo Nocera), Giacomo Bulgarelli, Paolo Barison. Trainer: Edmondo Fabbri
WALES: David Michael Hollins, Colin Robert Green, Graham Evan Williams, Cyril Lea, Harold Michael England, Barrington Gerard Hole, Clifford William Jones, Ivor John Allchurch, Brian Cameron Godfrey, Thomas Royston Vernon, Ronald Raymond Rees.   Trainer: David Bowen
Goals: Giovanni Lodetti (24, 76), Paolo Barison (62), Cosimo Nocera (90) / Brian Cameron Godfrey (80)

264. 30.05.1965   8th World Cup Qualifiers
SOVIET UNION v WALES 2-1 (1-0)
Lenin, Moskva
Referee: Helmut Fritz (West Germany)   Attendance: 86,015
SOVIET UNION: Viktor Bannikov, Vladimir Ponomarev, Vasiliy Danilov, Albert Shesternev, Valeriy Voronin, Georgiy Ryabov, Slava Metreveli, Valentin Ivanov (Cap), Boris Kazakov, Galimzyan Khusainov, Mikhail Meskhi.
Trainer: Nikolay Morozov
WALES: Anthony Horace Millington, Colin Robert Green, Graham Evan Williams, William Terence Hennessey, Harold Michael England, Barrington Gerard Hole, Clifford William Jones, Ivor John Allchurch, Ronald Wyn Davies, William John Charles, Ronald Raymond Rees.   Trainer: David Bowen
Goals: Valentin Ivanov (39), Graham Williams (48 own goal) / Ronald Wyn Davies (69)

265. 02.10.1965   British Championship
WALES v ENGLAND 0-0
Ninian Park, Cardiff
Referee: Archibald Webster (Scotland)   Attendance: 30,000
WALES: Gareth Sprake, Peter Joseph Rodrigues, Colin Robert Green, William Terence Hennessey, Harold Michael England, Barrington Gerard Hole, Ronald Raymond Rees, Thomas Royston Vernon, Ronald Wyn Davies, Ivor John Allchurch, Gilbert Ivor Reece.
ENGLAND: Ronald Derrick Springettt, George Reginald Cohen, Ramon Wilson, Norbert Peter Stiles, John "Jack" Charlton, Robert Frederick Moore (Cap), Terence Lionel Paine, James Peter Greaves, Alan Peacock, Robert Charlton, John Michael Connelly.   Manager: Alfred Ramsey

266. 27.10.1965   8th World Cup Qualifiers
WALES v SOVIET UNION 2-1 (1-1)
Ninian Park, Cardiff
Referee: Birger Nilsen (Norway)   Attendance: 24,626
WALES: Gareth Sprake, Peter Joseph Rodrigues, Colin Robert Green, William Terence Hennessey, Harold Michael England, Barrington Gerard Hole, Ronald Raymond Rees, Thomas Royston Vernon, Ronald Wyn Davies, Ivor John Allchurch, Gilbert Ivor Reece.   Trainer: David Bowen
SOVIET UNION: Anzor Kavazashvili, Valentin Afonin, Albert Shesternev, Vasiliy Danilov, Valeriy Voronin (Cap), Murtaz Khurtzilava, Slava Metreveli, Eduard Malofeev, Anatoliy Banishevskiy, Galimzyan Khusainov, Mikhail Meskhi.
Trainer: Nikolay Morozov
Goals: Thomas Royston Vernon (18), Ivor Allchurch (78) / Anatoliy Banishevskiy (17)

267. 24.11.1965   British Championship
SCOTLAND v WALES 4-1 (3-1)
Hampden Park, Glasgow
Referee: James Finney (England)   Attendance: 49,888
SCOTLAND: Robert Ferguson, John Greig, Edward Graham McCreadie, Robert White Murdoch, Ronald McKinnon, James Curran Baxter (Cap), William Henderson, Charles Cooke, James Forrest, Alan John Gilzean, William McClure Johnston.
Manager: John Stein
WALES: David Michael Hollins, Peter Joseph Rodrigues, Colin Robert Green, William Terence Hennessey, Harold Michael England, Barrington Gerard Hole, Ronald Raymond Rees, Thomas Royston Vernon, Ronald Wyn Davies, Ivor John Allchurch, Gilbert Ivor Reece.   Trainer: David Bowen
Goals: Robert Murdoch (10, 29), William Henderson (13), John Greig (86) / Ivor John Allchurch (12)

268. 01.12.1965   8th World Cup Qualifiers
WALES v DENMARK 4-2 (3-1)
The Racecourse, Wrexham
Referee: Michel Kitabdjian (France)   Attendance: 4,839
WALES: David Michael Hollins, Peter Joseph Rodrigues, Stuart Grenville Williams, William Terence Hennessey, Harold Michael England, Barrington Gerard Hole, Ronald Raymond Rees, Thomas Royston Vernon, Ronald Wyn Davies, Ivor John Allchurch, Keith David Pring.   Trainer: David Bowen
DENMARK: Max Møller, Johnny Hansen, Leif Hartwig, Jens Jørgen Hansen (Cap), Karl Hansen, Børge Enemark, Kaj Poulsen, Poul Bilde, Ole Fritsen, Egon Jensen, Ulrik Le Fevre.
Trainer: Poul Petersen
Goals: Ronald Wyn Davies (1), Thomas Vernon (11, 78), Ronald Raymond Rees (18) / Kaj Poulsen (4), Ole Fritsen (49)

269. 30.03.1966   British Championship
WALES v NORTHERN IRELAND 1-4 (0-2)
Ninian Park, Cardiff
Referee: Not recorded   Attendance: 12,860
WALES: Gareth Sprake, Peter Joseph Rodrigues, Graham Evan Williams, William Terence Hennessey, Harold Michael England, Barrington Gerard Hole, Ronald Raymond Rees, Thomas Royston Vernon, Ronald Wyn Davies, Graham Moore, Gilbert Ivor Reece.   Trainer: David Bowen
NORTHERN IRELAND: Patrick Anthony Jennings, Edward James Magill, Alexander Russell Elder, Martin Harvey, William John Terence Neill, James Joseph Nicholson, Eric Welsh, Samuel Wilson, William John Irvine, Alexander Derek Dougan, James Christopher McLaughlin.
Goals: Ronald Wyn Davies (#) / William John Irvine (#), Samuel Wilson (#), Eric Welsh (#), Martin Harvey (#)

270. 14.05.1966
BRAZIL v WALES 3-1 (2-1)
Maracanã, Rio de Janeiro
Referee: Thomas Wharton (Scotland)   Attendance: 64,000
BRAZIL: GILMAR dos Santos Neves, CARLOS ALBERTO Tôrres, Hércules BRITO Ruas, ORLANDO Peçanha de Carvalho, RILDO da Costa Menezes, DENÍLSON Custódio Machado, GÉRSON de Oliveira Nunes, Manoel Francisco dos Santos "Garrincha", SERVÍLIO de Jesus Filho, Wálter Machado da Silva, Ademir de Barros "Paraná".   Trainer: Vicente Feola
WALES: David Michael Hollins, Colin Robert Green, Peter Joseph Rodrigues, William Terence Hennessey, Edward Glyn James, Barrington Gerard Hole, Ronald Raymond Rees, Ronald Tudor Davies, Ronald Wyn Davies, Ivor John Allchurch, Graham Evan Williams.   Trainer: David Bowen
Goals: Wálter Machado da Silva (#), SERVÍLIO de Jesus Filho (#), Manoel Francisco dos Santos "Garrincha" (#) / Ronald Tudor Davies (#)

271. 18.05.1966
BRAZIL "B" v WALES 1-0 (0-0)
Mineirão, Belo Horizonte
Referee: Archibald F. Webster (Scotland)   Att: 25,000
BRAZIL: FÁBIO Arlindo Medeos, Paulo MURILO Frederico Ferreira, DJALMA Pereira DIAS Júnior, Sebastião Leônidas, ÉDSON de Souza Barbosa, Olegário Toloi de Oliveira "Dudu" (ROBERTO DIAS Branco), Antônio LIMA dos Santos, Jair Ventura Filho "Jairzinho", Eduardo Gonçalves de Andrade "Tostão", CÉLIO Taveira Filho (PAULO Luís BORGES), IVAIR Ferreira.   Trainer: Vicente Feola

WALES: Anthony Horace Millington, Colin Robert Green, Peter Joseph Rodrigues, William Terence Hennessey, Edward Glyn James, Barrington Gerard Hole, Ronald Raymond Rees (William Alan Durban), Ronald Tudor Davies, Ronald Wyn Davies, Ivor John Allchurch, Graham Evan Williams.
Trainer: David Bowen
Goal: Antônio LIMA dos Santos (#)

272. 22.05.1966
CHILE v WALES 2-0 (1-0)
Nacional, Santiago
Referee: Sérgio Bustamante González (Chile)   Att: 32,000
CHILE: Adán Godoy, Luis Armando Eyzaguirre, Humberto Cruz, Elías Ricardo Figueroa Brander, Hugo Villanueva, Guillermo Yávar, Rubén Marcos, Pedro Araya Toro (Francisco Valdés Muñoz), Armando Tobar (Orlando Ramírez), Alberto Fouilloux, Leonel Sánchez.   Trainer: Luis Alamos Luque
WALES: Anthony Horace Millington, Peter Joseph Rodrigues, Graham Evan Williams, William Terence Hennessey, Edward Glyn James (Frank Edward John Rankmore), Barrington Gerard Hole, Ronald Raymond Rees, Graham Moore, Ronald Tudor Davies, Ivor John Allchurch, Keith David Pring (Ronald Wyn Davies).   Trainer: David Bowen
Goals: Rubén Marcos (9), Armando Tobar (51)

273. 22.10.1966   3rd European Champs Qualifiers, British Championship
WALES v SCOTLAND 1-1 (0-0)
Ninian Park, Cardiff
Referee: Kenneth Dagnall (England)   Attendance: 33,269
WALES: Gareth Sprake, Peter Joseph Rodrigues, Graham Evan Williams, William Terence Hennessey, Harold Michael England, Barrington Gerard Hole, Gilbert Ivor Reece, Ronald Wyn Davies, Ronald Tudor Davies, Clifford William Jones, Alan Leslie Jarvis.   Trainer: David Bowen
SCOTLAND: Robert Ferguson, John Greig (Cap), Thomas Gemmell, William John Bremner, Ronald McKinnon, John Clark, James Connolly Johnstone, Denis Law, Joseph McBride, James Curran Baxter, William Henderson.
Manager: Malcolm MacDonald
Goal: Ronald Tudor Davies (77) / Denis Law (86)

274. 16.11.1966   3rd European Champs Qualifiers, British Championship
ENGLAND v WALES 5-1 (3-1)
Wembley, London

Referee: Thomas Wharton (Scotland)   Attendance: 75,380

ENGLAND: Gordon Banks, George Reginald Cohen, Ramon Wilson, Norbert Peter Stiles, John "Jack" Charlton, Robert Frederick Moore (Cap), Alan James Ball, Geoffrey Charles Hurst, Robert Charlton, Roger Hunt, Martin Stanford Peters.   Manager: Alfred Ramsey

WALES: Anthony Horace Millington, Colin Robert Green, Graham Evan Williams, William Terence Hennessey, Harold Michael England, Barrington Gerard Hole, Ronald Raymond Rees, Ronald Wyn Davies, Ronald Tudor Davies, Clifford William Jones, Alan Leslie Jarvis.   Trainer: David Bowen

Goals: Geoffrey Hurst (30, 34), Robert Charlton (43), William Terrence Hennessey (65 own goal), John "Jack" Charlton (84) / Ronald Wyn Davies (36)

275. 12.04.1967   3rd European Champs Qualifiers, British Championship
NORTHERN IRELAND v WALES 0-0
Windsor Park, Belfast

Referee: Kevin Howley (England)   Attendance: 17,770

NORTHERN IRELAND: Roderick McKenzie, David James Craig, Alexander Russell Elder, Arthur Stewart, William John Terence Neill, James Joseph Nicholson, Eric Welsh, Daniel Trainor, Alexander Derek Dougan, Walter Bruce, David Clements.

WALES: Anthony Horace Millington, Roderick John Thomas, Graham Evan Williams, Alan Leslie Jarvis, Edward Glyn James, Barrington Gerard Hole, Ronald Raymond Rees, William Alan Durban, Ronald Tudor Davies, Thomas Royston Vernon, Keith David Pring.   Trainer: Trainer: David Bowen

276. 21.10.1967   3rd European Champs Qualifiers, British Championship
WALES v ENGLAND 0-3 (0-1)
Ninian Park, Cardiff

Referee: John Robertson Gordon (Scotland)   Att: 44,960

WALES: Gareth Sprake, Peter Joseph Rodrigues, Colin Robert Green, William Terence Hennessey, Harold Michael England, Barrington Gerard Hole, Ronald Raymond Rees, William Alan Durban, John Francis Mahoney, Thomas Royston Vernon, Clifford William Jones.   Trainer: David Bowen

ENGLAND: Gordon Banks, George Reginald Cohen, Keith Robert Newton, Alan Patrick Mullery, John "Jack" Charlton, Robert Frederick Moore (Cap), Alan James Ball, Roger Hunt, Robert Charlton, Geoffrey Charles Hurst, Martin Stanford Peters.   Manager: Alfred Ramsey

Goals: Martin Stanford Peters (34), Robert Charlton (87), Alan James Ball (90 pen)

277. 22.11.1967   3rd European Champs Qualifiers, British Championship
SCOTLAND v WALES 3-2 (1-1)
Hampden Park, Glasgow

Referee: James Finney (England)   Attendance: 57,472

SCOTLAND: Robert Brown Clark, James Philip Craig, Edward Graham McCreadie, John Greig (Cap), Ronald McKinnon, James Curran Baxter, James Connolly Johnstone, William John Bremner, Alan John Gilzean, William McClure Johnston, Robert Lennox.   Manager: Robert Brown

WALES: Gareth Sprake, Peter Joseph Rodrigues, Colin Robert Green, William Terence Hennessey, Edward Glyn James, Barrington Gerard Hole, Ronald Raymond Rees, Ronald Wyn Davies, Ronald Tudor Davies, William Alan Durban, Clifford William Jones.   Trainer: David Bowen

Goals: Alan John Gilzean (15, 65), Ronald McKinnon (78) / Ronald Tudor Davies (18), William Alan Durban (57)

278. 28.02.1968   3rd European Champs Qualifiers, British Championship
WALES v NORTHERN IRELAND 2-0 (0-0)
The Racecourse, Wrexham

Referee: Robert Holley Davidson (Scotland)   Att: 17,548

WALES: Anthony Horace Millington, Peter Joseph Rodrigues, Colin Robert Green, William Terence Hennessey, Harold Michael England, Barrington Gerard Hole, Ronald Raymond Rees, Ronald Wyn Davies, Ronald Tudor Davies, William Alan Durban, Graham Evan Williams.   Trainer: David Bowen

NORTHERN IRELAND: Patrick Anthony Jennings, David James Craig, Alexander Russell Elder, Martin Harvey, Samuel John Todd, William McKeag, William John Irvine, Arthur Stewart, Alexander Derek Dougan, James Joseph Nicholson, John Terence Harkin.

Goals: Ronald Raymond Rees (75), Ronald Wyn Davies (84)

279. 08.05.1968
WALES v WEST GERMANY 1-1 (1-1)
Ninian Park, Cardiff

Referee: Gösta Lindberg (Sweden)   Attendance: 8,075

WALES: Anthony Horace Millington, Roderick John Thomas, Colin Robert Green, David Powell, Harold Michael England, Barrington Gerard Hole, Ronald Raymond Rees, Ronald Wyn Davies, Ronald Tudor Davies, William Alan Durban, Clifford William Jones.   Trainer: David Bowen

WEST GERMANY: Horst Wolter (26 Günter Bernard), Hans-Hubert Vogts, Horst-Dieter Höttges, Klaus Fichtel, Joachim Bäse, Wolfgang Weber, Herbert Laumen, Willi Neuberger, Siegfried Held, Wolfgang Overath (Cap) (50 Günter Netzer), Horst Köppel.   Trainer: Helmut Schön

Goal: Ronald Wyn Davies (26) / Wolfgang Overath (11)

280. 23.10.1968   9th World Cup Qualifiers
WALES v ITALY 0-1 (0-1)
Ninian Park, Cardiff
Referee: Joaquím Fernandes Campos (Portugal)
Attendance: 18,558

WALES: Anthony Horace Millington, Roderick John Thomas, Graham Evan Williams, Alwyn Derek Burton, David Powell, Barrington Gerard Hole, Ronald Raymond Rees, Ronald Wyn Davies, Ronald Tudor Davies, Colin Robert Green (62 Barrie Spencer Jones), Clifford William Jones.   Trainer: David Bowen

ITALY: Dino Zoff, Tarcisio Burgnich, Giacinto Facchetti (Cap), Roberto Rosato, Sandro Salvadore, Ernesto Castano, Angelo Domenghini, Gianni Rivera, Pietro Anastasi (52 Alessandro Mazzola), Giancarlo De Sisti, Luigi Riva.   Trainer: Ferruccio Valcareggi

Goal: Luigi Riva (44)

281. 26.03.1969
WEST GERMANY v WALES 1-1 (0-1)
Wald, Frankfurt/Main
Referee: Concetto Lo Bello (Italy)   Attendance: 40,000

WEST GERMANY: Josef Maier, Bernd Patzke, Hans-Hubert Vogts, Horst-Dieter Höttges, Willi Schulz (Cap), Max Lorenz, Reinhard Libuda, Lothar Ulsaß (74 Ludwig Müller), Gerhard Müller, Siegfried Held, Hans Rebele (46 Bernd Dörfel).   Trainer: Helmut Schön

WALES: Gareth Sprake, Roderick John Thomas, Stephen Clifford Derrett, David Powell, William Terence Hennessey, Barrington Gerard Hole, Barrie Spencer Jones, William Alan Durban, Ronald Tudor Davies, John Benjamin Toshack, Ronald Raymond Rees.   Trainer: David Bowen

Goals: Gerhard Müller (90) / Barrie Spencer Jones (34)

282. 16.04.1969   9th World Cup Qualifiers
EAST GERMANY v WALES 2-1 (1-0)
Heinz Steyer, Dresden
Referee: Frans Geluck (Belgium)   Attendance: 38,198

EAST GERMANY: Jürgen Croy, Otto Fräßdorf, Klaus Urbanczyk (Cap), Bernd Bransch, Klaus-Dieter Seehaus, Gerhard Körner, Helmut Stein, Hans-Jürgen Kreische, Wolfram Löwe (78 Peter Rock), Henning Frenzel, Eberhard Vogel.   Trainer: Harald Seeger

WALES: Anthony Horace Millington, Peter Joseph Rodrigues, Alwyn Derek Burton, William Terence Hennessey, Harold Michael England, Barrington Gerard Hole, Barrie Spencer Jones, William Alan Durban, John Benjamin Toshack, John Francis Mahoney, Ronald Raymond Rees.   Trainer: David Bowen

Goals: Wolfram Löwe (31), Peter Rock (89) / John Benjamin Toshack (57)

283. 03.05.1969   British Championship
WALES v SCOTLAND 3-5 (2-2)
The Racecourse, Wrexham
Referee: James Finney (England)   Attendance: 18,765

WALES: Gareth Sprake, Stephen Clifford Derrett (78 Ronald Raymond Rees), Colin Robert Green, Alwyn Derek Burton, David Powell, Graham Moore, William Alan Durban, John Benjamin Toshack, Ronald Tudor Davies, Ronald Wyn Davies, Barrie Spencer Jones.   Trainer: David Bowen

SCOTLAND: Thomas Johnstone Lawrence (46 James Herriot), Thomas Gemmell, Edward Graham McCreadie, William John Bremner (Cap), William McNeill, John Greig, Thomas McLean, Robert White Murdoch, Colin Anderson Stein, Alan John Gilzean, Charles Cooke.   Manager: Robert Brown

Goals: Ronald Tudor Davies (29, 57), John Toshack (44) / William McNeill (12), Colin Stein (16), Alan Gilzean (55), William John Bremner (72), Thomas McLean (87)

284. 07.05.1969   British Championship
ENGLAND v WALES 2-1 (0-1)
Wembley, London
Referee: John Adair (Northern Ireland)   Attendance: 70,000

ENGLAND: Gordon West, Keith Robert Newton, Terence Cooper, Robert Frederick Moore (Cap), John "Jack" Charlton, Norman Hunter, Francis Henry Lee, Colin Bell, Jeffrey Astle, Robert Charlton, Alan James Ball.   Manager: Alfred Ramsey

WALES: Gareth Sprake, Peter Joseph Rodrigues, Roderick John Thomas, William Alan Durban, David Powell, Alwyn Derek Burton, Ronald Tudor Davies, John Benjamin Toshack, Ronald Wyn Davies, Graham Moore, Barrie Spencer Jones.   Trainer: David Bowen

Goals: Robert Charlton (58), Francis Henry Lee (72) / Ronald Tudor Davies (18)

285. 10.05.1969   British Championship
NORTHERN IRELAND v WALES 0-0
Windsor Park, Belfast
Referee: Not recorded   Attendance: 12,500

NORTHERN IRELAND: Patrick Anthony Jennings, David James Craig, Alexander Russell Elder, Samuel John Todd, William John Terence Neill, James Joseph Nicholson, George Best, Alexander McMordie, Alexander Derek Dougan, Thomas Jackson, David Clements (John Terence Harkin).

WALES: Gareth Sprake, Peter Joseph Rodrigues (Colin Robert Green), Roderick John Thomas, William Alan Durban, David Powell, Alwyn Derek Burton, Ronald Tudor Davies, John Benjamin Toshack, Ronald Wyn Davies, Graham Moore, Barrie Spencer Jones.   Trainer: David Bowen

286. 28.07.1969
WALES
v REST OF THE UNITED KINGDOM 0-1 (0-1)
Ninian Park, Cardiff
Referee: Mervyn Griffiths (Wales)   Attendance: 13,605
WALES: Gareth Sprake, Peter Joseph Rodrigues, Roderick John Thomas, William Terence Hennessey, Harold Michael England, Graham Moore, Barrie Spencer Jones, Clifford William Jones, Ronald Tudor Davies, John Benjamin Toshack, Ronald Raymond Rees (Gilbert Ivor Reece).
Trainer: David Bowen
REST OF THE UNITED KINGDOM: Patrick Jennings, Thomas Gemmell, Terence Cooper (Keith Robert Newton), William Bremner, John Charlton, Alan Patrick Mullery, George Best, Francis Lee (William Henderson), Alexander Dougan, Robert Charlton, John Hughes.   Manager: Alfred Ramsey
Goal: Francis Lee (34)

287. 22.10.1969   9th World Cup Qualifiers
WALES v EAST GERMANY 1-3 (0-0)
Ninian Park, Cardiff
Referee: Roger Machin (France)   Attendance: 22,409
WALES: Gareth Sprake, Peter Joseph Rodrigues, Roderick John Thomas, William Terence Hennessey, Harold Michael England, David Powell, William Alan Durban, Richard Lech Krzywicki, Ronald Wyn Davies, John Benjamin Toshack, Ronald Raymond Rees.   Trainer: David Bowen
EAST GERMANY: Jürgen Croy, Otto Fräßdorf, Klaus Urbanczyk (Cap), Klaus-Dieter Seehaus, Bernd Bransch, Helmut Stein, Harald Irmscher, Gerhard Körner, Wolfram Löwe, Henning Frenzel, Eberhard Vogel.
Trainer: Harald Seeger
Goals: David Powell (82) / Eberhard Vogel (54), Wolfram Löwe (60), Henning Frenzel (62)

288. 04.11.1969   9th World Cup Qualifiers
ITALY v WALES 4-1 (1-0)
Olimpico, Roma
Referee: Tudor Betchirov (Bulgaria)   Attendance: 67,401
ITALY: Enrico Albertosi, Tarcisio Burgnich, Giacinto Facchetti (Cap), Mario Bertini (87 Antonio Juliano), Giorgio Puia, Sandro Salvadore, Angelo Domenghini, Gianni Rivera, Pietro Anastasi (46 Alessandro Mazzola), Giancarlo De Sisti, Luigi Riva.   Trainer: Ferruccio Valcareggi
WALES: Gareth Sprake, Roderick John Thomas, Stephen Clifford Derrett, William Alan Durban, Harold Michael England, Graham Moore, Barrington Gerard Hole, Terence Charles Yorath, Richard Lech Krzywicki, John Benjamin Toshack, Ronald Raymond Rees (69 Gilbert Ivor Reece).
Trainer: David Bowen
Goals: Luigi Riva (37, 73, 81), Alessandro Mazzola (55) / Harold Michael England (67)

289. 18.04.1970   British Championship
WALES v ENGLAND 1-1 (1-0)
Ninian Park, Cardiff
Referee: Thomas Wharton (Scotland)   Attendance: 50,000
WALES: Anthony Horace Millington, Peter Joseph Rodrigues, Roderick John Thomas, William Terence Hennessey, Harold Michael England, David Powell, Richard Lech Krzywicki, William Alan Durban, Ronald Tudor Davies, Graham Moore, Ronald Raymond Rees.   Trainer: David Bowen
ENGLAND: Gordon Banks, Thomas James Wright, Emlyn Walter Hughes, Alan Patrick Mullery, Brian Leslie Labone, Robert Frederick Moore (Cap), Francis Henry Lee, Alan James Ball, Robert Charlton, Geoffrey Charles Hurst, Martin Stanford Peters.   Manager: Alfred Ramsey
Goals: Richard Lech Krzywicki (40) / Francis Henry Lee (71)

290. 22.04.1970   British Championship
SCOTLAND v WALES 0-0
Hampden Park, Glasgow
Referee: David W. Smith (England)   Attendance: 30,434
SCOTLAND: James Fergus Cruickshank, William Thomas Callaghan, William Dickson, John Greig (Cap), Ronald McKinnon, Robert Moncur, Thomas McLean (70 Robert Lennox), David Hay, John O'Hare, Colin Anderson Stein, William McInnany Carr.   Manager: Robert Brown
WALES: Anthony Horace Millington, Peter Joseph Rodrigues, Roderick John Thomas, William Terence Hennessey, Harold Michael England, David Powell, Richard Lech Krzywicki, William Alan Durban, Ronald Tudor Davies, Graham Moore, Ronald Raymond Rees.   Trainer: David Bowen

291. 25.04.1970   British Championship
WALES v NORTHERN IRELAND 1-0 (1-0)
Vetch Field, Swansea
Referee: Not recorded   Attendance: 28,000
WALES: Anthony Horace Millington, Peter Joseph Rodrigues, Roderick John Thomas, William Terence Hennessey, Harold Michael England, David Powell, Richard Lech Krzywicki, William Alan Durban, Ronald Tudor Davies, Graham Moore, Ronald Raymond Rees.   Trainer: David Bowen
NORTHERN IRELAND: William Stewart McFaul, David James Craig, Samuel Nelson, William James O'Kane, William John Terence Neill (Cap), James Joseph Nicholson, William Gibson Campbell (Anthony O'Doherty), George Best, Desmond Dickson, Alexander McMordie, David Clements. Manager: William Bingham
Goal: Ronald Raymond Rees (#)

292. 11.11.1970   4th European Champs Qualifiers
WALES v ROMANIA 0-0
Ninian Park, Cardiff
Referee: Arie van Gemert (Holland)   Attendance: 19,882
WALES: Gareth Sprake, Peter Joseph Rodrigues, Harold Michael England, David Powell, Roderick John Thomas, William Alan Durban, Graham Moore, Barrington Gerard Hole, Richard Lech Krzywicki, Ronald Wyn Davies, Ronald Raymond Rees.   Trainer: David Bowen
ROMANIA: Răducanu Necula, Lajos Sătmăreanu, Nicolae Lupescu, Cornel Dinu (Cap) (46 Bujor Hălmăgeanu), Mihai Mocanu, Ion Dumitru, Radu Nunweiller VI, Alexandru Neagu, Nicolae Dobrin (76 Flavius Domide), Florea Dumitrache, Florian Dumitrescu.   Trainer: Angelo Niculescu

293. 21.04.1971   4th European Champs Qualifiers
WALES v CZECHOSLOVAKIA 1-3 (0-0)
Vetch Field, Swansea
Referee: Einar Boström (Sweden)   Attendance: 12,767
WALES: Anthony Horace Millington, Peter Joseph Rodrigues, Roderick John Thomas, Leighton Phillips, Edward Glyn James, John Thomas Walley, Ronald Raymond Rees, William Alan Durban, Ronald Tudor Davies, Ronald Wyn Davies, John Francis Mahoney (46 Arfon Trevor Griffiths).   Trainer: David Bowen
CZECHOSLOVAKIA: Ivo Viktor, Karel Dobiaš, Vladimír Hrivnák, Jozef Desiatnik, Vladimír Táborský, Jaroslav Pollák, Ladislav Kuna, Jozef Adamec (Cap), František Veselý, Pavel Stratil, Ján Čapkovič.
Trainers: Ladislav Novák & Ladislav Kačáni
Goals: Ronald Tudor Davies (59 pen) /
Ján Čapkovič (78, 82), Vladimír Táborský (80)

294. 15.05.1971   British Championship
WALES v SCOTLAND 0-0
Ninian Park, Cardiff
Referee: John Keith Taylor (England)   Attendance: 19,068
WALES: Gareth Sprake, Peter Joseph Rodrigues, Roderick John Thomas, Edward Glyn James, John Griffith Roberts, Terence Charles Yorath, Leighton Phillips, William Alan Durban, Ronald Tudor Davies, John Benjamin Toshack, Gilbert Ivor Reece.   Trainer: David Bowen
SCOTLAND: Robert Brown Clark, David Hay, James Andrew Brogan, William John Bremner (72 John Greig), Francis McLintock, Robert Moncur (Cap), Peter Patrick Lorimer, Peter Barr Cormack, Edwin Gray, David Thomson Robb, John O'Hare.   Manager: Robert Brown

295. 19.05.1971   British Championship
ENGLAND v WALES 0-0
Wembley, London
Referee: Malcolm Wright (Northern Ireland)   Att: 70,000
ENGLAND: Peter Leslie Shilton, Christopher Lawler, Terence Cooper, Thomas Smith, Laurence Valentine Lloyd, Emlyn Walter Hughes, Francis Henry Lee, Ralph Coates, Geoffrey Charles Hurst, Anthony John Brown (72 Allan John Clarke), Martin Stanford Peters (Cap).   Manager: Alfred Ramsey
WALES: Gareth Sprake, Peter Joseph Rodrigues, Roderick John Thomas, Edward Glyn James, John Griffith Roberts, Terence Charles Yorath, Leighton Phillips, William Alan Durban, Ronald Tudor Davies, John Benjamin Toshack, Gilbert Ivor Reece (Ronald Raymond Rees).
Trainer: David Bowen

296. 22.05.1971   British Championship
NORTHERN IRELAND v WALES 1-0 (1-0)
Windsor Park, Belfast
Referee: Not recorded   Attendance: 20,000
NORTHERN IRELAND: Patrick Anthony Jennings, Patrick James Rice, Samuel Nelson, William James O'Kane, Alan Hunter, James Joseph Nicholson (Martin Harvey), Bryan Hamilton, Alexander McMordie, Alexander Derek Dougan (Cap), David Clements, George Best.
Manager: William Bingham
WALES: Gareth Sprake, Peter Joseph Rodrigues, Roderick John Thomas, Edward Glyn James, John Griffith Roberts, Terence Charles Yorath, Leighton Phillips (Ronald Raymond Rees), William Alan Durban, Ronald Tudor Davies, John Benjamin Toshack, Gilbert Ivor Reece.
Trainer: David Bowen
Goal: Bryan Hamilton (#)

297. 26.05.1971   4th European Champs Qualifiers
FINLAND v WALES 0-1 (0-0)
Olympiastadion, Helsinki
Referee: Günter Männig (East Germany)   Att: 5,410
FINLAND: Lars Näsman, Timo Kautonen (Cap), Raimo Saviomaa, Vilho Rajantie, Jouko Suomalainen, Timo Nummelin, Pekka Heikkilä, Raimo Toivanen (Jarmo Flink), Matti Paatelainen, Arto Tolsa, Tommy Lindholm.   Trainer: Olavi Laaksonen
WALES: Anthony Horace Millington, Malcolm Edward Page, Stephen Clifford Derrett, John Griffith Roberts, Robert Mielczarek, Richard Lech Krzywicki, Philip Wayne Jones, William Alan Durban, Ronald Raymond Rees, John Benjamin Toshack, Gilbert Ivor Reece.   Trainer: David Bowen
Goal: John Benjamin Toshack (54)

298. 13.10.1971   4th European Champs Qualifiers
WALES v FINLAND 3-0 (1-0)
Ninian Park, Cardiff
Referee: Kaj Rasmussen (Denmark)   Attendance: 10,430
WALES: Gareth Sprake (46 Anthony Horace Millington), Peter Joseph Rodrigues, Roderick John Thomas, John Griffith Roberts, Harold Michael England, William Terence Hennessey, Brian Clifford Evans, Gilbert Ivor Reece, William Alan Durban, John Benjamin Toshack, Trevor Hockey.
Trainer: David Bowen
FINLAND: Lars Näsman, Seppo Kilponen (Cap), Raimo Saviomaa, Ari Mäkynen, Pekka Kosonen, Raimo Elo, Jarmo Flink, Miikka Toivola, Heikki Suhonen (30 Henry Bergström), Pekka Heikkilä, Tommy Lindholm.
Trainer: Olavi Laaksonen
Goals: William Alan Durban (10), John Toshack (43), Gilbert Ivor Reece (89)

299. 27.10.1971   4th European Champs Qualifiers
CZECHOSLOVAKIA v WALES 1-0 (0-0)
Sparta, Praha
Referee: Marino Medina Iglesias (Spain)   Att: 20,051
CZECHOSLOVAKIA: Ivo Viktor, Karel Dobiaš (Cap), Vladimír Hrivnák, Ľudovít Zlocha, Vladimír Táborský, Jaroslav Pollák, Ladislav Kuna, Karol Jokl (65 Ondrej Daňko), Bohumil Veselý (72 Zdeněk Nehoda), Pavel Stratil, Dušan Kabát.
Trainers: Ladislav Novák & Ladislav Kačáni
WALES: Anthony Horace Millington, Peter Joseph Rodrigues, Leighton Phillips, Alwyn Derek Burton, Roderick John Thomas, Terence Charles Yorath (66 Ronald Raymond Rees), William Terence Hennessey, William Alan Durban (78 Richard Lech Krzywicki), Brian Clifford Evans, Michael Richard Hill, Leighton James.   Trainer: David Bowen
Goal: Ladislav Kuna (60)

300. 24.11.1971   4th European Champs Qualifiers
ROMANIA v WALES 2-0 (1-0)
23 August, București
Referee: Alfred Delcourt (Belgium)   Attendance: 35,251
ROMANIA: Răducanu Necula, Lajos Sătmăreanu, Nicolae Lupescu, Cornel Dinu, Augustin Pax Deleanu, Ion Dumitru, Radu Nunweiller VI, Mircea Lucescu (Cap), Emerich Dembrovschi, Nicolae Dobrin, Anghel Iordănescu.
Trainer: Angelo Niculescu
WALES: Anthony Horace Millington, Peter Joseph Rodrigues, Leighton Phillips, Herbert John Williams, Roderick John Thomas, Gilbert Ivor Reece, Trevor Hockey, Ronald Raymond Rees, Michael Richard Hill (46 Cyril Davies), Ronald Tudor Davies, Leighton James.   Trainer: David Bowen
Goals: Nicolae Lupescu (9), Mircea Lucescu (74)

301. 20.05.1972   British Championship
WALES v ENGLAND 0-3 (0-1)
Ninian Park, Cardiff
Referee: William Joseph Mullan (Scotland)   Att: 34,000
WALES: Gareth Sprake, Peter Joseph Rodrigues, Roderick John Thomas, William Terence Hennessey, Harold Michael England, John Griffith Roberts (Gilbert Ivor Reece), Terence Charles Yorath, Ronald Tudor Davies, Ronald Wyn Davies, John Benjamin Toshack, William Alan Durban.
Trainer: David Bowen
ENGLAND: Gordon Banks, Paul Edward Madeley, Emlyn Walter Hughes, Peter Edwin Storey, Roy Leslie McFarland, Robert Frederick Moore (Cap), Michael George Summerbee, Colin Bell, Malcolm Ian Macdonald, Rodney William Marsh, Norman Hunter.   Manager: Alfred Ramsey
Goals: Emlyn Hughes (25), Rodney William Marsh (60), Colin Bell (61)

302. 24.05.1972   British Championship
SCOTLAND v WALES 1-0 (0-0)
Hampden Park, Glasgow
Referee: James Lawther (Northern Ireland)   Att: 21,332
SCOTLAND: Robert Brown Clark, Patrick Gordon Stanton, Martin McLean Buchan, Robert Moncur, William McNeill, Peter Patrick Lorimer, William John Bremner (Cap), Anthony Green, Archibald Gemmill (35 Richard Asa Hartford), John O'Hare (56 Luigi Macari), Denis Law.
Manager: Thomas Docherty
WALES: Gareth Sprake, Malcolm Edward Page, Roderick John Thomas, William Terence Hennessey (74 Leighton James), Harold Michael England, Terence Charles Yorath, William Alan Durban, Ronald Wyn Davies, Gilbert Ivor Reece, Ronald Tudor Davies, Leighton Phillips.
Trainer: David Bowen
Goal: Peter Patrick Lorimer (72)

303. 27.05.1972   British Championship
WALES v NORTHERN IRELAND 0-0
The Racecourse, Wrexham
Referee: John Taylor (England)   Attendance: 15,647
WALES: Gareth Sprake, Malcolm Edward Page, Roderick John Thomas, Harold Michael England, John Griffith Roberts, Terence Charles Yorath (Peter Joseph Rodrigues), William Alan Durban, Ronald Wyn Davies, Gilbert Ivor Reece, Ronald Tudor Davies, Leighton Phillips.   Trainer: David Bowen
NORTHERN IRELAND: Patrick Anthony Jennings, Patrick James Rice, Samuel Nelson, William John Terence Neill (Cap), Alan Hunter, David Clements, Daniel Hegan, Alexander McMordie, Alexander Derek Dougan (Martin Hugh Michael O'Neill), William John Irvine, Thomas Jackson.
Manager: Terence Neill

304. 15.11.1972   10th World Cup Qualifiers
WALES v ENGLAND 0-1 (0-1)
Ninian Park, Cardiff
Referee: William Joseph Mullan (Scotland)   Att: 36,384
WALES: Gareth Sprake, Peter Joseph Rodrigues (65 Gilbert Ivor Reece), Roderick John Thomas, William Terence Hennessey, Harold Michael England, Trevor Hockey, Leighton Phillips, John Francis Mahoney, Ronald Wyn Davies, John Benjamin Toshack, Leighton James.   Trainer: David Bowen
ENGLAND: Raymond Neal Clemence, Peter Edwin Storey, Emlyn Walter Hughes, Norman Hunter, Roy Leslie McFarland, Robert Frederick Moore (Cap), Kevin Joseph Keegan, Martin Harcourt Chivers, Rodney William Marsh, Colin Bell, Alan James Ball.   Manager: Alfred Ramsey
Goal: Colin Bell (35)

305. 24.01.1973   10th World Cup Qualifiers
ENGLAND v WALES 1-1 (1-1)
Wembley, London
Referee: Malcolm Wright (Northern Ireland)   Att: 62,273
ENGLAND: Raymond Neal Clemence, Peter Edwin Storey, Emlyn Walter Hughes, Norman Hunter, Roy Leslie McFarland, Robert Frederick Moore (Cap), Kevin Joseph Keegan, Colin Bell, Martin Harcourt Chivers, Rodney William Marsh, Alan James Ball.   Manager: Alfred Ramsey
WALES: Gareth Sprake, Peter Joseph Rodrigues (80 Malcolm Edward Page), Roderick John Thomas, Trevor Hockey, Harold Michael England, John Griffith Roberts, Brian Clifford Evans, John Francis Mahoney, John Benjamin Toshack, Terence Charles Yorath, Leighton James.   Trainer: David Bowen
Goal: Norman Hunter (41) / John Benjamin Toshack (23)

306. 28.03.1973   10th World Cup Qualifiers
WALES v POLAND 2-0 (0-0)
Ninian Park, Cardiff
Referee: Antonio Rigo-Sureda (Spain)   Attendance: 13,000
WALES: Gareth Sprake, Peter Joseph Rodrigues, Roderick John Thomas, David Frazer Roberts, John Griffith Roberts, Trevor Hockey, Brian Clifford Evans, John Francis Mahoney, John Benjamin Toshack, Terence Charles Yorath, Leighton James.   Trainer: David Bowen
POLAND: Jan Tomaszewski, Zbigniew Gut, Lesław Ćmikiewicz, Jerzy Gorgoń, Zygmunt Anczok, Henryk Kasperczak (46 Włodzimierz Wojciechowski), Kazimierz Deyna, Zygmunt Maszczyk, Jerzy Kraska, Włodzimierz Lubański (Cap), Robert Gadocha.   Trainer: Kazimierz Górski
Goals: Leighton James (46), Trevor Hockey (85)

307. 12.05.1973   British Championship
WALES v SCOTLAND 0-2 (0-1)
The Racecourse, Wrexham
Referee: James Lawther (Northern Ireland)   Att: 18,682
WALES: Gareth Sprake, Peter Joseph Rodrigues, Roderick John Thomas, Trevor Hockey, Harold Michael England, John Griffith Roberts, Brian Clifford Evans (78 Peter Anthony O'Sullivan), John Francis Mahoney, John Benjamin Toshack, Terence Charles Yorath (69 Ronald Wyn Davies), Leighton James.   Trainer: David Bowen
SCOTLAND: Peter McCloy, Daniel Fergus McGrain, William Donachie, James Allan Holton, Derek Joseph Johnstone, Patrick Gordon Stanton (Cap), George Graham, David Hay, William Morgan, Kenneth Mathieson Dalglish (84 Luigi Macari), Derek James Parlane (80 Colin Anderson Stein).   Manager: William Esplin Ormond
Goals: George Graham (18, 80)

308. 15.05.1973   British Championship
ENGLAND v WALES 3-0 (2-0)
Wembley, London
Referee: John Wright Paterson (Scotland)   Att: 38,000
ENGLAND: Peter Leslie Shilton, Peter Edwin Storey, Emlyn Walter Hughes, Colin Bell, Roy Leslie McFarland, Robert Frederick Moore (Cap), Alan James Ball, Michael Roger Channon, Martin Harcourt Chivers, Allan John Clarke, Martin Stanford Peters.   Manager: Alfred Ramsey
WALES: Thomas John Seymour Phillips, Peter Joseph Rodrigues, Roderick John Thomas, Trevor Hockey, Harold Michael England (David Frazer Roberts), John Griffith Roberts, John Francis Mahoney, John Benjamin Toshack, Malcolm Edward Page (William John Emanuel), Brian Clifford Evans, Leighton James.   Trainer: David Bowen
Goals: Martin Harcourt Chivers (23), Michael Roger Channon (30), Martin Stanford Peters (67)

309. 19.05.1973   British Championship
NORTHERN IRELAND v WALES 1-0 (1-0)
Goodison Park, Liverpool
Referee: Not recorded   Attendance: 4,946
NORTHERN IRELAND: Patrick Anthony Jennings, Patrick James Rice, David James Craig, William John Terence Neill (Cap), Alan Hunter, David Clements, Bryan Hamilton (Robert John Lutton), Thomas Jackson, Samuel John Morgan, Martin Hugh Michael O'Neill, Trevor Anderson (Robert Irvine Coyle).   Manager: Terence Neill
WALES: Gareth Sprake, Peter Joseph Rodrigues, Roderick John Thomas, Trevor Hockey (William John Emanuel), David Frazer Roberts, John Griffith Roberts, John Francis Mahoney, Malcolm Edward Page, Gilbert Ivor Reece, Ronald Wyn Davies, Leighton James.   Trainer: David Bowen
Goal: Bryan Hamilton (#)

310. 26.09.1973   10th World Cup Qualifiers
POLAND v WALES 3-0 (2-0)

Śląski, Chorzów

Referee: Ove Dahlberg (Sweden)   Attendance: 70,181

POLAND: Jan Tomaszewski, Antoni Szymanowski, Mirosław Bulzacki, Jerzy Gorgoń, Adam Musiał, Lesław Ćmikiewicz, Kazimierz Deyna (Cap), Henryk Kasperczak, Grzegorz Lato, Jan Domarski, Robert Gadocha.   Trainer: Kazimierz Górski

WALES: Gareth Sprake, Peter Joseph Rodrigues, Roderick John Thomas, John Francis Mahoney (80 Leighton Phillips), Harold Michael England, John Griffith Roberts, Brian Clifford Evans (78 Gilbert Ivor Reece), Terence Charles Yorath, Ronald Wyn Davies, Trevor Hockey, Leighton James.   Trainer: David Bowen

Goals: Robert Gadocha (29), Grzegorz Lato (34), Jan Domarski (53)

311. 11.05.1974   British Championship
WALES v ENGLAND 0-2 (0-1)

Ninian Park, Cardiff

Referee: Redmond McFadden   Attendance: 25,734

WALES: Thomas John Seymour Phillips, Philip Stanley Roberts (Leslie Cartwright), Roderick John Thomas, John Francis Mahoney, John Griffith Roberts (Cap), David Frazer Roberts, Gilbert Ivor Reece, Anthony Keith Villars, Ronald Tudor Davies (David Paul Smallman), Terence Charles Yorath, Leighton James.   Trainer: David Bowen

ENGLAND: Peter Leslie Shilton, David John Nish, Michael Pejic, Emlyn Walter Hughes (Cap), Roy Leslie McFarland, Colin Todd, Kevin Joseph Keegan, Colin Bell, Michael Roger Channon, Keith Weller, Stanley Bowles.   Manager: Joseph Mercer

Goals: Stanley Bowles (35), Kevin Joseph Keegan (47)

312. 14.05.1974   British Championship
SCOTLAND v WALES 2-0 (2-0)

Hampden Park, Glasgow

Referee: Malcolm Wright (Northern Ireland)   Att: 41,969

SCOTLAND: David Harvey, William Pullar Jardine, David Hay, Martin McLean Buchan (76 Daniel Fergus McGrain), James Allan Holton, James Connolly Johnstone, William John Bremner (Cap), Donald Ford, Thomas Hutchison (6 James Smith), Kenneth Mathieson Dalglish, Joseph Jordan.   Manager: William Esplin Ormond

WALES: Gareth Sprake, Roderick John Thomas, Malcolm Edward Page, John Francis Mahoney, John Griffith Roberts (Cap), David Frazer Roberts, Gilbert Ivor Reece (46 David Paul Smallman), Anthony Keith Villars, Terence Charles Yorath, Leslie Cartwright, Leighton James.   Trainer: David Bowen

Goals: Kenneth Mathieson Dalglish (24), William Pullar Jardine (44 pen)

313. 18.05.1974   British Championship
WALES v NORTHERN IRELAND 1-0 (1-0)

The Racecourse, Wrexham

Referee: Not recorded   Attendance: 9,311

WALES: Gareth Sprake, Malcolm Edward Page, Roderick John Thomas, John Francis Mahoney, John Griffith Roberts (Cap), Gilbert Ivor Reece, Terence Charles Yorath, David Paul Smallman (Anthony Keith Villars), Leighton Phillips, Leslie Cartwright, Leighton James.   Trainer: David Bowen

NORTHERN IRELAND: Patrick Anthony Jennings, Patrick James Rice, Hugh Oliver Dowd, William James O'Kane, Alan Hunter, David Clements (Cap), Bryan Hamilton (Thomas Jackson), Thomas Cassidy, Samuel Baxter McIlroy, Roland Christopher McGrath, Martin Hugh Michael O'Neill.   Manager: Terence Neill

Goal: David Paul Smallman (#)

314. 04.09.1974   5th European Champs Qualifiers
AUSTRIA v WALES 2-1 (0-1)

Prater, Wien

Referee: Dogan Babaçan (Turkey)   Attendance: 30,795

AUSTRIA: Herbert Rettensteiner, Johann Eigenstiller, Johannes Winklbauer, Eduard Krieger, Werner Kriess, Werner Walzer, August Starek, Rainer Schlagbauer (67 Helmut Köglberger), Josef Stering, Wilhelm Kreuz, Johann Krankl.   Trainer: Leopold Stastny

WALES: Gareth Sprake, Philip Stanley Roberts, Leighton Phillips, David Frazer Roberts, John Griffith Roberts (Cap), Terence Charles Yorath, John Francis Mahoney, Arfon Trevor Griffiths, Gilbert Ivor Reece, John Benjamin Toshack, Leighton James.   Manager: Michael Smith

Goals: Wilhelm Kreuz (63), Johann Krankl (74) / Arfon Trevor Griffiths (34)

315. 30.10.1974   5th European Champs Qualifiers
WALES v HUNGARY 2-0 (0-0)

Ninian Park, Cardiff

Referee: Antonio Da Silva Garrido (Portugal)   Attendance: 8,445

WALES: Gareth Sprake (84 Thomas John Seymour Phillips), Roderick John Thomas, Philip Stanley Roberts, Leighton Phillips, Harold Michael England, John Francis Mahoney, Arfon Trevor Griffiths, Terence Charles Yorath, Gilbert Ivor Reece, John Benjamin Toshack, Leighton James.   Manager: Michael Smith

HUNGARY: Ferenc Mészáros, Péter Török, László Bálint, József Mucha, Mihály Kántor, Zoltán Halmosi, László Fazekas, András Tóth (63 József Póczik), László Fekete, Tibor Kiss, László Nagy.   Trainer: Ede Moór

Goals: Arfon Trevor Griffiths (57), John Toshack (87)

316. 20.11.1974   5th European Champs Qualifiers
WALES v LUXEMBOURG 5-0 (1-0)
Vetch Field, Swansea
Referee: Preben Christofersen (Denmark)   Att: 10,539
WALES: Gareth Sprake, Roderick John Thomas, Harold Michael England, Philip Stanley Roberts, Leighton Phillips, John Francis Mahoney (77 Brian Flynn), Arfon Trevor Griffiths, Terence Charles Yorath, Gilbert Ivor Reece, John Benjamin Toshack, Leighton James.   Manager: Michael Smith
LUXEMBOURG: Lucien Thill, Roger Fandel, Joseph Hansen, René Flenghi, Robert Da Grava (73 Henri Roemer), Jean Zuang, Louis Pilot (Cap), Louis Trierweiler, Pierrot Langers (64 Jean-Paul Martin), Gilbert Dussier, Paul Philipp.
Trainer: Gilbert Legrand
Goals: John Toshack (34), Harold Michael England (53), Phillip Stanley Roberts (70), Arfon Trevor Griffiths (73), Terence Yorath (75)

317. 16.04.1975   5th European Champs Qualifiers
HUNGARY v WALES 1-2 (0-1)
Népstadion, Budapest
Referee: Pablo Augusto Sánchez Ibañez (Spain)   Att: 21,080
HUNGARY: Ferenc Mészáros, Péter Török, János Nagy, László Bálint, József Tóth, Károly Csapó (56 Ferenc Bene), Lajos Kocsis, József Horváth (46 Sándor Pintér), Mihály Kozma, László Branikovits, János Máté.   Trainer: János Szőcs
WALES: William David Davies, Roderick John Thomas, Malcolm Edward Page, Leighton Phillips, John Griffith Roberts (Cap), Terence Charles Yorath, John Francis Mahoney, Arfon Trevor Griffiths, Gilbert Ivor Reece (83 David Paul Smallman), John Benjamin Toshack, Leighton James (59 Brian Flynn).   Manager: Michael Smith
Goals: László Branikovits (77) /
John Benjamin Toshack (45), John Francis Mahoney (70)

318. 01.05.1975   5th European Champs Qualifiers
LUXEMBOURG v WALES 1-3 (1-2)
Municipal, Luxembourg
Referee: Jan Peeters (Belgium)   Attendance: 3,289
LUXEMBOURG: Jeannot Moes, Roger Fandel, Joseph Hansen, Louis Pilot (Cap), Jean-Louis Margue, Jean Zuang, Louis Trierweiler, Paul Philipp, Jean-Paul Martin (50 Jeannot Krecke, 80 Henri Roemer), Nicolas Braun, Gilbert Zender.
Trainer: Gilbert Legrand
WALES: William David Davies, Roderick John Thomas, Malcolm Edward Page, David Frazer Roberts, Leighton Phillips, Terence Charles Yorath, John Francis Mahoney, Arfon Trevor Griffiths (58 Brian Flynn), Gilbert Ivor Reece, John Benjamin Toshack, Leighton James.
Manager: Michael Smith
Goals: Paul Philipp (39 pen) /
Gilbert Ivor Reece (24), Leighton James (32, 83 pen)

319. 17.05.1975   British Championship
WALES v SCOTLAND 2-2 (2-0)
Ninian Park, Cardiff
Referee: Malcolm H. Wright (Northern Ireland)   Att: 23,509
WALES: William David Davies, Roderick John Thomas, Malcolm Edward Page, Terence Charles Yorath, John Griffith Roberts, Leighton Phillips, John Francis Mahoney, Brian Flynn, Gilbert Ivor Reece, John Benjamin Toshack, Leighton James.   Manager: Michael Smith
SCOTLAND: Stewart Kennedy, William Pullar Jardine (Cap), Daniel Fergus McGrain, Colin MacDonald Jackson (77 Francis Michael Munro), Gordon McQueen, Bruce David Rioch, Luigi Macari, Arthur Duncan, Kenneth Mathieson Dalglish, Derek James Parlane, Edward John MacDougall.
Manager: William Esplin Ormond
Goals: John Benjamin Toshack (28), Brian Flynn (35) /
Colin MacDonald Jackson (54), Bruce David Rioch (62)

320. 21.05.1975   British Championship
ENGLAND v WALES 2-2 (1-0)
Wembley, London
Referee: John Wright Paterson (Scotland)   Att: 53,000
ENGLAND: Raymond Neal Clemence, Steven Whitworth, Ian Terry Gillard, Gerald Charles James Francis, David Victor Watson, Colin Todd, Alan James Ball (Cap), Michael Roger Channon (70 Brian Little), David Edward Johnson, Colin Viljoen, David Thomas.   Manager: Donald Revie
WALES: William David Davies, Roderick John Thomas, Malcolm Edward Page, John Francis Mahoney, John Griffith Roberts, Leighton Phillips, Arfon Trevor Griffiths, Brian Flynn, David Paul Smallman (Derek Showers), John Benjamin Toshack, Leighton James.   Manager: Michael Smith
Goals: David Edward Johnson (10, 71) /
John Benjamin Toshack (55), Arfon Trevor Griffiths (56)

321. 24.05.1975   British Championship
NORTHERN IRELAND v WALES 1-0 (1-0)
Windsor Park, Belfast
Referee: Not recorded   Attendance: 17,000
NORTHERN IRELAND: Patrick Anthony Jennings, Peter William Scott, Patrick James Rice, Christopher James Nicholl, Alan Hunter, David Clements, Ronald Victor Blair, Thomas Jackson, Derek William Spence, Samuel Baxter McIlroy, Thomas Finney.
WALES: William David Davies, Roderick John Thomas, Malcolm Edward Page, John Francis Mahoney, David Frazer Roberts, Leighton Phillips, Arfon Trevor Griffiths, Brian Flynn, Gilbert Ivor Reece (David Paul Smallman), Derek Showers, Leighton James.   Manager: Michael Smith
Goal: Thomas Finney (33)

322. 19.11.1975   5th European Champs Qualifiers
WALES v AUSTRIA 1-0 (1-0)
The Racecourse, Wrexham
Referee: Sergio Gonella (Italy)   Attendance: 27,578
WALES: Brian William Lloyd, Roderick John Thomas, Joseph Patrick Jones, John Francis Mahoney, Ian Peter Evans, Leighton Phillips, Arfon Trevor Griffiths, Brian Flynn, Terence Charles Yorath, David Paul Smallman, Leighton James.   Manager: Michael Smith
AUSTRALIA: Friedrich Koncilia, Robert Sara, Johannes Winklbauer, Bruno Pezzey, Werner Kriess (29 Heinrich Strasser), Herbert Prohaska, Manfred Steiner, Johann Ettmayer, Kurt Welzl (70 Josef Stering), Johann Krankl, Kurt Jara.   Trainer: Branko Elsner
Goal: Arfon Trevor Griffiths (69)

323. 24.03.1976   British Championship
WALES v ENGLAND 1-2 (0-0)
The Racecourse, Wrexham
Referee: Ian Foote (Scotland)   Attendance: 20,927
WALES: Brian William Lloyd, Malcolm Edward Page, Joseph Patrick Jones, Leighton Phillips, Ian Peter Evans, Carl Stephen Harris, Terence Charles Yorath, Brian Flynn, Alan Thomas Curtis, John Griffith Roberts, Arfon Trevor Griffiths.   Manager: Michael Smith
ENGLAND: Raymond Neal Clemence, Trevor John Cherry (46 David Thomas Clement), Michael Dennis Mills, Philip George Neal, Philip Brian Thompson, Michael Doyle, Kevin Joseph Keegan (Cap), Michael Roger Channon (46 Peter John Taylor), Philip John Boyer, Trevor David Brooking, Raymond Kennedy.   Manager: Donald Revie
Goals: Alan Thomas Curtis (90) / Raymond Kennedy (70), Peter John Taylor (80)

324. 24.04.1976   5th European Championships, Quarter-Final
YUGOSLAVIA v WALES 2-0 (1-0)
Maksimir, Zagreb
Referee: Paul Schiller (Austria)   Attendance: 40,000
YUGOSLAVIA: Ognjen Petrović, Ivan Buljan, Džemal Hadžiabdić, Branko Oblak, Josip Katalinski, Dražen Mužinić, Drago Vabec, Danilo Popivoda, Momčilo Vukotić (60 Jure Jerković), Jovan Aćimović (Cap), Ivan Šurjak.   Trainer: Ante Mladinić
WALES: William David Davies, Roderick John Thomas, Malcolm Edward Page, John Francis Mahoney, Leighton Phillips, Ian Peter Evans, Arfon Trevor Griffiths, Terence Charles Yorath, Brian Flynn, John Benjamin Toshack, Leighton James (85 Alan Thomas Curtis).   Manager: Michael Smith
Goals: Momčilo Vukotić (1), Danilo Popivoda (54)

325. 06.05.1976   British Championship
SCOTLAND v WALES 3-1 (2-0)
Hampden Park, Glasgow
Referee: Malcolm H. Wright (Northern Ireland)   Att: 35,000
SCOTLAND: Alan Roderick Rough, Daniel Fergus McGrain, William Donachie, Thomas Forsyth, Colin MacDonald Jackson, Archibald Gemmill (Cap), Donald Sandison Masson, Bruce David Rioch, Edwin Gray, William H. Pettigrew, Joseph Jordan.   Manager: William Esplin Ormond
WALES: Brian William Lloyd, David Edward Jones, Joseph Patrick Jones, David Frazer Roberts, John Griffith Roberts, Terence Charles Yorath, Arfon Trevor Griffiths, Carl Stephen Harris (46 Leslie Cartwright), Alan Thomas Curtis, Peter Anthony O'Sullivan, Leighton James.   Manager: Michael Smith
Goals: William H. Pettigrew (38), Bruce David Rioch (44), Edwin Gray (69) / Arfon Trevor Griffiths (61 pen)

326. 08.05.1976   British Championship
WALES v ENGLAND 0-1 (0-0)
Ninian Park, Cardiff
Referee: Robert Holley Davidson (Scotland)   Att: 24,592
WALES: William David Davies, Roderick John Thomas (David Edward Jones), Malcolm Edward Page, John Francis Mahoney, Leighton Phillips, Ian Peter Evans, Terence Charles Yorath, Brian Flynn, Alan Thomas Curtis (Arfon Trevor Griffiths), John Benjamin Toshack, Leighton James.   Manager: Michael Smith
ENGLAND: Raymond Neal Clemence, David Thomas Clement, Michael Dennis Mills, Anthony Mark Towers, Brian Greenhoff, Philip Brian Thompson, Kevin Joseph Keegan, Gerald Charles James Francis (Cap), Stuart James Pearson, Raymond Kennedy, Peter John Taylor.   Manager: Donald Revie
Goal: Peter John Taylor (59)

327. 14.05.1976   British Championship
WALES v NORTHERN IRELAND 1-0 (1-0)
Vetch Field, Swansea
Referee: Not recorded   Attendance: 9,935
WALES: William David Davies, Leighton Phillips, Malcolm Edward Page, John Francis Mahoney, David Frazer Roberts, Ian Peter Evans, Arfon Trevor Griffiths, Brian Flynn, Terence Charles Yorath (Cap), Alan Thomas Curtis, Leighton James.   Manager: Michael Smith
NORTHERN IRELAND: Patrick Anthony Jennings, Peter William Scott, Patrick James Rice, Christopher James Nicholl, Alan Hunter, David Clements, Bryan Hamilton, Samuel Baxter McIlroy, Derek William Spence (Samuel John Morgan), Thomas Cassidy (James Michael Nicholl), David McCreery.
Goal: Leighton James (#)

328. 22.05.1976   5th European Championships, Quarter-Final
WALES v YUGOSLAVIA 1-1 (1-1)
Ninian Park, Cardiff
Referee: Rudolf Glöckner (East Germany)   Att: 30,306
WALES: William David Davies, Leighton Phillips, David Frazer Roberts, Ian Peter Evans, Malcolm Edward Page, Arfon Trevor Griffiths (Alan Thomas Curtis), Terence Charles Yorath (Cap), John Francis Mahoney, Brian Flynn, John Benjamin Toshack, Leighton James.   Manager: Michael Smith
YUGOSLAVIA: Enver Marić, Ivan Buljan (Cap), Džemal Hadžiabdić, Branko Oblak, Josip Katalinski, Dražen Mužinić, Slaviša Žungul (61 Franjo Vladić), Danilo Popivoda, Borislav Đorđević, Jure Jerković, Ivan Šurjak.   Trainer: Ante Mladinić
Goals: Ian Peter Evans (38) / Josip Katalinski (19 pen)

329. 06.10.1976
WALES v WEST GERMANY 0-2 (0-1)
Ninian Park, Cardiff
Referee: Robert Matthewson (England)   Att: 14,029
WALES: William David Davies, Malcolm Edward Page (Leslie Cartwright), Joseph Patrick Jones, Leighton Phillips, Ian Peter Evans, Arfon Trevor Griffiths (Brian Flynn), Terence Charles Yorath (Cap), John Francis Mahoney, Michael Reginald Thomas, Alan Thomas Curtis, Leighton James.   Manager: Michael Smith
WEST GERMANY: Rudi Kargus, Hans-Hubert Vogts, Herbert Zimmermann (46 Georg Schwarzenbeck), Franz Beckenbauer (Cap), Bernhard Dietz, Ulrich Stielike, Ulrich Hoeneß (74 Dieter Müller), Heinz Flohe, Karl-Heinz Rummenigge, Erich Beer (62 Rudolf Seliger), Josef Heynckes.   Trainer: Helmut Schön
Goal: Franz Beckenbauer (34), Josef Heynckes (73)

330. 17.11.1976   11th World Cup Qualifiers
SCOTLAND v WALES 1-0 (1-0)
Hampden Park, Glasgow
Referee: Ferdinand Biwersi (West Germany)   Att: 63,233
SCOTLAND: Alan Roderick Rough, Daniel Fergus McGrain, William Donachie, John Henderson Blackley, Gordon McQueen, Archibald Gemmill (Cap), Kenneth Burns, Bruce David Rioch (67 Richard Asa Hartford), Edwin Gray (84 William H. Pettigrew), Kenneth Mathieson Dalglish, Joseph Jordan.   Manager: William Esplin Ormond
WALES: William David Davies, Malcolm Edward Page, Joseph Patrick Jones, Leighton Phillips, Ian Peter Evans, Arfon Trevor Griffiths, Michael Reginald Thomas, Brian Flynn, Terence Charles Yorath, John Benjamin Toshack, Leighton James (76 Alan Thomas Curtis).   Manager: Michael Smith
Goal: Ian Evans (15 own goal)

331. 30.03.1977   11th World Cup Qualifiers
WALES v CZECHOSLOVAKIA 3-0 (1-0)
The Racecourse, Wrexham
Referee: Antonio Da Silva Garrido (Portugal)
Attendance: 18,022
WALES: William David Davies, Roderick John Thomas, Joseph Patrick Jones, Leighton Phillips, Ian Peter Evans, John Francis Mahoney, Peter Anthony Sayer, Brian Flynn, Terence Charles Yorath (Cap), Nicholas Simon Deacy, Leighton James.   Manager: Michael Smith
CZECHOSLOVAKIA: Alexander Vencel, Jan Pivarník, Ladislav Jurkemik, Pavel Biroš, Koloman Gögh, Jaroslav Pollák (Cap), Karel Dobiaš, Antonín Panenka, Marián Masný, Zdeněk Nehoda, Jozef Móder (46 Miroslav Gajdůšek).   Trainer: Václav Ježek
Goals: Leighton James (27, 75), Nicholas Simon Deacy (65)

332. 28.05.1977   British Championship
WALES v SCOTLAND 0-0
The Racecourse, Wrexham
Referee: Malcolm Moffatt (Northern Ireland)   Att: 14,468
WALES: William David Davies, Roderick John Thomas, Joseph Patrick Jones, Leighton Phillips, Ian Peter Evans, John Francis Mahoney, Peter Anthony Sayer, Brian Flynn, Terence Charles Yorath (Cap), Nicholas Simon Deacy, Leighton James (67 Michael Reginald Thomas).   Manager: Michael Smith
SCOTLAND: Alan Roderick Rough, Daniel Fergus McGrain, William Donachie, Thomas Forsyth, Gordon McQueen, Archibald Gemmill, Donald Sandison Masson, Bruce David Rioch (Cap) (65 William McClure Johnston), Richard Asa Hartford, Kenneth Mathieson Dalglish, Derek James Parlane (74 Kenneth Burns).   Manager: Alistair MacLeod

333. 31.05.1977   British Championship
ENGLAND v WALES 0-1 (0-1)
Wembley, London
Referee: John Robertson Gordon (Scotland)   Att: 48,000
ENGLAND: Peter Leslie Shilton, Philip George Neal, Michael Dennis Mills, Brian Greenhoff, David Victor Watson, Emlyn Walter Hughes, Kevin Joseph Keegan (Cap), Michael Roger Channon, Stuart James Pearson, Trevor David Brooking (79 Dennis Tueart), Raymond Kennedy.   Manager: Donald Revie
WALES: William David Davies, Roderick John Thomas, Joseph Patrick Jones, Leighton Phillips (David Frazer Roberts), Ian Peter Evans, John Francis Mahoney, Peter Anthony Sayer, Brian Flynn, Terence Charles Yorath, Nicholas Simon Deacy, Leighton James.   Manager: Michael Smith
Goal: Leighton James (44 pen)

334. 03.06.1977   British Championship
NORTHERN IRELAND v WALES 1-1 (0-1)
Windsor Park, Belfast
Referee: Not recorded   Attendance: 15,000
NORTHERN IRELAND: Patrick Anthony Jennings, James Michael Nicholl, Samuel Nelson, Christopher James Nicholl, Alan Hunter, Bryan Hamilton, Roland Christopher McGrath, Samuel Baxter McIlroy, Thomas Jackson, David McCreery (Gerard Joseph Armstrong), Trevor Anderson (Derek William Spence).
WALES: William David Davies, Roderick John Thomas, Joseph Patrick Jones, David Frazer Roberts, Ian Peter Evans, John Francis Mahoney, Peter Anthony Sayer (Alan Thomas Curtis), Brian Flynn, Terence Charles Yorath (Cap), Nicholas Simon Deacy, Leighton James (Michael Reginald Thomas). Manager: Michael Smith
Goal: Samuel Nelson (#) / Nicholas Simon Deacy (#)

335. 06.09.1977
WALES v KUWAIT 0-0
The Racecourse, Wrexham
Referee: Not recorded   Attendance: 3,132
WALES: William David Davies, Roderick John Thomas (Malcolm Edward Page), Joseph Patrick Jones, Leighton Phillips, David Frazer Roberts, John Francis Mahoney, Peter Anthony Sayer (Nicholas Simon Deacy), Brian Flynn, Terence Charles Yorath, John Benjamin Toshack, Leighton James. Manager: Michael Smith
KUWAIT: Altrabousi, Hussain, Jumah, Mayouf, Durehaim (Marafi), Farouk, Saad, Hammed, Feisal, Jassim, Alanbari.

336. 20.09.1977
KUWAIT v WALES 0-0
Al-Kuwait
Referee: Not recorded   Attendance: 6,000
KUWAIT: Altrabousi, Hussain, Jumah, Mayouf, Durehaim, Farouk, Saad, Hammed, Feisal, Jassim, Alanbari.
WALES: Thomas John Seymour Phillips, Malcolm Edward Page, Joseph Patrick Jones, Leighton Phillips, Ian Peter Evans, John Francis Mahoney, Peter Anthony Sayer, Brian Flynn, Terence Charles Yorath (David Frazer Roberts), John Benjamin Toshack (Robert Ian Edwards), Leighton James (Michael Reginald Thomas).   Manager: Michael Smith

337. 12.10.1977   11th World Cup Qualifiers
WALES v SCOTLAND 0-2 (0-0)
Anfield Road, Liverpool
Referee: Robert Charles Paul Wurtz (France)   Att: 50,850
WALES: William David Davies, Roderick John Thomas, Joseph Patrick Jones, David Edward Jones, Leighton Phillips, John Francis Mahoney, Peter Anthony Sayer (75 Nicholas Simon Deacy), Brian Flynn, Terence Charles Yorath (Cap), John Benjamin Toshack, Michael Reginald Thomas. Manager: Michael Smith
SCOTLAND: Alan Roderick Rough, William Pullar Jardine (57 Martin McLean Buchan), William Donachie, Thomas Forsyth, Gordon McQueen, Donald Sandison Masson (Cap), Richard Asa Hartford, Luigi Macari, William McClure Johnston, Kenneth Mathieson Dalglish, Joseph Jordan. Manager: Alistair MacLeod
Goals: Donald Masson (79 pen), Kenneth Dalglish (87)

338. 16.11.1977   11th World Cup Qualifiers
CZECHOSLOVAKIA v WALES 1-0 (1-0)
Sparta, Praha
Referee: Adolf Prokop (East Germany)   Attendance: 22,383
CZECHOSLOVAKIA: Zdeněk Hruška, Jozef Barmoš, Jan Fiala (67 Zdeněk Prokeš), Rostislav Vojáček (Cap), Koloman Gögh, Ivan Bilský, Karel Jarůšek, Miroslav Gajdůšek, Marián Masný (87 Ján Kozák), Karel Kroupa, Zdeněk Nehoda. Trainer: Václav Ježek
WALES: William David Davies, Roderick John Thomas, Joseph Patrick Jones, David Edward Jones, Leighton Phillips, John Francis Mahoney, Donato Nardiello, Brian Flynn, Terence Charles Yorath (Cap), John Benjamin Toshack, Michael Reginald Thomas (73 Nicholas Simon Deacy). Manager: Michael Smith
Goal: Zdeněk Nehoda (12)

339. 14.12.1977
WEST GERMANY v WALES 1-1 (0-0)
Westfalen, Dortmund
Referee: Charles George Rainier Corver (Holland)
Attendance: 57,000
WEST GERMANY: Josef Maier, Hans-Hubert Vogts (Cap), Rolf Rüssmann Franz-Josef Tenhagen, Bernhard Dietz, Rainer Bonhof, Heinz Flohe, Manfred Burgsmüller, Rudiger Abramczik, Klaus Fischer (76 Wolfgang Seel), Bernd Hölzenbein.   Trainer: Helmut Schön
WALES: William David Davies, Malcolm Edward Page, Joseph Patrick Jones, David Edward Jones, Leighton Phillips, Carl Stephen Harris, Brian Flynn, Terence Charles Yorath (Cap), Nicholas Simon Deacy, Leighton James, Alan Thomas Curtis (Donato Nardiello).   Manager: Michael Smith
Goals: Klaus Fischer (46) / David Edward Jones (78)

340. 18.04.1978
IRAN v WALES 0-1

Teheran

Referee: Not recorded   Attendance: 50,000

IRAN: Nasser Hejazi, Hassan Nazari, Hossein Kazerani, Nasrollah Abdollahi, Andranik Eskanderian (Panjali), Hassan Nayeb-Agha, Ali Parvin, Mohammed Sadeghi, Ebrahim Ghassempour, Ghafoor D'jahani (Hassan Rowshan), Adelkhani (Hossein Faraki).

WALES: William David Davies, Malcolm Edward Page, Joseph Patrick Jones, Gareth Davies, David Edward Jones, John Francis Mahoney (Brian Flynn), Carl Stephen Harris (Leslie Cartwright), Terence Charles Yorath, Phillip John Dwyer, Nicholas Simon Deacy, Michael Reginald Thomas. Manager: Michael Smith

Goal: Phillip John Dwyer (#)

341. 13.05.1978   British Championship
WALES v ENGLAND 1-3 (0-1)

Ninian Park, Cardiff

Referee: Malcolm Moffatt (Northern Ireland)   Att: 17,698

WALES: William David Davies, Malcolm Edward Page, Joseph Patrick Jones, Leighton Phillips, David Edward Jones (Gareth Davies), Terence Charles Yorath (46 John Francis Mahoney), Brian Flynn, Carl Stephen Harris, Alan Thomas Curtis, Phillip John Dwyer, Michael Reginald Thomas. Manager: Michael Smith

ENGLAND: Peter Leslie Shilton, Michael Dennis Mills (Cap), Trevor John Cherry (16 Anthony William Currie), Brian Greenhoff, David Victor Watson, Raymond Colin Wilkins, Steven James Coppell, Trevor John Francis, Robert Dennis Latchford (32 Paul Mariner), Trevor David Brooking, Peter Simon Barnes. Manager: Ronald Greenwood

Goals: Phillip John Dwyer (63) / Robert Latchford (8), Anthony William Currie (82), Peter Simon Barnes (89)

342. 17.05.1978   British Championship
SCOTLAND v WALES 1-1 (1-0)

Hampden Park, Glasgow

Referee: Malcolm H. Wright (Northern Ireland)   Att: 70,241

SCOTLAND: James Anton Blyth, Stuart Robert Kennedy, William Donachie, Kenneth Burns, Gordon McQueen (32 Thomas Forsyth), Archibald Gemmill (Cap), Graeme James Souness, Richard Asa Hartford, William McClure Johnston (85 John Neilson Robertson), Kenneth Mathieson Dalglish, Derek Joseph Johnstone. Manager: Alistair MacLeod

WALES: William David Davies, Malcolm Edward Page (76 Nicholas Simon Deacy), Joseph Patrick Jones, David Frazer Roberts, Leighton Phillips, Terence Charles Yorath (Cap), John Francis Mahoney, Brian Flynn, Carl Stephen Harris, Alan Thomas Curtis, Phillip John Dwyer. Manager: Michael Smith

Goals: Derek Joseph Johnstone (12) / William Donachie (89 own goal)

343. 20.05.1978   British Championship
WALES v NORTHERN IRELAND 1-0 (0-0)

The Racecourse, Wrexham

Referee: Not recorded   Attendance: 9,077

WALES: William David Davies, William Byron Stevenson, Joseph Patrick Jones, David Frazer Roberts, Gareth Davies, Terence Charles Yorath (Cap) (Michael Reginald Thomas), John Francis Mahoney, Brian Flynn, Carl Stephen Harris, Phillip John Dwyer, Nicholas Simon Deacy. Manager: Michael Smith

NORTHERN IRELAND: James Archibald Platt, Bryan Hamilton, Peter William Scott (Thomas Eugene Connell), Christopher James Nicholl, James Michael Nicholl, Martin Hugh Michael O'Neill, David McCreery, Samuel Baxter McIlroy, Trevor Anderson (George Terence Cochrane), Gerard Joseph Armstrong, Roland Christopher McGrath.

Goal: Nicholas Simon Deacy (# penalty)

344. 25.10.1978   6th European Champs Qualifiers
WALES v MALTA 7-0 (3-0)

The Racecourse, Wrexham

Referee: Magnus Petúrson (Iceland)   Attendance: 11,475

WALES: William David Davies, William Byron Stevenson, Joseph Patrick Jones, Leighton Phillips, Malcolm Edward Page, Michael Reginald Thomas, Carl Stephen Harris, Brian Flynn, Robert Ian Edwards, Robert Mark James, Leslie Cartwright (16 Peter Anthony O'Sullivan).   Manager: Michael Smith

MALTA: Robert Gatt, George Ciantar, Edwin Farrugia (Constantino Consiglio), Simon Tortell, Mario Schembri, John Holland (Cap), Vincent Magro, Richard Aquilina (46 Ernest Spiteri-Gonzi), George Xuereb, Raymond Xuereb, Carlo Seychell.   Trainer: Victor Scerri

Goals: Robert Ian Edwards (17, 45, 48, 50), Peter Anthony O'Sullivan (20), Michael Reginald Thomas (70), Brian Flynn (73)

345. 29.11.1978   6th European Champs Qualifiers
WALES v TURKEY 1-0 (0-0)
The Racecourse, Wrexham
Referee: Alojzy Jargus (Poland)   Attendance: 11,794
WALES: William David Davies, William Byron Stevenson, Joseph Patrick Jones, Leighton Phillips, Terence Charles Yorath (Cap), Michael Reginald Thomas, Carl Stephen Harris, Brian Flynn, Nicholas Simon Deacy, Phillip John Dwyer, Leighton James.   Manager: Michael Smith
TURKEY: Şenol Güneş, Turgay Semercioğlu, Cem Pamiroğlu, Necati Özçağlayan, Erdoğan Arica, Fatih Terim, Mehmet Ekşi, Önder Mustafaoğlu, Necdet Ergün, Sedat III Özden, Ahmet Ceylan (Isa Ertürk).   Trainer: Sabri Kiraz
Goal: Nicholas Simon Deacy (70)

346. 02.05.1979   6th European Champs Qualifiers
WALES v WEST GERMANY 0-2 (0-1)
The Racecourse, Wrexham
Referee: Alberto Michelotti (Italy)   Attendance: 26,900
WALES: William David Davies, Malcolm Edward Page, Joseph Patrick Jones, Leighton Phillips, George Frederick Berry, John Francis Mahoney, Terence Charles Yorath (Cap) (73 Robert Mark James), Carl Stephen Harris, Robert Ian Edwards (59 John Benjamin Toshack), Alan Thomas Curtis, Michael Reginald Thomas.   Manager: Michael Smith
WEST GERMANY: Josef Maier (Cap), Manfred Kaltz, Ulrich Stielike (88 Bernd Martin), Karlheinz Förster, Bernhard Dietz, Rainer Bonhof, Bernhard Cullmann, Herbert Zimmermann, Klaus Fischer, Karl-Heinz Rummenigge, Klaus Allofs.
Trainer: Josef Derwall
Goal: Herbert Zimmermann (30), Klaus Fischer (52)

347. 19.05.1979   British Championship
WALES v SCOTLAND 3-0 (2-0)
Ninian Park, Cardiff
Referee: Patrick Partridge (England)   Attendance: 20,371
WALES: William David Davies, William Byron Stevenson, Joseph Patrick Jones, Leighton Phillips, Phillip John Dwyer, John Francis Mahoney, Terence Charles Yorath (Cap) (89 Peter Nicholas), Brian Flynn, Robert Mark James, John Benjamin Toshack, Alan Thomas Curtis.   Manager: Michael Smith
SCOTLAND: Alan Roderick Rough, George Elder Burley, Francis Tierney Gray, Alan David Hansen, Paul Anthony Hegarty, John Wark, Richard Asa Hartford, Graeme James Souness, Arthur Graham, Kenneth Mathieson Dalglish (Cap), Ian Andrew Wallace (55 Joseph Jordan).
Manager: John Stein
Goals: John Benjamin Toshack (28, 35, 75)

348. 23.05.1979   British Championship
ENGLAND v WALES 0-0
Wembley, London
Referee: Malcolm Moffatt (Northern Ireland)   Att: 70,220
ENGLAND: Joseph Thomas Corrigan, Trevor John Cherry, Kenneth Graham Sansom, Raymond Colin Wilkins (75 Trevor David Brooking), David Victor Watson, Emlyn Walter Hughes (Cap), Kevin Joseph Keegan (68 Steven James Coppell), Anthony William Currie, Robert Dennis Latchford, Terence McDermott, Laurence Paul Cunningham.
Manager: Ronald Greenwood
WALES: William David Davies, William Byron Stevenson, Joseph Patrick Jones, Leighton Phillips, Phillip John Dwyer, John Francis Mahoney, Terence Charles Yorath (Cap), Brian Flynn, Robert Mark James, John Benjamin Toshack (80 Carl Stephen Harris), Alan Thomas Curtis.
Manager: Michael Smith

349. 25.05.1979   British Championship
NORTHERN IRELAND v WALES 1-1 (1-0)
Windsor Park, Belfast
Referee: Not recorded   Attendance: 6,500
NORTHERN IRELAND: Patrick Anthony Jennings, Patrick James Rice, Samuel Nelson, Christopher James Nicholl, Alan Hunter, James Michael Nicholl, David McCreery (46 Thomas Sloan), Samuel Baxter McIlroy, Gerard Joseph Armstrong, Derek William Spence, Bryan Hamilton.
WALES: William David Davies, William Byron Stevenson, Joseph Patrick Jones, Leighton Phillips, Phillip John Dwyer, John Francis Mahoney, Terence Charles Yorath (Cap), Brian Flynn, Robert Mark James, John Benjamin Toshack, Alan Thomas Curtis (76 Peter Nicholas).
Manager: Michael Smith
Goal: Derek William Spence / Robert Mark James

350. 02.06.1979   6th European Champs Qualifiers
MALTA v WALES 0-2 (0-1)
Empire, Gzira
Referee: Nikolaos Lagoyannis (Greece)   Attendance: 8,358
MALTA: Charles Sciberras, David Buckingham, Edwin Farrugia, John Holland (Cap), Norman Buttigieg, Emanuel Farrugia, Vincent Magro, Joe Xuereb (John Joseph Aquilina), Ernest Spiteri-Gonzi (Emanuel 'Leli' Fabri), Raymond Xuereb, George Xuereb.   Trainer: Victor Scerri
WALES: William David Davies, William Byron Stevenson, Joseph Patrick Jones, Leighton Phillips, Peter Nicholas, John Francis Mahoney, Carl Stephen Harris (65 Michael Reginald Thomas), Brian Flynn (89 Phillip John Dwyer), Robert Mark James, John Benjamin Toshack, Alan Thomas Curtis.
Manager: Michael Smith
Goals: Peter Nicholas (15), Brian Flynn (51)

351. 11.09.1979
WALES v REPUBLIC OF IRELAND 2-1 (1-1)
Vetch Field, Swansea
Referee: Stevens (England)   Attendance: 6,825
WALES: William David Davies, Peter Nicholas, Joseph Patrick Jones, Leighton Phillips, George Frederick Berry, John Francis Mahoney, Terence Charles Yorath, Brian Flynn, Ian Patrick Walsh, Alan Thomas Curtis, Michael Reginald Thomas.   Manager: Michael Smith
IRELAND: Gerald Joseph Peyton, Eamonn Gregg, David Anthony O'Leary, Michael Paul Martin, Patrick Martin Mulligan (Cap), Anthony Patrick Grealish, William Brady, Jeremiah Michael Murphy, Francis Anthony Stapleton, Brendan Richard O'Callaghan, Gerard Joseph Ryan.   Manager: John Michael Giles
Goals: Ian Patrick Walsh (#), Alan Thomas Curtis (#) / Joseph Patrick Jones (# own goal)

352. 17.10.1979   6th European Champs Qualifiers
WEST GERMANY v WALES 5-1 (4-0)
Müngersdorfer, Köln
Referee: Johannes Nicolaas Ignatius "Jan" Keizer (Holland)   Attendance: 61,000
WEST GERMANY: Dieter Burdenski, Manfred Kaltz, Bernhard Cullmann, Karlheinz Förster, Bernhard Dietz (Cap), Rainer Bonhof, Bernd Schuster (64 Herbert Zimmermann), Hans Müller, Karl-Heinz Rummenigge (75 Hans-Peter Briegel), Klaus Fischer, Klaus Allofs.   Trainer: Josef Derwall
WALES: William David Davies, William Byron Stevenson, Joseph Patrick Jones (15 George Frederick Berry), Leighton Phillips, Phillip John Dwyer, Peter Nicholas, John Francis Mahoney, Brian Flynn, Alan Thomas Curtis, John Benjamin Toshack (64 Michael Reginald Thomas), Robert Mark James.   Manager: Michael Smith
Goals: Klaus Fischer (23, 38), Manfred Kaltz (32), Karl-Heinz Rummenigge (41), Karlheinz Förster (83) / Alan Thomas Curtis (85)

353. 21.11.1979   6th European Champs Qualifiers
TURKEY v WALES 1-0 (0-0)
Kemal Atatürk, Izmir
Referee: Constantin Ghiţă (Romania)   Attendance: 50,000
TURKEY: Şenol Güneş, Turgay Semercioğlu, Cem Pamiroğlu, Erol Togay, Fatih Terim, Mehmet Ekşi, Arif Güney, Erhan Önal, Sedat III Özden, Isa Ertürk (Mustafa Turgat), Mustafa Denizli (Sadullah Acele).   Trainer: Sabri Kiraz

WALES: William David Davies, William Byron Stevenson, Joseph Patrick Jones, Leighton Phillips, George Frederick Berry, Terence Charles Yorath (Cap), Gordon John Davies (71 John Francis Mahoney), Peter Nicholas, Alan Thomas Curtis, Ian Patrick Walsh (65 Robert Ian Edwards), Michael Reginald Thomas.   Manager: Michael Smith
Sent off: William Byron Stevenson (69)
Goal: Erhan Önal (80)

354. 17.05.1980   British Championship
WALES v ENGLAND 4-1 (2-1)
The Racecourse, Wrexham
Referee: Ian Foote (Scotland)   Attendance: 24,386
WALES: William David Davies, Peter Nicholas, Joseph Patrick Jones, David Edward Jones (46 Keith Pontin), Paul Terence Price, Terence Charles Yorath (Cap), David Charles Giles, Brian Flynn, Ian Patrick Walsh, Leighton James, Michael Reginald Thomas.   Trainer: Harold Michael England
ENGLAND: Raymond Neal Clemence, Philip George Neal (20 Kenneth Graham Sansom), Trevor John Cherry, Philip Brian Thompson (Cap), Laurence Valentine Lloyd (80 Raymond Colin Wilkins), Raymond Kennedy, Steven James Coppell, Glenn Hoddle, Paul Mariner, Trevor David Brooking, Peter Simon Barnes.   Manager: Ronald Greenwood
Goal: Michael Reginald Thomas (19), Ian Patrick Walsh (30), Leighton James (60), Philip Brian Thompson (66 own goal) / Paul Mariner (16)

355. 21.05.1980   British Championship
SCOTLAND v WALES 1-0 (1-0)
Hampden Park, Glasgow
Referee: Hugh Wilson (Northern Ireland)   Att: 31,359
SCOTLAND: Alan Roderick Rough, Daniel Fergus McGrain, Alexander Fordyce Munro, Paul Anthony Hegarty, Alexander McLeish, William Fergus Miller, Gordon David Strachan, Archibald Gemmill (Cap), Peter Russell Weir (84 Robert Sime Aitken), Kenneth Mathieson Dalglish, Joseph Jordan.   Manager: John Stein
WALES: William David Davies, Peter Nicholas, Joseph Patrick Jones, Keith Pontin (46 Leighton Phillips), Paul Terence Price, Terence Charles Yorath (Cap), David Charles Giles, Brian Flynn, Ian Patrick Walsh (15 Ian James Rush), Leighton James, Michael Reginald Thomas.   Trainer: Harold Michael England
Goal: William Fergus Miller (26)

356. 23.05.1980   British Championship
WALES v NORTHERN IRELAND   0-1 (0-1)
Ninian Park, Cardiff
Referee: Not recorded   Attendance: 12,913
WALES: William David Davies, Peter Nicholas, Joseph Patrick Jones, Terence Charles Yorath (Cap), Leighton Phillips, Paul Terence Price, David Charles Giles, Brian Flynn (Carl Stephen Harris), Ian James Rush, Leighton James, Michael Reginald Thomas.   Trainer: Harold Michael England
NORTHERN IRELAND: James Archibald Platt, James Michael Nicholl, Malachy Martin Donaghy, Christopher James Nicholl, John Patrick O'Neill, Thomas Cassidy (David McCreery), Samuel Baxter McIlroy, William Robert Hamilton (George Terence Cochrane), Gerard Joseph Armstrong, Thomas Finney, Noel Brotherston.   Manager: W. Bingham
Goal: Noel Brotherston (#)

357. 02.06.1980   12th World Cup Qualifiers
ICELAND v WALES   0-4 (0-1)
Laugardalsvöllur, Reykjavík
Referee: Rolf Nyhus (Norway)   Attendance: 10,254
ICELAND: Þorsteinn Ólafsson, Sævar Jónsson (85 Árni Sveinsson), Trausti Haraldsson, Marteinn Geirsson (Cap), Sidurdur Halldórsson (85 Dýri Guðmundsson), Janus Guðlaugsson, Arnór Guðjohnsen, Atli Eðvaldsson, Pétur Pétursson, Karl Þórðarson, Guðmundur Þorbjörnsson.
Trainer: Guðni Kjartansson
WALES: William David Davies, Peter Nicholas, Joseph Patrick Jones, Paul Terence Price, Leighton Phillips, Terence Charles Yorath (Cap) (75 William Byron Stevenson), David Charles Giles, Brian Flynn, Ian Patrick Walsh, Leighton James, Gordon John Davies (80 Carl Stephen Harris).
Trainer: Harold Michael England
Goals: Ian Patrick Walsh (45, 75), David Charles Giles (53), Brian Flynn (61 pen)

358. 15.10.1980   12th World Cup Qualifiers
WALES v TURKEY   4-0 (2-0)
Ninian Park, Cardiff
Referee: Torben Mansson (Denmark)   Attendance: 11,770
WALES: William David Davies, Peter Nicholas, Joseph Patrick Jones, Paul Terence Price, Leighton Phillips, Terence Charles Yorath (Cap), David Charles Giles, Brian Flynn, Carl Stephen Harris, Ian Patrick Walsh, Leighton James.
Trainer: Harold Michael England
TURKEY: Şenol Güneş, Turgay Semercioğlu, Cem Pamiroğlu, Hüsnü Özkara, Fatih Terim, Erhan Önal, Necdet Ergün, Güngör Şahinkaya, Tuncay Soyak, Sedat III Özden (80 Serdar Bali), Halil Ibrahim Eren.   Trainer: Sabri Kiraz
Sent off: Tuncay Soyak (78)
Goals: Brian Flynn (19), Leighton James (37 pen, 85), Ian Patrick Walsh (79)

359. 19.11.1980   12th World Cup Qualifiers
WALES v CZECHOSLOVAKIA   1-0 (1-0)
Ninian Park, Cardiff
Referee: Walter Eschweiler (West Germany)   Att: 20,175
WALES: William David Davies, Peter Nicholas, Kevin Ratcliffe, Paul Terence Price, Leighton Phillips, Terence Charles Yorath (Cap), Michael Reginald Thomas, David Charles Giles, Brian Flynn, Ian Patrick Walsh (49 Carl Stephen Harris), Jeremy Melvyn Charles.
Trainer: Harold Michael England
CZECHOSLOVAKIA: Zdeněk Hruška, Jozef Barmoš, Libor Radimec, Rostislav Vojáček, Luděk Macela, Ján Kozák, Ladislav Jurkemik (72 Petr Janečka), Antonín Panenka, Marián Masný, Zdeněk Nehoda (Cap), Ladislav Vízek.
Trainer: Jozef Vengloš
Goal: David Charles Giles (10)

360. 24.02.1981
REPUBLIC OF IRELAND v WALES   1-3 (1-2)
Tolka Park, Dublin
Referee: Peter Geoffrey Reeves (England)   Att: 15,000
IRELAND: James Martin McDonagh, David Francis Langan, Brendan Richard O'Callaghan, James Paul Holmes, Christopher William Gerard Hughton, Anthony Patrick Grealish (Cap), Gerard Anthony Daly, Gary Patrick Waddock, Daniel Joseph Givens (46 Kevin Bernard Moran), Eamonn Gerard O'Keefe, Stephen Derek Heighway.
Manager: Eoin Hand
WALES: William David Davies, Peter Nicholas, Kevin Ratcliffe, Paul Terence Price, Joseph Patrick Jones, Terence David John Boyle, Terence Charles Yorath (Cap), Carl Stephen Harris, Brian Flynn, Ian Patrick Walsh, Leighton James.
Trainer: Harold Michael England
Goals: Anthony Patrick Grealish (#) / Paul Terence Price (#), Terence David John Boyle (#), Terence Charles Yorath (#)

361. 25.03.1981   12th World Cup Qualifiers
TURKEY v WALES   0-1 (0-0)
19 Mayis, Ankara
Referee: Sándor Kuti (Hungary)   Attendance: 35,000
TURKEY: Şenol Güneş, Onur Alp Kayador, Muammer Birdal (Sedat Karaoğlu), Necati Özçağlayan, Hüsnü Özkara, Sedat III Özden, Güngör Şahinkaya, Volkan Yayim (76 Şevket Kesler), Necdet Ergün, Tuncay Mesçi, Halil Ibrahim Eren.
Trainer: Özkan Sümer
WALES: William David Davies, Peter Nicholas, Kevin Ratcliffe, Paul Terence Price, Leighton Phillips, Joseph Patrick Jones, Carl Stephen Harris (75 David Charles Giles), Terence Charles Yorath (Cap), Brian Flynn, Ian Patrick Walsh (58 Jeremy Melvyn Charles), Leighton James.
Trainer: Harold Michael England
Goal: Carl Stephen Harris (67)

362. 16.05.1981   British Championship
WALES v SCOTLAND 2-0 (2-0)
Vetch Field, Swansea

Referee: Oliver Donnelly (Northern Ireland)   Att: 18,985

WALES: William David Davies, Joseph Patrick Jones (71 Terence David John Boyle), Peter Nicholas, Kevin Ratcliffe, Paul Terence Price, Leighton Phillips, Carl Stephen Harris, Brian Flynn (Cap), Ian Patrick Walsh (76 Jeremy Melvyn Charles), Leighton James, Michael Reginald Thomas.
Trainer: Harold Michael England

SCOTLAND: Alan Roderick Rough, Raymond Strean McDonald Stewart, Francis Tierney Gray (46 Daniel Fergus McGrain), David Narey, Gordon McQueen, William Fergus Miller, David Alexander Provan, Kenneth Burns, Richard Asa Hartford (Cap), Arthur Graham (85 Paul Whitehead Sturrock), Joseph Jordan.   Manager: John Stein

Goal: Ian Patrick Walsh (17, 20)

363. 20.05.1981   British Championship
ENGLAND v WALES 0-0
Wembley, London

Referee: Brian Robert McGinlay (Scotland)   Att: 34,280

ENGLAND: Joseph Thomas Corrigan, Vivian Alexander Anderson, Kenneth Graham Sansom, Bryan Robson, David Victor Watson (Cap), Raymond Colin Wilkins, Steven James Coppell, Glenn Hoddle, Peter Withe (82 Anthony Stewart Woodcock), Graham Rix, Peter Simon Barnes.
Manager: Ronald Greenwood

WALES: William David Davies, Joseph Patrick Jones, Kevin Ratcliffe, Peter Nicholas, Leighton Phillips, Paul Terence Price, Carl Stephen Harris (60 David Charles Giles), Brian Flynn (Cap), Ian Patrick Walsh, Leighton James (65 Ian James Rush), Michael Reginald Thomas.
Trainer: Harold Michael England

364. 30.05.1981   12th World Cup Qualifiers
WALES v SOVIET UNION 0-0
The Racecourse, Wrexham

Referee: Bruno Galler (Switzerland)   Attendance: 29,366

WALES: William David Davies, Joseph Patrick Jones, Kevin Ratcliffe, Leighton Phillips, Paul Terence Price, Peter Nicholas, Brian Flynn (Cap), Terence Charles Yorath, Ian Patrick Walsh (70 Jeremy Melvyn Charles), Michael Reginald Thomas, Carl Stephen Harris (75 David Charles Giles).
Trainer: Harold Michael England

SOVIET UNION: Rinat Dasaev, Tengiz Sulakvelidze, Aleksandr Chivadze (Cap), Sergey Borovskiy, Sergey Baltacha, Khoren Oganesyan, Vladimir Bessonov, Leonid Buryak, Sergey Andreev, David Kipiani (84 Yuriy Gavrilov), Oleg Blokhin.
Trainer: Konstantin Beskov

365. 09.09.1981   12th World Cup Qualifiers
CZECHOSLOVAKIA v WALES 2-0 (1-0)
Stahov, Praha

Referee: Franz Wöhrer (Austria)   Attendance: 38,000

CZECHOSLOVAKIA: Stanislav Seman, Přemysl Bičovský, Libor Radimec, Rostislav Vojáček, Jozef Barmoš, Ján Kozák, Ladislav Jurkemik, Jan Berger, Antonín Panenka (26 Werner Lička), Ladislav Vízek, Zdeněk Nehoda (Cap).
Trainer: Jozef Vengloš

WALES: William David Davies, William Byron Stevenson, Kevin Ratcliffe, Joseph Patrick Jones, Leighton Phillips (73 Ian Patrick Walsh), Brian Flynn (Cap), Peter Nicholas, Michael Reginald Thomas (62 Robert Mark James), Leighton James, Carl Stephen Harris, Alan Thomas Curtis.
Trainer: Harold Michael England

Goals: William Davies (26 own goal), Werner Lička (68)

366. 14.10.1981   12th World Cup Qualifiers
WALES v ICELAND 2-2 (1-0)
Vetch Field, Swansea

Referee: Arto Ravander (Finland)   Attendance: 20,000

WALES: William David Davies, Kevin Ratcliffe, Joseph Patrick Jones, John Francis Mahoney, Peter Nicholas, Alan Thomas Curtis, Robert Mark James, Ian Patrick Walsh, Jeremy Melvyn Charles, Carl Stephen Harris (67 Ian James Rush), Leighton James.   Trainer: Harold Michael England

ICELAND: Guðmundur Baldursson, Viðar Halldórsson, Örn Óskarsson, Marteinn Geirsson (Cap), Sævar Jónsson, Magnús Bergs, Janus Guðlaugsson, Atli Eðvaldsson, Arnór Guðjohnsen, Ásgeir Sigurvinsson, Pétur Ormslev.
Trainer: Guðni Kjartansson

Goals: Robert Mark James (25), Alan Thomas Curtis (54) / Ásgeir Sigurvinsson (41, 61)

367. 18.11.1981   12th World Cup Qualifiers
SOVIET UNION v WALES 3-0 (2-0)
Dinamo, Tbilisi

Referee: Johannes Nicolaas Ignatius "Jan" Keizer (Holland)
Attendance: 80,000

SOVIET UNION: Rinat Dasaev, Sergey Borovskiy, Yuriy Susloparov, Sergey Baltacha, Anatoliy Demyanenko, Vitaliy Daraselia, Tengiz Sulakvelidze, Leonid Buryak, Ramaz Shengeliya, Yuriy Gavrilov (71 Vladimir Gutzaev), Oleg Blokhin (Cap).   Trainer: Konstantin Beskov

WALES: William David Davies, Kevin Ratcliffe, Joseph Patrick Jones (85 Steven John Lovell), Peter Nicholas, Leighton Phillips, Paul Terence Price, Alan Thomas Curtis, Brian Flynn (Cap), Ian James Rush, John Francis Mahoney (46 Michael Reginald Thomas), Leighton James.
Trainer: Harold Michael England

Goals: Vitaliy Daraselia (13), Oleg Blokhin (18), Yuriy Gavrilov (64)

368. 24.03.1982
SPAIN v WALES 1-1 (1-0)

Luis Casanova, Valencia

Referee: Enzo Barbaresco (Italy)   Attendance: 15,000

SPAIN: Luis Miguel Arkonada (Cap), José Antonio Camacho, Miguel Tendillo, José Ramón Alexanco, Rafael Gordillo, José Vicente Sánchez, Juan José Estella, Ricardo Gallego, Enrique Saura, Jesús María Satrústegui, Roberto López Ufarte. Trainer: José Emilio Santamaría

WALES: William David Davies, Christopher Marustik, Joseph Patrick Jones, Paul Terence Price, Kevin Ratcliffe, Peter Nicholas, Robert Mark James, Michael Reginald Thomas (62 David Charles Giles), William Byron Stevenson, Ian Patrick Walsh (81 Gordon John Davies), Alan Thomas Curtis. Trainer: Harold Michael England

Goals: Satrústegui (25) / Robert Mark James (51)

369. 27.04.1982   British Championship
WALES v ENGLAND 0-1 (0-0)

Ninian Park, Cardiff

Referee: Oliver Donnely (Northern Ireland)   Att: 25,000

WALES: William David Davies, Christopher Marustik, Kevin Ratcliffe, Peter Nicholas, Nigel Charles Ashley Stevenson, Joseph Patrick Jones, Alan Thomas Curtis, Brian Flynn (Cap) (77 Carl Stephen Harris), Ian James Rush, Michael Reginald Thomas (46 Leighton James), Robert Mark James. Trainer: Harold Michael England

ENGLAND: Joseph Thomas Corrigan, Philip George Neal, Kenneth Graham Sansom, Philip Brian Thompson (Cap), Terence Ian Butcher, Bryan Robson, Raymond Colin Wilkins, Trevor John Francis (80 Cyrille Regis), Peter Withe, Glenn Hoddle (52 Terence McDermott), Anthony William Morley. Manager: Ronald Greenwood

Goal: Trevor John Francis (74)

370. 24.05.1982   British Championship
SCOTLAND v WALES 1-0 (1-0)

Hampden Park, Glasgow

Ref: Frederick McKnight (Northern Ireland)   Att: 25,284

SCOTLAND: Alan Roderick Rough, Raymond Strean McDonald Stewart (72 George Elder Burley), Francis Tierney Gray, David Narey, Alan David Hansen, Thomas Burns, Graeme James Souness (Cap), Richard Asa Hartford, Kenneth Mathieson Dalglish, Alan Bernard Brazil, Joseph Jordan (72 Paul Whitehead Sturrock).   Manager: John Stein

WALES: William David Davies, Christopher Marustik, Joseph Patrick Jones, Peter Nicholas, Nigel Charles Ashley Stevenson, William Byron Stevenson, Alan Thomas Curtis (75 Ian Patrick Walsh), Robert Mark James, Brian Flynn (Cap) (75 Michael Reginald Thomas), Ian James Rush, Leighton James. Trainer: Harold Michael England

Goal: Richard Asa Hartford (7)

371. 27.05.1982   British Championship
WALES v NORTHERN IRELAND 3-0 (1-0)

The Racecourse, Wrexham

Referee: Not recorded   Attendance: 2,315

WALES: Neville Southall, Christopher Marustik, Joseph Patrick Jones, Peter Nicholas, Nigel Charles Ashley Stevenson, William Byron Stevenson, Alan Thomas Curtis (Ian Patrick Walsh), Robert Mark James, Brian Flynn (Cap), Ian James Rush, Leighton James (Michael Reginald Thomas). Trainer: Harold Michael England

NORTHERN IRELAND: Patrick Anthony Jennings (46 James Archibald Platt), James Michael Nicholl, Malachy Martin Donaghy, John McClelland, Christopher James Nicholl, James Cleary (Robert McFaul Campbell), Noel Brotherston, Patrick Joseph Healy, Gerard Joseph Armstrong, Samuel Baxter McIlroy (Cap), William Robert Hamilton. Manager: William Bingham

Goals: Alan Thomas Curtis (#), Ian James Rush (#), Peter Nicholas (#)

372. 02.06.1982
FRANCE v WALES 0-1 (0-0)

Municipal, Toulouse

Referee: Viriato Graça Oliva (Portugal)   Attendance: 26,671

FRANCE: Jean Castaneda, Patrick Battiston, Marius Trésor (46 Philippe Mahut), Christian Lopez, Maxime Bossis, Jean-François Larios (64 Jean Amadou Tigana), Alain Giresse, Michel Platini (Cap), Alain Couriol, Gérard Soler, Didier Six (56 Bruno Bellone).   Trainer: Michel Hidalgo

WALES: William David Davies, Christopher Marustik, Paul Terence Price, William Byron Stevenson, Joseph Patrick Jones, Peter Nicholas, Robert Mark James, Brian Flynn (Cap), Ian Patrick Walsh (71 Gordon John Davies), Ian James Rush, Leighton James.   Trainer: Harold Michael England

Goal: Ian James Rush (55)

373. 22.09.1982   7th European Champs Qualifiers
WALES v NORWAY 1-0 (1-0)

Vetch Field, Swansea

Referee: Joël Quiniou (France)   Attendance: 4,340

WALES: Neville Southall, Christopher Marustik, Joseph Patrick Jones, Kenneth Francis Jackett, Nigel Charles Ashley Stevenson, Paul Terence Price (Cap), Alan Thomas Curtis (62 Jeremy Melvyn Charles), Brian Flynn, Ian James Rush, Michael Reginald Thomas, Robert Mark James. Trainer: Harold Michael England

NORWAY: Per Egil Nygård, Bjarne Berntsen, Terje Kojedal, Åge Hareide, Svein Grøndalen, Roger Albertsen, Tom Lund, Erik Solér, Arne Erlandsen (78 Stein Kollshaugen), Arne Larsen Økland, Hallvar Thoresen.   Trainer: Tor Røste Fossen

Goal: Ian James Rush (30)

374. 15.12.1982   7th European Champs Qualifiers
YUGOSLAVIA v WALES 4-4 (3-2)
Pod Goricom, Titograd
Referee: Alexis Ponnet (Belgium)   Attendance: 17,000
YUGOSLAVIA: Ratko Svilar, Nenad Stojković (Cap), Zvjezdan Cvetković, Aleksandar Trifunović, Nijaz Ferhatović (82 Boško Đurovski), Faruk Hadžibegić, Stjepan Deverić (59 Miodrag Ješić), Slavoljub Nikolić, Zlatko Kranjčar, Ivan Gudelj, Zvonko Živković.   Trainer: Todor Veselinović
WALES: William David Davies, Joseph Patrick Jones, Kevin Ratcliffe, Peter Nicholas (77 Nigel Mark Vaughan), Paul Terence Price (Cap), Kenneth Francis Jackett, Robert Mark James, Brian Flynn, Ian James Rush, Michael Reginald Thomas (57 Jeremy Melvyn Charles), John Francis Mahoney.   Trainer: Harold Michael England
Goals: Zvjezdan Cvetković (16), Zvonko Živković (19), Zlatko Kranjčar (37), Miodrag Ješić (66) / Brian Flynn (6), Ian Rush (39), Joseph Patrick Jones (70), Robert Mark James (80)

375. 23.02.1983   British Championship
ENGLAND v WALES 2-1 (1-1)
Wembley, London
Referee: Robert Valentine (Scotland)   Attendance: 24,000
ENGLAND: Peter Leslie Shilton (Cap), Philip George Neal, Derek James Statham, Samuel Lee, Alvin Edward Martin, Terence Ian Butcher, Luther Loide Blissett, Gary Vincent Mabbutt, Paul Mariner, Gordon Sidney Cowans, Alan Ernest Devonshire.   Manager: Robert Robson
WALES: Neville Southall, Joseph Patrick Jones (44 George Frederick Berry), Kevin Ratcliffe, Paul Terence Price (Cap), Kenneth Francis Jackett, Brian Flynn, Gordon John Davies, Robert Mark James, Ian James Rush, Michael Reginald Thomas, John Francis Mahoney (80 Leighton James).   Trainer: Harold Michael England
Goals: Terence Ian Butcher (39), Philip George Neal (78 pen) / Ian James Rush (14)

376. 27.04.1983   7th European Champs Qualifiers
WALES v BULGARIA 1-0 (0-0)
The Racecourse, Wrexham
Referee: Siegfried Kirschen (East Germany)   Att: 9,006
WALES: Neville Southall, Joseph Patrick Jones, Kevin Ratcliffe, Paul Terence Price, Kenneth Francis Jackett, Peter Nicholas (Cap), Brian Flynn, Robert Mark James, Ian James Rush (69 Jeremy Melvyn Charles), Michael Reginald Thomas, Gordon John Davies.   Trainer: Harold Michael England

BULGARIA: Georgi Velinov, Plamen Nikolov, Nikolai Arabov, Petar Petrov, Sasho Borisov, Radoslav Zdravkov, Tsvetan Ionchev (83 Bojidar Iskrenov), Todor Iordanov (75 Georgi Slavkov), Spas Djevizov, Anio Sadkov, Stoicho Mladenov.   Trainer: Ivan Vutsov
Goal: Jeremy Melvyn Charles (79)

377. 28.05.1983   British Championship
WALES v SCOTLAND 0-2 (0-1)
Ninian Park, Cardiff
Referee: Malcolm Moffatt (Northern Ireland)   Att: 14,100
WALES: Neville Southall, Joseph Patrick Jones, Neil John Slatter, Kevin Ratcliffe, Paul Terence Price, Peter Nicholas (Cap), Brian Flynn (57 Steven Robert Lowndes), Kenneth Francis Jackett, Jeremy Melvyn Charles, Michael Reginald Thomas, Gordon John Davies.
Trainer: Harold Michael England
SCOTLAND: James Leighton, Richard Charles Gough, Francis Tierney Gray, David Narey, Alexander McLeish, Gordon David Strachan, William Fergus Miller, Graeme James Souness (Cap), Eamonn John Peter Bannon, Andrew Mullen Gray, Alan Bernard Brazil.   Manager: John Stein
Goals: Andrew Mullen Gray (11), Alan Bernard Brazil (67)

378. 31.05.1983   British Championship
NORTHERN IRELAND v WALES 0-1 (0-0)
Windsor Park, Belfast
Referee: Hugh Alexander (Scotland)   Attendance: 8,000
NORTHERN IRELAND: Patrick Anthony Jennings, James Michael Nicholl, Malachy Martin Donaghy, John McClelland, Christopher James Nicholl, Samuel Baxter McIlroy, Noel Brotherston, Gerald Mullan (James Cleary), Gerard Joseph Armstrong, William Robert Hamilton, Ian Edwin Stewart.   Manager: William Bingham
WALES: Neville Southall, Jeffrey Hopkins, Joseph Patrick Jones, Kevin Ratcliffe, Paul Terence Price (72 David Charles Giles), Peter Nicholas (Cap), Brian Flynn, Gordon John Davies, Jeremy Melvyn Charles, Michael Reginald Thomas, Alan Davies.   Trainer: Harold Michael England
Goal: Gordon John Davies (#)

379. 12.06.1983
WALES v BRAZIL 1-1 (1-0)
Ninian Park, Cardiff
Referee: Jan Redelfs (West Germany)   Attendance: 35,000
WALES: Neville Southall, Jeffrey Hopkins, Joseph Patrick Jones, Kevin Ratcliffe, Brian Flynn, Jeremy Melvyn Charles (62 Dudley Keith Lewis), Gordon John Davies, Nigel Mark Vaughan, David Charles Giles (83 Steven Robert Lowndes), Michael Reginald Thomas, Alan Davies.
Trainer: Harold Michael England
BRAZIL: Émerson Leão, Roberto Taylor Santos Morais "Betão", MÁRCIO Antônio ROSSINI, Luiz Carlos Ferreira "Luisinho", Pedro Luís Vicençote "Pedrinho", João BATISTA da Silva, SÓCRATES Brasileiro Sampaio Vieira de Oliveira (Cap), Edvaldo Oliveira Chaves "Pita" (PAULO ISIDORO de Jesus), Carlos Alberto Borges (Jorge Antônio Putinatti "Jorginho"), Antônio de Oliveira Filho "Careca", ÉDER Aleixo de Assis.   Trainer: Carlos Alberto Gomes Parreira
Goals: Brian Flynn (#) / Paulo Isidoro (#)

380. 21.09.1983   7th European Champs Qualifiers
NORWAY v WALES 0-0
Ullevaal, Oslo
Referee: Vojtech Christov (Czechoslovakia)   Att: 17,575
NORWAY: Erik Thorstvedt, Terje Kojedal, Svein Fjælberg, Åge Hareide, Svein Grøndalen, Roger Albertsen, Vidar Davidsen, Erik Solér, Hallvar Thoresen, Arne Dokken, Stein Kollshaugen.   Trainer: Tor Røste Fossen
WALES: Neville Southall, Jeffrey Hopkins, Joseph Patrick Jones, Kevin Ratcliffe, Paul Terence Price, Peter Nicholas (Cap), Brian Flynn, Nigel Mark Vaughan, Kenneth Francis Jackett, Robert Mark James, Ian James Rush.
Trainer: Harold Michael England

381. 12.10.1983
WALES v ROMANIA 5-0 (3-0)
The Racecourse, Wrexham
Referee: Robert Charles Paul Wurtz (France)   Att: 4,161
WALES: Neville Southall (46 David Wynne Felgate), Jeffrey Hopkins, Joseph Patrick Jones, Kevin Ratcliffe, Paul Terence Price, Brian Flynn (Cap), Robert Mark James (77 Alan Thomas Curtis), Nigel Mark Vaughan, Ian James Rush (75 Gordon John Davies), Michael Reginald Thomas, Kenneth Francis Jackett.   Trainer: Harold Michael England
ROMANIA: Silviu Lung (46 Dumitru Moraru), Mircea Rednic, Gino Iorgulescu (65 Ioan Andone), Costică Ștefănescu (Cap), Nicolae Ungureanu, Aurel Țicleanu (63 Ionel Augustin), Ladislau Bölöni, Michael Klein (67 Mircea Irimescu), Marcel Coraș, Romulus Gabor, Rodion Gorun Cămătaru.
Trainer: Mircea Lucescu
Goals: Ian James Rush (14, 30), Michael Thomas (25), Robert Mark James (72), Alan Thomas Curtis (90)

382. 16.11.1983   7th European Champs Qualifiers
BULGARIA v WALES 1-0 (0-0)
Vasil Levski, Sofia
Referee: Dieter Pauly (West Germany)   Attendance: 8,000
BULGARIA: Borislav Mihailov, Nasko Sirakov, Nikolai Arabov, Petar Petrov, Georgi Dimitrov, Radoslav Zdravkov, Bojidar Iskrenov, Anio Sadkov, Tsvetan Danov (46 Rusi Gochev), Jivko Gospodinov (88 Sasho Borisov), Stoicho Mladenov.   Trainer: Ivan Vutsov
WALES: Neville Southall, Jeffrey Hopkins, Joseph Patrick Jones, Kevin Ratcliffe, Paul Terence Price, Brian Flynn (Cap), Peter Nicholas (59 Jeremy Melvyn Charles), Nigel Mark Vaughan, Ian James Rush, Michael Reginald Thomas, Robert Mark James.   Trainer: Harold Michael England
Goal: Rusi Gochev (53)

383. 14.12.1983   7th European Champs Qualifiers
WALES v YUGOSLAVIA 1-1 (0-0)
Ninian Park, Cardiff
Referee: Erik Fredriksson (Sweden)   Attendance: 24,000
WALES: Neville Southall, Jeffrey Hopkins, Paul Terence Price, Kevin Ratcliffe, Joseph Patrick Jones, Brian Flynn (Cap) (82 Jeremy Melvyn Charles), Kenneth Francis Jackett, Nigel Mark Vaughan, Ian James Rush, Michael Reginald Thomas, Robert Mark James.   Trainer: Harold Michael England
YUGOSLAVIA: Zoran Simović, Zoran Vujović, Branislav Drobnjak, Srećko Katanec, Luka Peruzović, Ljubomir Radanović, Zlatko Vujović (Cap) (89 Zvjezdan Cvetković), Ivan Gudelj, Safet Sušić, Mehmed Baždarević, Marko Mlinarić (67 Sulejman Halilović).   Trainer: Todor Veselinović
Goal: Robert Mark James (52) / Mehmed Baždarević (82)

384. 28.02.1984   British Championship
SCOTLAND v WALES 2-1 (1-0)
Hampden Park, Glasgow
Referee: Jack Poucher (Northern Ireland)   Att: 21,542
SCOTLAND: James Leighton, Richard Charles Gough, Arthur Richard Albiston, William Fergus Miller, Alexander McLeish, Paul Michael Lyons McStay (64 Robert Sime Aitken), Graeme James Souness (Cap), James Bett, David Cooper, Paul Whitehead Sturrock, Francis Peter McGarvey (46 Maurice Johnston).   Manager: John Stein
WALES: Neville Southall, Jeffrey Hopkins, Kevin Ratcliffe, Joseph Patrick Jones, Jeremy Melvyn Charles, Brian Flynn, Kenneth Francis Jackett, Alan Thomas Curtis (84 Paul Terence Price), Ian James Rush (64 Gordon John Davies), Michael Reginald Thomas, Robert Mark James.
Trainer: Harold Michael England
Goals: David Cooper (37 pen), Maurice Johnston (78) / Robert Mark James (47)

385. 02.05.1984   British Championship
WALES v ENGLAND 1-0 (1-0)

The Racecourse, Wrexham

Referee: David Syme (Scotland)   Attendance: 14,250

WALES: Neville Southall, David Owen Phillips, Joseph Patrick Jones, Kevin Ratcliffe, Jeffrey Hopkins, Robert Mark James, Gordon John Davies, Alan Davies, Ian James Rush, Michael Reginald Thomas, Mark Leslie Hughes.
Trainer: Harold Michael England

ENGLAND: Peter Leslie Shilton, Michael Duxburyy, Alan Philip Kennedy, Samuel Lee, Alvin Edward Martin (80 Terence William Fenwick), Mark Wright, Raymond Colin Wilkins (Cap), John Charles Gregory, Paul Anthony Walsh, Anthony Stewart Woodcock, David Armstrong (77 Luther Loide Blissett).   Manager: Robert Robson

Goal: Mark Leslie Hughes (17)

386. 22.05.1984   British Championship
WALES v NORTHERN IRELAND 1-1 (0-0)

Vetch Field, Swansea

Referee: Brian Robert McKinley (Scotland)   Att: 7,845

WALES: Neville Southall, David Owen Phillips, Joseph Patrick Jones, Kevin Ratcliffe, Jeffrey Hopkins, Alan Davies, Robert Mark James, Kenneth Francis Jackett, Gordon John Davies (Nigel Mark Vaughan), Ian James Rush, Mark Leslie Hughes.   Trainer: Harold Michael England

NORTHERN IRELAND: Patrick Anthony Jennings (38 James Archibald Platt), Malachy Martin Donaghy, Nigel Worthington, John McClelland, Gerard McElhinney, Martin Hugh Michael O'Neill (Cap), Samuel Baxter McIlroy, Gerard Joseph Armstrong, Norman Whiteside, William Robert Hamilton, Ian Edwin Stewart.   Manager: William Bingham

Goals: Mark Hughes (51) / Gerard Joseph Armstrong (75)

387. 06.06.1984
NORWAY v WALES 1-0 (0-0)

Lerkendal, Trondheim

Referee: Håkan Lundgren (Sweden)   Attendance: 15,970

NORWAY: Erik Thorstvedt, Svein Fjælberg (79 Tom Sundby), Terje Kojedal, Åge Hareide, Svein Grøndalen, Kai Erik Herlovsen, Anders Giske (66 Vidar Davidsen), Per Egil Ahlsen, Sverre Brandhaug, Arne Larsen Økland, Hallvar Thoresen (38 Arne Dokken).   Trainer: Tor Røste Fossen

WALES: Neville Southall, David Owen Phillips (30 Neil John Slatter), Joseph Patrick Jones, Kevin Ratcliffe, Jeffrey Hopkins, Brian Flynn, Robert Mark James, Peter Nicholas, Colin James Pascoe (60 Anthony Andrew Rees), Nigel Mark Vaughan (71 Glyn Peter Hodges), Kenneth Francis Jackett.
Trainer: Harold Michael England

Goal: Arne Larsen Økland (75)

388. 10.06.1984
ISRAEL v WALES 0-0

National, Ramat Gan, Tel Aviv

Referee: Gerardus Geurds (Holland)   Attendance: 3,000

ISRAEL: Boni Ginzburg, Gabriel Lasri (78 Shlomo Kirat), Nissim Barda, Avi Cohen, Hanan Azulay, Nissim Cohen (46 Uri Malmilian), Rifat Turk (46 Eli Yani), Yaacov Ekhoiz, Moshe Sinai, Gili Landau, Eli Ohana (68 Zahi Armeli).
Trainer: Yosef Mirmovich

WALES: Neville Southall, Neil John Slatter, Joseph Patrick Jones, Kevin Ratcliffe, Jeffrey Hopkins, Brian Flynn, Robert Mark James, Peter Nicholas, Colin James Pascoe (73 Andrew Ian Holden), Nigel Mark Vaughan, Kenneth Francis Jackett (67 Glyn Peter Hodges).   Trainer: Harold Michael England

389. 12.09.1984   13th World Cup Qualifiers
ICELAND v WALES 1-0 (0-0)

Laugardalsvöllur, Reykjavík

Referee: Erik Sten Jensen (Denmark)   Attendance: 10,837

ICELAND: Bjarni Sigurðsson, Þorgrímur Þráinsson, Árni Sveinsson, Magnús Bergs, Sævar Jónsson, Janus Guðlaugsson, Pétur Pétursson, Atli Eðvaldsson, Sigurður Grétarsson, Ásgeir Sigurvinsson (Cap), Guðmundur Þorbjörnsson.
Trainer: Anthony Knapp

WALES: Neville Southall, Neil John Slatter, Joseph Patrick Jones, Kevin Ratcliffe, Jeffrey Hopkins, Gordon John Davies (60 Jeremy Melvyn Charles), Kenneth Francis Jackett, Michael Reginald Thomas, Alan Davies, Robert Mark James, Mark Leslie Hughes.   Trainer: Harold Michael England

Goal: Magnús Bergs (52)

390. 17.10.1984   13th World Cup Qualifiers
SPAIN v WALES 3-0 (1-0)

Benito Villamarín, Sevilla

Referee: Erik Fredriksson (Sweden)   Attendance: 42,500

SPAIN: Luis Miguel Arkonada (Cap), Juan Antonio Señor, Andoni Goikoetxea, Antonio Maceda, José Antonio Camacho, Víctor Muñoz, Francisco Javier López (33 Roberto Fernández), Rafael Gordillo, Francisco José Carrasco, Emilio Butragueño, Hipólito Rincón (81 Julio Alberto Moreno).
Trainer: Miguel Muñoz

WALES: Neville Southall, Neil John Slatter, David Owen Phillips, Kevin Ratcliffe, Jeremy Melvyn Charles, Kenneth Francis Jackett, Robert Mark James, Peter Nicholas, Michael Reginald Thomas (60 Nigel Mark Vaughan), Mark Leslie Hughes, Alan Thomas Curtis.
Trainer: Harold Michael England

Goals: Hipólito Rincón (7), Francisco José Carrasco (83), Emilio Butragueño (89)

391. 14.11.1984   13th World Cup Qualifiers
WALES v ICELAND 2-1 (1-0)
Ninian Park, Cardiff

Referee: Eamonn Farrell (Republic of Ireland)   Att: 10,506

WALES: Neville Southall, Neil John Slatter, David Owen Phillips, Kevin Ratcliffe, Jeremy Melvyn Charles (30 Jeffrey Hopkins), Kenneth Francis Jackett, Robert Mark James, Alan Davies, Michael Reginald Thomas, Ian James Rush, Mark Leslie Hughes.   Trainer: Harold Michael England

ICELAND: Bjarni Sigurðsson, Þorgrímur Þráinsson, Árni Sveinsson, Magnús Bergs, Sævar Jónsson, Siðurdur Jónsson, Pétur Pétursson (Cap), Ragnar Margeirsson (82 Gunnar Gíslason), Sigurður Grétarsson (67 Njáll Eiðsson), Arnór Guðjohnsen, Guðmundur Þorbjörnsson.
Trainer: Anthony Knapp

Goals: Michael Reginald Thomas (35), Mark Hughes (63) / Pétur Pétursson (55)

392. 26.02.1985
WALES v NORWAY 1-1 (1-1)
The Racecourse, Wrexham

Referee: Robert Stewart (Northern Ireland)   Att: 4,532

WALES: Neville Southall, Neil John Slatter, Joseph Patrick Jones, Kevin Ratcliffe (Cap), Kenneth Francis Jackett, Robert Mark James, Alan Davies (46 Howard Keith Pritchard), Peter Nicholas, Alan Thomas Curtis, Ian James Rush, Mark Leslie Hughes.   Trainer: Harold Michael England

NORWAY: Erik Thorstvedt, Hans Hermann Henriksen, Terje Kojedal (53 Svein Fjælberg), Åge Hareide, Per Edmund Mordt, Vidar Davidsen, Per Egil Ahlsen, Kjetil Osvold, Arne Larsen Økland, Ulf Moen (63 Joar Vaadal, 88 Egil Johansen), Hallvar Thoresen.   Trainer: Tor Røste Fossen

Goals: Ian James Rush (#) / Per Egil Ahlsen (6)

393. 27.03.1985   13th World Cup Qualifiers
SCOTLAND v WALES 0-1 (0-1)
Hampden Park, Glasgow

Referee: Alexis Ponnet (Belgium)   Attendance: 62,424

SCOTLAND: James Leighton, Stephen Nicol, Arthur Richard Albiston (57 Alan David Hansen), William Fergus Miller, Alexander McLeish, David Cooper, Graeme James Souness (Cap), Paul Michael Lyons McStay (75 Charles Nicholas), James Bett, Kenneth Mathieson Dalglish, Maurice Johnston.
Manager: John Stein

WALES: Neville Southall, Neil John Slatter, Joseph Patrick Jones, Kevin Ratcliffe, Kenneth Francis Jackett, David Owen Phillips, Robert Mark James, Peter Nicholas, Michael Reginald Thomas, Ian James Rush, Mark Leslie Hughes.
Trainer: Harold Michael England

Goal: Ian James Rush (37)

394. 30.04.1985   13th World Cup Qualifiers
WALES v SPAIN 3-0 (1-0)
The Racecourse, Wrexham

Referee: Johannes Nicolaas Ignatius "Jan" Keizer (Holland)   Attendance: 23,494

WALES: Neville Southall, Neil John Slatter, Patrick William Roger Van Den Hauwe, Kevin Ratcliffe (Cap), Kenneth Francis Jackett, David Owen Phillips, Robert Mark James, Peter Nicholas, Michael Reginald Thomas, Ian James Rush, Mark Leslie Hughes.   Trainer: Harold Michael England

SPAIN: Luis Miguel Arkonada (Cap), Gerardo Miranda, Andoni Goikoetxea, Antonio Maceda, Julio Alberto Moreno, Jesús Iñigo Liceranzu, Víctor Muñoz, Ricardo Gallego (46 Ramón María Calderé), Rafael Gordillo, José Francisco Rojo, Hipólito Rincón (57 Francisco Javier Clos).
Trainer: Miguel Muñoz Mozún

Goals: Ian James Rush (44, 86), Mark Leslie Hughes (53)

395. 05.06.1985
NORWAY v WALES 4-2 (3-1)
Brann, Bergen

Referee: Ulf Eriksson (Sweden)   Attendance: 5,596

NORWAY: Ola By Rise, Hans Hermann Henriksen (74 Hans Martin Brandtun), Trond Sollied, Åge Hareide, Per Edmund Mordt, Arne Erlandsen, Per Egil Ahlsen, Kai Erik Herlovsen, Vidar Davidsen, Arne Larsen Økland (79 Sverre Brandhaug), Pål Jacobsen.   Trainer: Tor Røste Fossen

WALES: Neville Southall (67 Andrzej Edward Niedzwiecki), Neil John Slatter, Jeffrey Hopkins (46 Clayton Graham Blackmore), Joseph Patrick Jones (Cap), Robert Mark James, Kenneth Francis Jackett, David Owen Phillips (67 Steven Robert Lowndes), Peter Nicholas, Mark Leslie Hughes, Michael Reginald Thomas, Steven John Lovell (67 Alan Thomas Curtis).   Trainer: Harold Michael England

Goals: Trond Sollied (3), Arne Larsen Økland (9), Neil Slatter (18 own goal), Pål Jacobsen (54) / Steven John Lovell (#), Mark Leslie Hughes (#)

396. 10.09.1985   13th World Cup Qualifiers
WALES v SCOTLAND   1-1 (1-0)
Ninian Park, Cardiff
Referee: Johannes Nicolaas Ignatius "Jan" Keizer (Holland)
Attendance: 39,500

WALES: Neville Southall, Joseph Patrick Jones, Patrick William Roger Van Den Hauwe, Kevin Ratcliffe (Cap), Kenneth Francis Jackett, Robert Mark James (80 Steven John Lovell), David Owen Phillips, Peter Nicholas, Mark Leslie Hughes, Michael Reginald Thomas (83 Clayton Graham Blackmore), Ian James Rush.
Trainer: Harold Michael England

SCOTLAND: James Leighton (46 Alan Roderick Rough), Richard Charles Gough, Maurice Daniel Robert Malpas, William Fergus Miller (Cap), Alexander McLeish, Gordon David Strachan (61 David Cooper), Stephen Nicol, Robert Sime Aitken, James Bett, David Robert Speedie, Graeme Marshall Sharp.   Manager: John Stein

Goals: Mark Leslie Hughes (13) / David Cooper (81 pen)

397. 16.10.1985
WALES v HUNGARY   0-3 (0-1)
Ninian Park, Cardiff
Referee: George Hyndes (Northern Ireland)   Att: 3,505

WALES: Neville Southall, Joseph Patrick Jones (56 Neil John Slatter), Patrick William Roger Van Den Hauwe, Kevin Ratcliffe (Cap), Kenneth Francis Jackett, David Owen Phillips, Peter Nicholas, Alan Davies (56 Clayton Graham Blackmore), Mark Leslie Hughes, Michael Reginald Thomas, Alan Thomas Curtis (71 Steven John Lovell).
Trainer: Harold Michael England

HUNGARY: Péter Disztl, László Disztl, Antal Róth, Imre Garaba, Zoltán Péter, Sándor Sallai, Tibor Nyilasi, Antal Nagy (46 László Gyimesi), Lajos Détári, Márton Esterházy (75 Kálmán Kovács), Gyula Hajszán.   Trainer: György Mezey

Goals: Márton Esterházy (8), Gyula Hajszán (52), Lajos Détári (89)

398. 25.02.1986
SAUDI ARABIA v WALES   1-2 (0-0)
Dahran
Referee: Farid Rabie (Saudi Arabia)   Attendance: 20,000

SAUDI ARABIA: Samir Suleiman, Nasser Al-Mansour, Ahmed Jamil, Samir Abdul Sattar, Essam Sefian, Yousef Khamis (56 Abdul Gamad), Yousef Al-Thani, Ismail Hatemi, Jamal Mohammed (81 Abdullah Zaki), Abdullah Al-Harbi, Saeed Al-Nefisa.

WALES: Neville Southall, Neil John Slatter, Kevin Ratcliffe, Kenneth Francis Jackett, Mark Aizlewood, Robert Mark James (62 Steven Robert Lowndes), Peter Nicholas, David Owen Phillips (78 David Michael Williams), Clayton Graham Blackmore (62 Michael Reginald Thomas), Gordon John Davies (85 Malcolm Allen), Ian James Rush.
Trainer: Harold Michael England

Goals: Al-Thani (66 pen) /
Neil John Slatter (47), Gordon John Davies (60)

399. 26.03.1986
REPUBLIC OF IRELAND v WALES   0-1 (0-1)
Lansdowne Road, Dublin
Referee: Kenneth Johnston Hope (Scotland)   Att: 16,500

IRELAND: Gerald Joseph Peyton, David Francis Langan, James Martin Beglin, John Christopher Patrick Anderson (50 Michael Joseph McCarthy), David Anthony O'Leary, William Brady (Cap), Paul McGrath, Raymond James Houghton, John William Aldridge, Michael John Robinson (66 Patrick Byrne II), Ronald Andrew Whelan.   Manager: John Charlton

WALES: Neville Southall (66 Anthony Joseph Norman), Robert Mark James, Kenneth Francis Jackett, Peter Nicholas, Jeremy Melvyn Charles, Joseph Patrick Jones, Steven Robert Lowndes, David Owen Phillips, Ian James Rush, Clayton Graham Blackmore, Gordon John Davies (61 Dean Nicholas Saunders).   Trainer: Harold Michael England

Goal: Ian James Rush (17)

400. 21.04.1986
WALES v URUGUAY   0-0
The Racecourse, Wrexham
Referee: Oliver Donnelly (Northern Ireland)   Att: 11,154

WALES: Anthony Joseph Norman, Robert Mark James, Clayton Graham Blackmore, Kevin Ratcliffe, Joseph Patrick Jones, David Michael Williams, Steven Robert Lowndes, Peter Nicholas, Ian James Rush, David Owen Phillips, Mark Leslie Hughes.   Trainer: Harold Michael England

URUGUAY: Rodolfo Sergio Rodríguez, Víctor Hugo Diogo, José Alberto Batista, Nelson Daniel Gutiérrez, Eduardo Mario Acevedo, Miguel Angel Bossio (Mario Daniel Saralegui), Antonio Alzamendi, Jorge Walter Barrios, Enzo Francéscoli, Sergio Rodolfo Santín, Jorge Orosmán Da Silva.
Trainer: Omar Borrás

401. 10.05.1986
CANADA v WALES 2-0 (2-0)
Varsity, Toronto
Referee: D. Brummitt (Canada)   Attendance: 13,142
CANADA: Paul Dolan, Colin Fyfe Miller, Randy Ragan, Randolph Fitzgerald Samuel, Bruce Wilson, Gregory Ion, Jamie Lowery, Gerard Gray, Paul James, Dale William Mitchell (George Pakos), Igor Vrablic.
Trainer: Anthony Keith Waiters
WALES: Anthony Joseph Norman (Andrew Gerald Dibble), Robert Mark James, Neil John Slatter (Mark Rosslyn Bowen), Kenneth Francis Jackett, Joseph Patrick Jones, David Michael Williams, Steven Robert Lowndes, Peter Nicholas, Dean Nicholas Saunders, Mark Aizlewood, Malcolm Allen (Steven John Lovell).   Trainer: Harold Michael England
Goals: Igor Vrablic (#), Gerard Gray (#)

402. 19.05.1986
CANADA v WALES 0-3 (0-1)
Swangard, Burnaby, Vancouver
Referee: James Douglas (Canada)   Attendance: 9,007
CANADA: Paul Dolan, Robert Lenarduzzi, Ian Bridge (Randolph Fitzgerald Samuel), Terence Moore, Bruce Wilson, Gerard Gray, Randy Ragan, Mike Sweeney (David McDonald Norman), Carl Valentine, Igor Vrablic (George Pakos), Dale William Mitchell (Branko Segota).
Trainer: Anthony Keith Waiters
WALES: Andrew Gerald Dibble, Robert Mark James, Joseph Patrick Jones, Kenneth Francis Jackett, Neil John Slatter, Steven Robert Lowndes, Peter Nicholas, David Michael Williams (Mark Rosslyn Bowen), Mark Aizlewood, Dean Nicholas Saunders, Steven John Lovell (Malcolm Allen).
Trainer: Harold Michael England
Goals: Dean Nicholas Saunders (11, 49), Malcolm Allen (81)

403. 10.09.1986   8th European Champs Qualifiers
FINLAND v WALES 1-1 (1-0)
Olympiastadion, Helsinki
Referee: Gerald Losert (Austria)   Attendance: 9,840
FINLAND: Kari Laukkanen, Jari Europaeus, Esa Pekonen, Jukka Ikäläinen (Cap), Erkka Petäjä, Pasi Tauriainen, Markus Törnvall, Kari Ukkonen, Ari Hjelm, Mika Lipponen (76 Ari Valvee), Jari Rantanen.   Trainer: Martti Kuusela
WALES: Martin Richard Thomas, Kenneth Francis Jackett, Kevin Ratcliffe, Jeremy Melvyn Charles, Robert Mark James, Peter Nicholas, Clayton Graham Blackmore (81 Steven Robert Lowndes), Mark Aizlewood, David Michael Williams (52 Neil John Slatter), Ian James Rush, Dean Nicholas Saunders.
Trainer: Harold Michael England
Goals: Ari Hjelm (11) / Neil John Slatter (68)

404. 18.02.1987
WALES v SOVIET UNION 0-0
Vetch Field, Swansea
Referee: Andrew Ritchie (Northern Ireland)   Att: 17,617
WALES: Neville Southall, Robert Mark James, Clayton Graham Blackmore, Kevin Ratcliffe (Cap), Patrick William Roger Van Den Hauwe, Alan Thomas Curtis (58 Dean Nicholas Saunders), Peter Nicholas, Mark Aizlewood, Glyn Peter Hodges, Ian James Rush, Mark Leslie Hughes.
Trainer: Harold Michael England
SOVIET UNION: Viktor Chanov, Tengiz Sulakvelidze, Aleksandr Chivadze, Sergey Baltacha, Anatoliy Demyanenko (Cap), Oleg Kuznetzov, Pavel Yakovenko, Vasiliy Ratz, Aleksandr Zavarov, Vadim Evtushenko (63 Sergey Gotzmanov), Igor Belanov (72 Oleg Protasov).
Trainer: Valeriy Lobanovskiy

405. 01.04.1987   8th European Champs Qualifiers
WALES v FINLAND 4-0 (2-0)
The Racecourse, Wrexham
Referee: Ignatius van Swieten (Holland)   Attendance: 7,696
WALES: Neville Southall, Kenneth Francis Jackett, Clayton Graham Blackmore, Patrick William Roger Van Den Hauwe (11 Mark Aizlewood), Kevin Ratcliffe (Cap), David Owen Phillips, Peter Nicholas, Robert Mark James, Glyn Peter Hodges, Ian James Rush, Andrew Mark Jones.
Trainer: Harold Michael England
FINLAND: Kari Laukkanen, Jari Europaeus, Esa Pekonen, Jukka Ikäläinen (Cap), Erkka Petäjä, Hannu Turunen (70 Ismo Lius), Erik Holmgren, Pasi Tauriainen, Petri Tiainen (60 Mika Lipponen), Ari Hjelm, Jari Rantanen.
Trainer: Martti Kuusela
Goals: Ian James Rush (14), Glyn Peter Hodges (28), David Owen Phillips (64), Andrew Mark Jones (73)

406. 29.04.1987   8th European Champs Qualifiers
WALES v CZECHOSLOVAKIA 1-1 (0-0)
The Racecourse, Wrexham
Referee: Krzysztof Czemarmazowicz (Poland)   Att: 14,150
WALES: Neville Southall, Neil John Slatter, Clayton Graham Blackmore, Patrick William Roger Van Den Hauwe, Kevin Ratcliffe (Cap), Peter Nicholas, David Owen Phillips, Robert Mark James, Glyn Peter Hodges, Ian James Rush, Mark Leslie Hughes (76 Andrew Mark Jones).
Trainer: Harold Michael England
CZECHOSLOVAKIA: Luděk Mikloško, Ivan Hašek, František Straka, Jan Fiala (Cap), Josef Novák, Luboš Kubík, Petr Janečka (88 Milan Luhový), Jozef Chovanec, Tomáš Skuhravý (81 Miroslav Kadlec), Karel Kula, Ivo Knoflíček.
Trainer: Josef Masopust
Goals: Ian James Rush (83) / Ivo Knoflíček (75)

407. 09.09.1987   8th European Champs Qualifiers
WALES v DENMARK 1-0 (1-0)
Ninian Park, Cardiff
Referee: Siegfried Kirschen (East Germany)   Att: 20,535
WALES: Neville Southall, Neil John Slatter, Clayton Graham Blackmore, Kevin Ratcliffe (Cap), Patrick William Roger Van Den Hauwe, David Owen Phillips, Robert Mark James (88 Barry Horne), Peter Nicholas, Andrew Mark Jones, Mark Leslie Hughes, Glyn Peter Hodges (73 Mark Aizlewood). Trainer: Harold Michael England
DENMARK: Troels Rasmussen, John Sivebæk, Ivan Nielsen, Morten Olsen (Cap), Kent Nielsen, Søren Lerby, Klaus Berggreen, Jens Jørn Bertelsen, Flemming Povlsen (66 Claus Nielsen), Preben Elkjær-Larsen, Michael Laudrup (46 John Jensen).   Trainer: Josef Piontek
Goal: Mark Leslie Hughes (19)

408. 14.10.1987   8th European Champs Qualifiers
DENMARK v WALES 1-0 (0-0)
Idraetsparken, København
Referee: Ion Igna (Romania)   Attendance: 44,500
DENMARK: Troels Rasmussen, John Sivebæk, Morten Olsen (Cap), Ivan Nielsen, Jan Heintze (46 Flemming Povlsen), Per Frimann, John Jensen, Søren Lerby, Jesper Olsen, Michael Laudrup (85 Lars Olsen), Preben Elkjær-Larsen. Trainer: Josef Piontek
WALES: Andrzej Edward Niedzwiecki, Neil John Slatter, Clayton Graham Blackmore, Kevin Ratcliffe (Cap), Patrick William Roger Van Den Hauwe, David Owen Phillips, Robert Mark James (73 Andrew Mark Jones), Peter Nicholas, Ian James Rush, Mark Leslie Hughes, Kenneth Francis Jackett (65 Glyn Peter Hodges).   Trainer: Harold Michael England
Goal: Preben Elkjær-Larsen (50)

409. 11.11.1987   8th European Champs Qualifiers
CZECHOSLOVAKIA v WALES 2-0 (1-0)
Sparta, Praha
Referee: Erik Fredriksson (Sweden)   Attendance: 6,443
CZECHOSLOVAKIA: Luděk Mikloško, Josef Novák, Miroslav Kadlec, František Straka, Stanislav Levý, Ivan Hašek, Jozef Chovanec (Cap), Ľubomír Moravčík (71 Karel Kula), Michal Bílek, Tomáš Skuhravý, Ivo Knoflíček. Trainer: Josef Masopust
WALES: Neville Southall, Neil John Slatter (46 Andrew Mark Jones), Kenneth Francis Jackett, Kevin Ratcliffe (Cap), Patrick William Roger Van Den Hauwe, David Owen Phillips, David Geraint Williams, Peter Nicholas, Ian James Rush, Mark Leslie Hughes, Clayton Graham Blackmore (66 Glyn Peter Hodges). Trainer: Harold Michael England
Goals: Ivo Knoflíček (32), Michal Bílek (90)

410. 23.03.1988
WALES v YUGOSLAVIA 1-2 (1-1)
Vetch Field, Swansea
Referee: Robert Stewart (Northern Ireland)   Att: 5,985
WALES: Neville Southall, Barry Horne (80 Gareth David Hall), Clayton Graham Blackmore, Patrick William Roger Van Den Hauwe, Kenneth Francis Jackett, David Owen Phillips, David Geraint Williams, Peter Nicholas (Cap), Ian James Rush, Robert Mark James (68 Mark Rosslyn Bowen), Dean Nicholas Saunders.   Trainer: David Williams
YUGOSLAVIA: Vladan Radača, Zoran Vulić, Dragoljub Brnović, Srećko Katanec, Faruk Hadžibegić, Ljubomir Radanović, Dragan Stojković (85 Miodrag Krivokapić), Dejan Savićević, Dragan Jakovljević, Mehmed Baždarević (Cap), Haris Škoro (74 Darko Pančev).   Trainer: Ivan Osim
Goals: Dean Nicholas Saunders (7) / Dragan Stojković (43), Dragan Jakovljević (71)

411. 27.04.1988
SWEDEN v WALES 4-1 (2-1)
Råsunda, Stockholm
Referee: Gerald Losert (Austria)   Attendance: 11,656
SWEDEN: Thomas Ravelli, Roland Nilsson, Glenn Ingvar Hysén, Peter Larsson, Dennis Schiller, Jonas Thern, Glenn Peter Strömberg (80 Stefan Rehn), Robert Prytz, Anders Erik Limpár, Hans Eskilsson, Hans Holmqvist. Trainer: Olle Nordin
WALES: Neville Southall, David Owen Phillips, Clayton Graham Blackmore, Mark Aizlewood, Kenneth Francis Jackett, David Geraint Williams, Glyn Peter Hodges, Peter Nicholas (Cap) (78 Barry Horne), Ian James Rush, Mark Leslie Hughes, Dean Nicholas Saunders (78 Steven Robert Lowndes). Manager: Terence Charles Yorath
Goals: Hans Holmqvist (18, 56), Glenn Peter Strömberg (24), Hans Eskilsson (67) / Glyn Peter Hodges (27)

412. 01.06.1988
MALTA v WALES 2-3 (2-1)
National, Ta'Qali
Referee: Edgar Azzopardi (Malta)   Attendance: 4,836
MALTA: David Cluett, Edwin Camilleri, Alex Azzopardi, Joseph Galea, Joseph Brincat (75 Martin Scicluna), John Buttigieg (Cap), Carmel Busuttil, Charles Scerri, David Carabott (60 Leo Refalo), Charles Micallef II (36 Emanuel Lowell), Michael Degiorgio.   Trainer: Horst Heese
WALES: Anthony Joseph Norman, Gareth David Hall, Clayton Graham Blackmore, David Geraint Williams, Mark Aizlewood, Neil John Slatter, Dean Nicholas Saunders (78 Glyn Peter Hodges), Barry Horne, Ian James Rush (Cap), Mark Leslie Hughes, Alan Davies. Manager: Terence Charles Yorath
Goals: Carmel Busuttil (14, 21) / Barry Horne (9), Mark Hughes (53), Ian James Rush (74)

413. 04.06.1988
ITALY v WALES 0-1 (0-1)

Rigamonti, Brescia

Referee: Karl-Heinz Tritschler (West Germany)   Att: 18,931

ITALY: Walter Zenga, Giuseppe Bergomi (Cap), Paolo Maldini, Franco Baresi, Riccardo Ferri, Carlo Ancelotti (57 Luigi De Agostini), Roberto Donadoni (70 Ruggiero Rizzitelli), Fernando De Napoli, Roberto Mancini, Giuseppe Giannini, Gianluca Vialli (46 Alessandro Altobelli).
Trainer: Azeglio Vicini

WALES: Anthony Joseph Norman, Gareth David Hall, Clayton Graham Blackmore, David Geraint Williams (75 Dean Nicholas Saunders), Patrick William Roger Van Den Hauwe, Neil John Slatter, Alan Davies, Barry Horne (60 Glyn Peter Hodges), Ian James Rush (Cap), Mark Leslie Hughes, Mark Aizlewood.   Manager: Terence Charles Yorath

Goal: Ian James Rush (38)

414. 14.09.1988   14th World Cup Qualifiers
HOLLAND v WALES 1-0 (0-0)

Olympisch, Amsterdam

Referee: Jan Damgaard (Denmark)   Attendance: 58,000

HOLLAND: Hans van Breukelen, Ronald Koeman, Frank Rijkaard, Adri van Tiggelen, Berry van Aerle, Jan Wouters, Erwin Koeman, Gerald Vanenburg (67 Wim Kieft), Hendrie Krüzen, Ruud Gullit (Cap), Marco van Basten.
Trainer: Thijs Lijbregts

WALES: Neville Southall, Gareth David Hall, Clayton Graham Blackmore, Peter Nicholas, Alan Richard Knill, David Geraint Williams, Barry Horne, Alan Davies, Mark Aizlewood, Ian James Rush (Cap), Mark Leslie Hughes (76 Dean Nicholas Saunders).   Manager: Terence Charles Yorath

Goal: Ruud Gullit (83)

415. 19.10.1988   14th World Cup Qualifiers
WALES v FINLAND 2-2 (2-2)

Ninian Park, Cardiff

Referee: Guðmundur Haraldsson (Iceland)   Att: 9,603

WALES: Neville Southall, Gareth David Hall (59 Mark Rosslyn Bowen), Clayton Graham Blackmore, Peter Nicholas, Patrick William Roger Van Den Hauwe, Kevin Ratcliffe (Cap), Colin James Pascoe, Dean Nicholas Saunders, Ian James Rush, Mark Leslie Hughes, Barry Horne.
Manager: Terence Charles Yorath

FINLAND: Olavi Huttunen, Esa Pekonen, Aki Lahtinen, Jari Europaeus, Markku Kanerva, Marko Myyry (86 Mika Lipponen), Erik Holmgren, Kari Ukkonen, Erkka Petäjä (61 Jari Rantanen), Mika-Matti Paatelainen, Ari Hjelm.
Trainer: Jukka Vakkila

Goals: Dean Saunders (24 pen), Aki Lahtinen (40 own goal) / Kari Ukkonen (8), Mika-Matti Paatelainen (45)

416. 08.02.1989
ISRAEL v WALES 3-3 (2-1)

National, Ramat Gan, Tel Aviv

Referee: Ulf Eriksson (Sweden)   Attendance: 6,000

ISRAEL: Shuli Gilardi, Eitan Aharoni, Yehuda Amar, Nir Alon, David Pizanti, Efraim Davidi, Nir Klinger, Moshe Sinai, Nir Levin (80 Reuoven Atar), Roni Rosenthal, Igal Menahem (46 Eli Driks).   Trainers: Itzhak Shneor & Yaacov Grundman

WALES: Andrew Gerald Dibble, Gareth David Hall (68 Neil John Slatter), Mark Rosslyn Bowen, Peter Nicholas, Kevin Ratcliffe (Cap), David Geraint Williams (68 Malcolm Allen), Barry Horne, Clayton Graham Blackmore, Mark Leslie Hughes, Dean Nicholas Saunders, Colin James Pascoe.
Manager: Terence Charles Yorath

Goals: Barry Horne (11), Eitan Aharoni (57 own goal), Malcolm Allen (87)

417. 26.04.1989
WALES v SWEDEN 0-2 (0-1)

The Racecourse, Wrexham

Referee: John Purcell (Republic of Ireland)   Att: 7,292

WALES: Neville Southall, David Owen Phillips (62 Mark Aizlewood), Mark Rosslyn Bowen, Peter Nicholas, Patrick William Roger Van Den Hauwe, Kevin Ratcliffe (Cap), Dean Nicholas Saunders, Barry Horne, Ian James Rush, Mark Leslie Hughes, David Geraint Williams.
Manager: Terence Charles Yorath

SWEDEN: Thomas Ravelli, Roland Nilsson, Peter Lönn, Dennis Schiller, Roger Ljung, Anders Erik Limpár, Jonas Thern, Robert Prytz, Joakim Nilsson, Mats Magnusson (52 Johnny Ekström), Stefan Pettersson.   Trainer: Olle Nordin

Goal: Dennis Schiller (30), Kevin Ratcliffe (56 own goal)

418. 31.05.1989   14th World Cup Qualifiers
WALES v WEST GERMANY 0-0

The Arms Park, Cardiff

Referee: Carlos da Silva Valente (Portugal)   Att: 30,000

WALES: Neville Southall, David Owen Phillips, Clayton Graham Blackmore, Kevin Ratcliffe (Cap) (80 Mark Rosslyn Bowen), Mark Aizlewood, Peter Nicholas, Barry Horne, David Geraint Williams (80 Colin James Pascoe), Dean Nicholas Saunders, Ian James Rush, Mark Leslie Hughes.
Manager: Terence Charles Yorath

WEST GERMANY: Bodo Illgner, Thomas Berthold, Stefan Reuter, Alois Reinhardt, Guido Buchwald, Andreas Brehme, Thomas Häßler, Holger Fach, Andreas Möller, Karlheinz Riedle (78 Jürgen Klinsmann), Rudolf Völler (Cap).
Trainer: Franz Beckenbauer

419. 06.09.1989   14th World Cup Qualifiers
FINLAND v WALES 1-0 (0-0)
Olympiastadion, Helsinki
Referee: Siegfried Kirschen (East Germany)   Att: 7,480
FINLAND: Kari Laukkanen, Aki Lahtinen, Ari Heikkinen, Jari Europaeus, Erik Holmgren, Kimmo Tarkkio, Kari Ukkonen (82 Pasi Tauriainen), Jukka Ikäläinen, Mika-Matti Paatelainen (65 Markus Törnvall), Mika Lipponen, Marko Myyry.   Trainer: Jukka Vakkila
WALES: Neville Southall, David Owen Phillips, Clayton Graham Blackmore, Kevin Ratcliffe (Cap), Mark Aizlewood, Peter Nicholas (88 Gavin Terence Maguire), Dean Nicholas Saunders, David Geraint Williams (80 Mark Rosslyn Bowen), Ian James Rush, Mark Leslie Hughes, Alan Davies. Manager: Terence Charles Yorath

Goal: Mika Lipponen (50)

420. 11.10.1989   14th World Cup Qualifiers
WALES v HOLLAND 1-2 (0-1)
Ninian Park, Cardiff
Referee: Helmut Kohl (Austria)   Attendance: 9,025
WALES: Neville Southall (Cap), Mark Rosslyn Bowen, Clayton Graham Blackmore, Peter Nicholas, Jeffrey Hopkins, Gavin Terence Maguire, Dean Nicholas Saunders, David Owen Phillips, Iwan Wyn Roberts (64 Andrew Mark Jones), David Geraint Williams (85 Colin James Pascoe), Malcolm Allen. Manager: Terence Charles Yorath
HOLLAND: Hans van Breukelen, Graeme Rutjes, Ronald Koeman (Cap), Addick Koot, Berry van Aerle, Jan Wouters, Johnny van't Schip, Wim Hofkens, Wim Kieft, Frank Rijkaard (46 Johnny Bosman), Rob Witschge (71 Marco van Basten). Trainer: Thijs Lijbregts

Goal: Mark Rosslyn Bowen (87) /
Graeme Rutjes (12), Johnny Bosman (72)

421. 15.11.1989   14th World Cup Qualifiers
WEST GERMANY v WALES 2-1 (1-1)
Müngersdorfer, Köln
Referee: Michel Vautrot (France)   Attendance: 60,000
WEST GERMANY: Bodo Illgner, Klaus Augenthaler (46 Alois Reinhardt), Stefan Reuter, Guido Buchwald, Andreas Brehme, Thomas Häßler, Hans Dorfner, Andreas Möller (82 Uwe Bein), Pierre Littbarski (Cap), Jürgen Klinsmann, Rudolf Völler.   Trainer: Franz Beckenbauer
WALES: Neville Southall (Cap), Mark Rosslyn Bowen (65 Barry Horne), Clayton Graham Blackmore, David Owen Phillips, Mark Aizlewood, Andrew Roger Melville (80 Colin James Pascoe), Dean Nicholas Saunders, Peter Nicholas, Mark Leslie Hughes, Malcolm Allen, Gavin Terence Maguire. Manager: Terence Charles Yorath

Goals: Rudolf Völler (25), Thomas Häßler (48) /
Malcolm Allen (11)

422. 28.03.1990
REPUBLIC OF IRELAND v WALES 1-0 (0-0)
Lansdowne Road, Dublin
Referee: Alan Gunn (England)   Attendance: 41,350
IRELAND: Patrick Bonner, Christopher Barry Morris, Michael Joseph McCarthy, Kevin Bernard Moran (75 David Anthony O'Leary), Stephen Staunton (67 Christopher William Gerard Hughton), Ronald Andrew Whelan (Cap) (46 Kevin Mark Sheedy), Andrew David Townsend, John Frederick Byrne, Bernard Joseph Slaven, Anthony Guy Cascarino, John Joseph Sheridan.   Manager: John Charlton
WALES: Neville Southall, Gareth David Hall, David Owen Phillips, Peter Nicholas (Cap), Mark Aizlewood, Andrew Roger Melville, Gavin Terence Maguire, Barry Horne, Ian James Rush, Malcolm Allen, Alan Davies. Manager: Terence Charles Yorath

Goal: Bernard Joseph Slaven (86)

423. 25.04.1990
SWEDEN v WALES 4-2 (2-1)
Råsunda, Stockholm
Referee: Simo Ruokonen (Finland)   Attendance: 13,981
SWEDEN: Thomas Ravelli, Roland Nilsson, Glenn Ingvar Hysén, Peter Larsson, Roger Ljung, Leif Engqvist, Anders Erik Limpár, Klas Ingesson, Stefan Schwarz, Tomas Brolin, Mats Magnusson (69 Stefan Pettersson).   Trainer: Olle Nordin
WALES: Neville Southall (Cap), David Owen Phillips, Mark Rosslyn Bowen, Andrew Roger Melville, Brian John Law, Gavin Terence Maguire, Peter Nicholas, Barry Horne, Malcolm Allen, Dean Nicholas Saunders, Glyn Peter Hodges. Manager: Terence Charles Yorath

Goals: Tomas Brolin (19, 25), Klas Ingesson (54, 73) /
Dean Nicholas Saunders (14, 59)

424. 20.05.1990
WALES v COSTA RICA 1-0 (1-0)
Ninian Park, Cardiff
Referee: Arturo Martino (Switzerland)   Attendance: 5,977
WALES: Neville Southall (Cap), Paul John Bodin (75 Gary Andrew Speed), Clayton Graham Blackmore, Peter Nicholas, Eric Young (70 Andrew Roger Melville), Mark Aizlewood, Jeffrey Hopkins, Barry Horne, Dean Nicholas Saunders, Mark Leslie Hughes (75 Malcolm Allen), Glyn Peter Hodges. Manager: Terence Charles Yorath
COSTA RICA: Gabelo Conejo, Germán Chavarría, Mauricio Montero, Róger Flores, José Carlos Chaves, Héctor Marchena, Juan Cayasso, Aléxandre Guimarães (46 Rónald Marín), Miguel Davis, Oscar Ramírez (85 Rónald González), Hernán Medford (46 José Jaikel).   Trainer: Bora Milutinović

Goal: Dean Nicholas Saunders (10)

425. 11.09.1990
DENMARK v WALES 1-0 (0-0)

Idraetsparken, København

Referee: Esa Palsi (Finland)   Attendance: 8,700

DENMARK: Peter Schmeichel, John Sivebæk, Kent Nielsen, Lars Olsen (Cap), Henrik Andersen, John Larsen, Jan Bartram (73 Jesper Olsen), Kim Vilfort, Flemming Povlsen, Bent Christensen (46 Jan Mølby), Brian Laudrup.
Trainer: Richard Møller Nielsen

WALES: Neville Southall, David Owen Phillips, Paul John Bodin, Mark Aizlewood, Eric Young, Kevin Ratcliffe, Dean Nicholas Saunders, Barry Horne, Ian James Rush, Mark Leslie Hughes, Gary Andrew Speed (69 Peter Nicholas).
Manager: Terence Charles Yorath

Goal: Brian Laudrup (64)

426. 17.10.1990   9th European Champs Qualifiers
WALES v BELGIUM 3-1 (1-1)

The Arms Park, Cardiff

Referee: Kurt Röthlisberger (Switzerland)   Att: 12,000

WALES: Neville Southall, Paul John Bodin, Clayton Graham Blackmore, Mark Aizlewood, Eric Young, Kevin Ratcliffe, Dean Nicholas Saunders, Barry Horne, Peter Nicholas, Ian James Rush, Mark Leslie Hughes, Dean Nicholas Saunders.
Manager: Terence Charles Yorath

BELGIUM: Michel Preud'homme, Eric Gerets, Georges Grün, Michel De Wolf, Bruno Versavel, Marc Emmers, Stéphane Demol, Frank Richard Vander Elst, Luc Nilis (73 Marc Wilmots), Vincenzo Scifo, Jan Ceulemans (Cap).
Trainer: Guy Thys

Goals: Ian James Rush (29), Dean Nicholas Saunders (86), Mark Leslie Hughes (88) / Bruno Versavel (27)

427. 14.11.1990   9th European Champs Qualifiers
LUXEMBOURG v WALES 0-1 (0-1)

Municipal, Luxembourg

Referee: Jiří Ulrich (Czechoslovakia)   Attendance: 7,000

LUXEMBOURG: John van Rijswijck, Théo Malget, Marcel Bossi, Marc Birsens, Pierre Petry, Patrick Morocutti (59 Armin Krings), Guy Hellers, Jean-Paul Girres, Jeff Saibene, Carlo Weis, Robert Langers.   Trainer: Paul Philipp

WALES: Neville Southall, Paul John Bodin, Clayton Graham Blackmore, Mark Aizlewood, Eric Young, Kevin Ratcliffe, Barry Horne, Peter Nicholas, Ian James Rush (83 Gary Andrew Speed), Mark Leslie Hughes, Dean Nicholas Saunders (89 Malcolm Allen).   Manager: Terence Charles Yorath

Goal: Ian James Rush (15)

428. 06.02.1991
WALES v REPUBLIC OF IRELAND 0-3 (0-1)

The Racecourse, Wrexham

Referee: Frederick McKnight (Northern Ireland)   Att: 9,168

WALES: Neville Southall, Gareth David Hall, Paul John Bodin, Mark Aizlewood, Eric Young (46 Gary Andrew Speed), Kevin Ratcliffe, Barry Horne, Peter Nicholas, Ian James Rush (51 Malcolm Allen), Dean Nicholas Saunders, Colin James Pascoe.   Manager: Terence Charles Yorath

IRELAND: Patrick Bonner, Joseph Dennis Irwin, Kevin Bernard Moran (Cap), Paul McGrath, Stephen Staunton, Alan Francis McLoughlin, Andrew David Townsend, John Frederick Byrne, Niall John Quinn, Bernard Joseph Slaven (68 David Thomas Kelly), Kevin Mark Sheedy.
Manager: John Charlton

Goals: Niall John Quinn (24, 66), John Frederick Byrne (86)

429. 27.03.1991   9th European Champs Qualifiers
BELGIUM v WALES 1-1 (0-0)

Parc Astrid, Bruxelles

Referee: Emilio Soriano Aladren (Spain)   Att: 25,000

BELGIUM: Michel Preud'homme, Eric Gerets (Cap), Georges Grün, Phillipe Albert, Léo Albert Clijsters, Bruno Versavel, Frank Richard Vander Elst, Erwin Vanderbergh, Marc Degryse, Vincenzo Scifo, Marc Wilmots.
Trainer: Guy Thys

WALES: Neville Southall, David Owen Phillips, Paul John Bodin, Mark Aizlewood, Eric Young, Kevin Ratcliffe (Cap), Peter Nicholas, Dean Nicholas Saunders, Ian James Rush, Mark Leslie Hughes, Barry Horne.
Manager: Terence Charles Yorath

Goals: Marc Degryse (49) / Dean Nicholas Saunders (58)

430. 01.05.1991
WALES v ICELAND 1-0 (1-0)

Ninian Park, Cardiff

Referee: Andrew Ritchie (Northern Ireland)   Att: 3,656

WALES: Neville Southall (Cap), David Owen Phillips, Paul John Bodin, Mark Aizlewood, Andrew Roger Melville, Kevin Ratcliffe, Jeremy Goss, Barry Horne, Dean Nicholas Saunders, Mark Leslie Hughes (69 Colin James Pascoe), Gary Andrew Speed.   Manager: Terence Charles Yorath

ICELAND: Bjarni Sigurðsson, Gunnar Gíslason, Atli Eðvaldsson (Cap), Sævar Jónsson, Guðni Bergsson, Þorvaldur Örlygsson (75 Hlynur Stefánsson), Sigurður Grétarsson, Ólafur Þórðarson, Rúnar Kristinsson, Arnór Guðjohnsen, Anthony Gregory (70 Ólafur H. Kristjánsson).
Trainer: Bo Johansson

Goal: Paul John Bodin (35 pen)

431. 29.05.1991
POLAND v WALES 0-0
Radomiak, Radom

Referee: Heinz Holzmann (Austria)   Attendance: 13,000

POLAND: Jarosław Bako (46 Józef Wandzik), Dariusz Kubicki, Czesław Jakołcewicz, Piotr Soczyński, Dariusz Wdowczyk (80 Michał Gębura), Krzysztof Warzycha (46 Roman Szewczyk), Janusz Nawrocki, Ryszard Tarasiewicz (Cap), Jacek Ziober, Roman Kosecki (73 Tomasz Cebula), Jan Furtok.   Trainer: Andrzej Strejlau

WALES: Neville Southall, David Owen Phillips, Paul John Bodin, Mark Aizlewood, Andrew Roger Melville, Kevin Ratcliffe (Cap), Peter Nicholas (67 Jeremy Goss), Dean Nicholas Saunders, Ian James Rush, Mark Leslie Hughes, Barry Horne.   Manager: Terence Charles Yorath

432. 05.06.1991   9th European Champs Qualifiers
WALES v GERMANY 1-0 (0-0)
The Arms Park, Cardiff

Referee: Bo Karlsson (Sweden)   Attendance: 38,000

WALES: Neville Southall, David Owen Phillips, Paul John Bodin, Mark Aizlewood, Andrew Roger Melville, Kevin Ratcliffe (Cap), Peter Nicholas, Dean Nicholas Saunders (90 Gary Andrew Speed), Ian James Rush, Mark Leslie Hughes, Barry Horne.   Manager: Terence Charles Yorath

GERMANY: Bodo Illgner, Thomas Berthold, Stefan Reuter, Thomas Helmer, Jürgen Kohler, Andreas Brehme, Lothar Herbert Matthäus (Cap) (46 Thomas Doll), Guido Buchwald, Matthias Sammer (74 Stefan Effenberg), Jürgen Klinsmann, Rudolf Völler.   Trainer: Hans-Hubert Vogts

Sent off: Thomas Berthold (60)

Goal: Ian James Rush (66)

433. 11.09.1991
WALES v BRAZIL 1-0 (0-0)
The Arms Park, Cardiff

Referee: Emilio Soriano Aladren (Spain)   Att: 20,000

WALES: Neville Southall, Mark Anthony Pembridge, Paul John Bodin (67 Mark Rosslyn Bowen), Mark Aizlewood, Andrew Roger Melville, Kevin Ratcliffe (87 Gavin Terence Maguire), Colin James Pascoe (76 Glyn Peter Hodges), Barry Horne, Dean Nicholas Saunders, Mark Leslie Hughes, Gary Andrew Speed.   Manager: Terence Charles Yorath

BRAZIL: Cláudio André Mergen Taffarel, Marcos Evangelista de Moraes "Cafu" (59 CÁSSIO Alves de Barros), CLÉBER Américo da Conceição, MÁRCIO Roberto dos SANTOS, Jorge de Amorim Campos "Jorginho", Mauro Silva, MOACIR Rodrigues dos Santos (59 VALDEIR Celso Moreira), GEOVANI Faria da Silva (72 Waldemar Aureliano de Oliveira Filho "Mazinho Oliveira"), José Roberto Gama de Oliveira "Bebeto", Antônio de Oliveira Filho "Careca", Sérgio Donizete Luís "João Paulo".   Trainer: Ernesto Paulo

Goal: Dean Nicholas Saunders (58)

434. 16.10.1991   9th European Champs Qualifiers
GERMANY v WALES 4-1 (3-0)
Franken, Nürnberg

Referee: Joël Quiniou (France)   Attendance: 43,000

GERMANY: Bodo Illgner, Manfred Binz, Guido Buchwald, Jürgen Kohler, Andreas Brehme, Stefan Reuter, Thomas Doll (78 Stefan Effenberg), Lothar Herbert Matthäus (Cap), Andreas Möller, Karlheinz Riedle (65 Thomas Häßler), Rudolf Völler.   Trainer: Hans-Hubert Vogts

WALES: Neville Southall, Gavin Terence Maguire (46 Gary Andrew Speed), Mark Rosslyn Bowen, Andrew Roger Melville, Eric Young (84 Ryan Joseph Giggs), Kevin Ratcliffe, Barry Horne, Dean Nicholas Saunders, Ian James Rush, Mark Leslie Hughes, Paul John Bodin.   Manager: Terence Charles Yorath

Sent off: Dean Nicholas Saunders (51)

Goals: Andreas Möller (34), Rudolf Völler (39), Karlheinz Riedle (45), Thomas Doll (73) / Paul John Bodin (83 pen)

435. 13.11.1991   9th European Champs Qualifiers
WALES v LUXEMBOURG 1-0 (0-0)
The Arms Park, Cardiff

Referee: Sándor Puhl (Hungary)   Attendance: 20,000

WALES: Neville Southall, David Owen Phillips, Mark Rosslyn Bowen (72 Paul John Bodin), Mark Aizlewood, Eric Young, Andrew Roger Melville (62 Ryan Joseph Giggs), Barry Horne, Peter Nicholas, Ian James Rush, Mark Leslie Hughes, Gary Andrew Speed.   Manager: Terence Charles Yorath

LUXEMBOURG: John van Rijswijck, Marcel Bossi, Marc Birsens, Pierre Petry, Thomas Wolf, Jean-Paul Girres (88 Gérard Jeitz), Guy Hellers, Carlo Weis, Joël Groff, Robert Langers (68 Armin Krings), Théo Malget.   Trainer: Paul Philipp

Goal: Paul John Bodin (82 pen)

436. 19.02.1992
REPUBLIC OF IRELAND v WALES 0-1 (0-0)
Royal Society Showground, Dublin

Referee: Serge Muhmenthaler (Switzerland)   Att: 15,100

IRELAND: Patrick Bonner, Christopher Barry Morris, Joseph Dennis Irwin, David Anthony O'Leary, Liam Sean Daish, Andrew David Townsend (Cap) (46 Alan Francis McLoughlin), Terence Michael Phelan (55 John William Aldridge), John Frederick Byrne, Roy Maurice Keane, Anthony Guy Cascarino (67 Niall John Quinn), Kevin Mark Sheedy.   Manager: John Charlton

WALES: Neville Southall, David Owen Phillips, Mark Rosslyn Bowen, Mark Aizlewood, Eric Young (63 Paul John Bodin), Christopher Jeremiah Symons, Barry Horne, Mark Anthony Pembridge (76 Glyn Peter Hodges), Dean Nicholas Saunders (86 Alan Bruce Neilson), Mark Leslie Hughes, Gary Andrew Speed (46 Clayton Graham Blackmore).
Manager: Terence Charles Yorath
Goal: Mark Andrew Pembridge (72)

437. 29.04.1992
AUSTRIA v WALES 1-1 (0-0)
Prater, Wien
Referee: Sándor Piller (Hungary)   Attendance: 53,000
AUSTRALIA: Michael Konsel, Michael Streiter, Leopold Rotter, Thomas Flögel, Manfred Zsak, Christian Prosenik, Andreas Ogris (46 Ralph Hasenhüttl), Peter Stöger, Anton Polster, Andreas Herzog (79 Peter Schöttel), Herbert Gager (46 Michael Baur).   Trainer: Ernst Happel
WALES: Neville Southall, David Owen Phillips, Mark Rosslyn Bowen, Mark Aizlewood, Eric Young (59 Christopher Coleman), Clayton Graham Blackmore, Jeremy Goss (87 Jason Mark Rees), Malcolm Allen (76 Lee Martin Nogan), Iwan Wyn Roberts, Barry Horne, Glyn Peter Hodges (59 Gareth David Hall).   Manager: Terence Charles Yorath
Goals: Michael Baur (58) / Christopher Coleman (83)

438. 20.05.1992   15th World Cup Qualifiers
ROMANIA v WALES 5-1 (5-0)
Naţional, Bucureşti
Referee: Fabio Baldas (Italy)   Attendance: 23,000
ROMANIA: Bogdan Stelea, Dan Petrescu, Gheorghe Mihali, Miodrag Belodedici, Dorinel Munteanu, Ioan Ovidiu Sabau (77 Ion Timofte), Gheorghe Popescu, Ionuţ Angelo Lupescu, Gheorghe Hagi (Cap) (70 Gábor Gerstenmájer), Marius Lăcătuş, Gavril Pelé Balint.   Trainer: Cornel Dinu
WALES: Neville Southall, David Owen Phillips, Mark Rosslyn Bowen (79 Clayton Graham Blackmore), Mark Aizlewood, Andrew Roger Melville, Mark Anthony Pembridge (57 Ryan Joseph Giggs), Dean Nicholas Saunders, Barry Horne (Cap), Mark Leslie Hughes, Ian James Rush, Gary Andrew Speed.
Manager: Terence Charles Yorath
Goals: Gheorghe Hagi (5, 34), Ionuţ Angelo Lupescu (7, 25), Gavril Pelé Balint (31) / Ian James Rush (50)

439. 30.05.1992
HOLLAND v WALES 4-0 (2-0)
Galgenwaard, Utrecht
Referee: Esa Palsi (Finland)   Attendance: 18,000
HOLLAND: Hans van Breukelen, Danny Blind (Cap), Berry van Aerle, Adri van Tiggelen (16 Frank de Boer), Jan Wouters (73 Wim Jonk), Frank Rijkaard (46 Aron Winter), Ruud Gullit (46 Johnny van't Schip), Rob Witschge, Dennis Bergkamp (64 Peter Bosz), Marco van Basten (46 Wim Kieft), Bryan Roy.
Trainer: Rinus Michels
WALES: Neville Southall, Paul John Bodin (52 David Owen Phillips), Christopher Jeremiah Symons, Mark Aizlewood, Andrew Roger Melville, Clayton Graham Blackmore (82 Ceri Morgan Hughes), Barry Horne (Cap), Mark Anthony Pembridge (60 Mark Rosslyn Bowen), Dean Nicholas Saunders, Mark Leslie Hughes, Gary Andrew Speed.
Manager: Terence Charles Yorath
Goals: Bryan Roy (15), Marco van Basten (36), Aron Winter (73), Wim Jonk (83)

440. 03.06.1992   Kirin Cup
ARGENTINA v WALES 1-0 (0-0)
Gifu Memorial Centre, Gifu (Japan)
Referee: Kichiro Tachi (Japan)   Attendance: 31,000
ARGENTINA: Luis Alberto Islas, Fabián Armando Basualdo, Ricardo Daniel Altamirano, Sergio Fabián Vázquez, Oscar Alfredo Ruggeri, Leonardo Adrián Rodríguez (60 Alberto Federico Acosta), José Luis Villareal, Diego Sebastián Cagna, Darío Javier Franco, Claudio Paul Caniggia, Gabriel Omar Batistuta.   Trainer: Alfio Oscar Basile
WALES: Neville Southall, Paul John Bodin, Clayton Graham Blackmore, Mark Aizlewood, Christopher Jeremiah Symons, David Owen Phillips, Barry Horne (Cap), Iwan Wyn Roberts, Dean Nicholas Saunders, Mark Leslie Hughes, Gary Andrew Speed.   Manager: Terence Charles Yorath
Goal: Gabriel Omar Batistuta (87)

441. 07.06.1992   Kirin Cup
JAPAN v WALES 0-1 (0-1)
Ehime Sports Complex, Matsuyama
Referee: Samuel Chan Yam-Ming (Hong Kong)   Att: 30,000
JAPAN: Kazuya Maekawa, Toshinobu Katsuya, Takumi Horiike, Tetsuji Hashiratani (Cap), Satoshi Tsunami, Masami Ihara, Hiroshi Hirakawa (61 Mitsunori Yoshida), Hajime Moriyasu, Tsuyoshi Kitazawa (61 Takuya Takagi), Nobuhiro Takeda, Kazuyoshi Miura.   Trainer: Hans Ooft
WALES: Neville Southall, David Owen Phillips, Clayton Graham Blackmore, Mark Aizlewood (68 Andrew Roger Melville), Christopher Jeremiah Symons, Mark Rosslyn Bowen, Barry Horne (Cap), Iwan Wyn Roberts, Dean Nicholas Saunders (80 Mark Anthony Pembridge), Mark Leslie Hughes, Gary Andrew Speed.   Manager: Terence Charles Yorath
Sent off: Iwan Wyn Roberts (60)
Goal: Mark Rosslyn Bowen (40)

442. 09.09.1992   15th World Cup Qualifiers
WALES v FAROE ISLANDS 6-0 (3-0)
The Arms Park, Cardiff
Referee: Jorge Monteiro Coroado (Portugal)   Att: 7,000
WALES: Neville Southall, David Owen Phillips, Clayton Graham Blackmore, Eric Young, Christopher Jeremiah Symons, Mark Rosslyn Bowen (66 Ryan Joseph Giggs), Barry Horne (Cap), Dean Nicholas Saunders, Ian James Rush, Mark Leslie Hughes, Gary Andrew Speed.
Manager: Terence Charles Yorath
FAROE ISLANDS: Jens Martin Knudsen, Jóannes Jakobsen (Cap), Tummas Eli Hansen, Mikkjal Danielsen, Allan Mørkøre, Jan Dam (46 Alvi Justinussen), Kári Reynheim, Todi Jónsson, Øssur Hansen, Jakup Símun Simonsen, Jan Allan Müller.
Trainer: Páll Gudlaugsson
Goals: Ian James Rush (5, 64, 89), Dean Saunders (28), Mark Rosslyn Bowen (37), Clayton Blackmore (71)

443. 14.10.1992   15th World Cup Qualifiers
CYPRUS v WALES 0-1 (0-0)
Tsireio, Limassol
Referee: László Vágner (Hungary)   Attendance: 12,000
CYPRUS: Mihális Hristofi, Kóstas Konstantínou, Kóstas Kosta, Haralampos Píttas (71 Loukás Hatziloukas), Floros Nikoláou, Giannakis Giagkoudakis, Mários Haralámpous, Dimitris Ioannou, Giórgos Savvidis, Antros Sotiriou (59 Giannos Ioannou), Nikodimos Papavasileiou.
Trainer: Andreas Mihailidis
WALES: Neville Southall, David Owen Phillips, Clayton Graham Blackmore, Eric Young, Christopher Jeremiah Symons, Mark Rosslyn Bowen, Barry Horne (Cap), Dean Nicholas Saunders, Ian James Rush, Mark Leslie Hughes, Gary Andrew Speed.   Manager: Terence Charles Yorath
Goal: Mark Leslie Hughes (51)

444. 18.11.1992   15th World Cup Qualifiers
BELGIUM v WALES 2-0 (0-0)
Parc Astrid, Bruxelles
Referee: Jan Damgaard (Denmark)   Attendance: 21,000
BELGIUM: Michel Preud'homme, Dirk Medved, Georges Grün (Cap), Phillipe Albert, Rudy Smidts, Lorenzo Staelens (85 Marc Wilmots), Frank Richard Vander Elst, Danny Boffin, Marc Degryse, Vincenzo Scifo, Alexander Czerniatynski (46 Luc Nilis).   Trainer: Paul Van Himst
WALES: Neville Southall, David Owen Phillips, Clayton Graham Blackmore, Eric Young, Christopher Jeremiah Symons, Mark Rosslyn Bowen (70 Ryan Joseph Giggs), Barry Horne, Dean Nicholas Saunders, Ian James Rush, Mark Leslie Hughes, Gary Andrew Speed (80 Mark Anthony Pembridge).
Manager: Terence Charles Yorath
Goals: Lorenzo Staelens (54), Marc Degryse (59)

445. 17.02.1993
REPUBLIC OF IRELAND v WALES 2-1 (0-1)
Tolka Park, Dublin
Referee: Bo Karlsson (Sweden)   Attendance: 9,500
IRELAND: Patrick Bonner (46 Alan Thomas Kelly), Christopher Barry Morris, Edward John Paul McGoldrick, Brian Patrick Carey, David Anthony O'Leary (Cap) (7 Ronald Andrew Whelan, 46 Kevin Mark Sheedy), Roy Maurice Keane, Liam Francis O'Brien, John Frederick Byrne, Anthony Guy Cascarino (82 Bernard Joseph Slaven), David Thomas Kelly (69 Thomas Coyne), Alan Francis McLoughlin.   Manager: John Charlton
WALES: Neville Southall (83 Anthony Mark Roberts), David Owen Phillips, Paul John Bodin, Mark Aizlewood, Eric Young (46 Christopher Coleman), Christopher Jeremiah Symons, Barry Horne, David Geraint Williams (73 Malcolm Allen), Mark Leslie Hughes, Mark Anthony Pembridge, Gary Andrew Speed.   Manager: Terence Charles Yorath
Goals: Kevin Mark Sheedy (75), Thomas Coyne (81) / Mark Leslie Hughes (18)

446. 31.03.1993   15th World Cup Qualifiers
WALES v BELGIUM 2-0 (2-0)
The Arms Park, Cardiff
Referee: Aron Schmidhuber (Germany)   Att: 27,002
WALES: Neville Southall, Barry Horne, Paul John Bodin, Mark Aizlewood, Eric Young, Kevin Ratcliffe, Gary Andrew Speed (87 David Owen Phillips), Dean Nicholas Saunders, Ian James Rush, Mark Leslie Hughes, Ryan Joseph Giggs (89 Mark Rosslyn Bowen).   Manager: Terence Charles Yorath

BELGIUM: Michel Preud'homme, Dirk Medved (46 Luis Airton Oliveira Barosso), Georges Grün (Cap), Phillipe Albert, Rudy Smidts, Lorenzo Staelens, Vincenzo Scifo, Frank Richard Vander Elst, Danny Boffin, Marc Degryse, Alexander Czerniatynski (65 Francis Severeyns).
Trainer: Paul Van Himst
Goals: Ryan Joseph Giggs (18), Ian James Rush (39)

447. 28.04.1993   15th World Cup Qualifiers
CZECHOSLOVAKIA v WALES 1-1 (1-1)
Bazalý, Ostrava
Referee: Joël Quiniou (France)   Attendance: 16,000
CZECHOSLOVAKIA: Petr Kouba, Miloš Glonek (67 Radek Bejbl), Miroslav Kadlec, Jiří Novotný, Petr Vrabec, Radoslav Látal, Jiří Němec (81 Peter Dubovský), Václav Němeček (Cap), Luboš Kubík, Pavel Kuka, Ľubomír Luhový.
Trainer: Václav Ježek
WALES: Neville Southall, David Owen Phillips, Paul John Bodin (52 Mark Rosslyn Bowen), Clayton Graham Blackmore, Andrew Roger Melville, Christopher Jeremiah Symons, Barry Horne, Dean Nicholas Saunders, Ian James Rush, Mark Leslie Hughes, Ryan Joseph Giggs.
Manager: Terence Charles Yorath
Goals: Radoslav Látal (38) / Mark Leslie Hughes (29)

448. 06.06.1993   15th World Cup Qualifiers
FAROE ISLANDS v WALES 0-3 (0-2)
Svankasgard, Toftir
Referee: Vadim Zhuk (Belarus)   Attendance: 4,209
FAROE ISLANDS: Jens Martin Knudsen, Jóannes Jakobsen, Tummas Eli Hansen, Óli Johannesen, Jan Dam, Alvi Justinussen, Kári Reynheim (60 Jens Erik Rasmussen), Páll Reynatugvu (49 Gunnar Mohr), Torkil Nielsen, Ábraham Hansen, Uni Arge.   Trainer: Páll Gudlaugsson
WALES: Neville Southall, David Owen Phillips, Paul John Bodin, Mark Aizlewood, Eric Young (49 Andrew Roger Melville), Christopher Jeremiah Symons, Barry Horne, Dean Nicholas Saunders, Ian James Rush, Mark Leslie Hughes (75 Gary Andrew Speed), Ryan Joseph Giggs.
Manager: Terence Charles Yorath
Goals: Dean Nicholas Saunders (22), Eric Young (31), Ian James Rush (69)

449. 08.09.1993   15th World Cup Qualifiers
WALES v CZECHOSLOVAKIA 2-2 (2-1)
The Arms Park, Cardiff
Referee: Juan Ansuategui Roca (Spain)   Attendance: 37,558
WALES: Neville Southall, David Owen Phillips, Mark Rosslyn Bowen (75 Gary Andrew Speed), Mark Aizlewood (78 Andrew Roger Melville), Eric Young, Christopher Jeremiah Symons, Barry Horne, Dean Nicholas Saunders, Ian James Rush, Mark Leslie Hughes, Ryan Joseph Giggs.
Manager: Terence Charles Yorath
CZECHOSLOVAKIA: Petr Kouba, Jan Suchopárek, Miroslav Kadlec, Jiří Novotný, Radoslav Látal (59 Tomáš Skuhravý), Ivan Hašek, Václav Němeček (Cap), Pavel Hapal, Ľubomír Moravčík, Peter Dubovský, Pavel Kuka.   Trainer: Václav Ježek
Goals: Ryan Joseph Giggs (21), Ian James Rush (35) / Pavel Kuka (17), Peter Dubovský (68)

450. 13.10.1993   15th World Cup Qualifiers
WALES v CYPRUS 2-0 (0-0)
The Arms Park, Cardiff
Referee: Phillip Don (England)   Attendance: 30,825
WALES: Neville Southall, David Owen Phillips, Barry Horne, Mark Aizlewood, Eric Young, Christopher Jeremiah Symons (70 Jeremy Goss), Gary Andrew Speed, Dean Nicholas Saunders, Ian James Rush, Mark Leslie Hughes, Ryan Joseph Giggs.   Manager: Terence Charles Yorath
CYPRUS: Antros Petridis, Kóstas Kosta, Kóstas Konstantínou, Haralampos Píttas (77 Paníkos Xiouroupas), Evagoras Hristofi, Dimitris Ioannou, Giannakis Giagkoudakis (71 Giórgos Panayi), Neofytos Larkou, Mários Haralámpous, Antros Sotiriou, Nikodimos Papavasileiou.
Trainer: Andreas Mihailidis
Sent off: Kóstas Kosta (50), Evagoras Hristofi (81)
Goals: Dean Nicholas Saunders (70), Ian James Rush (82)

451. 17.11.1993   15th World Cup Qualifiers
WALES v ROMANIA 1-2 (0-1)
The Arms Park, Cardiff
Referee: Kurt Röthlisberger (Switzerland)   Att: 40,000
WALES: Neville Southall, David Owen Phillips, Paul John Bodin (69 Malcolm Allen), Andrew Roger Melville, Eric Young, Christopher Jeremiah Symons (53 Jeremy Goss), Barry Horne, Dean Nicholas Saunders, Ian James Rush, Gary Andrew Speed, Ryan Joseph Giggs.
Manager: Terence Charles Yorath
ROMANIA: Florian Prunea, Dan Petrescu, Daniel Claudiu Prodan, Miodrag Belodedici, Tibor Selymes (74 Dorinel Munteanu), Ioan Ovidiu Sabău, Gheorghe Popescu, Ionuț Angelo Lupescu, Gheorghe Hagi (Cap), Florin Răducioiu, Ilie Dumitrescu (89 Gheorghe Mihali).
Trainer: Anghel Iordănescu
Goals: Dean Nicholas Saunders (60) / Gheorghe Hagi (33), Florin Răducioiu (83)

452. 09.03.1994
WALES v NORWAY 1-3 (0-1)
The Arms Park, Cardiff
Referee: John Ferry (Northern Ireland)   Attendance: 10,000
WALES: Neville Southall, Jason Perry, Andrew Roger Melville, Eric Young, Christopher Coleman, David Owen Phillips, Barry Horne, Nathan Alexander Blake (59 Mark Anthony Pembridge), Ian James Rush, Mark Leslie Hughes (46 Ceri Morgan Hughes), Gary Andrew Speed (59 Dean Nicholas Saunders).   Manager: John Benjamin Toshack

NORWAY: Frode Grodås, Karl Petter Løken, Tore Pedersen, Henning Berg, Stig Inge Bjørnebye, Erik Mykland, Lars Bohinen, Jostein Flo, Kjetil Rekdal (68 Ståle Solbakken), Jahn Ivar Jakobsen, Jan Åge Fjørtoft (79 Geir Frigård).
Trainer: Egil Olsen

Goals: Christopher Coleman (89) /
Jostein Flo (6), Erik Mykland (49), Jahn Ivar Jakobsen (51)

453. 20.04.1994
WALES v SWEDEN 0-2 (0-0)
The Racecourse, Wrexham
Referee: Brendan Shorte (Republic of Ireland)   Att: 4,694
WALES: Neville Southall, Alan Bruce Neilson, Paul John Bodin, Andrew Roger Melville, Mark Rosslyn Bowen (60 Clayton Graham Blackmore), Jeremy Goss (81 Nathan Alexander Blake), David Owen Phillips, Barry Horne, Ian James Rush, Iwan Wyn Roberts (81 Ceri Morgan Hughes), Gary Andrew Speed.   Manager: Michael Smith

SWEDEN: Thomas Ravelli, Roland Nilsson (72 Mikael Nilsson), Patrik Jonas Andersson, Joachim Björklund, Roger Ljung, Anders Erik Limpár (60 Jesper Blomqvist), Klas Ingesson (83 Stefan Rehn), Stefan Schwarz, Henrik Larsson, Tomas Brolin, Kennet Andersson (81 Niklas Kindvall).
Trainer: Tommy Svensson

Goal: Henrik Larsson (83), Tomas Brolin (90)

454. 23.05.1994
ESTONIA v WALES 1-2 (0-0)
Kadriorg, Tallinn
Referee: Romans Lajuks (Latvia)   Attendance: 3,500
ESTONIA: Mart Poom, Risto Kallaste, Urmas Kaljend, Marek Lemsalu, Igopr Prins, Indro Olumets (78 Mati Pari), Marko Kristal, Tarmo Linnumäe, Martin Reim, Dzintar Klavan, Meelis Lindmaa.   Trainer: Roman Ubakivi

WALES: Neville Southall, Adrian Williams, Andrew Roger Melville (72 Paul John Bodin), Alan Bruce Neilson, Christopher Coleman, David Owen Phillips, Barry Horne, Jason Peter Bowen, Ian James Rush, Ceri Morgan Hughes, Ryan Anthony Jones.   Manager: Michael Smith

Goals: Martin Reim (86 pen) /
Ian James Rush (56), David Owen Phillips (83)

455. 07.09.1994
WALES v ALBANIA 2-0 (1-0)
The Arms Park, Cardiff
Referee: Gianni Beschin (Italy)   Attendance: 15,791
WALES: Neville Southall, Adrian Williams, Andrew Roger Melville, Christopher Coleman, Paul John Bodin, Jeremy Goss (74 Mark Anthony Pembridge), David Owen Phillips, Gary Andrew Speed, Ryan Joseph Giggs, Ian James Rush, Nathan Alexander Blake (80 Iwan Wyn Roberts).
Manager: Michael Smith

ALBANIA: Foto Strakosha, Rudi Vata, Arian Xhumba, Ilir Shulku, Salvator Kaçaj, Agustin Kola (52 Indrit Fortuzi), Arjan Bellai, Bledar Kola, Ledio Pano, Ylli Shehu (81 Edmond Dosti), Sulejman Demollari.   Trainer: Neptun Bajko

Goals: Christopher Coleman (9), Ryan Joseph Giggs (67)

456. 12.10.1994   10th European Champs Qualifiers
MOLDOVA v WALES 3-2 (2-1)
Republican, Chişinău
Referee: István Vad (Hungary)   Attendance: 12,000
MOLDOVA: Vasile Coşelev, Serghei Secu, Serghei Belous (86 Emil Caras), Valeriu Pogorelov, Radu Rebeja, Serghei Stroenco, Igor Oprea, Alexandru Curtianu, Serghei Nani, Alexandru Spiridon, Iurie Miterev (46 Vladimir Kosse).
Trainer: Ion Caras

WALES: Neville Southall, Mark Rosslyn Bowen, Adrian Williams, Christopher Coleman, Christopher Jeremiah Symons, Barry Horne (Cap), David Owen Phillips, Nathan Alexander Blake (87 Andrew Roger Melville), Iwan Wyn Roberts, Mark Anthony Pembridge, Gary Andrew Speed.
Manager: Michael Smith

Goals: Serghei Belous (8), Serghei Secu (20), Valeriu Pogorelov (78) /
Gary Andrew Speed (6), Nathan Alexander Blake (70)

457. 16.11.1994   10th European Champs Qualifiers
GEORGIA v WALES 5-0 (2-0)
Boris Paichadze, Tbilisi
Referee: Alain Sars (France)   Attendance: 45,000
GEORGIA: Akaki Devadze, Zaza Revishvili, Kakhaber Tskhadadze, Murtaz Shelia, Giorgi Chikhradze, Kakhaber Gogichaishvili, Giorgi Nemsadze (42 Gela Inalishvili), Gocha Gogrichiani, Temur Ketsbaia (75 Mikheil Kavelashvili), Giorgi Kinkladze, Shota Arveladze.   Trainer: Aleksandr Chivadze

WALES: Neville Southall, Alan Bruce Neilson (46 Christopher Jeremiah Symons), Mark Rosslyn Bowen, Andrew Roger Melville, Christopher Coleman, Barry Horne (Cap), David Owen Phillips, Dean Nicholas Saunders, Ian James Rush, Mark Leslie Hughes, Gary Andrew Speed.
Manager: Michael Smith

Goals: Temur Ketsbaia (31, 49), Giorgi Kinkladze (41), Gocha Gogrichiani (59), Shota Arveladze (67)

82

458. 14.12.1994 10th European Champs Qualifiers
WALES v BULGARIA 0-3 (0-2)
The Arms Park, Cardiff
Referee: Leif Sundell (Sweden)   Attendance: 20,000

WALES: Neville Southall, David Owen Phillips, Mark Rosslyn Bowen, Mark Aizlewood, Christopher Coleman, Andrew Roger Melville, Vincent Peter Jones, Dean Nicholas Saunders, Ian James Rush, Mark Leslie Hughes, Gary Andrew Speed.
Manager: Michael Smith

BULGARIA: Borislav Mihailov, Emil Kremenliev, Trifon Ivanov, Tsanko Tsvetanov, Zlatko Yankov, Ivailo Iordanov, Emil Kostadinov (74 Ilian Kiriakov), Hristo Stoichkov, Liuboslav Penev (74 Nasko Sirakov), Krasimir Balakov, Iordan Lechkov.
Trainer: Dimitar Penev

Goals: Trifon Ivanov (5), Emil Kostadinov (16), Hristo Stoichkov (51)

459. 29.03.1995 10th European Champs Qualifiers
BULGARIA v WALES 3-1 (1-0)
Vasil Levski, Sofia
Referee: Michel Piraux (Belgium)   Attendance: 60,000

BULGARIA: Borislav Mihailov, Emil Kremenliev, Trifon Ivanov, Tsanko Tsvetanov (65 Ilian Kiriakov), Petar Hubchev, Zlatko Yankov, Emil Kostadinov, Hristo Stoichkov, Liuboslav Penev, Krasimir Balakov, Iordan Lechkov.
Trainer: Dimitar Penev

WALES: Neville Southall, David Owen Phillips, Mark Rosslyn Bowen, Christopher Jeremiah Symons, Christopher Coleman, Vincent Peter Jones (78 John Michael Cornforth), Barry Horne, Gary Andrew Speed, John Hartson, Dean Nicholas Saunders, Ryan Joseph Giggs.   Manager: Michael Smith

Goals: Krasimir Balakov (37), Liuboslav Penev (70, 82) / Dean Nicholas Saunders (83)

460. 26.04.1995 10th European Champs Qualifiers
GERMANY v WALES 1-1 (1-1)
Rhein, Düsseldorf
Referee: José María García-Aranda Encinar (Spain)
Attendance: 45,000

GERMANY: Andreas Köpke, Stefan Reuter, Dieter Eilts, Markus Babbel, Steffen Freund, Mario Basler (76 Mehmet Scholl), Thomas Häßler, Christian Ziege (86 Stefan Kuntz), Ralf Weber, Heiko Herrlich, Jürgen Klinsmann (Cap).
Trainer: Hans-Hubert Vogts

WALES: Neville Southall, David Owen Phillips, Mark Rosslyn Bowen, Christopher Jeremiah Symons, Christopher Coleman (46 Adrian Williams), Barry Horne (Cap), Vincent Peter Jones, Dean Nicholas Saunders, Ian James Rush, Mark Leslie Hughes (90 John Hartson), Gary Andrew Speed.
Manager: Michael Smith

Goals: Heiko Herrlich (42) / Dean Nicholas Saunders (7)

461. 07.06.1995 10th European Champs Qualifiers
WALES v GEORGIA 0-1 (0-0)
The Arms Park, Cardiff
Referee: Ilkka Koho (Finland)   Attendance: 6,500

WALES: Neville Southall, David Owen Phillips, Mark Rosslyn Bowen, Adrian Williams, Christopher Jeremiah Symons, Barry Horne (Cap), Vincent Peter Jones, Dean Nicholas Saunders (84 Mark Anthony Pembridge), Ian James Rush, Mark Leslie Hughes (84 John Hartson), John Michael Cornforth.
Manager: Michael Smith

GEORGIA: Akaki Devadze, Besik Beradze, Kakhaber Tskhadadze, Murtaz Shelia, Giorgi Chikhradze, Kakhaber Gogichaishvili, Gela Inalishvili, Mikheil Kavelashvili (73 Levan Tskitishvili), Temur Ketsbaia, Giorgi Kinkladze, Shota Arveladze (86 Giorgi Kilasonia).
Trainer: Aleksandr Chivadze

Goal: Giorgi Kinkladze (72)

462. 06.09.1995 10th European Champs Qualifiers
WALES v MOLDOVA 1-0 (0-0)
The Arms Park, Cardiff
Referee: Gylfi Orasson (Iceland)   Attendance: 5,000

WALES: Neville Southall, Adrian Williams, Mark Rosslyn Bowen, Christopher Jeremiah Symons, Christopher Coleman, Barry Horne (Cap), Mark Anthony Pembridge, Lee Martin Nogan (46 David Owen Phillips), Ian James Rush (69 John Hartson), Mark Leslie Hughes, Gary Andrew Speed.
Manager: Robert Gould

MOLDOVA: Evgheni Ivanov, Oleg Fistican, Ion Testimițanu, Vitali Culibaba, Radu Rebeja (84 Vadim Gavriliuc), Serghei Stroenco, Igor Oprea, Serghei Belous, Serghei Nani (76 Alexandru Suharev), Boris Cebotari, Serghei Cleșcenco.
Trainer: Ion Caras

Sent off: Oleg Fistican (88)

Goal: Gary Andrew Speed (55)

463. 11.10.1995 10th European Champs Qualifiers
WALES v GERMANY 1-2 (0-0)
The Arms Park, Cardiff
Referee: Ion Crăciunescu (Romania)   Attendance: 25,000

WALES: Neville Southall, Stephen Robert Jenkins (70 Paul Jonathan Mardon), Mark Rosslyn Bowen, Andrew Roger Melville, Christopher Jeremiah Symons, Barry Horne (Cap), Mark Anthony Pembridge (82 Glyn Peter Hodges), Nathan Alexander Blake (82 David Geraint Williams), Dean Nicholas Saunders, Gary Andrew Speed, Ryan Joseph Giggs.
Manager: Robert Gould

GERMANY: Andreas Köpke, Matthias Sammer, Markus Babbel (46 Christian Wörns), Thomas Helmer, Steffen Freund, Thomas Häßler, Dieter Eilts, Andreas Möller, Christian Ziege, Jürgen Klinsmann (Cap), Heiko Herrlich (74 Stefan Kuntz).
Trainer: Hans-Hubert Vogts

Goal: Thomas Helmer (78 own goal) /
Andrew Roger Melville (75 own goal), Jürgen Klinsmann (81)

464. 15.11.1995   10th European Champs Qualifiers
ALBANIA v WALES 1-1 (1-1)
Qemal Stafa, Tiranë
Referee: David Suheil (Israel)   Attendance: 6,000
ALBANIA: Foto Strakosha, Hysen Zmijani, Artur Lekbello, Rudi Vata, Saimir Malko, Ilir Shulku, Gjergj Dëma (83 Arben Milori), Ledio Pano, Kliton Bozgo (78 Alvaro Zalla), Sokol Kushta (57 Alban Bushi), Altin Rraklli.
Trainer: Neptun Bajko
WALES: Neville Southall, Stephen Robert Jenkins, Mark Rosslyn Bowen, Eric Young, Andrew Roger Melville, David Owen Phillips, Mark Anthony Pembridge, Dean Nicholas Saunders, Gareth Keith Taylor (84 John Robert Campbell Robinson), Robert William Savage (63 Ceri Morgan Hughes), Ryan Joseph Giggs.   Manager: Robert Gould
Goals: Sokol Kushta (3 pen) / Mark Anthony Pembridge (43)

465. 24.01.1996
ITALY v WALES 3-0 (1-0)
Libero Liberati, Terni
Referee: Guy Goethals (Belgium)   Attendance: 16,095
ITALY: Angelo Peruzzi (46 Francesco Toldo), Ciro Ferrara (46 Moreno Torricelli), Amedeo Carboni, Demetrio Albertini, Luigi Apolloni, Alessandro Costacurta (Cap), Angelo Di Livio (79 Massimo Crippa), Roberto Di Matteo (23 Antonio Conte I), Gianfranco Zola, Alessandro Del Piero (73 Pier Luigi Casiraghi), Fabrizio Ravanelli.   Trainer: Arrigo Sacchi
WALES: Neville Southall, Stephen Robert Jenkins, Christopher Coleman, David Owen Phillips, Adrian Williams, Christopher Jeremiah Symons, Barry Horne, Glyn Peter Hodges (57 Marcus Trevor Browning), Ian James Rush (64 Gareth Keith Taylor), Mark Leslie Hughes, Gary Andrew Speed (77 Nathan Alexander Blake).
Manager: Robert Gould
Goals: Alessandro Del Piero (1), Fabrizio Ravanelli (50), Pier Luigi Casiraghi (77)

466. 24.04.1996
SWITZERLAND v WALES 2-0 (2-0)
Cornaredo, Lugano
Referee: Loris Stafoggia (Italy)   Attendance: 8,500
SWITZERLAND: Marco Pascolo (84 Stéphane Lehmann), Johann Vogel (46 Marc Hottiger), Ramon Vega, Stéphane Henchoz, Yvan Quentin, Christophe Ohrel (64 Massimo Lombardo), Ciriaco Sforza, Raphaël Wicky (84 Marcel Koller), Kubilay Türkyilmaz (85 Alexandre Comisetti), Marco Grassi (76 Adrian Knup), Stéphane Chapuisat (64 Alain Sutter).
Trainer: Artur Jorge Braga Melo Teixeira

WALES: Daniel Coyne (46 Andrew Marriott), John Robert Campbell Robinson, Christopher Jeremiah Symons, Mark Rosslyn Bowen, Christopher Coleman (88 Christian Nicholas Howells Edwards), Andrew Legg (30 Gary Andrew Speed), Vincent Peter Jones 865 Robert William Savage), Barry Horne (74 Jeremy Goss), Mark Anthony Pembridge, John Hartson, Gareth Keith Taylor (46 Simon Ithel Davies).
Manager: Robert Gould
Goals: Christopher Coleman (32 own goal), Kubilay Türkyilmaz (42 pen)

467. 02.06.1996   16th World Cup Qualifiers
SAN MARINO v WALES 0-5 (0-3)
Olimpico, Serravalle
Referee: Ľuboš Michel (Slovakia)   Attendance: 1,613
SAN MARINO: Stefano Muccioli, Leone Gasperoni, Luca Gobbi, Waldes Pasolini (71 Riccardo Muccioli), William Guerra, Mauro Valentini, Alessandro Casadei (75 Claudio Peverani), Pierangelo Manzaroli, Paolo Montagna, Marco Mazza, Marco Mularoni (46 Vittorio Valentini).
Trainer: Massimo Bonini
WALES: Neville Southall, Mark Rosslyn Bowen, Mark Anthony Pembridge, Marcus Trevor Browning (75 Jeremy Goss), Andrew Roger Melville, Christopher Coleman, Barry Horne (83 Robert William Savage), Dean Nicholas Saunders, John Robert Campbell Robinson (80 Andrew Legg), Mark Leslie Hughes, Ryan Joseph Giggs.   Manager: Robert Gould
Goals: Andrew Melville (22), Mark Leslie Hughes (32, 42), Ryan Joseph Giggs (50), Mark Anthony Pembridge (85)

468. 31.08.1996   16th World Cup Qualifiers
WALES v SAN MARINO 6-0 (4-0)
The Arms Park, Cardiff
Referee: Alain Hamer (Luxembourg)   Attendance: 15,150
WALES: Neville Southall (76 Anthony Mark Roberts), Mark Rosslyn Bowen, Mark Anthony Pembridge, Marcus Trevor Browning, Andrew Roger Melville, Christopher Coleman (80 Gareth Keith Taylor), Barry Horne, Dean Nicholas Saunders, John Robert Campbell Robinson (77 Gary Andrew Speed), Mark Leslie Hughes, Ryan Joseph Giggs.
Manager: Robert Gould
SAN MARINO: Stefano Muccioli, Leone Gasperoni (65 Ivan Matteoni), Luca Gobbi, Vittorio Valentini, William Guerra, Mirco Gennari, Nicola Bacciocchi (43 Fabio Francini), Pierangelo Manzaroli, Paolo Montagna, Marco Mazza (79 Waldes Pasolini), Bryan Gasperoni.
Trainer: Massimo Bonini
Sent off: Pierangelo Manzaroli (90)
Goals: Dean Saunders (1, 74), Mark Leslie Hughes (25, 54), Andrew Melville (34), John Robert Campbell Robinson (45)

469. 05.10.1996   16th World Cup Qualifiers
WALES v HOLLAND 1-3 (1-0)

The Arms Park, Cardiff

Referee: Antonio Jesús López Nieto (Spain)   Att: 34,560

WALES: Neville Southall, Mark Rosslyn Bowen, Mark Anthony Pembridge (68 Andrew Legg), Marcus Trevor Browning (83 Stephen Robert Jenkins), Andrew Roger Melville, Christopher Jeremiah Symons, Barry Horne, Dean Nicholas Saunders, John Robert Campbell Robinson, Mark Leslie Hughes, Gary Andrew Speed.
Manager: Robert Gould

HOLLAND: Edwin van der Sar, Ferdy Vierklau (69 Pierre van Hooijdonk), Stan Valckx, Frank de Boer (Cap), Winston Bogarde, Ronald de Boer (88 Giovanni van Bronckhorst), Wim Jonk, Clarence Seedorf, Aron Winter, Philip Cocu, Jordi Cruijff (46 Roy Makaay).   Trainer: Guus Hiddink

Goal: Dean Nicholas Saunders (17) /
Pierre van Hooijdonk (70, 74), Ronald de Boer (78)

470. 09.11.1996   16th World Cup Qualifiers
HOLLAND v WALES 7-1 (4-1)

Philips, Eindhoven

Referee: Vítor Manuel Melo Pereira (Portugal)   Att: 26,210

HOLLAND: Edwin van der Sar, Michael Reiziger, Jaap Stam, Frank de Boer (Cap), Arthur Numan, Wim Jonk (81 Giovanni van Bronckhorst), Clarence Seedorf (68 Pierre van Hooijdonk), Aron Winter, Philip Cocu, Ronald de Boer (57 Marc Overmars), Dennis Bergkamp.   Trainer: Guus Hiddink

WALES: Neville Southall, Alan Bruce Neilson, Mark Anthony Pembridge, Vincent Peter Jones (Cap), Andrew Roger Melville, Christopher Jeremiah Symons, Mark Rosslyn Bowen, Dean Nicholas Saunders, Jason Peter Bowen (56 John Robert Campbell Robinson), John Hartson (66 Gareth Keith Taylor), Gary Andrew Speed.   Manager: Robert Gould

Goals: Dennis Bergkamp (22, 72, 78), Ronald de Boer (33), Wim Jonk (34), Frank de Boer (44), Philip Cocu (61) /
Dean Nicholas Saunders (38)

471. 14.12.1996   16th World Cup Qualifiers
WALES v TURKEY 0-0

The Arms Park, Cardiff

Referee: Aron Huzu (Romania)   Attendance: 14,206

WALES: Neville Southall, Stephen Robert Jenkins, Robert John Page, Vincent Peter Jones, Andrew Roger Melville, Mark Anthony Pembridge, Barry Horne, Dean Nicholas Saunders (81 John Hartson), Gary Andrew Speed, Mark Leslie Hughes, Ryan Joseph Giggs.   Manager: Robert Gould

TURKEY: Engin İpekoğlu, Recep Çetin, Bülent Korkmaz, Alpay Özalan, İlker Yağcıoğlu (88 Saffet Akbaş), Ogün Temizkanoğlu, Tugay Kerimoğlu, Kemalettin Şentürk (88 Tolunay Kafkas), Abdullah Ercan, Arif Erdem (70 Oktay Derelioğlu), Hakan Şükür.   Trainer: Mustafa Denizli

472. 11.02.1997
WALES v REPUBLIC OF IRELAND 0-0

The Arms Park, Cardiff

Referee: William S G. Young (Scotland)   Attendance: 7,000

WALES: Mark Geoffrey Crossley, Karl Ready, Gary Andrew Speed, Christopher Jeremiah Symons, Mark Anthony Pembridge, Andrew Legg, Vincent Peter Jones (73 Ceri Morgan Hughes), Barry Horne, John Robert Campbell Robinson (62 Mark Rosslyn Bowen), John Hartson (69 Gareth Keith Taylor), Mark Leslie Hughes (88 Robert William Savage).   Manager: Robert Gould

IRELAND: Keith Graham Branagan, Terence Michael Phelan, Kenneth Edward Cunningham, Paul McGrath, Jason Wynn McAteer, Stephen Staunton, Alan Francis McLoughlin (52 Garry Kelly), Ian Patrick Harte, Roy Maurice Keane (75 David Thomas Kelly), Anthony Guy Cascarino, Jonathan Goodman.
Manager: Michael Joseph McCarthy

473. 29.03.1997   16th World Cup Qualifiers
WALES v BELGIUM 1-2 (0-2)

The Arms Park, Cardiff

Referee: Christer Faellström (Sweden)   Attendance: 15,000

WALES: Neville Southall, Clayton Graham Blackmore, Vincent Peter Jones, Mark Anthony Pembridge, Christopher Jeremiah Symons, Robert John Page, Mark Leslie Hughes, Ryan Joseph Giggs, Gary Andrew Speed, Barry Horne, Dean Nicholas Saunders (65 John Hartson).
Manager: Robert Gould

BELGIUM: Filip De Wilde, Bertrand Crasson, Eric Van Meir, Albert De Roover, Rudy Smidts, Lorenzo Staelens, Frank Richard Vander Elst (Cap), Dominique Lemoine, Nico Van Kerckhoven, Emile Lokonda Mpenza (65 Mbo Jerôme Mpenza), Luis Airton Oliveira Barosso (80 Vincenzo Scifo).   Trainer: Georges Leekens

Goal: Gary Andrew Speed (60) /
Bertrand Crasson (24), Lorenzo Staelens (45)

474. 27.05.1997
SCOTLAND v WALES 0-1 (0-0)
Rugby Park, Kilmarnock
Referee: Alan Snoddy (Northern Ireland)   Att: 8,000
SCOTLAND: Neil Sullivan (80 James Leighton), David Weir, Thomas Boyd, Christian Eduard Dailly (74 John McNamara), Brian McAllister, Scot Gemmill, Gary McAllister (Cap), Thomas Valley McKinlay, William Dodds, Darren Jackson (46 John Spencer), Kevin William Gallacher (80 Simon Donnelly). Manager: Craig Brown
WALES: Andrew Marriott (46 Paul Steven Jones), Stephen Robert Jenkins, Paul Jonathan Trollope, Robert John Page, Christopher Jeremiah Symons, John Robert Campbell Robinson (88 Marcus Trevor Browning), Robert William Savage, Dean Nicholas Saunders (88 Philip Lee Jones), John Hartson (71 Simon Owen Haworth), Mark Anthony Pembridge, Gary Andrew Speed.   Manager: Robert Gould
Goal: John Hartson (46)

475. 20.08.1997   16th World Cup Qualifiers
TURKEY v WALES 6-4 (3-3)
Ali Sami Yen, Istanbul
Referee: Marek Kowalczyk (Poland)   Attendance: 30,000
TURKEY: Rüştü Reçber, Alpay Özalan, Bülent Korkmaz, Ilker Yağcıoğlu, Ogün Temizkanoğlu (63 Fatih Akyel), Tolunay Kafkas, Oğuz Çetin, Abdullah Ercan (83 Ergün Penbe), Arif Erdem, Hakan Şükür, Saffet Akyüz (58 Hamı Mandıralı). Trainer: Mustafa Denizli
WALES: Neville Southall (46 Paul Steven Jones), Stephen Robert Jenkins, Ceri Morgan Hughes (68 Robert William Edwards), Robert John Page, Andrew Roger Melville, Gary Andrew Speed, Robert William Savage, Nathan Alexander Blake, Dean Nicholas Saunders (83 Philip Lee Jones), Mark Leslie Hughes, Ryan Joseph Giggs.   Manager: Robert Gould
Goals: Hakan Şükür (5, 37, 77, 82), Saffet Akyüz (8), Oğuz Çetin (60) / Nathan Alexander Blake (18), Robert William Savage (20), Dean Nicholas Saunders (31), Andrew Roger Melville (52)

476. 11.10.1997   16th World Cup Qualifiers
BELGIUM v WALES 3-2 (3-0)
Roi Baudouin, Bruxelles
Referee: Vítor Manuel Melo Pereira (Portugal)   Att: 18,233
BELGIUM: Filip De Wilde, Eric Deflandre, Albert De Roover (64 Mike Verstraeten), Lorenzo Staelens, Rudy Smidts, Frank Richard Vander Elst (Cap), Marc Wilmots, Nico Van Kerckhoven (82 Vital Borkelmans), Danny Boffin, Luis Airton Oliveira Barosso, Gert Claessens (68 Luc Nilis). Trainer: Georges Leekens

WALES: Andrew Marriott, Stephen Robert Jenkins, Ceri Morgan Hughes (84 Robert John Page), Robert William Edwards, Karl Ready, John Robert Campbell Robinson, Robert William Savage (90 John Morgan Oster), John Hartson (84 Gareth Keith Taylor), Dean Nicholas Saunders, Mark Anthony Pembridge, Ryan Joseph Giggs.   Manager: Robert Gould
Goals: Lorenzo Staelens (4 pen), Gert Claessens (33), Marc Wilmots (40) / Mark Anthony Pembridge (53), Ryan Joseph Giggs (66)

477. 11.11.1997
BRAZIL v WALES 3-0 (2-0)
Mané Garrincha, Brasilia
Referee: Javier Castrilli (Argentina)   Attendance: 30,000
BRAZIL: Cláudio André Mergen Taffarel, Marcos Evangelista de Moraes "Cafu" (70 José Marcelo Ferreira "Zé Maria"), ALDAIR Nascimento Santos, ANDRÉ Alves da CRUZ (69 Raimundo Ferreira Ramos Júnior "Júnior Baiano"), José "Zé" ROBERTO da Silva Junior, Dorival Guidoni Júnior "Doriva", Flávio Conceição (70 ÉMERSON Ferreira da Rosa), Crizam César de Oliveira Filho "Zinho", RIVALDO Vitor Borba Ferreira, Luís Antônio Corrêa da Costa "Müller", Ricardo Lucas "Dodô" (46 RODRIGO Fabbri).
Trainer: Mário Jorge Lobo Zagallo
WALES: Paul Steven Jones (81 Andrew Marriott), Stephen Robert Jenkins (81 Andrew Phillip Williams), Christopher Coleman, Mark Anthony Pembridge (52 Paul Jonathan Trollope), Karl Ready, Robert John Page, John Robert Campbell Robinson, Dean Nicholas Saunders, Simon Owen Haworth (60 Adrian Williams), Gary Andrew Speed, John Morgan Oster.   Manager: Robert Gould
Goals: Crizam César de Oliveira Filho "Zinho" (32), RIVALDO Vitor Borba Ferreira (37), RODRIGO Fabbri (50)

478. 25.03.1998
WALES v JAMAICA 0-0
Ninian Park, Cardiff
Referee: Stuart Dougal (Scotland)   Attendance: 13,349
WALES: Paul Steven Jones, Stephen Robert Jenkins, Darren Sean Barnard, Mark Anthony Pembridge, Adrian Williams, Christopher Coleman, John Morgan Oster, Robert William Savage, John Hartson (77 Simon Owen Haworth), Gary Andrew Speed (46 Paul Jonathan Trollope), Gareth Keith Taylor (58 Craig Douglas Bellamy).   Manager: Robert Gould
JAMAICA: Aaron Lawrence (46 Warren Barrett), Steve Malcolm (73 Dean Sewell), Linval Dixon, Ian Goodison, Christopher Dawes, Ricardo Gardner, Fitzroy Simpson (67 Darryl Powell), Robbie Earle (59 Andrew Williams), Peter Cargill, Paul Hall (76 Onandi Lowe), Deon Burton (46 Marcus Gayle).   Trainer: René Simões
Sent off: Onandi Lowe (81)

479. 03.06.1998
MALTA v WALES 0-3 (0-1)
National, Ta'Qali
Referee: Pasquale Rodomonti (Italy)   Attendance: 2,500
MALTA: Mario Muscat, Darren Debono, David Camilleri (80 Stefan Giglio), Jeffrey Chetcuti (69 Massimo Grima), Jonathan Magri-Overend (46 Pierre Aquilina), Joseph Brincat, Antoine Zahra, Noel Turner (61 Richard Buhagiar), Carmel Busuttil (Cap) (70 Daniel Theuma), Stefan Sultana (46 Chucks Nwoko), Nicholas Saliba (Cap).   Trainer: Josif Ilić
WALES: Paul Steven Jones, Ryan Green, Paul Jonathan Trollope, Craig Douglas Bellamy (76 Robert William Edwards), Karl Ready, Christopher Coleman, Andrew Phillip Williams (76 Christopher Mark Llewellyn), Dean Nicholas Saunders, John Hartson (72 Simon Owen Haworth), Gary Andrew Speed, Mark Anthony Pembridge.
Manager: Robert Gould
Goals: Craig Douglas Bellamy (25), John Hartson (67), Mark Anthony Pembridge (78 pen)

480. 06.06.1998
TUNISIA v WALES 4-0 (2-0)
Olympique El Menzah, Tunis
Referee: Mourad Ben Dadi (Algeria)   Attendance: 80,000
TUNISIA: Chokri El Ouaer, Ferid Chouchane (46 Sabri Jaballah), Hatem Trabelsi (46 Zoubier Beya), Khais Ghodbane (46 Mehdi Ben Slimane), Sirajeddine Chihi, Skander Souayah (46 Tarek Thabet), Adel Sellimi (46 Mourad Melki), José Clayton (76 Faycal Ben Ahmed), Khaled Badra, Imed Ben Younes (46 Riadh Bouazizi), Sami Trabelsi.
Trainer: Henryk Kasperczak
WALES: Andrew Marriott, Karl Ready, Ryan Green, Christopher Coleman, Robert William Savage, Gary Andrew Speed, Craig Douglas Bellamy (70 Simon Owen Haworth), Mark Anthony Pembridge, Paul Jonathan Trollope, Dean Nicholas Saunders (78 Christopher Mark Llewellyn), John Hartson (60 Robert William Edwards).
Manager: Robert Gould
Goals: Imed Ben Younes (19), Khaled Badra (27, 83 pen), Sabri Jaballah (69)

481. 05.09.1998   11th European Champs Qualifiers
WALES v ITALY 0-2 (0-1)
Anfield Road, Liverpool
Referee: Terje Hauge (Norway)   Attendance: 23,160
WALES: Paul Steven Jones, John Robert Campbell Robinson, Darren Sean Barnard, Christopher Jeremiah Symons, Adrian Williams, Christopher Coleman, Andrew James Johnson, Gary Andrew Speed (Cap), Nathan Alexander Blake (65 Dean Nicholas Saunders), Mark Leslie Hughes (80 Robert William Savage), Ryan Joseph Giggs.   Manager: Robert Gould

ITALY: Angelo Peruzzi, Christian Panucci, Gianluca Pessotto, Diego Fuser, Fabio Cannavaro, Mark Iuliano, Eusebio Di Francesco (85 Michele Serena), Dino Baggio, Alessandro Del Piero (75 Roberto Baggio I), Demetrio Albertini (Cap) (66 Luigi Di Biagio), Christian Vieri.   Trainer: Dino Zoff
Goals: Diego Fuser (17), Christian Vieri (77)

482. 10.10.1998   11th European Champs Qualifiers
DENMARK v WALES 1-2 (0-0)
Parken, København
Referee: Sándor Piller (Hungary)   Attendance: 36,000
WALES: Paul Steven Jones, Robert William Savage, Darren Sean Barnard, Christopher Jeremiah Symons, Christopher Coleman, Adrian Williams, Andrew James Johnson (54 Mark Anthony Pembridge), Dean Nicholas Saunders (80 John Robert Campbell Robinson), Nathan Alexander Blake (69 Craig Douglas Bellamy), Mark Leslie Hughes, Gary Andrew Speed.   Manager: Robert Gould
DENMARK: Mogens Krogh, Ole Tobiasen, Marc Rieper, Jes Høgh (Cap), Jan Heintze, Thomas Helveg, Per Frandsen (76 Thomas Gravesen), Brian Steen Nielsen, Martin Jørgensen, Søren Frederiksen, Mikkel Beck (66 Ebbe Sand).
Trainer: Bo Johansson
Goals: Søren Frederiksen (58) /
Adrian Williams (59), Craig Douglas Bellamy (86)

483. 14.10.1998   11th European Champs Qualifiers
WALES v BELARUS 3-2 (1-1)
Ninian Park, Cardiff
Referee: Lawrence Sammut (Malta)   Attendance: 11,975
WALES: Paul Steven Jones, Darren Sean Barnard, Robert William Savage, Christopher Jeremiah Symons, Christopher Coleman, Andrew James Johnson, John Robert Campbell Robinson, Dean Nicholas Saunders, Nathan Alexander Blake, Mark Leslie Hughes (Cap), Mark Anthony Pembridge.
Manager: Robert Gould
BELARUS: Andrey Satsunkevich, Erik Yakhimovich, Andrey Ostrovskiy, Andrey Lavrik, Sergey Shtanyuk, Vasiliy Baranov (69 Sergey Gerasimets), Aleksandr Khatskevich, Vyacheslav Gerashchenko (88 Maxym Romashchenko), Sergey Gurenko, Valentin Belkevich, Vladimir Makovskiy (72 Petr Kachuro).
Trainer: Mikhail Vergeyenko
Goals: John Robinson (14), Christopher Coleman (53), Christopher Jeremiah Symons (84) /
Sergey Gurenko (20), Valentin Belkevich (48)

484. 31.03.1999   11th European Champs Qualifiers
SWITZERLAND v WALES 2-0 (1-0)
Letzigrund, Zürich
Referee: Miroslav Liba (Czech Republic)   Att: 13,500
SWITZERLAND: Martin Brunner, Sébastien Jeanneret, Stéphane Henchoz, Stefan Wolf, Patrick Müller, Johann Vogel, Ciriaco Sforza, Sébastien Fournier, Raphaël Wicky, Stéphane Chapuisat, Alexandre Comisetti (68 Patrick Bühlmann).
Trainer: Gilbert Gress
WALES: Paul Steven Jones (26 Mark Geoffrey Crossley), John Robert Campbell Robinson, Mark Anthony Pembridge, Robert William Savage, Christopher Jeremiah Symons, Christopher Coleman, Andrew James Johnson, Dean Nicholas Saunders, Nathan Alexander Blake (64 John Hartson), Mark Leslie Hughes (72 Craig Douglas Bellamy), Gary Andrew Speed.
Manager: Robert Gould
Goals: Stéphane Chapuisat (4, 70)

485. 05.06.1999   11th European Champs Qualifiers
ITALY v WALES 4-0 (3-0)
Renato Dall'Ara, Bologna
Referee: Edgar Steinborn (Germany)   Attendance: 12,392
ITALY: Gianluigi Buffon, Christian Panucci, Paolo Negro, Fabio Cannavaro, Paolo Maldini, Diego Fuser (69 Angelo Di Livio), Demetrio Albertini, Antonio Conte, Eusebio Di Francesco, Christian Vieri (46 Vincenzo Montella), Filippo Inzaghi (80 Enrico Chiesa).   Trainer: Dino Zoff
WALES: Paul Steven Jones, John Robert Campbell Robinson (77 Stephen Robert Jenkins), Darren Sean Barnard, Robert John Page, Andrew Roger Melville, Adrian Williams, Craig Douglas Bellamy (80 Mark Anthony Pembridge), Dean Nicholas Saunders (46 John Hartson), Ryan Joseph Giggs, Mark Leslie Hughes, Gary Andrew Speed (Cap).
Manager: Robert Gould
Goals: Christian Vieri (6), Filippo Inzaghi (37), Paolo Maldini (40), Enrico Chiesa (89)

486. 09.06.1999   11th European Champs Qualifiers
WALES v DENMARK 0-2 (0-0)
Anfield Road, Liverpool
Referee: Armand Ancion (Belgium)   Attendance: 10,000
WALES: Paul Steven Jones, Stephen Robert Jenkins, Darren Sean Barnard (90 Andrew Legg), John Robert Campbell Robinson (86 Mark Anthony Pembridge), Andrew Roger Melville, Christopher Coleman, Gary Andrew Speed, Dean Nicholas Saunders, John Hartson (87 Craig Douglas Bellamy), Mark Leslie Hughes, Ryan Joseph Giggs.
Manager: Mark Leslie Hughes
DENMARK: Peter Schmeichel (Cap), Søren Colding, René Henriksen, Jes Høgh, Jan Heintze, Bjarne Goldbaek, Allan Nielsen (83 Stig Tøfting), Jesper Grønkjær, Martin Jørgensen (90 Per Frandsen), Ebbe Sand, Miklos Molnar (70 Jon Dahl Tomasson).   Trainer: Bo Johansson
Goal: Jon Dahl Tomasson (84), Stig Tøfting (90 pen)

487. 04.09.1999   11th European Champs Qualifiers
BELARUS v WALES 1-2 (1-1)
Dinamo, Minsk
Referee: Tom Henning Øvrebø (Norway)   Att: 25,000
BELARUS: Gennadiy Tumilovich, Igor Tarlovskiy, Andrey Lavrik, Aleksandr Lukhvich, Andrey Ostrovskiy, Sergey Gurenko, Vasiliy Baranov, Aleksandr Chayka, Aleksandr Kulchiy, Radislav Orlovskiy (60 Maxym Romashchenko), Vladimir Makovskiy.   Trainer: Mikhail Vergeyenko
WALES: Paul Steven Jones, Robert John Page, Darren Sean Barnard, Andrew Roger Melville, Christopher Coleman, Mark Anthony Pembridge (80 Carl Phillip Robinson), John Robert Campbell Robinson, Dean Nicholas Saunders, Nathan Alexander Blake, Gary Andrew Speed, Ryan Joseph Giggs.
Manager: Mark Leslie Hughes
Goals: Vasiliy Baranov (30) /
Dean Nicholas Saunders (42), Ryan Joseph Giggs (86)

488. 09.10.1999   11th European Champs Qualifiers
WALES v SWITZERLAND 0-2 (0-1)
The Racecourse, Wrexham
Referee: Spiridon Papadakos (Greece)   Attendance: 5,064
WALES: Paul Steven Jones, Mark Delaney, Darren Sean Barnard, Robert John Page, Christopher Coleman, Robert William Savage, John Robert Campbell Robinson, Dean Nicholas Saunders (67 John Hartson), Nathan Alexander Blake (78 Neil Wyn Roberts), Gary Andrew Speed, John Morgan Oster (78 Matthew Jones).
Manager: Mark Leslie Hughes
SWITZERLAND: Pascal Zuberbühler, Bernt Haas, Sébastien Jeanneret, Franco Di Jorio, Stéphane Henchoz, Marc Hodel, Johann Vogel, David Sesa, Christophe Jaquet (70 Thomas Wyss), Alexandre Rey (66 Alexandre Comisetti), Patrick Bühlmann.   Trainer: Gilbert Gress
Goals: Alexandre Rey (16), Patrick Bühlmann (60)

489. 23.02.2000
QATAR v WALES 0-1 (0-1)
Al-Saad, Doha
Referee: Abdul Aziz Hamed (Bahrain)   Attendance: 2,000
QATAR: Khalil, Almobi, Zamel Al-Kuwari, Rahman Al-Kuwari, Jassim Al-Tamimi, Fahad Al-Kuwari, Nadno, Mohamed, Hassab, Jassim, Fath.   Trainer: Jamal Hadji
WALES: Paul Steven Jones, Mark Delaney, Darren Sean Barnard (89 Christopher Jeremiah Symons), Robert John Page, Andrew Roger Melville, Christopher Coleman, John Robert Campbell Robinson, Gary Andrew Speed, Nathan Alexander Blake, Mark Anthony Pembridge, Matthew Jones.
Manager: Mark Leslie Hughes
Goal: John Robert Campbell Robinson (10)

490. 29.03.2000
WALES v FINLAND 1-2 (0-2)
Millennium, Cardiff

Referee: Michael Thomas Ross (N. Ireland)   Att: 66,500

WALES: Mark Geoffrey Crossley, John Robert Campbell Robinson, Darren Sean Barnard (67 Gareth Roberts), Robert John Page, Christopher Coleman, Andrew Roger Melville, Robert William Savage (79 Andrew James Johnson), Mark Anthony Pembridge (86 Iwan Wyn Roberts), Nathan Alexander Blake (79 Dean Nicholas Saunders), Gary Andrew Speed, Ryan Joseph Giggs.   Manager: Mark Leslie Hughes

FINLAND: Peter Enckelman (46 Teuvo Moilanen), Juha Reini, Sami Hyypiä, Jarmo Saastamoinen (48 Marko Tuomela), Hannu Tihinen, Aki Riihilahti, Mika Nurmela, Simo Valakari (64 Jarkko Wiss), Jari Litmanen (Cap) (69 Mika Lehkosuo), Joonas Kolkka, Mikael Forssell (46 Mika-Matti Paatelainen).
Trainer: Antti Muurinen

Goals: Ryan Joseph Giggs (60) /
Jari Litmanen (21), Nathan Blake (42 own goal)

491. 23.05.2000
WALES v BRAZIL 0-3 (0-0)
Millennium, Cardiff

Referee: Vítor Manuel Melo Pereira (Portugal)   Att: 72,250

WALES: Roger Freestone, Mark Delaney, Gareth Roberts, Robert John Page, Andrew Roger Melville, Matthew Jones (75 Andrew James Johnson), Robert William Savage (75 Craig Douglas Bellamy), Dean Nicholas Saunders (84 Darren Sean Barnard), Iwan Wyn Roberts, Gary Andrew Speed, John Robert Campbell Robinson.   Manager: Mark Leslie Hughes

BRAZIL: Nélson de Jesus Silva "Dida", Marcos Evangelista de Moraes "Cafu" (84 EVANÍLSON Aparecido Ferreira), ANTÔNIO CARLOS Zago, ALDAIR Nascimento Santos (84 ÉMERSON CARVALHO da Silva), Sylvio Mendes Campos Júnior "Silvinho", ÉMERSON Ferreira da Rosa, Carlos Campos CÉSAR SAMPAIO, José "Zé" ROBERTO da Silva Junior, RIVALDO Vitor Borba Ferreira (84 MARCOS dos Santos ASSUNÇÃO), ÉLBER Giovane de Souza (71 DENÍLSON de Oliveira), Francoaldo Sena de Souza "França".
Trainer: Wanderley Luxemburgo da Silva

Goals: ÉLBER Giovane de Souza (63), Marcos Evangelista de Moraes "Cafu" (70), RIVALDO Vitor Borba Ferreira (73)

492. 02.06.2000
PORTUGAL v WALES 3-0 (2-0)
Municipal, Chavés

Referee: Frank de Bleeckere (Belgium)   Attendance: 11,000

PORTUGAL: VÍTOR Manuel Martins BAÍA (Cap), Carlos Alberto Oliveira "Secretário" (59 Francisco José Rodrigues Costa "Costinha"), FERNANDO Manuel Silva COUTO, JORGE Paulo COSTA Almeida, DIMAS Manuel Marques Teixeira (68 RUI JORGE de Sousa Dias Macedo de Oliveira), Luis Filipe Madeira Caeiro "Figo" (59 Nuno Fernando Gonçalves Rocha "Capucho"), PAULO Jorge Gomes BENTO, RUI Manuel César COSTA, José Luís da Cruz Vidigal (46 SÉRGIO Paulo Marceneiro CONCEIÇÃO), João Manuel Vieira Pinto (77 Pedro Miguel Carreiro Resendes "Pauleta"), Ricardo Manuel Silva Sá Pinto (62 NUNO Miguel Soares Pereira Ribeiro "GOMES").   Trainer: Humberto Manuel de Jesus Coelho

WALES: Darren Ward, Mark Delaney, Gareth Roberts (84 Rhys Weston), Robert John Page, Andrew Roger Melville, Matthew Jones, John Robert Campbell Robinson, Craig Douglas Bellamy, Iwan Wyn Roberts, Gary Andrew Speed (31 Andrew James Johnson), Darren Sean Barnard (68 Carl Phillip Robinson).   Manager: Mark Leslie Hughes

Goals: Luis Filipe Madeira Caeiro "Figo" (21),
Ricardo Manuel Silva Sá Pinto (44),
Nuno Fernando Gonçalves Rocha "Capucho" (66)

493. 02.09.2000   17th World Cup Qualifiers
BELARUS v WALES 2-1 (1-0)
Dinamo, Minsk

Referee: Alfredo Trentalange (Italy)   Attendance: 32,000

BELARUS: Gennadiy Tumilovich, Erik Yakhimovich, Aleksandr Lukhvich, Sergey Shtanyuk, Sergey Gurenko, Sergey Yaskovich (70 Vladimir Shuneiko), Radislav Orlovskiy (85 Vadim Skripchenko), Valentin Belkevich, Aleksandr Khatskevich, Maxym Romashchenko (28 Nikolay Ryndyuk), Roman Vasilyuk.   Trainer: Eduard Malofeyev

WALES: Paul Steven Jones, Robert John Page, Gareth Roberts, Andrew Roger Melville, Christopher Coleman, Robert William Savage, John Robert Campbell Robinson, Craig Douglas Bellamy, Iwan Wyn Roberts (73 Nathan Alexander Blake), Gary Andrew Speed, Ryan Joseph Giggs.
Manager: Mark Leslie Hughes

Sent off: Craig Douglas Bellamy (65)

Goals: Aleksandr Khatskevich (39), Valentin Belkevich (56) /
Gary Andrew Speed (90)

494. 07.10.2000   17th World Cup Qualifiers
WALES v NORWAY 1-1 (0-0)
Millennium, Cardiff
Referee: Hartmut Strampe (Germany)   Attendance: 53,360
WALES: Paul Steven Jones, Mark Delaney, Robert John Page, Andrew Roger Melville, Christopher Coleman, Robert William Savage, John Robert Campbell Robinson, John Hartson (87 Iwan Wyn Roberts), Nathan Alexander Blake, Gary Andrew Speed, Ryan Joseph Giggs.   Manager: Mark Leslie Hughes
NORWAY: Frode Olsen, Christer Basma, Henning Berg, Ronny Johnsen, Stig Inge Bjørnebye, Stefen Iversen (58 Tore André Flo), Erik Mykland, Roar Strand, Øyvind Leonhardsen, Eirik Bakke (78 Thorstein Helstad), Ole Gunnar Solskjær.   Trainer: Nils Johan Semb
Goals: Nathan Alexander Blake (60) / Thorstein Helstad (80)

495. 11.10.2000   17th World Cup Qualifiers
POLAND v WALES 0-0
Wojska Polskiego, Warszawa
Referee: Lucillio Cortez Cardoso Batista (Portugal)   Attendance: 10,067
POLAND: Jerzy Dudek, Tomasz Kłos, Tomasz Wałdoch (Cap), Jacek Zieliński, Michał Żewłakow, Bartosz Karwan, Jacek Krzynówek (69 Tomasz Rząsa), Radosław Kałużny, Piotr Świerczewski, Andrzej Juskowiak (75 Emmanuel Olisadebe), Radosław Gilewicz (58 Paweł Kryszałowicz).   Trainer: Jerzy Engel
WALES: Paul Steven Jones, Mark Delaney, Robert John Page, Andrew Roger Melville, Christopher Coleman, Robert William Savage, John Robert Campbell Robinson, John Hartson (74 Matthew Jones), Nathan Alexander Blake, Gary Andrew Speed, Ryan Joseph Giggs.   Manager: Mark Leslie Hughes

496. 24.03.2001   17th World Cup Qualifiers
ARMENIA v WALES 2-2 (1-1)
Razdan, Yerevan
Referee: Georgios Kasnaferis (Greece)   Attendance: 7,000
ARMENIA: Harutyun Abrahamyan, Albert Sargisyan, Sargis Hovsepyan, Harutyun Vardanyan, Artak Minasyan (39 Hovhannes Demirchyan), Karen Dokhoyan, Felix Khodzhoyan (57 Artavazd Karamyan), Aram Voskanyan, Artur Petrosyan, Armen Shahgeldyan, Andrei Movsesyan.   Trainer: Varuzhan Sukiasyan
WALES: Paul Steven Jones, Mark Delaney, Andrew Legg, Andrew Roger Melville, Robert John Page, Mark Anthony Pembridge (46 Matthew Jones), John Robert Campbell Robinson, Dean Nicholas Saunders (71 Carl Phillip Robinson), John Hartson (80 Iwan Wyn Roberts), Gary Andrew Speed, Craig Douglas Bellamy.   Manager: Mark Leslie Hughes
Sent off: Albert Sargisyan (81)
Goals: Artak Minasyan (39), Andrei Movsesyan (67) / John Hartson (40, 48)

497. 28.03.2001   17th World Cup Qualifiers
WALES v UKRAINE 1-1 (1-0)
Millennium, Cardiff
Referee: Eric Romain (Belgium)   Attendance: 48,014
WALES: Paul Steven Jones, Mark Delaney, Darren Sean Barnard, Andrew Roger Melville, Robert John Page, Carl Phillip Robinson, Matthew Jones (54 Simon Davies), Craig Douglas Bellamy, John Hartson (69 Dean Nicholas Saunders), Gary Andrew Speed (Cap), Ryan Joseph Giggs.   Manager: Mark Leslie Hughes
UKRAINE: Oleksandr Shovkovskiy, Oleh Luzhniy (Cap), Andriy Nesmachniy, Oleksandr Holovko, Vladislav Vaschuk, Anatoliy Tymoschuk, Serhiy Popov (69 Oleksandr Melashchenko), Andriy Vorobei, Artyom Yashkin, Andriy Shevchenko, Serhiy Rebrov (46 Vasyl Kardash).   Trainer: Valeriy Lobanovskiy
Goals: John Hartson (12) / Andriy Shevchenko (52)

498. 02.06.2001   17th World Cup Qualifiers
WALES v POLAND 1-2 (1-1)
Millennium, Cardiff
Referee: Erol Ersoy (Turkey)   Attendance: 48,500
WALES: Paul Steven Jones, Christopher Jeremiah Symons, Darren Sean Barnard (78 Matthew Jones), Andrew Roger Melville, Robert John Page (84 Stephen Robert Jenkins), Mark Anthony Pembridge, Robert William Savage, Nathan Alexander Blake, John Hartson, Gary Andrew Speed (Cap), Ryan Joseph Giggs.   Manager: Mark Leslie Hughes
POLAND: Jerzy Dudek, Tomasz Kłos, Tomasz Hajto, Jacek Bąk, Michał Żewłakow, Tomasz Iwan, Arkadiusz Bąk, Marek Koźmiński, Tomasz Zdebel (62 Jacek Krzynówek), Emmanuel Olisadebe (90 Marcin Żewłakow), Andrzej Juskowiak (Cap) (54 Paweł Kryszałowicz).   Trainer: Jerzy Engel
Goals: Nathan Alexander Blake (14) / Emmanuel Olisadebe (32), Paweł Kryszałowicz (72)

499. 06.06.2001   17th World Cup Qualifiers
UKRAINE v WALES 1-1 (1-0)
Olympiyskiy, Kyiv
Referee: Joaquím Gómes (Portugal)   Attendance: 33,000
UKRAINE: Oleksandr Shovkovskiy (86 Maxym Levytskiy), Mykhailo Starostyak (46 Oleh Luzhniy), Dmytro Parfyonov, Oleksandr Holovko, Vladislav Vaschuk, Yuriy Dmitrulin (46 Andriy Nesmachniy), Anatoliy Tymoschuk, Hennadiy Zubov, Andriy Vorobei, Serhiy Rebrov, Andriy Shevchenko.   Trainer: Valeriy Lobanovskiy
WALES: Paul Steven Jones, Mark Delaney (37 Stephen Robert Jenkins), Darren Sean Barnard, Andrew Roger Melville, Robert John Page, Mark Anthony Pembridge, Simon Davies, Nathan Alexander Blake (72 Jason Koumas), John Hartson, Gary Andrew Speed, Ryan Joseph Giggs.   Manager: Mark Leslie Hughes
Goals: Hennadiy Zubov (44) / Mark Anthony Pembridge (72)

500. 01.09.2001   17th World Cup Qualifiers
WALES v ARMENIA   0-0
Millennium, Cardiff

Referee: Joseph Attard (Malta)   Attendance: 20,000

WALES: Paul Steven Jones, Mark Delaney, Stephen Robert Jenkins (80 Darren Sean Barnard), Andrew Roger Melville, Christopher Jeremiah Symons, Carl Phillip Robinson (80 Matthew Jones), Robert William Savage, Craig Douglas Bellamy, Iwan Wyn Roberts, Simon Davies, Ryan Joseph Giggs. Manager: Mark Leslie Hughes

ARMENIA: Roman Berezovski, Yervand Sukiasyan, Sargis Hovsepyan, Harutyun Vardanyan, Romik Khachatryan, Aram Voskanyan (66 Ararat Harutyunyan), Artur Petrosyan (89 Hovhannes Demirchyan), Karen Dokhoyan, Arkadi Dokhoyan, Armen Shahgeldyan (75 Gagik Simonyan), Andrei Movsesyan. Trainer: Varuzhan Sukiasyan

501. 05.09.2001   17th World Cup Qualifiers
NORWAY v WALES 3-2 (1-2)
Ullevaal, Oslo

Referee: Fritz Stuchlik (Austria)   Attendance: 18,211

NORWAY: Thomas Myhre, Christer Basma, Ronny Johnsen, Henning Berg, John Arne Riise, Roar Strand, Jan Derek Sørensen (46 Frode Johnsen), Øyvind Leonhardsen (90 Pål Strand), Petter Rudi, Ole Gunnar Solskjær, Steffen Iversen (5 John Carew).   Trainer: Nils Johan Semb

WALES: Paul Steven Jones, Mark Delaney, Stephen Robert Jenkins, Robert John Page, Christopher Jeremiah Symons, Carl Phillip Robinson (84 Matthew Jones), Robert William Savage, Craig Douglas Bellamy, John Hartson (84 Nathan Alexander Blake), Simon Davies (77 John Robert Campbell Robinson), Ryan Joseph Giggs.   Manager: Mark Leslie Hughes

Sent off: Ryan Joseph Giggs (86)

Goals: Ronny Johnsen (17), John Carew (65), Frode Johnsen (82) /
Robert William Savage (10), Craig Douglas Bellamy (28)

502. 06.10.2001   17th World Cup Qualifiers
WALES v BELARUS 1-0 (0-0)
Millennium, Cardiff

Referee: Pasquale Rodomonti (Italy)   Attendance: 10,201

WALES: Paul Steven Jones, Mark Delaney, Mark Anthony Pembridge, Andrew Roger Melville, Christopher Jeremiah Symons (16 Robert John Page), John Robert Campbell Robinson, Matthew Jones (61 Carl Phillip Robinson), Craig Douglas Bellamy, John Hartson (90 Iwan Wyn Roberts), Gary Andrew Speed, Simon Davies.
Manager: Mark Leslie Hughes

BELARUS: Gennadiy Tumilovich, Erik Yakhimovich, Sergey Yaskovich, Aleksandr Lukhvich, Sergey Shtanyuk, Sergey Gurenko, Vasiliy Baranov (66 Aleksandr Hleb), Aleksandr Kulchiy, Vladimir Shuneiko, Petr Kachuro (43 Nikolay Ryndyuk), Roman Vasilyuk.   Trainer: Eduard Malofeyev

Goal: John Hartson (47)

503. 13.02.2002
WALES v ARGENTINA   1-1 (1-0)
Millennium, Cardiff

Referee: Paul McKeon (Republic of Ireland)   Att: 65,000

WALES: Paul Steven Jones (46 Mark Geoffrey Crossley), Mark Delaney, Andrew Roger Melville, Robert John Page, Gary Andrew Speed (Cap), Simon Davies, Robert William Savage (90 Carl Phillip Robinson), Ryan Joseph Giggs (61 John Robert Campbell Robinson), Mark Anthony Pembridge, Craig Douglas Bellamy, John Hartson.
Manager: Mark Leslie Hughes

ARGENTINA: Sebastián Diego Saja, Nelson David Vivas, José Antonio Chamot, Diego Rodolfo Placente, Claudio Daniel Husaín, Juan Román Riquelme (73 Pablo César Aimar), Juan Pablo Sorín, Julio Ricardo Cruz (73 Javier Pedro Saviola), Juan Sebastián Verón (Cap), Claudio Paul Caniggia (90 Luciano Martín Galletti), Cristián Alberto González.
Trainer: Marcelo Alberto Bielsa

Goals: Craig Douglas Bellamy (34) / Julio Ricardo Cruz (62)

504. 27.03.2002
WALES v CZECH REPUBLIC 0-0
Millennium, Cardiff

Referee: Claus Bo Larsen (Denmark)   Attendance: 20,000

WALES: Darren Ward (46 Daniel Coyne), Mark Delaney, Andrew Roger Melville, Robert John Page, Daniel Gabbidon, Simon Davies, Robert William Savage (73 Paul Simon Evans), John Robert Campbell Robinson, Jason Koumas, Nathan Alexander Blake (62 Paul Jonathan Trollope), John Hartson (73 Gareth Keith Taylor).   Manager: Mark Leslie Hughes

CZECH REPUBLIC: Petr Čech (46 Martin Vaniak), Milan Fukal, Jiří Novotný (Cap) (46 Petr Johana), Marek Jankulovski (82 Miroslav Holeňák), Tomáš Galásek (61 Václav Koloušek), Tomáš Ujfaluši, Vladimír Šmicer, Karel Poborský, Vratislav Lokvenc (46 Jan Koller), Tomáš Rosický (46 Tomáš Hübschman), Jiří Štajner (46 Libor Sionko).
Trainer: Karel Brückner

505. 14.05.2002
WALES v GERMANY 1-0 (0-0)
Millennium, Cardiff
Referee: Roy Helge Olsen (Norway)   Attendance: 36,920
WALES: Mark Geoffrey Crossley, Mark Delaney, Andrew Roger Melville, Robert John Page, Gary Andrew Speed (Cap), Simon Davies, Robert William Savage, Mark Anthony Pembridge, Ryan Joseph Giggs, Robert Earnshaw (90 Christopher Coleman), John Hartson.
Manager: Mark Leslie Hughes
GERMANY: Oliver Kahn (Cap), Thomas Linke, Christoph Metzelder, Jörg Heinrich, Christian Ziege (63 Marco Bode), Jens Jeremies, Dietmar Hamann (73 Sebastian Kehl), Sebastian Deisler (63 Gerald Asamoah), Torsten Frings, Oliver Bierhoff (72 Carsten Jancker), Miroslav Klose.
Trainer: Rudolf Völler
Goal: Robert Earnshaw (46)

506. 21.08.2002
CROATIA v WALES 1-1 (0-1)
Varteks, Varaždin
Referee: Lutz-Michael Fröhlich (Germany)   Att: 6,000
CROATIA: Stipe Pletikosa (46 Tomislav Butina), Boris Živković (61 Stjepan Tomas), Filip Tapalović (75 Marko Babić), Josip Šimunić, Robert Kovač (61 Jurica Vranješ), Niko Kovač (46 Jerko Leko), Danijel Šarić, Davor Vugrinec (46 Silvio Marić), Goran Vlaović (46 Mladen Petrić), Milan Rapaić (61 Mario Bazina), Tomislav Marić (46 Marijo Marić).
Trainer: Otto Barić
WALES: Paul Steven Jones, Mark Delaney, Daniel Gabbidon, Andrew Roger Melville (Cap), Darren Sean Barnard (60 Rhys Weston), Mark Anthony Pembridge, Carl Phillip Robinson (70 Paul Simon Evans), Andrew James Johnson, Simon Davies, John Hartson (60 Gareth Keith Taylor), Robert Earnshaw (80 Paul Jonathan Trollope).   Manager: Mark Leslie Hughes
Goal: Simon Davies (10)

507. 07.09.2002   12th European Champs Qualifiers
FINLAND v WALES 0-2 (0-1)
Olympiastadion, Helsinki
Referee: Konrad Plautz (Austria)   Attendance: 35,833
FINLAND: Antti Niemi, Kaj Wilhelm Nylund (69 Jonatan Johansson), Janne Saarinen (78 Peter Kopteff), Sami Hyypiä, Hannu Tihinen, Aki Riihilahti, Mika Nurmela (86 Mika Kottila), Teemu Tainio, Shefki Kuqi, Jari Litmanen (Cap), Joonas Kolkka.   Trainer: Antti Muurinen
WALES: Paul Steven Jones, Mark Delaney, Gary Andrew Speed (Cap), Andrew Roger Melville, Daniel Gabbidon, Mark Anthony Pembridge, Robert William Savage, Andrew James Johnson (76 Craig Douglas Bellamy), John Hartson, Simon Davies, Ryan Joseph Giggs.   Manager: Mark Leslie Hughes
Goals: John Hartson (30), Simon Davies (72)

508. 16.10.2002   12th European Champs Qualifiers
WALES v ITALY 2-1 (1-1)
Millennium, Cardiff
Referee: Gilles Veissière (France)   Attendance: 72,500
WALES: Paul Steven Jones, Mark Delaney, Gary Andrew Speed (Cap), Andrew Roger Melville, Daniel Gabbidon, Mark Anthony Pembridge, Robert William Savage, Craig Douglas Bellamy (90 Nathan Alexander Blake), John Hartson, Simon Davies, Ryan Joseph Giggs.   Manager: Mark Leslie Hughes
ITALY: Gianluigi Buffon, Christian Panucci, Luciano Zauri, Luigi Di Biagio (64 Gennaro Gattuso, 84 Massimo Marazzina), Fabio Cannavaro (Cap), Alessandro Nesta, Alessandro Del Piero, Massimo Ambrosini, Vincenzo Montella (70 Massimo Maccarone), Andrea Pirlo, Damiano Tommasi.
Trainer: Giovanni Trapattoni
Goals: Simon Davies (11), Craig Douglas Bellamy (70) / Alessandro Del Piero (32)

509. 20.11.2002   12th European Champs Qualifiers
AZERBAIJAN v WALES 0-2 (0-1)
Tofik Bakhramov, Baku
Referee: Luc Huyghe (Belgium)   Attendance: 12,000
AZERBAIJAN: Dzhakhangir Hasanzade, Aslan Kerimov (46 Fizuli Mamedov), Ilgham Yadullayev, Tarlan Akhmedov (75 Arif Asadov), Adagim Niftaliyev, Rashad Sadygov, Makhmud Kurbanov (62 Farrukh Ismaylov), Emin Imamaliyev, Kurban Kurbanov, Vadim Vasilyev, Samir Aliyev.
Trainer: Asker Abdullayev
WALES: Paul Steven Jones, Mark Delaney (71 Rhys Weston), Darren Sean Barnard, Andrew Roger Melville, Robert John Page, Gary Andrew Speed (Cap), Carl Phillip Robinson (90 Paul Jonathan Trollope), Robert Earnshaw (90 Neil Wyn Roberts), John Hartson, Simon Davies, Ryan Joseph Giggs.
Manager: Mark Leslie Hughes
Goals: Gary Andrew Speed (10), John Hartson (68)

510. 12.02.2003
WALES v BOSNIA-HERZEGOVINA 2-2 (1-1)
Millenium, Cardiff
Referee: David Malcolm (Northern Ireland)   Att: 22,000
WALES: Darren Ward (46 Mark Geoffrey Crossley), Rhys Weston (60 Matthew Jones), Robert John Page, Andrew Roger Melville, Gary Andrew Speed (Cap), Mark Anthony Pembridge, Simon Davies, Robert William Savage (88 John Morgan Oster), Craig Douglas Bellamy, Robert Earnshaw (73 Jason Koumas), John Hartson (81 Gareth Keith Taylor).
Manager: Mark Leslie Hughes

BOSNIA-HERZEGOVINA: Kenan Hasagić, Džemal Berberović, Mirsad Bešlija, Muhamed Konjić, Mirsad Hibić, Vedin Mušić, Bulend Biščević (90 Admir Velagić), Vladan Grujić (78 Mirko Hrgović), Sergej Barbarez (81 Nenad Misković), Elvir Baljić (78 Siniša Mulina), Elvir Bolić (89 Nedim Halilović).   Trainer: Blaž Sliškovič

Goals: Robert Earnshaw (8), John Hartson (74) / Elvir Baljić (5), Sergej Barbarez (64)

511.   29.03.2003   12th European Champs Qualifiers
WALES v AZERBAIJAN 4-0 (3-0)
Millennium, Cardiff

Referee: Philippe Leuba (Switzerland)   Attendance: 73,500

WALES: Paul Steven Jones, John Morgan Oster, Gary Andrew Speed (Cap) (46 Paul Jonathan Trollope), Andrew Roger Melville, Robert John Page, Mark Anthony Pembridge, Robert William Savage (19 Carl Phillip Robinson), Craig Douglas Bellamy (71 Robert Edwards), John Hartson, Simon Davies, Ryan Joseph Giggs.   Manager: Mark Leslie Hughes

AZERBAIJAN: Dzhakhangir Hasanzade, Tarlan Akhmedov, Avtandil Gadzhiev (46 Fizuli Mamedov), Ruslan Musaev, Emin Guliyev (46 Ilghan Yadullayev), Kamal Guliyev, Makhmud Kurbanov, Khagani Mamedov, Kurban Kurbanov, Emin Imamaliyev, Samir Aliyev (78 Zaur Tagizade).   Trainer: Asker Abdullayev

Goals: Craig Douglas Bellamy (1), Gary Andrew Speed (40), John Hartson (43), Ryan Joseph Giggs (52)

512.   26.05.2003
UNITED STATES v WALES 2-0 (1-0)
Spartan, San José

Referee: Benito Archundia (Mexico)   Attendance: 12,282

UNITED STATES: Nick Rimando, Ryan Suarez (78 Michael Petke), Charles Brown, Jeff Agoos (Cap), Gregory Vanney, Earnest Stewart (83 Manuel Lagos), Richard Mulrooney, Robert Francis Convey (75 Brian Ching), Edward Lewis, Jovan Kirovski (89 Alecko Eskandarian), Landon Timothy Donovan.   Trainer: Bruce Arena

WALES: Paul Steven Jones (46 Darren Ward), David Vaughan, Andrew Roger Melville (Cap), Adrian Williams, Mark Anthony Pembridge (78 Carl Phillip Robinson), Andrew James Johnson, Simon Davies, Matthew Jones, Jason Koumas, John Morgan Oster (70 David Pipe), Gareth Keith Taylor (57 Neil Wyn Roberts).   Manager: Mark Leslie Hughes

Sent off: Matthew Jones (48)

Goals: Landon Donovan (41 pen), Edward Lewis (59)

513.   20.08.2003   12th European Champs Qualifiers
SERBIA & MONTENEGRO v WALES 1-0 (0-0)
Crvena zvezda, Beograd

Referee: Anders Frisk (Sweden)   Attendance: 22,000

SERBIA & MONTENEGRO: Dragoslav Jevrić, Ivica Dragutinović, Mladen Krstajić, Milivoje Ćirković, Dragan Mladenović, Dejan Stefanović, Goran Gavrančić, Zvonimir Vukić (67 Saša Ilić), Mateja Kežman (71 Savo Milošević), Dejan Stanković (81 Predrag Đorđević), Darko Kovačević.   Trainer: Ilija Petković

WALES: Paul Steven Jones, Mark Delaney, Gary Andrew Speed (Cap), Daniel Gabbidon, Robert John Page, Mark Anthony Pembridge, Robert William Savage, Craig Douglas Bellamy, Nathan Alexander Blake (78 Robert Earnshaw), Simon Davies, Ryan Joseph Giggs.   Manager: Mark Hughes

Goal: Dragan Mladenović (73)

514.   06.09.2003   12th European Champs Qualifiers
ITALY v WALES 4-0 (0-0)
Giuseppe Meazza, Milano

Referee: Dr. Markus Merk (Germany)   Attendance: 68,000

ITALY: Gianluigi Buffon, Christian Panucci (58 Massimo Oddo), Alessandro Nesta, Fabio Cannavaro, Gianluca Zambrotta, Mauro German Camoranesi, Cristiano Zanetti, Simone Perrotta (85 Stefano Fiore), Alessandro Del Piero, Christian Vieri, Filippo Inzaghi (73 Gennaro Gattuso).   Coach: Giovanni Trapattoni

WALES: Paul Steven Jones, Mark Delaney, Gary Andrew Speed (Cap), Jason Koumas (71 Robert Earnshaw), Robert John Page, Mark Anthony Pembridge (78 Andrew James Johnson), Robert William Savage, Craig Douglas Bellamy, John Hartson (82 Nathan Alexander Blake), Simon Davies, Ryan Joseph Giggs.   Manager: Mark Leslie Hughes

Goals: Filippo Inzaghi (59, 63, 70), Alessandro del Piero (75 pen)

515.   10.09.2003   12th European Champs Qualifiers
WALES v FINLAND 1-1 (1-0)
Millennium, Cardiff

Referee: Arturo Daudén Ibáñez (Spain)   Attendance: 73,411

WALES: Paul Steven Jones, Rhys Weston (73 Andrew James Johnson), Gary Andrew Speed (Cap), Andrew Roger Melville, Robert John Page, Mark Anthony Pembridge, Jason Koumas, Robert Earnshaw, John Hartson (82 Nathan Alexander Blake), Simon Davies, Ryan Joseph Giggs.   Manager: Mark Hughes

FINLAND: Antti Niemi, Petri Pasanen (82 Peter Kopteff), Janne Saarinen (46 Juha Reini), Sami Hyypiä, Hannu Tihinen, Aki Riihilahti, Mika Nurmela, Teemu Tainio, Mikael Forssell, Mika Väyrynen (58 Shefki Kuqi), Joonas Kolkka.   Trainer: Antti Muurinen

Sent off: Jason Koumas (64)

Goals: Simon Davies (3) / Mikael Forssell (78)

516. 11.10.2003   12th European Champs Qualifiers
WALES v SERBIA & MONTENEGRO 2-3 (1-1)
Millennium, Cardiff
Referee: Fritz Stuchlik (Austria)   Attendance: 72,514
WALES: Paul Steven Jones, Mark Delaney, Gary Andrew Speed (Cap), Daniel Gabbidon, Rhys Weston (73 Robert Edwards), Carl Phillip Robinson (89 John Morgan Oster), Robert Earnshaw, Craig Douglas Bellamy, John Hartson (86 Nathan Alexander Blake), Darren Sean Barnard, Ryan Joseph Giggs.   Manager: Mark Leslie Hughes
SERBIA & MONTENEGRO: Dragoslav Jevrić, Milivoje Ćirković (75 Nenad Brnović), Dragan Šarac, Dragan Mladenović, Goran Bunjevčević, Goran Gavrančić, Mateja Kežman (60 Savo Milošević), Zvonimir Vukić, Branko Bošković, Nenad Đorđević, Darko Kovačević (79 Danijel Ljuboja).   Trainer: Ilija Petković
Goals: John Hartson (26 pen), Robert Earnshaw (90) / Zvonimir Vukić (6), Savo Milošević (82), Danijel Ljuboja (88)

517. 15.11.2003   12th European Champs Play-Offs
RUSSIA v WALES 0-0
Lokomotiv, Moskva
Referee: Lucillio Cortez Cardoso Batista (Portugal)
Attendance: 29,000
RUSSIA: Sergey Ovchinnikov, Vadim Yevseyev, Dmitriy Sennikov, Aleksey Smertin (59 Rolan Gusev), Dmitriy Alenichev, Sergey Ignashevich, Viktor Onopko (Cap), Dmitriy Loskov, Dmitriy Bulykin, Aleksandr Mostovoi, Dmitriy Sychev (46 Marat Izmailov).   Trainer: Georgiy Yartsev
WALES: Paul Steven Jones, Mark Delaney, Darren Sean Barnard, Andrew Roger Melville, Daniel Gabbidon, Andrew James Johnson, Robert William Savage, Jason Koumas, Gary Andrew Speed (Cap), John Hartson (83 Nathan Alexander Blake), Ryan Joseph Giggs.   Manager: Mark Leslie Hughes

518. 19.11.2003   12th European Champs Play-Offs
WALES v RUSSIA 0-1 (0-1)
Millennium, Cardiff
Referee: Manuel Enrique Mejuto González (Spain)
Attendance: 73,062
WALES: Paul Steven Jones, Mark Delaney, Darren Sean Barnard, Andrew Roger Melville, Daniel Gabbidon, Andrew James Johnson (57 Robert Earnshaw), Robert William Savage, Jason Koumas (73 Nathan Alexander Blake), Gary Andrew Speed (Cap), John Hartson, Ryan Joseph Giggs.   Manager: Mark Leslie Hughes
RUSSIA: Vyacheslav Malafeyev, Vadim Yevseyev, Dmitriy Sennikov, Aleksey Smertin, Dmitriy Alenichev, Sergey Ignashevich, Viktor Onopko (Cap), Rolan Gusev, Yegor Titov (59 Vladislav Radimov), Dmitriy Bulykin, Marat Izmailov.   Trainer: Georgiy Yartsev
Goal: Vadim Yevseyev (22)

519. 18.02.2004
WALES v SCOTLAND 4-0 (2-0)
Millennium, Cardiff
Referee: Michael Thomas Ross (N. Ireland)   Att: 47,124
WALES: Mark Geoffrey Crossley (46 Darren Ward), Robert Edwards, Daniel Gabbidon, Robert John Page, Andrew Roger Melville (87 Christopher Jeremiah Symons), Simon Davies (33 Paul Parry), John Morgan Oster, Gary Andrew Speed (Cap) (72 Carl Phillip Robinson), Robert William Savage (72 Carl Neil Fletcher), Ryan Joseph Giggs (46 Gareth Keith Taylor), Robert Earnshaw.   Manager: Mark Leslie Hughes
SCOTLAND: Robert Douglas, John McNamara, Gary Naysmith (46 Graeme Stuart Murty), Christian Eduard Dailly (Cap), Stephen Caldwell, Paul Ritchie, Darren Fletcher (85 Andrew Webster), Colin Cameron (67 Paul Gallagher), Stephen Pearson (46 James McFadden), Kenneth Miller, Paul Dickov.   Manager: Hans-Hubert Vogts
Goals: Robert Earnshaw (1, 35, 58), Gareth Keith Taylor (78)

520. 31.03.2004
HUNGARY v WALES 1-2 (1-1)
Puskás Ferenc, Budapest
Referee: Florian Meyer (Germany)   Attendance: 8,000
HUNGARY: Gábor Babos, Ádám Komlósi (89 Zsolt Dvéri), Péter Stark, Zoltán Pető, László Bodnár, Krisztián Lisztes (52 Balázs Tóth), Balázs Molnár (80 Attila Böjte), Zsolt Lőw (89 Boldizsár Bodor), Zoltán Gera, Krisztián Kenesei (46 Imre Szabics), Sándor Torghelle (70 József Sebők).   Trainer: Lothar Herbert Matthäus
WALES: Paul Steven Jones (46 Daniel Coyne), Daniel Gabbidon, Benjamin David Thatcher, Andrew Roger Melville (Cap), Robert John Page, Carl Phillip Robinson (89 Carl Neil Fletcher), Robert William Savage, Jason Koumas, Gareth Keith Taylor (53 Robert Edwards), Robert Earnshaw, David Vaughan (66 Gareth Roberts).   Manager: Mark Leslie Hughes
Goals: Krisztián Kenesei (18 pen) / Jason Koumas (20), Robert Earnshaw (81)

521. 27.05.2004
NORWAY v WALES 0-0
Ullevaal, Oslo
Referee: Martin Hansson (Sweden)   Attendance: 14,137
NORWAY: Thomas Myhre, Christer Basma, Ronny Johnsen (88 Trond Andersen), Henning Berg (18 Claus Lundekvam), John Arne Riise, Martin Andresen, Magne Hoseth, Thorstein Helstad (61 Jan Gunnar Solli), Ole Gunnar Solskjær (61 Tore Andre Flo), Morten Gamst Pedersen (46 André Bergdølmo), Bengt Sæternes (46 Rune Lange).   Trainer: Åge Hareide

WALES: Daniel Coyne, Mark Delaney (Cap), James Collins, Daniel Gabbidon, Benjamin David Thatcher, John Morgan Oster (90 Darren Sean Barnard), Carl Phillip Robinson (75 Robert Edwards), Carl Neil Fletcher, Paul Parry (71 Gareth Roberts), Craig Douglas Bellamy (86 Christopher Mark Llewellyn), Robert Earnshaw (71 Neil Wyn Roberts). Manager: Mark Leslie Hughes

522. 30.05.2004
WALES v CANADA 1-0 (1-0)
The Racecourse, Wrexham
Referee: David McKeown (Republic of Ireland)   Att: 10,805
WALES: Daniel Coyne (46 Martyn Walter Margetson), Mark Delaney, James Collins, Daniel Gabbidon, Benjamin David Thatcher, John Morgan Oster, Carl Phillip Robinson (79 Robert Edwards), Carl Neil Fletcher, Paul Parry (68 Robert Earnshaw), Craig Douglas Bellamy, Ryan Joseph Giggs (90 Christopher Mark Llewellyn).
Manager: Mark Leslie Hughes
CANADA: Patrick Stewart Onstad, Daniel Imhof, Ante Jazic, Mark Watson, Jason deVos, Julián de Guzmán, Atiba Hutchinson (46 Marc Bircham), James Brennan (46 Paolo Pasquale Peschisolido), Iain Hume (76 Olivier Occean), Tomasz Radzinski (73 Kevin McKenna), Dwayne De Rosario (80 Michael Klukowski).   Trainer: Frank Yallop
Goal: Paul Parry (21)

523. 18.08.2004
LATVIA v WALES 0-2 (0-0)
Skonto, Riga
Referee: Valentin Ivanov (Russia)   Attendance: 6,500
LATVIA: Aleksandrs Koliņko, Igors N. Stepanovs, Valentīns Lobaņovs, Mihails Zemļinskis, Juris Laizāns, Oļegs Blagonadeždins (74 Igors Korabļovs), Aleksandrs Isakovs, Mihails Miholaps (61 Igors Semjonovs), Andrejs Rubins, Māris Verpakovskis, Andrejs Prohorenkovs (66 Vits Rimkus).
Trainer: Aleksandrs Starkovs
WALES: Paul Steven Jones (46 Mark Geoffrey Crossley), Mark Delaney, Benjamin David Thatcher, Andrew Roger Melville (24 James Collins), Robert John Page, Mark Anthony Pembridge (69 Gareth Roberts), Robert William Savage (46 Andrew James Johnson), Craig Douglas Bellamy, John Hartson (87 Gareth Keith Taylor), Gary Andrew Speed (Cap), Jason Koumas (88 Carl Phillip Robinson).
Manager: Mark Leslie Hughes
Goals: John Hartson (82), Craig Douglas Bellamy (89)

524. 04.09.2004   18th World Cup Qualifiers
AZERBAIJAN v WALES 1-1 (0-0)
Tofik Bahramov, Baku
Referee: Edo Trivković (Croatia)   Attendance: 8,000
AZERBAIJAN: Dmitriy Kramarenko, Avtandil Gadzhiev, Rashad Sadygov, Emin Agaev, Mahir Shukurov, Vusal Huseynov (73 Ismayil Mammadov), Aslan Kerimov, Makhmud Kurbanov, Anatoli Ponomarev (83 Ilgar Kurbanov), Kurban Kurbanov, Samir Aliyev (71 Nadir Nabiyev).
Trainer: Carlos Alberto Torres
WALES: Paul Steven Jones, Mark Delaney, Andrew Roger Melville, Robert John Page, Daniel Gabbidon, Jason Koumas (88 Robert Earnshaw), Robert William Savage, Gary Andrew Speed (Cap), Mark Anthony Pembridge (46 John Morgan Oster), Craig Douglas Bellamy, John Hartson.
Manager: Mark Leslie Hughes
Goals: Rashad Sadygov (55) / Gary Andrew Speed (47)

525. 08.09.2004   18th World Cup Qualifiers
WALES v NORTHERN IRELAND 2-2 (1-2)
Millenium, Cardiff
Referee: Domenico Messina (Italy)   Attendance: 63,500
WALES: Paul Steven Jones, Mark Delaney (25 Robert Earnshaw), James Collins, Daniel Gabbidon, Benjamin David Thatcher (63 Paul Parry), John Morgan Oster, Robert William Savage, Gary Andrew Speed (Cap), Jason Koumas, John Hartson, Craig Douglas Bellamy.
Manager: Mark Leslie Hughes
NORTHERN IRELAND: Maik Stefan Taylor, Aaron William Hughes, Colin James Murdock, Mark Stuart Williams, Anthony Capaldi (90 George McCartney), Damien Michael Johnson, Jeffrey Whitley, Michael Eamonn Hughes, Mark Clyde, David Healy, Stephen James Quinn (56 Andrew Smith, 87 Paul McVeigh).   Manager: Lawrie Sanchez
Sent off: Robert Savage (9), Michael Eamonn Hughes (9), David Healy (21)
Goals: John Hartson (32), Robert Earnshaw (75) / Jeffrey Whitley (10), David Healy (21)

526. 09.10.2004   18th World Cup Qualifiers
ENGLAND v WALES 2-0 (1-0)
Old Trafford, Manchester

Referee: Terje Hauge (Norway)   Attendance: 65,244

ENGLAND: Paul Robinson, Gary Alexander Neville, Sol Campbell, Rio Gavin Ferdinand, Ashley Cole, David Beckham (Cap) (85 Owen Hargreaves), Nicholas Butt, Frank James Lampard, Wayne Rooney (87 Ledley King), Jermain Defoe (70 Alan Smith), Michael James Owen.
Manager: Sven-Göran Eriksson

WALES: Paul Steven Jones, Mark Delaney, Daniel Gabbidon, Benjamin David Thatcher, Simon Davies, Jason Koumas (74 Robert Earnshaw), Craig Douglas Bellamy, Mark Anthony Pembridge (59 Carl Phillip Robinson), Gary Andrew Speed (Cap), Ryan Joseph Giggs, John Hartson.
Manager: Mark Leslie Hughes

Goals: Frank James Lampard (4), David Beckham (76)

527. 13.10.2004   18th World Cup Qualifiers
WALES v POLAND 2-3 (0-0)
Millennium, Cardiff

Referee: Alain Sars (France)   Attendance: 56,685

WALES: Paul Steven Jones, Mark Delaney, Benjamin David Thatcher, James Collins, Daniel Gabbidon, Simon Davies, Robert William Savage, Gary Andrew Speed (79 John Hartson), Jason Koumas (86 Paul Parry), Craig Douglas Bellamy, Robert Earnshaw.   Manager: Mark Leslie Hughes

POLAND: Jerzy Dudek, Marcin Baszczyński, Tomasz Hajto, Jacek Bąk (48 Tomasz Kłos), Tomasz Rząsa, Kamil Kosowski, Radosław Kałużny (71 Sebastian Mila), Mirosław Szymkowiak, Jacek Krzynówek, Maciej Żurawski, Piotr Włodarczyk (60 Tomasz Frankowski).   Trainer: Paweł Janas

Goals: Robert Earnshaw (56), John Hartson (90) /
Tomasz Frankowski (72), Maciej Żurawski (81),
Jacek Krzynówek (85)

528. 09.02.2005
WALES v HUNGARY 2-0 (0-0)
Millennium, Cardiff

Referee: Charles Richmond (Scotland)   Attendance: 16,672

WALES: Daniel Coyne, Robert Edwards (50 Rhys Weston), Robert John Page, David Partridge (65 Daniel Collins), Daniel Gabbidon, Simon Davies, Carl Phillip Robinson (90 Stephen Roberts), Carl Neil Fletcher, Samuel Ricketts, Robert Earnshaw (85 Gareth Roberts), Craig Douglas Bellamy.
Manager: John Benjamin Toshack

HUNGARY: Gábor Király, Gábor Gyepes (82 Ottó Vincze), Attila Dragóner, Roland Juhász, László Bodnár, György Korsós (65 Dénes Rósa), Péter Lipcsei (68 Péter Kovács), Tamás Hajnal (58 Leandro de Almeida), Szabolcs Huszti, Zoltán Gera, Sándor Torghelle (82 Krisztián Kenesei).
Trainer: Lothar Herbert Matthäus

Goals: Craig Douglas Bellamy (64, 80)

529. 26.03.2005   18th World Cup Qualifiers
WALES v AUSTRIA 0-2 (0-0)
Millennium, Cardiff

Referee: Paul Allaerts (Belgium)   Attendance: 47,760

WALES: Daniel Coyne, Mark Delaney, Daniel Gabbidon, Robert John Page, Samuel Ricketts, Carl Phillip Robinson, Carl Neil Fletcher, Simon Davies (75 Robert Earnshaw), Ryan Joseph Giggs, Craig Douglas Bellamy, John Hartson.
Manager: John Benjamin Toshack

AUSTRIA: Helge Payer, Markus Katzer, Emanuel Pogatetz, Anton Ehmann, Martin Stranzl, René Aufhauser, Ernst Dospel, Roland Kirchler, Andreas Ivanschitz (90 Mario Hieblinger), Christian Mayrleb (87 Wolfgang Mair), Mario Haas (78 Ivica Vastic).   Trainer: Johann Krankl

Goal: Ivica Vastic (82), Martin Stranzl (86)

530. 30.03.2005   18th World Cup Qualifiers
AUSTRIA v WALES 1-0 (0-0)
Ernst Happel, Wien

Referee: Manuel Mejuto González (Spain)   Att: 30,000

AUSTRIA: Helge Payer, Markus Katzer, Martin Stranzl, Ernst Dospel (84 Markus Kiesenebner), Anton Ehmann, René Aufhauser, Roland Kirchler (78 Wolfgang Mair), Dietmar Kühbauer, Andreas Ivanschitz, Christian Mayrleb, Mario Haas (55 Ivica Vastic).   Trainer: Johann Krankl

WALES: Daniel Coyne, Mark Delaney, Samuel Ricketts, Daniel Gabbidon, James Collins (58 Robert John Page), Carl Phillip Robinson, Carl Neil Fletcher, Simon Davies, Ryan Joseph Giggs, Craig Douglas Bellamy, David Partridge.
Manager: John Benjamin Toshack

Goal: René Aufhauser (87)

531. 17.08.2005
WALES v SLOVENIA 0-0
New Stadium, Swansea

Referee: Ian Stokes (Ireland)   Attendance: 11,087

WALES: Danny Coyne, Richard Duffy (73 Rob Edwards), Daniel Gabbidon, Robert John Page, Samuel Ricketts, David Partridge (89 Gareth Roberts), Carl Fletcher, Carl Phillip Robinson (85 Craig Davies), John Hartson (Cap), Robert Earnshaw (61 Gavin Williams), David Vaughan (68 Paul Parry).   Manager: John Benjamin Toshack

SLOVENIA: Borut Mavrič (62 Samir Handanovich), Boštjan Cesar, Suad Filekovič, Matej Mavrič (46 Goran Šukalo), Aleksander Knavs (Cap), Milenko Ačimovič (46 Sebastjan Cimirotič), Anton Žlogar, Nastja Čeh, Jalen Pokorn (56 Branko Ilič), Klemen Lavrič (46 Aleksandar Rodič), Andrej Komac (87 Andrej Pečnik).   Trainer: Branko Oblak

532. 03.09.2005   18th World Cup Qualifiers
WALES v ENGLAND 0-1 (0-0)
Millenium, Cardiff
Referee: Brian Hall (United States)   Attendance: 70,795
WALES: Danny Coyne, Richard Duffy, Robert John Page (65 James Collins), Daniel Gabbidon, Samuel Ricketts, David Partridge, Carl Neil Fletcher, Carl Phillip Robinson (54 Jason Koumas), Simon Davis (70 Robert Earnshaw), Ryan Giggs (Cap), John Hartson.   Manager: John Benjamin Toshack
ENGLAND: Paul Robinson, Luke Young, Ashley Cole, James Lee Carragher, Rio Gavin Ferdinand, Steven Gerrard (85 Kieran Richardson), David Beckham (Cap), Frank James Lampard, Wayne Rooney, Shaun Wright-Phillips (68 Jermain Defoe), Joseph Cole (76 Owen Hargreaves).   Manager: Sven-Göran Eriksson
Goal: Joseph Cole (53)

533. 07.09.2005   18th World Cup Qualifiers
POLAND v WALES 1-0 (0-0)
Wojska Polskiego, Warszawa
Referee: Claus Larsen (Denmark)   Attendance: 14,000
POLAND: Artur Boruc, Marcin Baszczyński, Jacek Bąk, Mariusz Jop, Tomasz Rząsa, Kamil Kosowski (79 Arkadiusz Radomski), Radosław Sobolewski, Mirosław Szymkowiak, Euzebiusz Smolarek (86 Michał Żewłakow), Grzegorz Rasiak (65 Tomasz Frankowski), Maciej Żurawski.
Trainer: Paweł Janas
WALES: Danny Coyne, James Collins, Rob Edwards (46 Richard Duffy), Daniel Gabbidon, David Partridge, Samuel Ricketts, Simon Davies, Carl Neil Fletcher, Jason Koumas (69 Craig Davies), Robert Earnshaw (81 Joseph Ledley), Ryan Giggs (Cap).   Manager: John Benjamin Toshack
Goal: Maciej Żurawski (54 pen)

534. 08.10.2005   18th World Cup Qualifiers
NORTHERN IRELAND v WALES 2-3 (0-2)
Windsor Park, Belfast
Referee: Ruud Bossen (Holland)   Attendance: 13,451
NORTHERN IRELAND: Maik Stefan Taylor, Michael Duff (82 Stephen Jones), Anthony Capaldi, Colin James Murdock, Stephen Craigan, Steven Davis, Keith Robert Gillespie, Damien Michael Johnson, David Healy, Stephen James Quinn, Stuart Elliott (65 Christopher Brunt).   Manager: Lawrie Sanchez
WALES: Paul Jones, James Collins (51 Richard Duffy), Mark Delaney, David Partridge, Samuel Ricketts (87 Daniel Collins), Carl Neil Fletcher, Carl Phillip Robinson, Simon Davies, Ryan Giggs (Cap), Robert Earnshaw (77 David Vaughan), John Hartson.   Manager: John Toshack
Goals: Michael Duff (47), Steve Davis (50)

535. 12.10.2005   18th World Cup Qualifiers
WALES v AZERBAIJAN 2-0 (1-0)
Millenium, Cardiff
Referee: Martin Hansson (Sweden)   Attendance: 32,628
WALES: Paul Jones, Richard Duffy, James Collins, Daniel Gabbidon, Daniel Collins (53 Samuel Ricketts), Carl Neil Fletcher (68 Andrew Crofts), David Vaughan, Carl Phillip Robinson, Simon Davies, Ryan Giggs (Cap) (73 David Cotterill), John Hartson.   Manager: John Toshack
AZERBAIJAN: Dmitriy Kramarenko, Rafael Amirbekov, Rashad Sadygov, Emin Rafael Agaev (79 Elmar Bakhshiyev), Mahir Shukurov, Vugar Guliyev, Aslan Kerimov, Yuriy Muzika, Emin Imamaliyev (88 Ruslan Poladov), Farrukh Ismaylov (68 Samir Aliyev), Zaur Tagizade.   Trainer: Vagif Sadykov
Goals: Ryan Giggs (3, 51)

536. 16.11.2005
CYPRUS v WALES 1-0 (1-0)
Tsireio, Limassol
Referee: Haim Jakov (Israel)   Attendance: 1,000
CYPRUS: Mihális Morfís (71 Antónis Giorgallídis), Stélios Okkarídis, Lambros Lambrou (79 Loukás Louká), Hrýsis Mihaíl, Konstantínos Haralámpidis, Mários Ilía (70 Hristos Theofilou), Aléxis Garpózis (59 Ilias Haralambous), Asimakis Krassas (59 Stathis Aloneftis), Konstantinos Makrídis, Giánnis Okkás (Cap), Giasemákis Giasemí (76 Alekos Alekou).
Trainer: Aggelos Anastasiadis
WALES: Lewis Price, Richard Duffy (76 Rob Edwards), Daniel Gabbidon (Cap), Robert John Page, Daniel Collins (46 Gavin Williams), Samuel Ricketts (83 Gareth Roberts), Carl Neil Fletcher, Carl Phillip Robinson, David Vaughan (67 Robert Earnshaw), Craig Douglas Bellamy, John Hartson.   Manager: John Toshack
Goal: Hrýsis Mihaíl (42 pen)

537. 01.03.2006
WALES v PARAGUAY 0-0
Millennium, Cardiff
Referee: Douglas McDonald (Scotland)   Attendance: 12,324
WALES: Paul Jones (66 Lewis Price), James Collins, Daniel Gabbidon, Lewin Nyatanga, Rob Edwards, Simon Davies (76 Andrew Crofts), Carl Neil Fletcher (75 Carl Phillip Robinson), Jason Koumas (69 Joseph Ledley), Samuel Ricketts, Ryan Giggs (85 David Cotterill), Craig Douglas Bellamy (78 Robert Earnshaw).   Manager: John Toshack
PARAGUAY: Justo Wilmar Villar Viveros, Denis Ramón Caniza, Juan Daniel Cáceres, Delio César Toledo, Paulo César Da Silva Barrios, Carlos Humberto Paredes, Edgar Osvaldo Barreto Cáceres, Julio Daniel Dos Santos Rodríguez (67 Cristián Miguel Riveros Núñez), Roberto Miguel Acuña Cabello, César Augusto Ramírez Caje (77 Salvador Cabañas Ortega), Nelson Antonio Haedo Valdéz (71 José Saturnino Cardozo).   Trainer: Aníbal Ruíz Leites

97

538. 27.05.2006
WALES v TRINIDAD & TOBAGO 2-1 (1-1)
Graz
Referee: S. Massner (Austria)   Attendance: 8,000

WALES: Jason Brown (46 Glyn Garner), James Collins, Daniel Gabbidon, David Partridge (46 Lewin Nyatanga), Carl Phillip Robinson, Simon Davies (77 Arron Davies), Carl Neil Fletcher (46 Andrew Crofts), David Vaughan (54 Gareth Bale), Joseph Ledley, David Cotterill (46 Craig Davies), Robert Earnshaw.   Manager: John Toshack

TRINIDAD & TOBAGO: Kelvin Jack, Cyd Gray, Marvin Andrews (34 Collin Samuel), Dennis Lawrence, Avery John, Carlos Edwards, Chris Birchall, Dwight Yorke, Densill Theobald (78 Whitley), Kenwyne Jones (61 Russell Latapy), Stern John.   Trainer: Leo Beenhakker

Goals: Robert Earnshaw (38, 87) / Stern John (32)

539. 15.08.2006
WALES v BULGARIA 0-0
Liberty, Swansea
Referee: Joseph Attard (Malta)   Attendance: 8,200

WALES: Paul Jones, Mark Delaney (60 Richard Duffy), Daniel Gabbidon (74 Rob Edwards), James Collins, Samuel Ricketts (69 David Vaughan), Simon Davies, Carl Phillip Robinson, Carl Neil Fletcher (52 Joseph Ledley), Ryan Giggs (Cap) (52 Lewin Nyatanga), Robert Earnshaw, Craig Douglas Bellamy (72 Paul Parry).   Manager: John Toshack

BULGARIA: Georgi Petkov (46 Dimitar Ivankov), Stanislav Angelov (81 Georgi Iliev), Igor Tomašić, Rosen Kirilov, Lúcio Wagner, Stiliyan Petrov (Cap), Radostin Kishishev (73 Yordan Todorov), Georgi Peev (56 Blagoy Georgiev), Zoran Janković (64 Svetoslav Todorov), Martin Petrov (57 Zdravko Lazarov), Dimitar Berbatov.   Trainer: Hristo Stoitchkov

540. 02.09.2006   13th European Champs Qualifiers
CZECH REPUBLIC v WALES 2-1 (0-0)
Na Stínadlech, Teplice
Referee: Jonas Eriksson (Sweden)   Attendance: 16,204

CZECH REPUBLIC: Petr Čech, Tomáš Ujfaluši, Martin Jiránek, David Rozehnal, Marek Jankulovski, Jiří Štajner (46 Libor Sionko), Tomáš Galásek (88 Radoslav Kováč), Tomáš Rosický (Cap), Jaroslav Plašil, Jan Koller, Marek Kulič (75 David Lafata).   Trainer: Karel Brückner

WALES: Paul Jones, Mark Delaney (79 David Cotterill), James Collins, Daniel Gabbidon, Lewin Nyatanga, Samuel Ricketts (79 Robert Earnshaw), Simon Davies, Carl Phillip Robinson, Carl Neil Fletcher (46 Joseph Ledley), Craig Douglas Bellamy, Ryan Giggs (Cap).   Manager: John Toshack

Goals: David Lafata (76, 89) / Martin Jiránek (85 own goal)

541. 05.09.2006
WALES v BRAZIL 0-2 (0-0)
White Harte Lane, London
Referee: Michael Riley (England)   Attendance: 22,008

WALES: Paul Jones, Richard Duffy (64 Rob Edwards), Gareth Bale (46 Samuel Ricketts), Daniel Gabbidon, James Collins, Lewin Nyatanga, Craig Douglas Bellamy, Robert Earnshaw (77 David Cotterill), Carl Phillip Robinson (53 Carl Neil Fletcher), Simon Davies (68 David Vaughan), Ryan Giggs (46 Joseph Ledley).   Manager: John Toshack

BRAZIL: Heurelho da Silva Gomes, MAICON Douglas Sisenando (59 Cicero João de Cezare "Cicinho"), Anderson Luiz da Silva "Luisão", ALEX Rodrigo Dias da Costa, MARCELO Vieira da Silva Júnior (74 GILBERTO da Silva Melo), EDMÍLSON José Gomes de Moraes (46 GILBERTO Aparecido da SILVA), Alessandro Silva de Souza "Dudu Cearense", JÚLIO César BAPTISTA (78 RAFAEL Augusto SÓBIS), Ricardo Izecson dos Santos Leite "Kaká" (72 ELANO Blumer), Ronaldo de Assis Moreira "Ronaldinho" (67 Robson de Souza "Robinho"), VÁGNER Silveira de Souza "Love".   Trainer: Carlos Caetano Bledorn Verri "Dunga"

Goals: Marcelo (61), Vágner "Love" (74)

542. 07.10.2006   13th European Champs Qualifiers
WALES v SLOVAKIA 1-5 (1-3)
Millenium, Cardiff
Referee: Dick van Egmond (Holland)   Attendance: 28,500

WALES: Paul Jones, Richard Duffy, Rob Edwards (58 Joseph Ledley), Daniel Gabbidon, Lewin Nyatanga, Gareth Bale, Simon Davies (88 David Cotterill), Carl Phillip Robinson, Jason Koumas, Craig Douglas Bellamy (Cap), Robert Earnshaw (46 Paul Parry).   Manager: John Toshack

SLOVAKIA: Kamil Čontofalský, Peter Petráš, Roman Kratochvíl, Stanislav Varga, Ján Ďurica, Martin Petráš, Miroslav Karhan (Cap) (67 Matej Krajčík), Ján Kozák, Dušan Švento, Marek Mintál (71 Ivan Hodúr), Róbert Vittek (77 Filip Hološko).   Trainer: Dušan Galis

Goals: Gareth Bale (37) /
Dušan Švento (14), Marek Mintál (32, 38),
Miroslav Karhan (51), Róbert Vittek (59)

543. 11.10.2006   13th European Champs Qualifiers
WALES v CYPRUS 3-1 (2-0)
Millenium, Cardiff
Referee: Jacek Granat (Poland)   Attendance: 20,456
WALES: Lewis Price, Richard Duffy (78 Rob Edwards), Craig Morgan, Daniel Gabbidon, Lewin Nyatanga, Gareth Bale, Simon Davies, Carl Phillip Robinson, Jason Koumas (76 Joseph Ledley), Craig Douglas Bellamy (Cap) (90 Paul Parry), Robert Earnshaw.   Manager: John Toshack
CYPRUS: Mikhályis Morfís, Yórghos Theodhótou, Lámbros Lámbrou, Loukás Louká, Aléxis Gharpózis (46 Ilyías Kharalámbous), Konstandínos Makrídhis, Marínos Satsiás (84 Yasemákyis Yasemí), Khrísis Mikhaíl (46 Konstandínos Kharalambídhis), Státhis Alonéftis, Yannákyis Okkás (Cap), Mikhályis Konstandínou.
Trainer: Ángyelos Anastasiádhis (Greece)
Goals: Jason Koumas (33), Robert Earnshaw (39), Craig Douglas Bellamy (72) / Yannakis Okkas (83)

544. 14.11.2006   13th European Champs Qualifiers
WALES v LIECHTENSTEIN 4-0 (2-0)
The Racecourse, Wrexham
Referee: Luc Wilmes (Luxembourg)   Attendance: 8,752
WALES: Jason Brown, Richard Duffy (46 Carl Neil Fletcher), Lewin Nyatanga, Steve Evans, Samuel Ricketts, Simon Davies (69 Mark Jones), Carl Phillip Robinson (80 Andrew Crofts), Jason Koumas (88 Craig Davies), Ryan Giggs (Cap) (46 Joseph Ledley), Craig Douglas Bellamy, Robert Earnshaw (59 Christopher Llewellyn).   Manager: John Toshack
LIECHTENSTEIN: Peter Jehle, Martin Telser, Daniel Hasler (Cap), Christof Ritter, Marco Ritzberger (59 Daniel Frick), Thomas Beck (88 Wolfgang Kieber), Martin Stocklasa, Martin Büchel, Franz Burgmeier, Mario Frick (82 Ronny Büchel), Fabio D'Elia (59 Raphael Rohrer).   Trainer: Urs Meier
Goals: Jason Koumas (8, 14), Craig Douglas Bellamy (77), Christopher Llewellyn (90)

545. 06.02.2007
NORTHERN IRELAND v WALES 0-0
Windsor Park, Belfast
Referee: Charlie Richmond (Scotland)   Attendance: 14,000
NORTHERN IRELAND: Maik Stefan Taylor (46 Michael Ingham), Michael Duff, Stephen Craigan (78 Sean Webb), Aaron Hughes, Anthony Capaldi, Keith Robert Gillespie, Steve Davis, Samuel Clingan (61 Grant McCann), Christopher Brunt, Kyle Lafferty (68 Peter Thompson), Ivan Sproule (68 Dean Shiels).   Manager: Lawrie Sanchez
WALES: Danny Coyne, Richard Duffy (46 David Cotterill, 71 Jermaine Easter), Steve Evans, Daniel Collins, Lewin Nyatanga, Simon Davies, Jason Koumas, Carl Phillip Robinson, Paul Parry (83 Andrew Crofts), David Vaughan (46 Samuel Ricketts), Craig Douglas Bellamy.   Manager: John Toshack

546. 24.03.2007   13th European Champs Qualifiers
REPUBLIC OF IRELAND v WALES 1-0 (1-0)
Croke Park, Dublin
Referee: Terje Hauge (Norway)   Attendance: 75,300
IRELAND: Shay Given, John O'Shea, Steve Finnan, Paul McShane, Richard Dunne, Lee Carsley, Stephen Ireland (59 Kevin Doyle), Jonathan Douglas (80 Stephen Hunt), Kevin Kilbane, Robbie Keane (89 Aidan McGeady), Damien Duff.
Manager: Stephen Staunton
WALES: Danny Coyne, Samuel Ricketts, Gareth Bale (74 Daniel Collins), James Collins, Steve Evans, Lewin Nyatanga, Joseph Ledley (46 Carl Neil Fletcher), Carl Phillip Robinson (90 Jermaine Easter), Simon Davies, Ryan Giggs, Craig Douglas Bellamy.   Manager: John Toshack
Goal: Stephen Ireland (39)

547. 28.03.2007   13th European Champs Qualifiers
WALES v SAN MARINO 3-0 (2-0)
Millenium, Cardiff
Referee: Ararat Tshagaryan (Armenia)   Attendance: 18,750
WALES: Danny Coyne, Samuel Ricketts, Steve Evans (63 Lewin Nyatanga), James Collins, Gareth Bale, Carl Neil Fletcher, Jason Koumas, Simon Davies, Ryan Giggs (73 Paul Parry), Craig Douglas Bellamy, Jermaine Easter (49 David Cotterill).   Manager: John Toshack
SAN MARINO: Aldo Simoncini, Carlo Valentini (85 Alan Toccaceli), Matteo Andreini, Nicola Albani, Riccardo Muccioli, Simone Bacciocchi, Cristian Negri (79 Federico Nanni), Marco Domeniconi (67 Matteo Bugli), Manuel Marani, Andy Selva, Alex Gasperoni.   Trainer: Giampaolo Mazza
Goals: Ryan Giggs (3), Gareth Bale (20), Jason Koumas (63 pen)

548. 26.05.2007
WALES v NEW ZEALAND 2-2 (2-2)
Wrexham
Referee: Tommy Fkjerven (Norway)   Attendance: 7,819
WALES: Danny Coyne (46 Wayne Robert Hennessey), James Collins, Daniel Gabbidon, Christopher Gunter (46 Steve Evans), Samuel Ricketts, Simon Davies (76 Andrew Crofts), Carl Neil Fletcher (46 Joseph Ledley), Ryan Giggs (76 Christopher Llewellyn), Carl Phillip Robinson, Craig Douglas Bellamy, Robert Earnshaw (64 Daniel Nardiello).   Manager: John Toshack
NEW ZEALAND: Mark Paston, Andrew Boyens, Ben Fignund, Tony Lochhead, James Pritchett, Leonidas Bertos (60 Andrew Barron), Tim Brown, Jeremy Christie (58 Jeffrey Campbell), Duncan Oughton, Chris James, Shane Smeltz.
Goals: Craig Douglas Bellamy (18, 38) / Shane Smeltz (2, 24)

99

549. 02.06.2007   13th European Champs Qualifiers
WALES v CZECH REPUBLIC   0-0
Millenium, Cardiff

Referee: Paul Allaerts (Belgium)   Attendance: 30,700

WALES: Wayne Robert Hennessey, Samuel Ricketts, Lewin Nyatanga, Daniel Gabbidon, James Collins, Carl Phillip Robinson, Joseph Ledley, Jason Koumas, Simon Davies, Ryan Giggs (89 Robert Earnshaw), Craig Douglas Bellamy.   Manager: John Toshack

CZECH REPUBLIC: Petr Cech, Tomáš Ujfaluši, Radoslav Kovác, Marek Jankulovski, David Rozehnal, Jan Polák (65 David Jarolim), Tomáš Sivok (83 Marek Matejovsky), Tomáš Rosický, Jaroslav Plašil, Jan Koller, Milan Baroš (46 Marek Kulic).   Trainer: Karel Brückner

550. 22.08.2007
BULGARIA v WALES   0-1 (0-1)
Naftex, Burgas

Referee: Germanakos (Greece)   Attendance: 15,000

BULGARIA: Dimitar Ivankov, Radostin Kishishev (52 Chavdar Yankov), Stanislav Angelov, Aleksander Tunchev, Igor Tomasic, Lucio Wagner (54 Petar Tzanev), Stilian Petrov, Dimitar Telkiyski, Hristo Yovov (66 Tsvetan Genkov), Georgi Chilikov, Martin Petrov.

WALES: Wayne Robert Hennessey, Samuel Ricketts (46 Neal Eardley), Daniel Gabbidon, Craig Morgan (46 Daniel Collins), Lewin Nyatanga, Joseph Ledley (46 Steve Evans), Gareth Bale (46 Mark Jones), Simon Davies (60 Daniel Nardiello), Andrew Crofts, David Vaughan, Freddy Eastwood (51 Robert Earnshaw).   Manager: John Toshack

Goal: Freddy Eastwood (45)

551. 08.09.2007   13th European Champs Qualifiers
WALES v GERMANY   0-2 (0-1)
Millennium, Cardiff

Referee: Manuel Mejuto González (Spain)   Att: 31,000

WALES: Wayne Robert Hennessey, Samuel Ricketts, Daniel Gabbidon, James Collins, Lewin Nyatanga, Joseph Ledley (46 Robert Earnshaw), Gareth Bale, Jason Koumas (67 Carl Neil Fletcher), Carl Phillip Robinson, Simon Davies (79 Andrew Crofts), Freddy Eastwood.   Manager: John Toshack

GERMANY: Jens Lehmann, Arne Friedrich, Per Mertesacker, Christoph Metzelder, Christian Pander (46 Piotr Trochowski), Roberto Hilbert, Thomas Hitzlsperger, Bastian Schweinsteiger, Marcell Jansen, Kevin Kuranyi (72 Lukas Podolski), Miroslav Klose (87 Patrick Helmes).   Trainer: Joachim Löw

Goals: Miroslav Klose (5, 60)

552. 12.09.2007   13th European Champs Qualifiers
SLOVAKIA v WALES   2-5 (1-3)
Antona Malatinského, Trnava

Referee: Laurent Duhamel (France)   Attendance: 5,500

SLOVAKIA: Štefan Senecký, Vratislav Greško (64 Igor Zofcak), Maroš Klimpl, Ján Durica, Marek Cech, Marek Hamšík, Peter Petráš, Marek Sapara, Marek Mintál, Stanislav Šesták (46 Branislav Obzera), Filip Hološko.
Trainer: Ján Kocian

WALES: Wayne Robert Hennessey, Samuel Ricketts, Daniel Gabbidon, Craig Morgan, James Collins, Gareth Bale, Simon Davies, Carl Phillip Robinson, Joseph Ledley (85 David Vaughan), Craig Douglas Bellamy, Freddy Eastwood (73 Carl Neil Fletcher).   Manager: John Toshack

Goals: Marek Mintál (12, 57) /
Freddy Eastwood (22), Craig Douglas Bellamy (34, 41), Ján Durica (78 own goal), Simon Davies (90)

553. 13.10.2007   13th European Champs Qualifiers
CYPRUS v WALES   3-1 (0-1)
GSP, Nicosia

Referee: Carlo Bertolini (Switzerland)   Attendance: 8,500

CYPRUS: Antonis Georgallides, Stelios Okkarides, Marinos Satsias (71 Christos Marangos), Marios Elia (63 Konstantinos Charalampidis), Chrysostomous Michail (46 Yiasoumi Yiasoumis), Paraskevas Christou, Alexandros Garpozis, Konstantinos Makridis, Marios Nikolaou, Efstathios Aloneftis, Yiannis Okkas.   Trainer: Angelos Anastasiadis

WALES: Danny Coyne, Samuel Ricketts (73 Jermaine Easter), James Collins (44 Craig Morgan), Daniel Gabbidon, Gareth Bale, Lewin Nyatanga, Joseph Ledley, Carl Phillip Robinson, Simon Davies, Craig Douglas Bellamy, Freddy Eastwood (58 Robert Earnshaw).   Manager: John Toshack

Goals: Yiannis Okkas (59, 68), K. Charalampidis (79) /
James Collins (21)

554. 17.10.2007   13th European Champs Qualifiers
SAN MARINO v WALES   1-2 (0-2)
Olimpico, Serravalle

Referee: Anthony Zammit (Malta)   Attendance: 1,300

SAN MARINO: Aldo Simoncini, Carlo Valentini, Damiano Vannucci (76 Matteo Bugli), Nicola Albani, Alessandro Della Valle, Luca Bonifazi (62 Giovanni Bonini), Davide Simoncini, Riccardo Muccioli, Matteo Andreini, Marco De Luigi (80 Matteo Vitaioli), Andy Selva.   Trainer: Giampaolo Mazza

WALES: Lewis Price, Gareth Bale, Neal Eardley, Daniel Gabbidon, Lewin Nyatanga, Carl Phillip Robinson, David Vaughan (62 Samuel Ricketts), Simon Davies, Joseph Ledley, Robert Earnshaw, Craig Douglas Bellamy.
Manager: John Toshack

Sent off: Nicola Albani (85)

Goals: Robert Earnshaw (13), Joseph Ledley (36) /
Andy Selva (73)

555. 17.11.2007   13th European Champs Qualifiers
WALES v REPUBLIC OF IRELAND 2-2 (1-1)
Millennium, Cardiff
Referee: Oleh Oriekhov (Ukraine)   Attendance: 24,600

WALES: Wayne Robert Hennessey, Neal Eardley (81 David Cotterill), James Collins, Daniel Gabbidon, Christopher Gunter, Joseph Ledley, Jason Koumas, Carl Phillip Robinson (37 David Edwards), Carl Neil Fletcher, Simon Davies, Freddy Eastwood (60 Jermaine Easter).   Manager: John Toshack

IRELAND: Shay Given, Steve Finnan, Paul McShane, John O'Shea, Kevin Kilbane, Aiden McGeady, Lee Carsley, Liam Miller (60 Stephen Hunt), Andy Reid (87 Darren Potter), Kevin Doyle, Robbie Keane.   Trainer: Donald Givens

Goals: Jason Koumas (23, 89 pen) / Robbie Keane (31), Kevin Doyle (60)

556. 21.11.2007   13th European Champs Qualifiers
GERMANY v WALES 0-0
Commerzbank Arena, Frankfurt am Main
Referee: Pavel Cristian Balaj (Romania)   Att: 49,300

GERMANY: Jens Lehmann, Gonzalo Castro (56 Roberto Hilbert), Per Mertesacker, Christoph Metzelder, Philipp Lahm, Clemens Fritz, Tim Borowski, Thomas Hitzlsperger (46 Simon Rolfes), Lukas Podolski, Mario Gómez (71 Oliver Neuville), Miroslav Klose.   Trainer: Joachim Löw

WALES: Wayne Robert Hennessey, Samuel Ricketts, Daniel Gabbidon, James Collins, Lewin Nyatanga, Christopher Gunter, Carl Neil Fletcher, Simon Davies, David Edwards (90 Andrew Crofts), Joseph Ledley, Robert Earnshaw (56 Jermaine Easter).   Manager: John Toshack

557. 06.02.2008
WALES v NORWAY 3-0 (1-0)
The Racecourse, Wrexham
Referee: McKeon (Ireland)   Attendance: 7,553

WALES: Wayne Robert Hennessey (46 Lewis Price), Samuel Ricketts (59 Neal Eardley), Craig Morgan, Lewin Nyatanga, Christopher Gunter, Simon Davies (59 David Cotterill), Carl Phillip Robinson (66 Andrew Crofts), Carl Neil Fletcher, Jason Koumas, Joseph Ledley (46 David Edwards), Freddie Eastwood (59 Craig Davies).   Manager: John Toshack

NORWAY: Håkon André Opdal (46 Rune Almenning Jarstein), Jarl-Andre Storbaek, Brede Hangeland (61 Frode Kippe), Pa Madou-Kah, John Arne Riise, Daniel Omoya Braaten, Martin Andresen, Fredrik Stromstad (46 Christian Grindheim), Erik Nevland (77 John Anders Buørkøy), Morten Gamst Pedersen, John Carew (46 Kristofer Haestad).   Trainer: Åge Hareide

Goals: Carl Neil Fletcher (15), Jason Koumas (62, 69)

558. 26.03.2008
LUXEMBOURG v WALES 0-2 (0-1)
Luxembourg
Referee: Bjorn Kuipers (Holland)   Attendance: 3,000

LUXEMBOURG: Jonathan Joubert, Benoit Lang (46 René Peters), Marko Mutsch, Kim Kintziger, Eric Hoffmann, Jean Wagner, Alphonse Leweck (66 Daniel Da Mota Alves), Jeff Strasser, Aurélien Joachim (66 Joël Kitenge), Sebastien Remy, Lars Gerson (90 Zarko Lukic).   Trainer: Guy Hellers

WALES: Lewis Price (46 Boaz Myhill), Neal Eardley (64 Richard Duffy), Samuel Ricketts, Ashley Williams, Craig Morgan, Lewin Nyatanga, Freddy Eastwood, Carl Neil Fletcher (74 David Cotterill), Jason Koumas (84 Daniel Nardiello), Simon Davies, Jermaine Easter (46 Owain Tudur-Jones).   Manager: John Toshack

Goals: Freddy Eastwood (38, 47)

559. 28.05.2008
ICELAND v WALES 0-1 (0-1)
Laugardalsvöllur, Reykjavík
Referee: Adrian McCourt (Northern Ireland)   Att: 5,322

ICELAND: Kjartan Sturluson, Birkir Mar Saevarsson, Atli Sveinn Thorarinsson, Aron Einar Gunnarsson (77 Jonas Saevarsson), Indridi Sigurdsson, Palmi Rafn Palmason, Kristjan Orn Sigurdsson, Eggert Jonsson (60 Hannes Sigurdsson), Emil Hallfredsson (70 Theodor Elmar Bjarnason), Stefan Thor Thordarson (60 Helgi Valur Danielsson), Gunnar Heidar Thorvaldsson (82 Arnor Smarason).   Trainer: Ólafur Jóhannesson

WALES: Wayne Robert Hennessey, Christopher Gunter, Joseph Ledley (49 Neal Eardley), Ashley Williams, Craig Morgan, Lewin Nyatanga, Carl Neil Fletcher (Cap)(41 Chedwyn Evans), Jack Collison (61 Owain Tudur-Jones), Freddy Eastwood (49 Samuel Vokes), Jason Koumas (89 Andrew Crofts), David Edwards (62 Craig Douglas Bellamy).   Manager: John Toshack

Goal: Chedwyn Evans (44)

560. 01.06.2008
HOLLAND v WALES 2-0 (1-0)

De Kuip, Rotterdam

Referee: Felix Brych (Germany)   Attendance: 48,500

HOLLAND: Edwin van der Sar, André Ooijer, John Heitinga (46 Mario Melchiot), Joris Mathijsen (80 Jan Vennegoor of Hesselink), Giovanni van Bronckhorst (46 Tim De Cler), Rafael van der Vaart (67 Ibrahim Afellay), Demy De Zeeuw (46 Nigel De Jong), Wesley Sneijder, Orlando Engelaar (46 Dirk Kuyt), Arjen Robben, Ruud van Nistelrooij. Trainer: Marco van Basten

WALES: Wayne Robert Hennessey, Samuel Ricketts (78 Andrew Crofts), Ashley Williams, Craig Morgan, Lewin Nyatanga, Christopher Gunter, Carl Phillip Robinson (46 Jack Collison), Jason Koumas (73 Samuel Vokes), David Edwards (57 Chedwyn Evans), Freddy Eastwood (57 Craig Douglas Bellamy), Joseph Ledley (89 Neal Eardley). Manager: John Toshack

Goals: Arjen Robben (35), Wesley Sneijder (54)

561. 20.08.2008
WALES v GEORGIA 1-2 (1-0)

Millenium, Cardiff

Referee: Matej Jug (Slovenia)   Attendance: 6,435

WALES: Boaz Myhill, Neal Eardley, Samuel Ricketts, Carl Phillip Robinson, Craig Morgan, Ashley Williams, Carl Neil Fletcher, Simon Davies, Paul Parry (70 David Vaughan), Jason Koumas, Freddy Eastwood (80 Robert Earnshaw). Manager: John Toshack

GEORGIA: Giorgi Loria, Ucha Lobjanidze, Zurab Khizanishvili, Malkhaz Asatiani, Zurab Menteshashvili, David Mujiri, Alexander Kvakhadze, David Odikadze (85 David Devdariani), Levan Kenia (77 Irakli Klimiashvili), Alexander Iashvili (79 Beka Gotsiridze), Levan Mchedlidze (30 Rati Aleksidze). Trainer: Hector Cuper

Goals: Koumas (16) / Levan Kenia (66), Beka Gotsiridze (90)

562. 06.09.2008   19th World Cup Qualifiers
WALES v AZERBAIJAN 1-0 (0-0)

Millenium, Cardiff

Referee: Aleksandar Stavrev (Makedonia)

WALES: Wayne Robert Hennessey, Christopher Gunter, Gareth Bale, Carl Neil Fletcher, Craig Morgan, Ashley Williams, Simon Davies (Cap), David Edwards (72 Samuel Vokes), Jason Koumas (82 Carl Phillip Robinson), Robert Earnshaw (62 Chedwyn Evans), Joseph Ledley. Manager: John Toshack

AZERBAIJAN: Kamran Agayev, Rail Malikov, Sasha Xxx, Elmar Bakshiev, Javid Huseynov (46 Agil Nabiyev), Samir Abasov, Branimir Subasic, Rashad Sadigov (Cap), Nodar Mammadov (77 Nduka Usim), Elvin Mammadov, Fabio Ramin. Trainer: Berti Vogts

Goal: Samuel Vokes (83)

563. 10.09.2008   19th World Cup Qualifiers
RUSSIA v WALES 2-1 (1-0)

Lokomotiv, Moscow

Referee: Damir Skomina (Slovenia)   Attendance: 28,000

RUSSIA: Igor Akinfeev, Alexander Anyukov, Denis Kolodin, Sergei Ignashevich, Dmitry Torbinskiy (60 Ivan Sayenko), Igor Semshov, Roman Pavlyuchenko (90 Vladimir Bystrov), Andrei Arshavin, Sergei Semak (73 Pavel Pogrebnyak), Konstantin Zyryanov, Yuri Zirkov. Trainer: Guus Hiddink

WALES: Wayne Robert Hennessey, Christopher Gunter, Gareth Bale, Carl Neil Fletcher, Craig Morgan, Ashley Williams, Simon Davies, David Edwards (77 Steven Evans), Samuel Vokes (62 Chedwyn Evans), Carl Phillip Robinson (46 Samuel Ricketts), Joseph Ledley. Manager: John Toshack

Goals: Roman Pavlyuchenko (22 pen), Pavel Pogrebnyak (81) / Joseph Ledley (67)

564. 11.10.2008   19th World Cup Qualifiers
WALES v LIECHTENSTEIN 2-0 (1-0)

Millenium, Cardiff

Referee: Thomas Vejlgaard (Denmark)   Attendance: 13,356

WALES: Wayne Robert Hennessey, Christopher Gunter, Gareth Bale, Carl Fletcher (56 Carl Robinson), Craig Morgan, Ashley Williams, Simon Davies, Craig Bellamy (80 James Collins), Jason Koumas, Samuel Vokes (51 Chedwyn Evans), David Edwards. Manager: John Toshack

LIECHTENSTEIN: Peter Jehle, Marco Ritzberger (67 Mathias Christen), Fabio D'Elia, Andreas Gerster, Martin Stocklasa, Benjamin Fischer, Thomas Beck, Mario Frick (Cap), Franz Burgmeier, Martin Buechel, Michele Polverino (80 Ronny Buechel). Trainer: Hanspeter Zaugg (Switzerland)

Goals: David Edwards (42), Mario Frick (80 own goal)

565. 15.10.2008   19th World Cup Qualifiers
GERMANY v WALES 1-0 (0-0)

Borussia Park, Mönchengladbach

Referee: Laurent Duhamel (France)   Attendance: 44,500

GERMANY: Rene Adler, Arne Friedrich (64 Clemens Fritz), Heiko Westermann, Bastian Schweinsteiger, Lukas Podolski (82 Mario Gomez), Miroslav Klose (46 Patrick Helmes), Michael Ballack (Cap), Piotr Trochowski, Thomas Hitzlsperger, Philipp Lahm, Per Mertesacker. Trainer: Joachim Loew

WALES: Wayne Hennessey, Christopher Gunter (86 Samuel Ricketts), Gareth Bale, Craig Morgan, James Collins, Ashley Williams, Simon Davies, Craig Bellamy (Cap), Jason Koumas, Carl Fletcher (77 Carl Phillip Robinson), David Edwards (77 Chedwyn Evans). Manager: John Toshack

Goal: Piotr Trochowski (72)

566. 19.11.2008
DENMARK v WALES 0-1 (0-0)
Parken, Brondby
Referee: Michael Weiner (Germany)   Attendance: 10,271
DENMARK: Thomas Sorensen (Cap), Kasper Bogelund (46 Soren Larsen), Per Kroldrup (60 Mathias Jorgensen), Daniel Agger, Thomas Rasmussen (46 Leon Andreasen), Hjalte Bo Norregaard, Thomas Kristensen (71 Martin Retov), Morten Nordstrand (46 Patrick Mtiliga), Nicklas Bendtner, Dennis Rommedahl, Michael Krohn-Dehli (60 Martin Vingaard).
Trainer: Morten Olsen
WALES: Boaz Myhill, Christopher Gunter, Gareth Bale (87 Neal Eardley), Ashley Williams, James Collins, Lewin Nyatanga, David Edwards (46 Samuel Ricketts), Craig Bellamy (Cap), Chedwyn Evans (60 Samuel Vokes), Aaron Ramsey (88 Owen Tudur Jones), Jack David Collison.
Manager: John Toshack
Goal: Craig Bellamy (77)

567. 11.02.2009
WALES v POLAND 0-1 (0-0)
Municipal de Vila Real, Vila Real de Santo António (Portugal)
Referee: BRUNO Miguel Duarte PAIXÃO (Portugal)
Attendance: 487
WALES: Wayne Hennessey (46 Glyn Oliver "Boaz" Myhill), Sam Ricketts, Lewin Nyatanga, Chris Gunter, Ashley Williams, Jack Collison (46 Aaron Ramsey), Joe Ledley (46 Carl Fletcher), Dave Edwards, Gareth Bale, Craig Bellamy (46 David Cotterill), Ched Evans (46 Sam Vokes).
Manager: John Toshack
POLAND: Lukasz Fabianski (46 Artur Boruc), Marcin Wasilewski, Michal Zewlakow, Jakub Wawrzyniak, Rafal Boguski (46 ROGER Guerreiro), Lukasz Gargula (46 Wojciech Lobodzinksi), Rafal Murawski (75 Lukasz Tralka), Mariusz Lewandowski, Jacek Krzynówek (46 Ebi Smolarek), Dariusz Dudka, Robert Lewandowski (62 Pawel Brozek).
Manager: Leo Beenhakker
Goal: ROGER Guerreiro (80)

568. 28.03.2009   19th World Cup Qualifier
WALES v FINLAND 0-2 (0-1)
Millennium, Cardiff
Referee: Eduardo Iturralde González (Spain)   Att: 22,604
WALES: Wayne Hennessey, Lewin Nyatanga, Chris Gunter, James Collins, Joe Ledley (71 Robert Earnshaw), Jason Koumas, Carl Fletcher (65 Carl Robinson), Dave Edwards (56 Aaron Ramsey), Simon Davies, Gareth Bale, Craig Bellamy.   Manager: John Toshack

FINLAND: Jussi Jääskeläinen, Hannu Tihinen, Petri Pasanen, Toni Kallio, Sami Hyypiä, Roman Eremenko, Markus Heikkinen, Alexei Eremenko (78 Daniel Sjölund), Jari Litmanen (90+2 Roni Porokara), Jonatan Johansson, Mikael Forssell (89 Shefki Kuqi).   Manager: Stuart Baxter
Goals: Jonatan Johansson (42), Shefki Kuqi (90+1)

569.   01.04.2009   19th World Cup Qualifier
WALES v GERMANY 0-2 (0-1)
Millennium, Cardiff
Referee: Terje Hauge (Norway)   Attendance: 26,064
WALES: Wayne Hennessey, Sam Ricketts (54 Chris Gunter), Lewin Nyatanga (75 David Cotterill), Ashley Williams, James Collins, Aaron Ramsey, Joe Ledley, Simon Davies, Gareth Bale, Sam Vokes (62 Ched Evans), Robert Earnshaw.   Manager: John Toshack
GERMANY: Robert Enke, Serdar Tasçi, Per Mertesacker, Philipp Lahm, Andreas Beck, Bastian Schweinsteiger (86 Patrick Helmes), Simon Rolfes (79 Heiko Westermann), Thomas Hitzlsperger, Michael Ballack, Lukas Podolski (72 Piotr Trochowski), Mario Gómez.   Manager: Joachim Löw
Goals: Michael Ballack (11), Ashley Williams (48 og)

570.   29.05.2009
WALES v ESTONIA 1-0 (1-0)
Stebonheath Park, Llanelli
Referee: Magnús Thórisson (Iceland)   Attendance: 4,071
WALES: Glyn Oliver "Boaz" Myhill (46 Wayne Hennessey), Lewin Nyatanga, Craig Morgan, Chris Gunter, Ashley Williams, Jack Collison (80 Joe Allen), Aaron Ramsey (67 Dave Edwards), Joe Ledley, Gareth Bale, Robert Earnshaw (59 Ched Evans, 89 Andy King), Sam Vokes (59 Simon Church).
Manager: John Toshack
ESTONIA: Artur Kotenko, Tihhon Sisov, Dmitriy Kruglov (78 Eino Puri), Alo Bärengrub, Igor Morozov, Sander Puri (65 Gert Kams), Martin Vunk, Konstantin Vassiljev, Taijo Teniste, Vitali Gussev (65 Oliver Konsa), Alo Dupikov (72 Kristian Marmor).   Manager: Tarmo Tüütli
Goal: Robert Earnshaw (26 pen)

571. 06.06.2009   19th World Cup Qualifier
AZERBAIJAN v WALES 0-1 (0-1)
Tofig Bakhramov, Baku
Referee: Markus Strömbergsson (Sweden)   Att: 25,000
AZERBAIJAN: Farhad Veliyev, Agil Nabiyev (50 Javid Hüseynov), Mahir Sükürov, Vladimir Levin, Rail Malikov, Rashad Sadygov, FÁBIO Luís Ramim (46 Branimir Subasic), Zeynal Zeynalov, Elmar Baxsiyev, Vagif Javadov, Daniel Akhtyamov (60 Vüqar Nadirov).   Manager: Berti Vogts
WALES: Wayne Hennessey, Neal Eardley, Lewin Nyatanga, Craig Morgan, Chris Gunter, Ashley Williams, Aaron Ramsey, Dave Edwards, Joe Ledley, Robert Earnshaw (70 Sam Vokes), Simon Church (83 Owain Tudur-Jones).
Manager: John Toshack
Goal: Dave Edwards (41)

572. 12.08.2009
MONTENEGRO v WALES 2-1 (2-0)
Pod Goricom, Podgorica
Referee: Milorad Mazic (Serbia)   Attendance: 5,000
MONTENEGRO: Vukasin Poleksic (46 Mladen Bozovic), Savo Pavicevic, Radoslav Batak (68 Luka Pejovic), Milan Jovanovic, Miodrag Dzudovic, Nikola Drincic, Vladimir Bozovic (72 Nemanja Nikolic), Simon Vukcevic (86 Mitar Novakovic), Milorad Pekovic (62 Mladen Kascelan), Stevan Jovetic, Radomir Djalovic (74 Fatos Beciraj).
Manager: Zoran Filipovic
WALES: Wayne Hennessey (46 Lewis Price), Sam Ricketts (57 Neal Eardley), Chris Gunter, James Collins (63 Craig Morgan), Daniel Gabbidon, Ashley Williams (46 Lewin Nyatanga), Aaron Ramsey (75 David Cotterill), Joe Ledley, Jack Collison, Robert Earnshaw, Simon Church (47 Sam Vokes).
Manager: John Toshack
Goals: Stevan Jovetic (31 pen), Radomir Djalovic (45) / Sam Vokes (52)

573. 09.09.2009   19th World Cup Qualifier
WALES v RUSSIA 1-3 (0-1)
Millennium, Cardiff
Referee: Manuel JORGE Neves Moreira de SOUSA (Portugal)
Attendance: 14,505
WALES: Wayne Hennessey, Sam Ricketts, Chris Gunter, Daniel Gabbidon (75 Sam Vokes), Ashley Williams, James Collins, Aaron Ramsey, Joe Ledley, Dave Edwards, Brian Stock, Craig Bellamy. Manager: John Toshack

RUSSIA: Igor Akinfeev, Sergey Ignashevich, Vasiliy Berezutskiy, Aleksandr Anyukov, Igor Semshov (71 Roman Pavlyuchenko), Konstantin Zyryanov, Renat Yanbaev, Sergey Semak, Vladimir Bystrov, Aleksandr Kerzhakov (84 Aleksey Rebko), Andrey Arshavin.   Manager: Guus Hiddink
Goals: James Collins (54) / Igor Semshov (36), Sergey Ignashevich (72), Roman Pavlyuchenko (90+1)

574. 10.10.2009   19th World Cup Qualifier
FINLAND v WALES 2-1 (1-1)
Olympiastadion, Helsinki
Referee: Milorad Mazic (Serbia)   Attendance: 14,000
FINLAND: Jussi Jääskeläinen, Hannu Tihinen, Petri Passanen, Niklas Moisander, Sami Hyypiä, Tim Sparv, Joonas Kolkka (68 Kasper Hämäläinen), Roman Eremenko, Roni Porokara, Jari Litmanen (90 Alexei Eremenko), Jonathan Johansson (88 Shefki Kuqi).   Manager: Stuart Baxter
WALES: Wayne Hennessey, Lewin Nyatanga (83 Neal Eardley), Chris Gunter, Ashley Williams, James Collins, David Vaughan, Aaron Ramsey, Dave Edwards, Gareth Bale, Simon Church (62 Sam Vokes), Craig Bellamy.
Manager: John Toshack
Goals: Roni Porokara (5), Niklas Moisander (77) / Craig Bellamy (17)

575. 14.10.2009   19th World Cup Qualifier
LIECHTENSTEIN v WALES 0-2 (0-1)
Rheinpark, Vaduz
Referee: Sten Kaldma (Estonia)   Attendance: 1,858
LIECHTENSTEIN: Peter Jehle, Marco Ritzberger, Martin Rechsteiner, Fabio D'Elia, Yves Oehri, Raphael Rohrer (36 Roger Beck), Wolfgang Kieber, Lucas Eberle, Ronny Büchel (70 Michele Polverino), Mario Frick, David Hasler (72 Mathias Christen).   Manager: Hans-Peter Zaugg
WALES: Glyn Oliver "Boaz" Myhill, Craig Morgan, Chris Gunter (87 Neal Eardley), James Collins, Ashley Williams, David Vaughan, Aaron Ramsey, Dave Edwards (82 Andy King), Gareth Bale (84 Lewin Nyatanga), Simon Church, Jermaine Easter.   Manager: John Toshack
Goals: David Vaughan (15), Aaron Ramsey (79)

104

576.   14.11.2009
WALES v SCOTLAND 3-0 (3-0)
Millennium, Cardiff
Referee: Cyril Zimmermann (Switzerland)   Att: 13,844
WALES: Wayne Hennessey, Sam Ricketts, Lewin Nyatanga (60 Daniel Gabbidon), Craig Morgan, Ashley Williams, Aaron Ramsey (56 Joe Allen), Joe Ledley (80 Andy King), Dave Edwards (88 David Cotterill), Gareth Bale, Ched Evans (46 Sam Vokes), Simon Church (46 Robert Earnshaw). Manager: John Toshack
SCOTLAND: David Marshall, Alan Hutton, Danny Fox (54 Lee Wallace), Stephen McManus, Gary Caldwell, Steven Naismith (62 Kevin Kyle), Darren Fletcher, Graham Dorrans (71 Barry Robson), Don Cowie (78 Derek Riordan), Kenny Miller (55 Steven Fletcher), James McFadden (62 Ross McCormack).   Manager: George Burley
Goals: Dave Edwards (17), Simon Church (32), Aaron Ramsey (35)

577.   03.03.2010
WALES v SWEDEN 0-1 (0-1)
Liberty Stadium, Swansea
Referee: Alan Black (Northern Ireland)   Attendance: 8,258
WALES: Glyn Oliver "Boaz" Myhill (46 Wayne Hennessey), Ashley Williams, Craig Morgan, Chris Gunter, James Collins, David Vaughan, Simon Davies (64 David Cotterill), Jack Collison (71 Andrew Crofts), Gareth Bale (67 Lewin Nyatanga), Ched Evans (46 Robert Earnshaw), Simon Church (53 Sam Vokes).   Manager: John Toshack
SWEDEN: Eddie Gustafsson, Olof Mellberg, Daniel Majstorovic, Behrang Safari (62 Oscar Wendt), Christian Wilhelmsson (73 Mikael Lustig), Anders Svensson, Kim Källström (80 Viktor Elm), Rasmus Elm (58 Pontus Wernbloom), Sebastian Larsson, Ola Toivonen, Johan Elmander (58 Tobias Hysén).   Manager: Erik Hamrén
Goal: Johan Elmander (44).

578.   23.05.2010
CROATIA v WALES 2-0 (1-0)
Gradski vrt, Osijek
Referee: Slavko Vincic (Slovenia)   Attendance: 12,000
CROATIA: Stipe Pletikosa, Ivan Strinic, Josip Simunic, Dejan Lovren, Ognjen Vukojevic (65 Tomislav Dujmovic), Darijo Srna (75 Domagoj Vida), Ivan Rakitic (76 Nikola Pokrivac), Luka Modric, Mladen Petric (46 Drago Gabric), Mario Mandzukic (90 Milan Badelj), Nikica Jelavic (46 Mate Bilic). Manager: Slaven Bilic

WALES: Wayne Hennessey (46 Glyn Oliver "Boaz" Myhill), Ashley Williams, Sam Ricketts, Lewin Nyatanga, Craig Morgan, Chris Gunter (81 Christian Ribeiro), Brian Stock (57 Mark Bradley), Dave Edwards, Andy Dorman (62 Neil Taylor), Robert Earnshaw (72 Hal Robson-Kanu), Simon Church (72 Sam Vokes).   Manager: John Toshack
Goals: Ivan Rakitic (45), Drago Gabric (81)

579.   11.08.2010
WALES v LUXEMBOURG 5-1 (1-1)
Parc-Y-Scarlets, Llanelli
Referee: Mattias Gestranius (Finland)   Attendance: 4.904
WALES: Wayne Hennessey (46 Glyn Oliver "Boaz" Myhill), Ashley Williams (85 Neal Eardley), Sam Ricketts, Craig Morgan, Chris Gunter, Brian Stock (46 Andy King), Joe Ledley, Craig Bellamy, Steve Morison, David Cotterill (82 Andrew Crofts), Robert Earnshaw (46 David Vaughan). Manager: John Toshack
LUXEMBOURG: Jonathan Joubert, Tom Schnell, Kim Kintziger, Mathias Jänisch (79 Dan Collette), Eric Hoffmann, Gilles Bettmer (86 Billy Bernard), Lars Gerson (59 Joël de Almeida Pedro), René Peters, Mario Mutsch, Joël Kitenge, Daniël Alves Da Mota (68 Tom Laterza). Manager: Luc Holtz
Sent off: Mario Mutsch (77)
Goals: David Cotterill (35), Joe Ledley (47 pen), Andy King (55), Ashley Williams (78), Craig Bellamy (82) / Joël Kitenge (44)

580.   03.09.2010   14th European Champs Qualifier
MONTENEGRO v WALES 1-0 (1-0)
Pod Goricom, Podgorica
Referee: Anastasios Kakos (Greece)   Attendance: 7,442
MONTENEGRO: Mladen Bozovic, Elsad Zverotic, Savo Pavicevic, Milan Jovanovic, Marko Basa, Miodrag Dzudovic, Simon Vukcevic (87 Fatos Beciraj), Milorad Pekovic, Branko Boskovic (73 Vladimir Bozovic), Mirko Vucinic, Radomir Djalovic (83 Mitar Novakovic).   Manager: Zlatko Kranjcar
WALES: Wayne Hennessey, Ashley Williams, Sam Ricketts, Chris Gunter, James Collins (75 Craig Morgan), David Vaughan, Joe Ledley, Dave Edwards (68 Robert Earnshaw), Gareth Bale, Steve Morison (78 Simon Church), Craig Bellamy. Manager: John Toshack
Goal: Mirko Vucinic (30)

581. 08.10.2010   14th European Champs Qualifier
WALES v BULGARIA 0-1 (0-0)
Cardiff City Stadium, Cardiff
Referee: Jonas Eriksson (Sweden)   Attendance: 14,061
WALES: Wayne Hennessey, Chris Gunter, James Collins, Danny Collins, Ashley Williams, Sam Ricketts, Joe Ledley (59 Andy King), Dave Edwards (68 Simon Church), David Vaughan, Gareth Bale, Steve Morison (82 Hal Robson-Kanu). Manager: Brian Flynn
BULGARIA: Nikolay Mihaylov, Petar Zanev, Ivan Ivanov, Valentin Iliev (37 Pavel Vidanov), Nikolaj Bodurov, Georgi Peev (72 Dimitar Rangelov), Stilian Petrov, Martin Petrov, Blagoy Georgiev, Dimitar Makriev (87 Chavdar Yankov), Ivelin Popov. Manager: Lothar Matthäus
Sent off: Chris Gunter (90)
Goal: Ivelin Popov (48)

582. 12.10.2010   14th European Champs Qualifier
SWITZERLAND v WALES 4-1 (2-1)
St. Jakob-Park, Basel
Referee: Alain Hamer (Luxembourg)   Attendance: 26,000
SWITZERLAND: Diego Benaglio (8 Marco Wölfli), Reto Ziegler, Steve von Bergen, Stephan Lichtsteiner, Stéphane Grichting, Valentin Stocker, Pirmin Schwegler (90 GÉLSON da Conceição Tavares FERNANDES), Gökhan Inler, Tranquillo Barnetta, Marco Streller, Alexander Frei (79 Eren Derdiyok). Manager: Ottmar Hitzfeld
WALES: Wayne Hennessey, Danny Collins, Andrew Crofts, Ashley Williams, James Collins, Andy King, David Vaughan (89 Shaun MacDonald), Dave Edwards (77 Steve Morison), Darcy Blake (54 Christian Ribeiro), Gareth Bale, Simon Church. Manager: Brian Flynn
Goals: Valentin Stocker (9, 89), Marco Streller (21), Gökhan Inler (82 pen) / Gareth Bale (13)

583. 08.02.2011   Nations Cup
REPUBLIC OF IRELAND v WALES 3-0 (0-0)
Aviva Stadium, Dublin
Referee: Mark Courtney (Northern Ireland)   Att: 19,783
REPUBLIC OF IRELAND: Shay Given, John O'Shea (85 Darren O'Dea), Séamus Coleman (58 Keith Fahey), Ciaran Clark, Sean St Ledger, Richard Dunne, Glenn Whelan (76 Paul Green), Darron Gibson (81 Marc Wilson), Damien Duff (71 Andy Keogh), Jon Walters, Kevin Doyle (46 Shane Long). Manager: Giovanni Trapattoni
WALES: Wayne Hennessey, Sam Ricketts (83 Lewin Nyatanga), Neal Eardley (46 Chris Gunter), Andrew Crofts, James Collins, Danny Collins, David Vaughan (61 Joe Ledley), Andy King, Robert Earnshaw (80 Jermaine Easter), Simon Church, Hal Robson-Kanu (68 Freddy Eastwood). Manager: Gary Speed
Goals: D. Gibson (60), Damien Duff (66), Keith Fahey (82)

584. 26.03.2011   14th European Champs Qualifier
WALES v ENGLAND 0-2 (0-2)
Millennium, Cardiff
Referee: OLEGARIO Manuel Bartolo Faustino BENQUERENÇA (Portugal)   Attendance: 68,959
WALES: Wayne Hennessey, Ashley Williams, Chris Gunter, Andrew Crofts, James Collins, Danny Collins, Aaron Ramsey, Joe Ledley, Andy King (65 David Vaughan), Steve Morison (65 Ched Evans), Craig Bellamy.   Manager: Gary Speed
ENGLAND: Joe Hart, John Terry, Michael Dawson, Ashley Cole, Glen Johnson, Ashley Young, Scott Parker (88 Phil Jagielka), Jack Wilshere (82 Stewart Downing), Frank Lampard, Darren Bent, Wayne Rooney (70 James Milner). Manager: Fabio Capello
Goals: Frank Lampard (7 pen), Darren Bent (15)

585. 25.05.2011   Nations Cup
WALES v SCOTLAND 1-3 (1-0)
Aviva Stadium, Dublin
Referee: Raymond Crangle (Northern Ireland)   Att: 6,036
WALES: Glyn Oliver "Boaz" Myhill, Neil Taylor (46 Chris Gunter), Craig Morgan, Neal Eardley (61 Adam Matthews), Owain Tudur-Jones (72 David Vaughan), Andy King (61 Aaron Ramsey), Andy Dorman (61 David Cotterill), Darcy Blake, Sam Vokes (73 Steve Morison), Jermaine Easter, Robert Earnshaw. Manager: Gary Speed
SCOTLAND: Allan McGregor, Steven Whittaker (80 Phil Bardsley), Stephen Crainey (81 Russell Martin), Gary Caldwell (86 Grant Hanley), Christophe Berra, Steven Naismith, James Morrison (74 Barry Robson), Scott Brown, Charlie Adam (88 James McArthur), Kenny Miller, Ross McCormack (74 Barry Bannan). Manager: Craig Levein
Goals: Robert Earnshaw (36) / James Morrison (56), Kenny Miller (65), Christophe Berra (71)

586. 27.05.2011   Nations Cup
WALES v NORTHERN IRELAND 2-0 (1-0)
Aviva Stadium, Dublin
Referee: Alan Kelly (Republic of Ireland)   Attendance: 529
WALES: Wayne Hennessey (75 Lewis Price), Chris Gunter (73 Adam Matthews), Daniel Gabbidon, Danny Collins, Neil Taylor, David Cotterill, Jack Collison (62 Owain Tudur-Jones), David Vaughan, Aaron Ramsey (90 Andy Dorman), Craig Bellamy (62 Robert Earnshaw), Steve Morison (80 Sam Vokes). Manager: Gary Speed
NORTHERN IRELAND: Jonny Tuffey, Colin Coates, Lee Hodson, Craig Cathcart (63 Stuart Dallas), Gareth McAuley, Johnny Gorman, Robert Garrett (76 Carl Winchester), Oliver Norwood, Niall McGinn (80 Jordan Owens), Warren Feeney (73 Liam Boyce), Josh Carson. Manager: Nigel Worthington
Goals: Aaron Ramsey (36), Robert Earnshaw (71)

587. 10.08.2011
WALES v AUSTRALIA 1-2 (0-1)
Cardiff City Stadium, Cardiff
Referee: Kristo Tohver (Estonia)   Attendance: 6,378
WALES: Wayne Hennessey, Ashley Williams, Neil Taylor, Chris Gunter (63 Adam Matthews), Daniel Gabbidon (46 Darcy Blake), David Vaughan (71 Joe Allen), Aaron Ramsey (46 Jack Collison), Joe Ledley, Gareth Bale, Robert Earnshaw (63 Steve Morison), Craig Bellamy.   Manager: Gary Speed
AUSTRALIA: Mark Schwarzer, Matthew Spiranovic, Lucas Neill, Michael Zullo (83 Adam Sarota), Tim Cahill (70 James Troisi), Luke Wilkshire (46 Robbie Kruse), Carl Valeri, Matt McKay, Neil Kilkenny, Brett Emerton (46 Rhys Williams), Scott McDonald (90 Mile Jedinak).   Manager: Holger Osieck
Goals: Darcy Blake (83) / Tim Cahill (44), Robbie Kruse (60)

588. 02.09.2011   14th European Champs Qualifier
WALES v MONTENEGRO 2-1 (1-0)
Cardiff City Stadium, Cardiff
Referee: Luca Banti (Italy)   Attendance: 8,194
WALES: Wayne Hennessey, Ashley Williams, Neil Taylor, Chris Gunter, David Vaughan, Aaron Ramsey (64 Andrew Crofts), Joe Ledley, Darcy Blake, Gareth Bale (90+2 Robert Earnshaw), Steve Morison (83 Hal Robson-Kanu), Craig Bellamy.   Manager: Gary Speed
MONTENEGRO: Mladen Bozovic, Elsad Zverotic, Stefan Savic, Radoslav Batak, Sasa Balic (83 Milan Jovanovic), Simon Vukcevic, Milorad Pekovic, Nikola Drincic, Mirko Vucinic (79 Andrija Delibasic), Stevan Jovetic, Radomir Djalovic (57 Dejan Damjanovic).   Manager: Zlatko Kranjcar
Goals: Steve Morison (29), Aaron Ramsey (50) / Stevan Jovetic (71)

589. 06.09.2011   14th European Champs Qualifier
ENGLAND v WALES 1-0 (1-0)
Wembley, London
Referee: Robert Schörgenhofer (Austria)   Att: 77,128
ENGLAND: Joe Hart, Ashley Cole, John Terry, Gary Cahill, Chris Smalling, Stewart Downing (79 Adam Johnson), Gareth Barry, Ashley Young, James Milner, Frank Lampard (73 Scott Parker), Wayne Rooney (89 Andy Carroll).
Manager: Fabio Capello
WALES: Wayne Hennessey, Chris Gunter, Andrew Crofts, Ashley Williams, Neil Taylor, Joe Ledley, Jack Collison (85 Andy King), Darcy Blake, Aaron Ramsey, Gareth Bale, Steve Morison (67 Robert Earnshaw).   Manager: Gary Speed
Goal: Ashley Young (35)

590. 07.10.2011   14th European Champs Qualifier
WALES v SWITZERLAND 2-0 (0-0)
Liberty Stadium, Swansea
Referee: Björn Kuipers (Netherlands)   Attendance: 12,317
WALES: Wayne Hennessey, Andrew Crofts (81 David Vaughan), Ashley Williams, Neil Taylor, Chris Gunter, Darcy Blake, Joe Allen, Aaron Ramsey, Gareth Bale, Craig Bellamy, Steve Morison (81 Simon Church).   Manager: Gary Speed
SWITZERLAND: Diego Benaglio, Timm Klose, Steve von Bergen, Reto Ziegler, Stephan Lichtsteiner, Fabian Frei (71 Innocent Emeghara), Granit Xhaka (81 Admir Mehmedi), Valon Behrami, Xherdan Shaqiri (62 Ricardo Rodríguez), Gökhan Inler, Eren Derdiyok.   Manager: Ottmar Hitzfeld
Sent off: Reto Ziegler (55)
Goals: Aaron Ramsey (60 pen), Gareth Bale (71)

591. 11.10.2011   14th European Champs Qualifier
BULGARIA v WALES 0-1 (0-1)
Vasil Levski, Sofia
Referee: Pawel Gil (Poland)   Attendance: 1,672
BULGARIA: Nikolay Mihaylov, Petar Zanev, Georgi Terziev, Yordan Miliev, Stanislav Manolev (52 Spas Delev), Ivan Ivanov, Aleksandar Tonev, Stilian Petrov, Vladimir Gadzhev, Valeri Domovchiyski (62 Valeri Bozhinov), Ivelin Popov (70 Dimitar Rangelov).   Manager: Mihail Madanski
WALES: Wayne Hennessey, Ashley Williams, Neil Taylor, Chris Gunter, Andrew Crofts, Aaron Ramsey, Darcy Blake (41 Adam Matthews), Joe Allen, Gareth Bale, Steve Morison (70 Simon Church), Craig Bellamy.   Manager: Gary Speed
Goal: Gareth Bale (45)

592. 12.11.2011
WALES v NORWAY 4-1 (2-0)
Cardiff City Stadium, Cardiff
Referee: Gerhard Grubelnik (Austria)   Attendance: 12,600
WALES: Wayne Hennessey, Ashley Williams, Adam Matthews, Chris Gunter, Andrew Crofts, Aaron Ramsey (90 Andy King), Darcy Blake, Joe Allen (76 Hal Robson-Kanu), Gareth Bale, Steve Morison (70 Sam Vokes), Craig Bellamy (90 Dave Edwards).   Manager: Gary Speed
NORWAY: Rune Jarstein (46 Espen Pettersen), Kjetil Wæhler (46 Vadim Demidov), Espen Ruud, John Arne Riise, Brede Hangeland, Erik Huseklepp, Ruben Jenssen (85 Jonathan Parr), Alexander Tettey, Morten Pedersen, Christian Grindheim (54 Simen Brenne), Mohammed Abdellaoue (77 Daniel Braaten).   Manager: Egil Olsen
Goals: Gareth Bale (11), C. Bellamy (16), Sam Vokes (88, 89) / Erik Huseklepp (61)

593. 29.02.2012
WALES v COSTA RICA 0-1 (0-1)
Cardiff City Stadium, Cardiff
Referee: Howard Webb (England)   Attendance: 23,193
WALES: Lewis Price, Adam Matthews (75 Sam Ricketts), Chris Gunter, Andrew Crofts, Ashley Williams (70 David Gabbidon), Darcy Blake, Joe Allen (63 Jack Collison), David Vaughan (70 Joe Ledley), Craig Bellamy (75 Robert Earnshaw), Steve Morison (69 Sam Vokes), Hal Robson-Kanu.   Manager: Chris Coleman
COSTA RICA: KEYLOR Antonio NAVAS Gamboa, BRYAN Josué OVIEDO Jiménez, ROY MILLER Hernández, MICHAEL UMAÑA Corrales, JOSÉ Andrés SALVATIERRA López, MICHAEL BARRANTES Rojas, RANDALL AZOFEIFA Corrales, RODNEY WALLACE (68 PABLO Daniel Antonio GABAS), KENNY Martin CUNNINGHAM Brown (88 JÚNIOR Enrique DÍAZ Campbell), JOEL Nathaniel CAMPBELL Samuels (79 JONATHAN Andrés McDONALD Porras), BRYAN Jafet RUIZ González.
Manager: JORGE Luis PINTO Afanador
Goal: JOEL Nathaniel CAMPBELL Samuels (6)

594. 27.05.2012
WALES v MEXICO 0-2 (0-1)
New Meadowlands, East Rutherford (USA)
Referee: Ricardo Salazar (USA)   Attendance: 35,518
WALES: Jason Brown, Ashley Williams, Neil Taylor (80 Jazz Richards), Adam Matthews (61 Sam Ricketts), Chris Gunter, Aaron Ramsey, Dave Edwards (71 Andy King), Joe Allen, Steve Morison (59 Sam Vokes), Craig Bellamy, Hal Robson-Kanu (59 Simon Church).   Manager: Chris Coleman
MEXICO: JOSÉ de Jesús CORONA Rodríguez, HÉCTOR Alfredo MORENO Herrera, SEVERO Efraín MEZA Mayorga, Francisco Javier Rodríguez Pinedo "Maza", CARLOS Arnoldo SALCIDO Flores, LUIS Ernesto PÉREZ Gómez (71 JORGE Emanuel TORRES Nilo), EDGAR Bismarck ANDRADE Renteria (89 ISRAEL Sabdi JIMÉNEZ Ñáñez), JESÚS Eduardo ZAVALA Castañeda (63 JESÚS Antonio MOLINA Granados), Jesús ALDO DE NIGRIS Guajardo, PABLO Edson BARRERA Acosta (76 RAFAEL MÁRQUEZ Álvarez), GIOVANI Alex DOS SANTOS Ramírez (71 ÁNGEL Eduardo REYNA Martínez).
Manager: JOSÉ Manuel DE LA TORRE Menchaca
Goals: Jesús ALDO DE NIGRIS Guajardo (43, 89)

595. 15.08.2012
WALES v BOSNIA-HERZEGOVINA 0-2 (0-1)
Parc-Y-Scarlets, Llanelli
Referee: Marco Borg (Malta)   Attendance: 6,253
WALES: Glyn Oliver "Boaz" Myhill, Andrew Crofts (88 Robert Earnshaw), Ashley Williams, Neil Taylor, Chris Gunter (69 Sam Ricketts), Aaron Ramsey, Darcy Blake (78 Joel Lynch), Joe Allen, Gareth Bale (62 Hal Robson-Kanu), Sam Vokes (69 Steve Morison), Simon Church (64 Craig Bellamy).   Manager: Chris Coleman
BOSNIA-HERZEGOVINA: Asmir Begovic, Boris Pandza (71 Toni Sunjic), Emir Spahic, Mensur Mujdza (86 Ognjen Vranjes), Adnan Zahirovic (86 Damir Vrancic), Miroslav Stevanovic (63 Muhamed Besic), Sejad Salihovic, Miralem Pjanic (82 Ivan Sesar), Senad Lulic, Vedad Ibisevic (74 Muamer Svraka), Edin Dzeko.   Manager: Safet Susic
Goals: Vedad Ibisevic (21), Miroslav Stevanovic (54)

596. 07.09.2012   20th World Cup Qualifier
WALES v BELGIUM 0-2 (0-1)
Cardiff City Stadium, Cardiff
Referee: Stefan Johannesson (Sweden)   Attendance: 16,557
WALES: Glyn Oliver "Boaz" Myhill, Ashley Williams, Adam Matthews, Chris Gunter, James Collins, Darcy Blake, Aaron Ramsey, Dave Edwards (79 Andy King), Gareth Bale, Steve Morison (72 Sam Vokes), Simon Church (71 Hal Robson-Kanu).   Manager: Chris Coleman
BELGIUM: Thibaut Courtois, Jan Vertonghen, Thomas Vermaelen, Vincent Kompany, Guillaume Gillet, Axel Witsel, Kevin Mirallas (46 Romelu Lukaku), Dries Mertens, Eden Hazard, Marouane Fellaini, Mousa Dembélé (64 Kevin De Bruyne).   Manager: Marc Wilmots
Sent off: James Collins (26)
Goals: Vincent Kompany (42), Jan Vertonghen (83)

597. 11.09.2012   20th World Cup Qualifier
SERBIA v WALES 6-1 (3-1)
Stadion Karadjordje, Novi Sad
Referee: DUARTE Nuno Pereira GOMES (Portugal)
Attendance: 10,660
SERBIA: Vladimir Stojkovic, Branislav Ivanovic, Milan Bisevac, Matija Nastasic, Aleksandar Kolarov, Aleksandar Ignjovski (85 Srdan Mijailovic), Ljubomir Fejsa, Filip Djuricic (81 Dejan Lekic), Zoran Tosic (70 Miralem Sulejmani), Dusan Tadic, Lazar Markovic.   Manager: Sinisa Mihajlovic
WALES: Glyn Oliver "Boaz" Myhill, Darcy Blake, Ashley Williams, Adam Matthews (46 Sam Ricketts), Chris Gunter, Dave Edwards (46 David Vaughan), Joe Allen (70 Andy King), Aaron Ramsey, Gareth Bale, Simon Church, Steve Morison.   Manager: Chris Coleman
Goals: Aleksandar Kolarov (16), Zoran Tosic (24), Filip Djuricic (37), Dusan Tadic (55), Branislav Ivanovic (80), Miralem Sulejmani (90) / Gareth Bale (31)

598.　12.10.2012　20th World Cup Qualifier
WALES v SCOTLAND 2-1 (0-1)
Cardiff City Stadium, Cardiff

Referee: Florian Meyer (Germany)　Attendance: 23,249

WALES: Lewis Price, Ashley Williams, Chris Gunter, Darcy Blake, Ben Davies, David Vaughan, Aaron Ramsey, Joe Ledley (71 Hal Robson-Kanu), Joe Allen, Gareth Bale, Steve Morison (65 Craig Davies).　Manager: Chris Coleman

SCOTLAND: Allan McGregor, Allan Hutton, Danny Fox, Gary Caldwell, Christophe Berra, James Morrison (85 Kenny Miller), Shaun Maloney, Darren Fletcher, Kris Commons (84 Jamie Mackie), Scott Brown (46 Charlie Adam), Steven Fletcher.　Manager: Craig Levein

Goals: Gareth Bale (81 pen, 89) / James Morrison (27)

599. 16.10.2012　20th World Cup Qualifier
CROATIA v WALES 2-0 (1-0)
Stadion Gradski vrt, Osijek

Referee: Alexandru Tudor (Romania)　Attendance: 17,500

CROATIA: Stipe Pletikosa, Ivan Strinic, Darijo Srna, Josip Simunic, Dejan Lovren (46 Gordon Schildenfeld), Ivan Rakitic, Ivan Perisic (85 Domagoj Vida), Luka Modric, Milan Badelj, Mario Mandzukic, EDUARDO Alves da Silva (78 Niko Kranjcar).　Manager: Igor Stimac

WALES: Lewis Price, Ashley Williams, Chris Gunter, Ben Davies, Darcy Blake, David Vaughan, Joe Ledley (82 Hal Robson-Kanu), Andy King (73 Sam Vokes), Joe Allen, Gareth Bale, Steve Morison (61 Simon Church).　Manager: Chris Coleman

Goals: Mario Mandzukic (27), EDUARDO Alves da Silva (58)

600.　06.02.2013
WALES v AUSTRIA 2-1 (1-0)
Liberty Stadium, Swansea

Referee: Menashe Masiah (Israel)　Attendance: 8,202

WALES: Glyn Oliver "Boaz" Myhill, Adam Matthews (73 Chris Gunter), Ashley Williams, Sam Ricketts, Ben Davies, Joe Ledley, Jack Collison (84 Simon Church), David Vaughan (46 Andy King), Joe Allen, Gareth Bale (60 Hal Robson-Kanu), Craig Bellamy (46 Sam Vokes).　Manager: Chris Coleman

AUSTRIA: Robert Almer, Markus Suttner (88 Franz Schiemer), Sebastian Prödl, Emanuel Pogatetz, Florian Klein, Veli Kavlak (76 Christoph Leitgeb), Andreas Ivanschitz (62 Zlatko Junuzovic), David Alaba, Marko Arnautovic, Andreas Weimann (62 Jakob Jantscher), Marc Janko.　Manager: Marcel Koller

Goals: Gareth Bale (21), Sam Vokes (52) / Marc Janko (75)

601.　22.03.2013　20th World Cup Qualifier
SCOTLAND v WALES 1-2 (1-0)
Hampden Park, Glasgow

Referee: Antony Gautier (France)　Attendance: 39,365

SCOTLAND: Allan McGregor, Grant Hanley, Gary Caldwell, Charlie Mulgrew, Alan Hutton, Graham Dorrans (64 Charlie Adam), Chris Burke (86 Jordan Rhodes), Robert Snodgrass, James McArthur, Shaun Maloney, Steven Fletcher (4 Kenny Miller).　Manager: Gordon Strachan

WALES: Glyn Oliver "Boaz" Myhill, Chris Gunter, Ben Davies, Ashley Williams, Sam Ricketts, Jack Collison (58 Andy King), Aaron Ramsey, Joe Ledley (89 Simon Church), Gareth Bale (46 Jonathan Williams), Craig Bellamy, Hal Robson-Kanu.　Manager: Chris Coleman

Sent off: Robert Snodgrass (72), Aaron Ramsey (90+4)

Goals: Grant Hanley (45+1) / Aaron Ramsey (72 pen), Hal Robson-Kanu (74)

602.　26.03.2013　20th World Cup Qualifier
WALES v CROATIA 1-2 (1-0)
Liberty Stadium, Swansea

Referee: Luca Banti (Italy)　Attendance: 11,534

WALES: Glyn Oliver "Boaz" Myhill, Ashley Williams, Chris Gunter, Ben Davies, James Collins, Joe Ledley, Andy King, Jonathan Williams (83 Simon Church), Gareth Bale, Craig Bellamy, Hal Robson-Kanu (64 Jazz Richards).　Manager: Chris Coleman

CROATIA: Stipe Pletikosa, Ivan Strinic (73 Ivica Olic), Darijo Srna, Dejan Lovren, Vedran Corluka, Jorge SAMMIR Cruz Campos (61 Mateo Kovacic), Ivan Rakitic, Luka Modric, Milan Badelj (46 Gordon Schildenfeld), Mario Mandzukic, EDUARDO Alves da Silva.　Manager: Igor Stimac

Goals: Gareth Bale (21 pen) / Dejan Lovren (77), EDUARDO Alves da Silva (87)

603.　14.08.2013
WALES v REPUBLIC OF IRELAND 0-0
Cardiff City Stadium, Cardiff

Referee: Pavel Královec (Czech Republic)　Att. 20,000

WALES: Glyn Oliver "Boaz" Myhill, Ashley Williams, Sam Ricketts, Chris Gunter, Ben Davies, Joe Ledley (59 Andy King), Jack Collison (81 Craig Davies), Joe Allen (86 Andrew Crofts), Jonathan Williams, Craig Bellamy (59 Sam Vokes), Hal Robson-Kanu (74 Neil Taylor).　Manager: Chris Coleman

REPUBLIC OF IRELAND: Keiren Westwood, Marc Wilson, John O'Shea (60 Darren O'Dea), Séamus Coleman, Ciaran Clark, Glenn Whelan (60 Paul Green), James McCarthy, Wes Hoolahan (69 Paddy Madden), Robbie Brady (46 James McClean), Jon Walters (84 Conor Sammon), Shane Long (74 Andy Keogh).　Manager: Giovanni Trapattoni

604. 06.09.2013   20th World Cup Qualifier
MACEDONIA v WALES 2-1 (1-1)
Filip II. Makedonski, Skopje

Referee: Sascha Kever (Switzerland)   Attendance: 18,000

MACEDONIA: Tome Pachovski, Vance Shikov, Nikolce Noveski, Daniel Georgievski (77 Aleksandar Lazevski), Darko Tasevski, Stefan Ristovski, Nikola Gligorov, Ivan Trichkovski, Goran Pandev, Jovan Kostovski (86 Daniel Mojsov), Agim Ibraimi (61 Aleksandar Trajkovski).
Manager: Cedomir Janevski

WALES: Glyn Oliver "Boaz" Myhill, Ashley Williams, Sam Ricketts, Chris Gunter, Ben Davies, David Vaughan (85 Sam Vokes), Aaron Ramsey, Joe Ledley, Jack Collison (79 Adam Matthews), Jonathan Williams (62 Andrew Crofts), Craig Bellamy.   Manager: Chris Coleman

Goals: Ivan Trichkovski (21), Aleksandar Trajkovski (80) / Aaron Ramsey (39 pen)

605. 10.09.2013   20th World Cup Qualifier
WALES v SERBIA 0-3 (0-2)
Cardiff City Stadium, Cardiff

Referee: Szymon Marciniak (Poland)   Attendance: 10,923

WALES: Glyn Oliver "Boaz" Myhill, Adam Matthews, Chris Gunter, Daniel Gabbidon, Ben Davies, Andrew Crofts (59 David Vaughan), Aaron Ramsey, Joe Ledley (75 Hal Robson-Kanu), Andy King (59 Gareth Bale), Sam Vokes, Craig Bellamy.
Manager: Chris Coleman

SERBIA: Vladimir Stojkovic, Matija Nastasic, Aleksandar Kolarov, Branislav Ivanovic, Milan Bisevac, Dusan Tadic (88 Nenad Krsticic), Ivan Radovanovic (67 Luka Milivojevic), Lazar Markovic, Ljubomir Fejsa (90+2 Radoslav Petrovic), Filip Djuricic, Filip Djordjevic.   Manager: Sinisa Mihajlovic

Goals: Filip Djordjevic (8), Aleksandar Kolarov (38), Lazar Markovic (55)

606. 11.10.2013   20th World Cup Qualifier
WALES v MACEDONIA 1-0 (0-0)
Cardiff City Stadium, Cardiff

Referee: Suren Baliyan (Armenia)   Attendance: 11,257

WALES: Wayne Hennessey, Neil Taylor, Chris Gunter, James Collins, David Vaughan, Aaron Ramsey, Andy King, Declan John, Simon Church (90+1 Jermaine Easter), Craig Bellamy, Hal Robson-Kanu. Manager: Chris Coleman

MACEDONIA: Tome Pachovski, Vance Shikov, Nikolce Noveski, Ezgjan Alioski, Ostoja Stjepanovic (75 Darko Tasevski), Stefan Ristovski, Predrag Randjelovic, Muhamed Demiri (85 Jovan Kostovski), Goran Pandev, Mirko Ivanovski (79 Aleksandar Trajkovski), Agim Ibraimi.
Manager: Zoran Stratev

Goal: Simon Church (67).

Aaron Ramsey missed a penalty kick in the 85th minute.

607. 15.10.2013   20th World Cup Qualifier
BELGIUM v WALES 1-1 (0-0)
Stade Roi Baudouin, Brussels

Referee: Sergey Karasev (Russia)   Attendance: 45,401

BELGIUM: Thibaut Courtois, Sébastien Pocognoli, Daniel Van Buyten (71 Jan Vertonghen), Thomas Vermaelen, Toby Alderweireld, Axel Witsel, Kevin Mirallas (77 Zakaria Bakkali), Mousa Dembélé, Kevin De Bruyne, Nacer Chadli (57 Eden Hazard), Romelu Lukaku.   Manager: Marc Wilmots

WALES: Wayne Hennessey, Neil Taylor, Chris Gunter, James Collins (56 James Wilson), David Vaughan, Jazz Richards, Aaron Ramsey, Andy King, Simon Church (70 Sam Vokes), Craig Bellamy, Hal Robson-Kanu (87 Harry Wilson).
Manager: Chris Coleman

Goals: Kevin De Bruyne (64) / Aaron Ramsey (88)

608. 16.11.2013
WALES v FINLAND 1-1 (0-0)
Cardiff City Stadium, Cardiff

Referee: Sebastien Delferière (Belgium)   Att: 11,809

WALES: Wayne Hennessey, Chris Gunter (72 Jazz Richards), Ashley Williams, Neil Taylor (72 Ben Davies), Sam Ricketts, Joe Ledley, Andy King, Joe Allen (90 Owain Tudur-Jones), Gareth Bale, Simon Church (63 Sam Vokes), Hal Robson-Kanu (84 David Cotterill).   Manager: Chris Coleman

FINLAND: Lukás Hrádecky, Juhani Ojala (46 Joona Toivio), Niklas Moisander (62 Petri Pasanen), Jere Uronen, Rasmus Schüller (70 Përparim Hetemaj), Riku Riski, Alexander Ring, Roman Eremenko, Kari Arkivuo (46 Veli Lampi, 70 Jukka Raitala), Tim Sparv, Teemu Pukki (63 Kasper Hämäläinen).
Manager: Mixu Paatelainen

Goals: Andy King (58) / Riku Riski (90+1)

609. 05.03.2014
WALES v ICELAND 3-1 (1-1)
Cardiff City Stadium, Cardiff

Referee: Eiko Saar (Estonia)   Attendance: 13,219

WALES: Wayne Hennessey, Ashley Williams (64 Sam Ricketts), Neil Taylor, Chris Gunter, James Collins (46 Daniel Gabbidon), Andy King (75 Jack Collison), Emyr Huws, Joe Allen, Sam Vokes, Hal Robson-Kanu (88 Ben Davies), Gareth Bale (71 Jonathan Williams).   Manager: Chris Coleman

ICELAND: Hannes Halldórsson, Ari Skúlason (81 Kristinn Jónsson), Ragnar Sigurdsson (46 Sölvi Ottesen), Aron Gunnarsson, Teddy Bjarnason, Kári Árnason, Gylfi Sigurdsson, Emil Hallfredsson, Jóhann Gudmundsson, Kolbeinn Sigthórsson (76 Björn Sverrisson), Alfred Finnbogason (46 Birkir Bjarnason).   Manager: Lars Lagerbäck

Goals: James Collins (12), Sam Vokes (64), Gareth Bale (70) / Ashley Williams (26 og)

610.   04.06.2014
NETHERLANDS v WALES 2-0 (1-0)
Amsterdam ArenA, Amsterdam
Referee: Bülent Yildirim (Turkey)   Attendance: 51,000
NETHERLANDS: Jasper Cillessen, Daryl Janmaat, Stefan de Vrij, Ron Vlaar, Bruno Martins Indi, Leroy Fer (46 Georginio Wijnaldum), Nigel de Jong (77 Klaas-Jan Huntelaar), Daley Blind, Wesley Sneijder, Robin van Persie (46 Jeremain Lens), Arjen Robben.   Manager: Louis van Gaal
WALES: Wayne Hennessey, Chris Gunter, Daniel Gabbidon, James Chester, Neil Taylor (83 Paul Dummett), Joe Ledley (62 Emyr Huws), Andy King (79 David Vaughan), Joe Allen, Simon Church (66 Jermaine Easter), Hal Robson-Kanu (60 Declan John), Jonathan Williams (70 George Christopher Williams).   Manager: Chris Coleman
Goals: Arjen Robben (32), Jeremain Lens (76)

611.   09.09.2014   15th European Champs Qualifier
ANDORRA v WALES 1-2 (1-1)
Estadi Nacional, Andorra la Vella
Referee: Slavko Vincic (Slovenia)   Attendance: 3,150
ANDORRA: FERRAN POL Pérez, EMILI Josep GARCÍA Miramontes, JORDI RUBIO Gómez, DAVID MANEIRO Ton, ILDEFONS LIMA Solà, José Manuel Díaz "JOSEP" AYALA (86 JULI SÁNCHEZ Soto), MARC VALES González, Gabriel "GABI" RIERA, Carlos Eduardo "EDU" PEPPE Britos (53 MÁRCIO VIEIRA de Vasconcelos), CRISTIAN MARTÍNEZ Alejo (83 ÓSCAR Masand SONEJEE), IVÁN LORENZO Roncero.   Manager: Jesús Luis Álvarez de Eulate Güergue "KOLDO"
WALES: Wayne Hennessey, James Chester, Ashley Williams, Neil Taylor, Chris Gunter, Ben Davies, Joe Allen, Aaron Ramsey (90+4 Emyr Huws), Andy King (76 George Christopher Williams), Simon Church (62 Joe Ledley), Gareth Bale.   Manager: Chris Coleman
Goals: ILDEFONS LIMA Solà (6 pen) / Gareth Bale (22, 81)

612.   10.10.2014   15th European Champs Qualifier
WALES v BOSNIA-HERZEGOVINA 0-0
Cardiff City Stadium, Cardiff
Referee: Vladislav Bezborodov (Russia)   Attendance: 30,741
WALES: Wayne Hennessey, Ashley Williams, Neil Taylor, Chris Gunter, Ben Davies, James Chester, Joe Ledley, Andy King, Simon Church (65 Hal Robson-Kanu), Jonathan Williams (83 George Christopher Williams), Gareth Bale.   Manager: Chris Coleman
BOSNIA-HERZEGOVINA: Asmir Begovic, Toni Sunjic, Mensur Mujdza, Muhamed Besic, Tino-Sven Susic, Miralem Pjanic, Senad Lulic, Anel Hadzic, Haris Medunjanin, Vedad Ibisevic (83 Izet Hajrovic), Edin Dzeko.   Manager: Safet Susic

613.   13.10.2014   15th European Champs Qualifier
WALES v CYPRUS 2-1 (2-1)
Cardiff City Stadium, Cardiff
Referee: Manuel Gräfe (Germany)   Attendance: 21,273
WALES: Wayne Hennessey, Ashley Williams, Neil Taylor, Chris Gunter, James Chester, Joe Ledley, Andy King, George Christopher Williams (58 Dave Edwards), Simon Church (6 David Cotterill), Hal Robson-Kanu (84 Jake Taylor), Gareth Bale.   Manager: Chris Coleman
CYPRUS: Tasos Kissas, Giorgios Merkis, DOSSA Momad Omar Hassamo JÚNIOR (29 Angelis Angeli, 85 Andreas Papathanasiou), Marios Antoniades, Mários Nikolaou (68 Nektarios Alexandrou), Konstantinos Makridis, Vincent Laban, Charis Kyriakou, Giorgos Efrem, Dimitris Christofi, Pieros Soteriou.   Manager: Pambos Christodoulou
Sent off: Andy King (47)
Goals: David Cotterill (13), Hal Robson-Kanu (23) / Vincent Laban (36)

614.   16.11.2014   15th European Champs Qualifier
BELGIUM v WALES 0-0
Stade Roi Baudouin, Brussels
Referee: Pavel Královec (Czech Republic)   Att: 41,535
BELGIUM: Thibaut Courtois, Jan Vertonghen, Anthony Vanden Borre, Nicolas Lombaerts, Toby Alderweireld, Axel Witsel, Marouane Fellaini, Kevin De Bruyne, Eden Hazard, Divock Origi (73 Dries Mertens, 89 Adnan Januzaj), Nacer Chadli (62 Christian Benteke).   Manager: Marc Wilmots
WALES: Wayne Hennessey, Ashley Williams, Neil Taylor, Chris Gunter, James Chester, Aaron Ramsey, Joe Ledley, David Cotterill (46 George Christopher Williams), Joe Allen, Hal Robson-Kanu (90+5 Emyr Huws), Gareth Bale.   Manager: Chris Coleman

615.   28.03.2015   15th European Champs Qualifier
ISRAEL v WALES 0-3 (0-1)
Sammy Ofer Stadium, Haifa
Referee: Milorad Mazic (Serbia)   Attendance: 30,200
ISRAEL: Ofir Marciano, Eitan Tibi, Orel Dgani, Omri Ben Harush, Tal Ben Haim, Sheran Yeini, Lior Refaelov, Bebars Natcho, Eran Zahavy (70 Ben Sahar), Omer Damari (45 Tomer Hemed), Tal Ben Haim (60 Nir Bitton).   Manager: Eli Guttmann
WALES: Wayne Hennessey, Ashley Williams, Neil Taylor, Chris Gunter, Ben Davies, James Collins, Aaron Ramsey (85 Shaun MacDonald), Joe Ledley (47 David Vaughan), Joe Allen, Hal Robson-Kanu (68 Sam Vokes), Gareth Bale.   Manager: Chris Coleman
Sent off: Eitan Tibi (51)
Goals: Aaron Ramsey (45+1), Gareth Bale (50, 77)

616. 12.06.2015   15th European Champs Qualifier
WALES v BELGIUM 1-0 (1-0)
Cardiff City Stadium, Cardiff
Referee: Dr. Felix Brych (Germany)   Attendance: 33,280
WALES: Wayne Hennessey, Ashley Williams, Neil Taylor, Chris Gunter, James Chester, Jazz Richards, Aaron Ramsey, Joe Ledley, Joe Allen, Hal Robson-Kanu (90+3 Andy King), Gareth Bale (87 Sam Vokes).   Manager: Chris Coleman
BELGIUM: Thibaut Courtois, Jan Vertonghen, Nicolas Lombaerts, Jason Denayer, Toby Alderweireld (77 Yannick Ferreira-Carrasco), Axel Witsel, Radja Nainggolan, Kevin De Bruyne, Eden Hazard, Dries Mertens (46 Romelu Lukaku), Christian Benteke.   Manager: Marc Wilmots
Goal: Gareth Bale (25)

617. 03.09.2015   15th European Champs Qualifier
CYPRUS v WALES 0-1 (0-0)
Neo GSP, Nicosia
Referee: Szymon Marciniak (Poland)   Attendance: 14,492
CYPRUS: Antonis Georgallides, Kostas Laifis, DOSSA Momad Omar Hassamo JÚNIOR, Jason Demetriou, Marios Antoniades, Mários Nikolaou, Andreas Makris (84 Pieros Soteriou), Konstantinos Makridis, Giorgos Economides, Costas Charalambides (74 Nikos Englezou), Nestoras Mitidis (65 Giorgos Kolokoudias).   Manager: Pambos Christodoulou
WALES: Wayne Hennessey, Ashley Williams, Neil Taylor, Chris Gunter, Ben Davies, Jazz Richards, Aaron Ramsey (90+3 Shaun MacDonald), Andy King, Dave Edwards, Hal Robson-Kanu (68 Sam Vokes), Gareth Bale (90 Simon Church). Manager: Chris Coleman
Goal: Gareth Bale (82)

618. 06.09.2015   15th European Champs Qualifier
WALES v ISRAEL 0-0
Cardiff City Stadium, Cardiff
Referee: Ivan Bebek (Croatia)   Attendance: 32,653
WALES: Wayne Hennessey, Ashley Williams, Neil Taylor, Chris Gunter, Ben Davies, Jazz Richards, Aaron Ramsey, Andy King (85 Sam Vokes), Dave Edwards, Gareth Bale, Hal Robson-Kanu (79 Simon Church).   Manager: Chris Coleman
ISRAEL: Ofir Marciano, Tal Ben Haim, Eitan Tibi, Orel Dgani, Elazar Dasa, Omri Ben Harush, Bebars Natcho, Biram Kayal (46 Tal Ben Haim), Nir Bitton, Eran Zahavy (90+3 Ben Sahar), Munas Dabbur (46 Tomer Hemed).
Manager: Eli Guttmann

619. 10.10.2015   15th European Champs Qualifier
BOSNIA-HERZEGOVINA v WALES 2-0 (0-0)
Stadion Bilino Polje, Zenica
Referee: Alberto Undiano Mallenco (Spain)   Att: 10,250
BOSNIA-HERZEGOVINA: Asmir Begovic, Mensur Mujdza, Ervin Zukanovic, Toni Sunjic, Emir Spahic (46 Edin Cocalic), Sejad Salihovic, Miralem Pjanic, Senad Lulic, Anel Hadzic (89 Ermin Bicakcic), Edin Visca (61 Milan Djuric), Vedad Ibisevic.
Manager: Mehmed Bazdarevic
WALES: Wayne Hennessey, Chris Gunter, Ben Davies, Ashley Williams, Neil Taylor, Aaron Ramsey, Joe Ledley (75 Sam Vokes), Joe Allen (85 Dave Edwards), Jazz Richards, Gareth Bale, Hal Robson-Kanu (84 Simon Church).
Manager: Chris Coleman
Goals: Milan Djuric (71), Vedad Ibisevic (90)

620. 13.10.2015   15th European Champs Qualifier
WALES v ANDORRA 2-0 (0-0)
Cardiff City Stadium, Cardiff
Referee: Kevin Blom (Netherlands)   Attendance: 33,280
WALES: Wayne Hennessey, Ashley Williams, Chris Gunter, Ben Davies, James Chester, David Vaughan, Aaron Ramsey, Sam Vokes, Jonathan Williams (86 Simon Church), Hal Robson-Kanu (23 Dave Edwards, 46 Tom Lawrence), Gareth Bale.   Manager: Chris Coleman
ANDORRA: FERRAN POL Pérez, MOISÉS SAN NICOLÁS Schellens, JESÚS RUBIO Gómez, ADRIÁ RODRÍGUES Gonçalves, MAX LLOVERA González-Adrio, ILDEFONS LIMA Solà, MÁRCIO VIEIRA de Vasconcelos, ÓSCAR Masand SONEJEE (70 José Manuel Díaz "JOSEP" AYALA), AARÓN SÁNCHEZ Alberquerque, VICTOR Hugo MOREIRA Teixeira (12 Gabriel "GABI" RIERA), IVÁN LORENZO Roncero (81 MARC García RENOM).
Manager: Jesús Luis Álvarez de Eulate Güergue "KOLDO"
Goals: Aaron Ramsey (51), Gareth Bale (86)

621. 13.11.2015
WALES v NETHERLANDS 2-3 (1-1)
Cardiff City Stadium, Cardiff
Referee: Benoît Bastien (France)   Attendance: 25,669
WALES: Wayne Hennessey (74 Owain Williams), James Chester, Ashley Williams (46 James Collins), Neil Taylor (65 Paul Dummett), Chris Gunter (65 Adam Henley), Ben Davies, Joe Allen, Joe Ledley (55 Emyr Huws), Andy King, Tom Lawrence, Jonathan Williams (60 George Christopher Williams).   Manager: Chris Coleman

112

NETHERLANDS: Jasper Cillessen, Jeffrey Bruma, Virgil van Dijk (46 Joël Veltman), Terence Kongolo, Daryl Janmaat, Daley Blind, Jordy Clasie (87 Riechedly Bazoer), Wesley Sneijder, Bas Dost, Arjen Robben, Quincy Promes (90+1 Georginio Wijnaldum).   Manager: Danny Blind

Goals: Joe Ledley (45+3), Emyr Huws (70) / Bas Dost (32), Arjen Robben (54, 81)

Joe Allen missed a penalty kick (45+3).

622.   24.03.2016
WALES v NORTHERN IRELAND 1-1 (0-0)
Cardiff City Stadium, Cardiff
Referee: Steven McLean (Scotland)   Attendance: 21,855
WALES: Wayne Hennessey (46 Danny Ward), Ashley Williams, Adam Matthews, Chris Gunter, James Chester, David Vaughan (71 Joe Allen), Joe Ledley (46 Andrew Crofts), David Cotterill, George Christopher Williams (62 Lloyd Isgrove), Sam Vokes (76 Simon Church), Tom Lawrence (62 Jonathan Williams).   Manager: Chris Coleman
NORTHERN IRELAND: Michael McGovern, Conor McLaughlin (81 Aaron Hughes), Gareth McAuley, Jonny Evans (73 Daniel Lafferty), Craig Cathcart, Oliver Norwood, Steven Davis, Stuart Dallas (90+2 Shane Ferguson), Paddy McNair (73 Paul Paton), Conor Washington (46 Jamie Ward), Kyle Lafferty (81 Billy McKay).   Manager: Michael O'Neill

Goals: Simon Church (89 pen) / Craig Cathcart (60)

623.   28.03.2016
UKRAINE v WALES 1-0 (1-0)
NKS Olimpijs'kyj, Kiev
Referee: Serdar Gözübüyük (Netherlands)   Att: 20,000
UKRAINE: Andriy Pyatov, Vyacheslav Shevchuk, Oleksandr Kucher, Evgen Khacheridi, Artem Fedetskiy, Taras Stepanenko, Ruslan Rotan (59 Sergiy Sydorchuk), Viktor Kovalenko, Denys Garmash, Roman Zozulya, Andriy Yarmolenko. Manager: Mikhail Fomenko
WALES: Wayne Hennessey, Ashley Williams (65 Jazz Richards), Neil Taylor (72 Adam Henley), Chris Gunter, Ben Davies, James Chester, Emyr Huws (79 Joe Ledley), Joe Allen, Tom Lawrence (73 Tom Bradshaw), Simon Church (61 Sam Vokes), Jonathan Williams (61 Shaun MacDonald).   Manager: Chris Coleman

Goal: Andriy Yarmolenko (27)

624.   05.06.2016
SWEDEN v WALES 3-0 (1-0)
Friends Arena, Solna
Referee: Tobias Welz (Germany)   Attendance: 37,942
SWEDEN: Andreas Isaksson (46 Robin Olsen), Martin Olsson (46 Ludwig Augustinsson), Mikael Lustig, Erik Johansson, Andreas Granqvist, Oscar Lewicki (61 Albin Ekdal), Sebastian Larsson, Kim Källström, Emil Forsberg (61 Jimmy Durmaz), Zlatan Ibrahimovic (61 Emir Kujovic), Marcus Berg (76 John Guidetti).
Managers: Erik Hamrén & Janne Andersson
WALES: Wayne Hennessey (46 Danny Ward), Ashley Williams, Neil Taylor, Chris Gunter, Ben Davies, James Chester (64 James Collins), Aaron Ramsey, David Vaughan (64 Dave Edwards), Andy King (64 Gareth Bale), Sam Vokes (73 Simon Church), Jonathan Williams (74 Emyr Huws).
Manager: Chris Coleman

Goals: Emil Forsberg (40), Mikael Lustig (57), John Guidetti (87)

625.   11.06.2016   15th European Champs Group B
WALES v SLOVAKIA 2-1 (1-0)
Stade Matmut-Atlantique, Bordeaux (France)
Referee: Svein Moen (Norway)   Attendance: 37,831
WALES: Danny Ward, Chris Gunter, Neil Taylor, Ben Davies, James Chester, Ashley Williams, Joe Allen, Aaron Ramsey (88 Jazz Richards), Dave Edwards (69 Joe Ledley), Gareth Bale, Jonathan Williams (71 Hal Robson-Kanu).
Manager: Chris Coleman
SLOVAKIA: Matús Kozácik, Peter Pekarík, Martin Skrtel, Ján Durica, Dusan Svento, Vladimír Weiss (83 Miroslav Stoch), Patrik Hrosovsky (60 Ondrej Duda), Marek Hamsík, Juraj Kucka, Róbert Mak, Michal Duris (60 Adam Nemec).
Manager: Ján Kozák

Goals: Gareth Bale (10), Hal Robson-Kanu (81) / Ondrej Duda (61)

626.   16.06.2016   15th European Champs Group B
ENGLAND v WALES 2-1 (0-1)
Stade Bollaert-Delelis, Lens (France)
Referee: Dr. Felix Brych (Germany)   Attendance: 34,033
ENGLAND: Joe Hart, Kyle Walker, Danny Rose, Gary Cahill, Chris Smalling, Raheem Sterling (46 Daniel Sturridge), Adam Lallana (73 Marcus Rashford), Wayne Rooney, Eric Dier, Dele Alli, Harry Kane (46 Jamie Vardy).   Manager: Roy Hodgson
WALES: Wayne Hennessey, Chris Gunter, Neil Taylor, Ben Davies, James Chester, Ashley Williams, Joe Allen, Aaron Ramsey, Joe Ledley (67 Dave Edwards), Hal Robson-Kanu (72 Jonathan Williams), Gareth Bale.   Manager: Chris Coleman

Goals: Jamie Vardy (56), Daniel Sturridge (90+1) / Gareth Bale (42)

627. 20.06.2016   15th European Champs Group B
RUSSIA v WALES 0-3 (0-2)
Stade Municipal, Toulouse (France)
Referee: Jonas Eriksson (Sweden)   Attendance: 28,840
RUSSIA: Igor Akinfeev, Igor Smolnikov, Sergey Ignashevich, Vasiliy Berezutskiy (46 Aleksey Berezutskiy), Denis Glushakov, Pavel Mamaev, Roman Shirokov (52 Aleksandr Golovin), Dmitriy Kombarov, Aleksandr Kokorin, Fedor Smolov (70 Aleksandr Samedov), Artem Dzyuba.
Manager: Leonid Slutskiy
WALES: Wayne Hennessey, Chris Gunter, Neil Taylor, Ben Davies, James Chester, Ashley Williams, Joe Allen (74 Dave Edwards), Aaron Ramsey, Joe Ledley (76 Andy King), Gareth Bale (83 Simon Church), Sam Vokes.
Manager: Chris Coleman
Goals: Aaron Ramsey (11), Neil Taylor (20), Gareth Bale (67)

628. 25.06.2016   15th Euro Champs Round of 16
WALES v NORTHERN IRELAND 1-0 (0-0)
Parc des Princes, Paris (France)
Referee: Martin Atkinson (England)   Attendance: 44,342
WALES: Wayne Hennessey, Chris Gunter, Neil Taylor, Ben Davies, James Chester, Ashley Williams, Joe Allen, Aaron Ramsey, Joe Ledley (63 Jonathan Williams), Gareth Bale, Sam Vokes (55 Hal Robson-Kanu).   Manager: Chris Coleman
NORTHERN IRELAND: Michael McGovern, Gareth McAuley (84 Josh Magennis), Jonny Evans, Aaron Hughes, Craig Cathcart, Steven Davis, Corry Evans, Stuart Dallas, Oliver Norwood (79 Niall McGinn), Kyle Lafferty, Jamie Ward (69 Conor Washington).   Manager: Michael O'Neill
Goal: Gareth McAuley (75 og)

629. 01.07.2016   15th Euro Champs Quarter-finals
WALES v BELGIUM 3-1 (1-1)
Stade Pierre-Mauroy, Villeneuve d'Ascq (France)
Referee: Damir Skomina (Slovenia)   Attendance: 45,936
WALES: Wayne Hennessey, Chris Gunter, Neil Taylor, Ben Davies, James Chester, Ashley Williams, Joe Allen, Aaron Ramsey (90 James Collins), Joe Ledley (78 Andy King), Hal Robson-Kanu (80 Sam Vokes), Gareth Bale.
Manager: Chris Coleman
BELGIUM: Thibaut Courtois, Toby Alderweireld, Jason Denayer, Thomas Meunier, Jordan Lukaku (75 Dries Mertens), Radja Nainggolan, Axel Witsel, Kevin De Bruyne, Eden Hazard, Yannick Ferreira-Carrasco (46 Marouane Fellaini), Romelu Lukaku (83 Michy Batshuayi).
Manager: Marc Wilmots
Goals: Ashley Williams (30), Hal Robson-Kanu (55), Sam Vokes (85) / Radja Nainggolan (13)

630. 06.07.2016   15th Euro Champs Semi-finals
PORTUGAL v WALES 2-0 (0-0)
Parc Olympique Lyonnais, Décines-Charpieu (France)
Referee: Jonas Eriksson (Sweden)   Attendance: 55,679
PORTUGAL: RUI Pedro dos Santos PATRÍCIO, BRUNO Eduardo Regufe ALVES, JOSÉ Miguel da Rocha FONTE, RAPHAËL Adelino José GUERREIRO, CÉDRIC Ricardo Alves SOARES, JOÃO MÁRIO Naval da Costa Eduardo, DANILO Luís Hélio Pereira, RENATO Júnior Luz SANCHES (74 ANDRÉ Filipe Tavares GOMES), ADRIEN Sebastian Perruchet SILVA (79 JOÃO Filipe Iria Santos MOUTINHO), CRISTIANO RONALDO dos Santos Aveiro, Luís Carlos Almeida da Cunha "NANI" (86 RICARDO Andrade QUARESMA Bernardo).
Manager: FERNANDO Manuel Fernandes da Costa SANTOS
WALES: Wayne Hennessey, Chris Gunter, Neil Taylor, James Chester, Ashley Williams, James Collins (66 Jonathan Williams), Joe Allen, Andy King, Joe Ledley (58 Sam Vokes), Hal Robson-Kanu (63 Simon Church), Gareth Bale.
Manager: Chris Coleman
Goals: CRISTIANO RONALDO dos Santos Aveiro (50), Luís Carlos Almeida da Cunha "NANI" (53)

631. 05.09.2016   21st World Cup Qualifier
WALES v MOLDOVA 4-0 (2-0)
Cardiff City Stadium, Cardiff
Referee: Liran Liany (Israel)   Attendance: 31,731
WALES: Wayne Hennessey, Chris Gunter, Ben Davies, James Chester, Ashley Williams (82 James Collins), Neil Taylor, Joe Allen, Joe Ledley (67 Emyr Huws), Andy King, Gareth Bale, Sam Vokes (75 Hal Robson-Kanu).
Manager: Chris Coleman
MOLDOVA: Ilie Cebanu, Adrian Cascaval, Igor Armas, Ion Jardan, Alexandru Epureanu, Andrei Cojocari, Eugen Cebotaru (75 Eugeniu Sidorenco), Artur Ionita, Alexandru Gatcan, Radu Gînsari (75 Igor Bugaiov), Alexandru Dedov (85 Maxim Mihaliov).   Manager: Igor Dobrovolskiy
Goals: S. Vokes (38), J. Allen (44), Gareth Bale (50, 90+5 pen)

632. 06.10.2016   21st World Cup Qualifier
AUSTRIA v WALES 2-2 (1-2)
Ernst-Happel-Stadion, Wien
Referee: Cüneyt Çakir (Turkey)   Attendance: 44,200
AUSTRIA: Robert Almer (58 Ramazan Özcan), Martin Hinteregger, Aleksandar Dragovic, Kevin Wimmer, Florian Klein, Julian Baumgartlinger, Marko Arnautovic (87 Louis Schaub), David Alaba, Zlatko Junuzovic (79 Alessandro Schöpf), Marcel Sabitzer, Marc Janko.
Manager: Marcel Koller

WALES: Wayne Hennessey, James Chester, Ashley Williams, Neil Taylor (90+1 Emyr Huws), Chris Gunter, Ben Davies, Joe Allen (56 Dave Edwards), Joe Ledley, Andy King, Gareth Bale, Sam Vokes (77 Hal Robson-Kanu). Manager: Chris Coleman

Goals: Marko Arnautovic (28, 48) / Joe Allen (22), Kevin Wimmer (45+1 og)

633.   09.10.2016   21st World Cup Qualifier
WALES v GEORGIA 1-1 (1-0)
Cardiff City Stadium, Cardiff

Referee: Paolo Mazzoleni (Italy)   Attendance: 32,652

WALES: Wayne Hennessey, Ashley Williams, Neil Taylor (70 David Cotterill), Chris Gunter, Ben Davies, James Chester, Joe Ledley (73 Emyr Huws), Andy King (61 Hal Robson-Kanu), Dave Edwards, Sam Vokes, Gareth Bale. Manager: Chris Coleman

GEORGIA: Giorgi Loria, Solomon Kverkvelia, Guram Kashia, Otar Kakabadze, Giorgi Navalovski, Valeriane Gvilia, Murtaz Daushvili, Jano Ananidze (90+3 Nika Kacharava), Valeri Qazaishvili, Tornike Okriashvili (90+1 Jambul Jighauri), Levan Mchedlidze (75 Vladimer Dvalishvili). Manager: Vladimir Weiss

Goals: Gareth Bale (10) / Tornike Okriashvili (57)

634.   12.11.2016   21st World Cup Qualifier
WALES v SERBIA 1-1 (1-0)
Cardiff City Stadium, Cardiff

Referee: Alberto Undiano Mallenco (Spain)   Att: 32,879

WALES: Wayne Hennessey, Chris Gunter, James Chester, Ashley Williams, Neil Taylor, Aaron Ramsey, Joe Ledley (84 Dave Edwards), Joe Allen, Gareth Bale, Sam Vokes, Hal Robson-Kanu (68 Tom Lawrence). Manager: Chris Coleman

SERBIA: Vladimir Stojkovic, Matija Nastasic, Nikola Maksimovic, Branislav Ivanovic, Antonio Rukavina, Ivan Obradovic, Luka Milivojevic, Nemanja Matic, Filip Kostic (70 Aleksandar Katai), Aleksandar Mitrovic (88 Nemanja Gudelj), Dusan Tadic. Manager: Slavoljub Muslin

Goals: Gareth Bale (30) / Aleksandar Mitrovic (85)

635.   24.03.2017   21st World Cup Qualifier
REPUBLIC OF IRELAND v WALES 0-0
Aviva Stadium, Dublin

Referee: Nicola Rizzoli (Italy)   Attendance: 49,989

REPUBLIC OF IRELAND: Darren Randolph, Richard Keogh, Séamus Coleman (72 Cyrus Christie), Stephen Ward, John O'Shea, Jeff Hendrick, David Meyler (79 Aiden McGeady), Glenn Whelan, Shane Long, Jon Walters, James McClean.   Manager: Martin O'Neill

WALES: Wayne Hennessey, Chris Gunter, Ben Davies, James Chester, Ashley Williams, Neil Taylor, Joe Allen, Aaron Ramsey, Joe Ledley (72 Jazz Richards), Gareth Bale, Hal Robson-Kanu (46 Sam Vokes).   Manager: Chris Coleman

Sent off: Neil Taylor (69)

636.   11.06.2017   21st World Cup Qualifier
SERBIA v WALES 1-1 (0-1)
Stadion Rajko Mitic, Beograd

Referee: Manuel JORGE Neves Moreira de SOUSA (Portugal) Attendance: 46,673

SERBIA: Vladimir Stojkovic, Jagos Vukovic, Antonio Rukavina, Matija Nastasic, Aleksandar Kolarov, Branislav Ivanovic, Luka Milivojevic (63 Nemanja Gudelj), Nemanja Matic, Filip Kostic (67 Aleksandar Prijovic), Dusan Tadic, Aleksandar Mitrovic.   Manager: Slavoljub Muslin

WALES: Wayne Hennessey, Ashley Williams, Chris Gunter, Ben Davies, James Chester, Jazz Richards, Aaron Ramsey, Joe Ledley, Dave Edwards (73 Emyr Huws), Joe Allen, Sam Vokes (86 Tom Lawrence).   Manager: Chris Coleman

Goals: Aleksandar Mitrovic (74) / Aaron Ramsey (35 pen)

637.   02.09.2017   21st World Cup Qualifier
WALES v AUSTRIA 1-0 (0-0)
Cardiff City Stadium, Cardiff

Referee: Ovidiu Hategan (Romania)   Attendance: 32,633

WALES: Wayne Hennessey, Ashley Williams, Chris Gunter, Ben Davies, James Chester, Jazz Richards (46 Andy King), Aaron Ramsey, Dave Edwards, Sam Vokes (69 Hal Robson-Kanu), Tom Lawrence (69 Benjamin Woodburn), Gareth Bale. Manager: Chris Coleman

AUSTRIA: Heinz Lindner, Sebastian Prödl (27 Kevin Danso), Stefan Lainer, Martin Hinteregger, Aleksandar Dragovic, Marcel Sabitzer (78 Michael Gregoritsch), Stefan Ilsanker, Martin Harnik (81 Marc Janko), Julian Baumgartlinger, Marko Arnautovic, David Alaba.   Manager: Marcel Koller

Goal: Benjamin Woodburn (74)

115

638. 05.09.2017   21st World Cup Qualifier
MOLDOVA v WALES 0-2 (0-0)

Stadionul Zimbru, Chisinau

Referee: Pawel Raczkowski (Poland)   Attendance: 10,272

MOLDOVA: Ilie Cebanu, Artiom Razgoniuc, Veaceslav Posmac, Alexandru Epureanu, Vitali Bordian, Aleksandr Pascenco (70 Andrei Cojocari), Artur Ionita (85 Igor Bugaiov), Dinu Graur (85 Vladimir Ambros), Gheorghe Anton, Radu Gînsari, Alexandru Dedov.   Manager: Igor Dobrovolskiy

WALES: Wayne Hennessey, Ashley Williams, Chris Gunter, Ben Davies, James Chester, Aaron Ramsey, Andy King (67 Sam Vokes), Joe Allen, Hal Robson-Kanu (88 Dave Edwards), Tom Lawrence (61 Benjamin Woodburn), Gareth Bale.   Manager: Chris Coleman

Goals: Hal Robson-Kanu (80), Aaron Ramsey (90+3)

639. 06.10.2017   21st World Cup Qualifier
GEORGIA v WALES 0-1 (0-0)

Boris Paichadze, Tbilisi

Referee: Jesús Gil Manzano (Spain)   Attendance: 20,000

GEORGIA: Giorgi Loria, Solomon Kverkvelia, Nika Kvekveskiri (76 Jambul Jighauri), Guram Kashia, Otar Kakabadze, Giorgi Navalovski, Giorgi Merebashvili, Jaba Kankava, Valeriane Gvilia (89 Davit Khotcholava), Valeri Qazaishvili, Giorgi Kvilitaia (76 Davit Skhirtladze).   Manager: Vladimir Weiss

WALES: Wayne Hennessey, Ashley Williams, Chris Gunter, Ben Davies, James Chester, Aaron Ramsey, Joe Ledley (81 Dave Edwards), Andy King, Joe Allen, Sam Vokes (74 Hal Robson-Kanu), Tom Lawrence (90+1 Benjamin Woodburn).   Manager: Chris Coleman

Goal: Tom Lawrence (49)

640. 09.10.2017   21st World Cup Qualifier
WALES v REPUBLIC OF IRELAND 0-1 (0-0)

Cardiff City Stadium, Cardiff

Referee: Damir Skomina (Slovenia)   Attendance: 33,000

WALES: Wayne Hennessey, Ashley Williams, Chris Gunter, Ben Davies, James Chester, Aaron Ramsey, Joe Ledley, Andy King (65 Benjamin Woodburn), Joe Allen (37 Jonathan Williams), Hal Robson-Kanu (71 Sam Vokes), Tom Lawrence.   Manager: Chris Coleman

REPUBLIC OF IRELAND: Darren Randolph, Stephen Ward, Shane Duffy, Ciaran Clark, Cyrus Christie, David Meyler, Jeff Hendrick, Robbie Brady, Harry Arter (78 Glenn Whelan), Daryl Murphy (90+2 Kevin Long), James McClean.   Manager: Martin O'Neill

Goal: James McClean (57)

641: 10.11.2017
FRANCE v WALES 2-0 (1-0)

Stade de France, Paris – St. Denis

Referee: Jorge Moreira de Sousa (Portugal)   Attendance: 50,000

FRANCE: Steve Mandanda, Samuel Umtiti, Layvin Kurzawa, Laurent Koscielny, Christophe Jallet (46 Benjamin Pavard), Corentin Tolisso (46 Steven N'Zonzi), Blaise Matuidi, Kingsley Coman (73 Anthony Martial), Kylian Mbappé (84 Florian Thauvin), Antoine Griezmann (63 Nabil Fekir), Olivier Giroud (73 Alexandre Lacazette).   Manager: Didier Deschamps

WALES: Wayne Hennessey, Neil Taylor, Chris Gunter, Ben Davies (63 Benjamin Woodburn), James Chester, Ashley Williams, Aaron Ramsey, Joe Ledley (64 Ethan Ampadu), Andy King (64 David Brooks), Joe Allen, Sam Vokes (83 Tom Lawrence).   Manager: Chris Coleman

Goals: Antoine Griezmann (19), Olivier Giroud (71)

642. 14.11.2017
WALES v PANAMA 1-1 (0-0)

Cardiff City Stadium, Cardiff

Referee: Bart Vertenten (Belgium)   Attendance: 13,747

WALES: Danny Ward, Neil Taylor, Chris Gunter, Ben Davies (46 Tom Lockyer), James Chester, Dave Edwards (62 Lee Evans), Ethan Ampadu (67 Andrew Crofts), Benjamin Woodburn (71 Ryan Hedges), Sam Vokes (46 Tom Bradshaw), Tom Lawrence, David Brooks (71 Marley Watkins).   Manager: Chris Coleman

PANAMA: JAIME Manuel PENEDO Cano, MICHAEL Amir MURILLO Bermúdez, FIDEL ESCOBAR Mendieta, FELIPE Abdiel BALOY Ramírez, MANUEL Alexander VARGAS Moreno (71 RICARDO Enrique BUITRAGO Medina), LUIS Carlos OVALLE Victoria, LESLIE HERÁLDEZ Sevillano (76 JOSÉ Del Carmen GONZÁLEZ Joly), ARMANDO Enrique COOPER, RICARDO Guardia ÁVILA (67 JEAN Carlos VARGAS Campo), GABRIEL Arturo TORRES Tejada (64 ISMAEL DÍAZ de León), BLAS Antonio Miguel PÉREZ Ortega (87 ALFREDO Horacio STEPHENS Francis).   Manager: HERNÁN Darío GÓMEZ Jaramillo

Goals: Tom Lawrence (75) /
ARMANDO Enrique COOPER (90+3)

Sam Vokes missed a penalty kick in the 42nd minute.

643. 22.03.2018   China Cup
CHINA v WALES 0-6 (0-4)
Guangxi Sports Center Stadium, Nanning
Referee: Mohd Amirul Izwan Bin Yaacob (Malaysia)
Attendance: 36,533
CHINA: Yan Junling, Feng Xiaoting (71 Deng Hanwen), Zheng Zheng, Wang Shenchao (46 Li Xuepeng), He Guan (46 Liu Yiming), Huang Bowen (46 He Chao), Hao Junmin, Yu Dabao (46 Zhao Xuri), Gao Lin (46 Yu Hanchao), Wu Lei, Wei Shihao. Manager: Marcello Lippi

WALES: Wayne Hennessey, Chris Gunter, Ashley Williams, James Chester (71 Tom Lockyer), Declan John, Ben Davies (70 Chris Mepham), Joe Allen (63 Lee Evans), Andy King, Gareth Bale (63 Benjamin Woodburn), Sam Vokes (63 Tom Bradshaw), Harry Wilson (71 Marley Watkins). Manager: Ryan Giggs

Goals: Gareth Bale (2, 21, 62), Sam Vokes (38, 58), Harry Wilson (45)

644. 26.03.2018   China Cup Final
URUGUAY v WALES 1-0 (0-0)
Guangxi Sports Center Stadium, Nanning
Referee: Salman Ahmad Falahi (Qatar)   Attendance: 41,016
URUGUAY: Néstor FERNANDO MUSLERA Micol, DIEGO Roberto GODÍN Leal, GUILLERMO VARELA Olivera, JOSÉ MARÍA GIMÉNEZ de Vargas (7 SEBASTIÁN COATES Nión), CRISTIAN Gabriel RODRÍGUEZ Barrotti (69 LUCAS TORREIRA Di Pascua), MATÍAS VECINO Falero, DIEGO Sebastián LAXALT Suárez, NAHITAN Michel NÁNDEZ Acosta (84 CRISTHIAN Ricardo STUANI Curbelo), RODRIGO BENTANCUR Colmán (77 GASTÓN Alexis SILVA Perdomo), LUIS Alberto SUÁREZ Díaz, EDINSON Roberto CAVANI Gómez (90+2 MAXIMILIANO GÓMEZ González).
Manager: ÓSCAR Washington TABÁREZ Silva

WALES: Wayne Hennessey, Chris Gunter (79 Adam Matthews), James Chester (75 Tom Lockyer), Ashley Williams, Ben Davies (90 Ryan Hedges), Andy King, Joe Allen, Sam Vokes (67 Billy Bodin), Gareth Bale, Declan John (59 Connor Roberts), Harry Wilson (72 Lee Evans).
Manager: Ryan Giggs

Goal: EDINSON Roberto CAVANI Gómez (48)

645. 28.05.2018
MEXICO v WALES 0-0
Rose Bowl, Pasadena (USA)
Referee: Armando Villareal (USA)   Attendance: 82,345
MEXICO: JOSÉ de Jesús CORONA Rodríguez, HUGO AYALA Castro, OSWALDO ALANÍS Pantoja (46 CARLOS Joel SALCEDO Hernández), EDSON Omar ÁLVAREZ Velázquez, JESÚS Antonio MOLINA Granados (46' JÜRGEN DAMM Rascón), JAVIER Ignacio AQUINO Carmona, HÉCTOR Miguel HERRERA López (61 JONATHAN DOS SANTOS Ramírez), ÉRICK Gabriel GUTIÉRREZ Galaviz (74 MARCO Jhonfai FABIÁN De La Mora), JESÚS Daniel GALLARDO Vasconcelos, JAVIER HERNÁNDEZ Balcázar (59 ORIBE PERALTA Morones), JESÚS Manuel CORONA Ruíz (69 GIOVANI DOS SANTOS Ramírez).
Manager: JUAN Carlos OSORIO Arbeláez

WALES: Wayne Hennessey, Chris Gunter (46 Connor Roberts), Ashley Williams (21 Tom Lockyer), Ben Davies, Chris Mepham, Andy King, Joe Ledley (46 Declan John), Aaron Ramsey, Tom Lawrence (81 Matthew Smith), Harry Wilson (64 Georges Thomas), Sam Vokes (46 David Brooks).
Manager: Ryan Giggs

646. 06.09.2018   UEFA Nations League Group B4
WALES v REPUBLIC OF IRELAND 4-1 (3-0)
Cardiff City Stadium, Cardiff
Referee: Clément Turpin (France)   Attendance: 25,657
WALES: Wayne Hennessey, Ashley Williams, Ben Davies (81 Paul Dummett), Ethan Ampadu (67 Matthew Smith), Chris Mepham, Joe Allen, Aaron Ramsey, Tom Lawrence, David Brooks, Connor Roberts, Gareth Bale (75 Tyler Roberts). Manager: Ryan Giggs

REPUBLIC OF IRELAND: Darren Randolph, Séamus Coleman, Stephen Ward (61 Enda Stevens), Ciaran Clark, Shane Duffy, Cyrus Christie, Conor Hourihane (57 Shaun Williams), Jeff Hendrick, Callum O'Dowda, Jon Walters, Callum Robinson (77 Daryl Horgan).
Manager: Martin O'Neill

Goals: Tom Lawrence (6), Gareth Bale (18), A. Ramsey (37), Connor Roberts (55) / Shaun Williams (66)

647. 09.09.2018   UEFA Nations League Group B4
DENMARK v WALES 2-0 (1-0)
Ceres Park & Arena, Aarhus
Referee: Deniz Aytekin (Germany)   Attendance: 17,506
DENMARK: Kasper Schmeichel, Simon Kjær, Mathias Jørgensen, Henrik Dalsgaard, Jens Stryger Larsen, Lasse Schøne, Thomas Delany, Christian Eriksen, Martin Braithwaite, Yussuf Poulsen (86 Andreas Cornelius), Pione Sisto (46 Viktor Fischer).   Manager: Åge Hareide
WALES: Wayne Hennessey, Chris Gunter, James Chester, Ben Davies, Ethan Ampadu (72 Tyler Roberts), Chris Mepham, Joe Allen, Aaron Ramsey, Tom Lawrence (79 Ben Woodburn), Connor Roberts (59 David Brooks), Gareth Bale. Manager: Ryan Giggs
Goals: Christian Eriksen (32, 63 pen)

648. 11.10.2018
WALES v SPAIN 1-4 (0-3)
Principality Stadium, Cardiff
Referee: Anthony Taylor (England)   Attendance: 50,232
WALES: Wayne Hennessey, Ben Davies (62 Jazz Richards), Ashley Williams (46 James Chester), Declan John (62 Tom Lawrence), Ethan Ampadu (50 Andy King), Joe Allen (62 Matthew Smith), Aaron Ramsey, Harry Wilson (46 David Brooks), Connor Roberts, Sam Vokes, Chris Gunter. Manager: Ryan Giggs
SPAIN: David DE GEA Quintana (46 KEPA Arrizabalaga Revuelta), SERGIO RAMOS García (46 MARC BARTRA Aregall), RAÚL ALBIOL Tortajada, CÉSAR AZPILICUETA Tanco (63 Jonathan "JONNY" CASTRO Otto), SAÚL Ñíguez Esclapez (46 Jorge Resurrección Merodio "KOKE"), Daniel "DANI" CEBALLOS Fernández, JOSÉ Luis GAYÁ Peña, Rodrigo "RODRI" HERNÁNDEZ Cascante, ÁLVARO Borja MORATA Martín, Francisco "PACO" ALCÁCER García (73 IAGO ASPAS Juncal), Jesús Joaquín Fernández Sáez de la Torre "SUSO" (81 RODRIGO Moreno Machado). Manager: LUIS ENRIQUE Martínez García
Goals: Sam Vokes (89) / "PACO" ALCÁCER García (8, 29), SERGIO RAMOS García (19), MARC BARTRA Aregall (74)

649. 16.10.2018   UEFA Nations League Group B4
REPUBLIC OF IRELAND v WALES 0-1 (0-0)
Aviva Stadium, Dublin
Referee: Björn Kuipers (Netherlands)   Attendance: 38,321
REPUBLIC OF IRELAND: Darren Randolph, Richard Keogh, Kevin Long (75 Scott Hogan), Shane Duffy, Cyrus Christie, Matt Doherty, Harry Arter, James McClean, Jeff Hendrick, Aiden O'Brien (56 Shane Long), Callum Robinson (60 Seán Maguire).   Manager: Martin O'Neill

WALES: Wayne Hennessey, Ashley Williams, James Chester, Ben Davies, Joe Allen, Tom Lawrence, Harry Wilson (85 Chris Gunter), Matthew Smith (75 George Thomas), Connor Roberts, Tyler Roberts, David Brooks (87 Andy King). Manager: Ryan Giggs
Goal: Harry Wilson (58)

650. 16.11.2018   UEFA Nations League Group B4
WALES v DENMARK 1-2 (0-1)
Cardiff City Stadium, Cardiff
Referee: Ivan Kruzliak (Slovakia)   Attendance: 32,354
WALES: Wayne Hennessey, Paul Dummett (39 Chris Gunter), Joe Allen, Ashley Williams, James Chester (50 Ethan Ampadu), Aaron Ramsey, Gareth Bale, Connor Roberts, Tom Lawrence, David Brooks, Tyler Roberts (68 Harry Wilson). Manager: Ryan Giggs
DENMARK: Kasper Schmeichel, Mathias Jørgensen, Henrik Dalsgaard, Jens Stryger Larsen, Andreas Christensen, Lasse Schøne (79 Lukas Lerager), Thomas Delany, Nicolai Jørgensen (70 Kasper Dolberg), Christian Eriksen, Martin Braithwaite, Yussuf Poulsen.   Manager: Åge Hareide
Goals: Gareth Bale (89) /
Nicolai Jørgensen (42), Martin Braithwaite (88)

651. 20.11.2018
ALBANIA v WALES 1-0 (0-0)
Elbasan Arena, Albasan
Referee: Dejan Jakimovski (Macedonia)   Attendance: 3,000
ALBANIA: Etrit Berisha, Mërgim Mavraj, Freddie Veseli, Elseid Hysaj, Ardian Ismajli, Andi Lila (59 Ledian Menushaj), Migjen Basha, Taulant Xhaka, Eros Grezda (69 Sabien Lilaj), Bekim Balaj, Myrto Uzuni.   Manager: Christian Panucci
WALES: Danny Ward, Chris Gunter, James Lawrence, Tom Lockyer, Andy King, Joe Allen (56 Aaron Ramsey), Daniel James (56 Ben Woodburn), Harry Wilson, David Brooks (59 Gareth Bale), Connor Roberts (78 Kieron Freeman), Sam Vokes (78 Rabbi Matondo).   Manager: Ryan Giggs
Goal: Bekim Balaj (58 pen)

652. 20.03.2019
WALES v TRINIDAD & TOBAGO 1-0 (0-0)
The Racecourse, Wrexham
Referee: Tim Marshall (Northern Ireland)   Attendance: 10,326

WALES: Danny Ward (46 Adam Davies), Chris Gunter, Neil Taylor, Ashley Williams (61 James Lawrence), Paul Dummett (61 Declan John), Will Vaulks, Lee Evans, Ben Woodburn, Ryan Hedges, George Thomas, Tyler Roberts (71 Rabbi Matondo).   Manager: Ryan Giggs

TRINIDAD & TOBAGO: Marvin Phillip, Aubrey David, Sheldon Bateau, Daneil Cyrus, Triston Hodge, Kevan George, Leston Paul (80 Neveal Hackshaw), Khaleem Hyland, Nathan Lewis, Levi Garcia (60 Lester Peltier), Willis Plaza (46 Cordell Cato).   Manager: Dennis Lawrence

Goal: Ben Woodburn (90+2)

653. 24.03.2019   16th European Champs Qualifiers
WALES v SLOVAKIA 1-0 (1-0)
Cardiff City Stadium, Cardiff
Referee: Felix Zwayer (Germany)   Attendance: 31,617

WALES: Wayne Hennessey, Chris Mepham, Ben Davies, James Lawrence, Harry Wilson (87 Will Vaulks), Joe Allen, Daniel James (72 Ashley Williams), David Brooks (60 Tyler Roberts), Connor Roberts, Matthew Smith, Gareth Bale.   Manager: Ryan Giggs

SLOVAKIA: Martin Dúbravka, Peter Pekarík (90 Pavol Safranko), Milan Skriniar, Denis Vavro, Dávid Hancko, Marek Hamsík, Juraj Kucka, Albert Rusnák, Róbert Mak (69 Miroslav Stoch), Stanislav Lobotka, Ondrej Duda (65 Michal Duris).   Manager: Pavel Hapal

Goal: Daniel James (5)

654. 08.06.2019   16th European Champs Qualifiers
CROATIA v WALES 2-1 (1-0)
Stadion Gradski Vrt, Osijek
Referee: Istvan Kovacs (Romania)   Attendance: 17,061

CROATIA: Dominik Livakovic, Domagoj Vida, Dejan Lovren, Tin Jedvaj, Marcelo Brozovic, Borna Barisic, Luka Modric, Ivan Perisic (90+3 Mile Skoric), Mateo Kovacic (76 Milan Badelj), Josip Brekalo (67 Mario Pasalic), Andrej Kramaric.   Manager: Zlatko Dalic

WALES: Wayne Hennessey, Ben Davies, James Lawrence, Chris Mepham, Harry Wilson, Joe Allen, Will Vaulks (66 Ethan Ampadu), Daniel James (79 Rabbi Matondo), Matthew Smith (65 David Brooks), Connor Roberts, Gareth Bale.   Manager: Ryan Giggs

Goals: James Lawrence (17 og), Ivan Perisic (48) / David Brooks (77)

655. 11.06.2019   16th European Champs Qualifiers
HUNGARY v WALES 1-0 (0-0)
Groupama Aréna, Budapest
Referee: Matej Jug (Slovenia)   Attendance: 18,350

HUNGARY: Péter Gulácsi, Mihály Korhut, Botond Baráth, Willi Orbán, Máté Pátkai, Balász Dzsudzsák (70 László Kleinheisler), Filip Holender (59 Roland Varga), Ádám Nagy, Dominik Szoboszlai (83 Barnabás Bese), Ádám Szalai, Gergö Lovrencsics.   Manager: Marco Rossi

WALES: Wayne Hennessey, Chris Gunter, Ashley Williams, Ben Davies, James Lawrence, Ethan Ampadu (54 Matthew Smith), Joe Allen, Tom Lawrence (79 Sam Vokes), David Brooks (73 Harry Wilson), Gareth Bale, Daniel James.   Manager: Ryan Giggs

Goal: Máté Pátkai (80)

656. 06.09.2019   16th European Champs Qualifiers
WALES v AZERBAIJAN 2-1 (1-0)
Cardiff City Stadium, Cardiff
Referee: Trustin Farrufia Cann (Malta)   Attendance: 28,385

WALES: Wayne Hennessey, Neil Taylor (80 Ben Davies), Joe Rodon, Ethan Ampadu (75 Sam Vokes), Chris Mepham, Joe Allen, Tom Lawrence, Daniel James, Harry Wilson (63 Jonathan Williams), Connor Roberts, Gareth Bale.   Manager: Ryan Giggs

AZERBAIJAN: Salahat Agayev, Pavel Pasayev, Maksim Medvedev, Qara Qarayev, Bahlul Mustafazade, Anton Krivotsyuk, Shahriyar Rahimov (73 Tamkin Khalilzade), Richard ALMEYDA de Oliveira (69 Rashad Eyyubov), Dima Nazarov (86 Agabala Ramazanov), Ramil Seydayev, Mahir Emreli.   Manager: Nikola Jurcevic

Goals: Pavel Pasayev (26 og), Gareth Bale (84) / Mahir Emreli (59)

657. 09.09.2019
WALES v BELARUS 1-0 (1-0)
Cardiff City Stadium, Cardiff
Referee: William Collum (Scotland)   Attendance: 7,666

WALES: Danny Ward, Ben Davies (90+1 Chris Gunter), Joe Rodon, Chris Mepham (77 Tom Lockyer), Joe Allen, Jonathan Williams, Daniel James (50 Gareth Bale), Joe Morrell, Harry Wilson (89 Will Vaulks), Connor Roberts, Kieffer Moore (75 Sam Vokes).   Manager: Ryan Giggs

BELARUS: Maksim Plotnikov, Sergey Politevich, Denis Polyakov, Dmitri Baga (71 Stanislau Dragun), Yuri Kovalev (46 Max Ebong Ngome), Evgeni Yablonskiy (46 Ivan Maevski), Ivan Bakhar (84 Vladislav Klimovich), Maksim Skavysh (76 Kirill Pechenin), Nikolay Signevich (70 Igor Stasevich), Nikolay Zolotov, Zakhar Volkov.
Managers: Igor Kriushenko & Mikhail Markhel

Goal: Daniel James (17)

658. 10.10.2019   16th European Champs Qualifiers
SLOVAKIA v WALES 1-1 (0-1)
Stadión Antona Malatinského, Trnava
Referee: Carlos del Cerro Grande (Spain)
Attendance: 18,071
SLOVAKIA: Martin Dúbravka, Peter Pekarík, Norbert Gyömbér, Milan Skriniar, Dávid Hancko, Marek Hamsík, Juraj Kucka, Róbert Mak (79 Lukás Haraslín), Albert Rusnák, Stanislav Lobotka, Róbert Bozeník (86 Pavol Safranko). Manager: Pavel Hapal
WALES: Wayne Hennessey, Ben Davies, Tom Lockyer, Joe Rodon, Ethan Ampadu (58 Joe Morrell), Joe Allen, Jonathan Williams (66 Harry Wilson), Daniel James, Connor Roberts, Gareth Bale, Kieffer Moore.   Manager: Ryan Giggs
Goals: Juraj Kucka (53) / Kieffer Moore (25)
Sent off: Norbert Gyömbér (88)

659. 13.10.2019   16th European Champs Qualifiers
WALES v CROATIA 1-1 (1-1)
Cardiff City Stadium, Cardiff
Referee: Björn Kuipers (Netherlands)   Attendance: 31,745
WALES: Wayne Hennessey, Ben Davies, Tom Lockyer, Joe Rodon, Ethan Ampadu (50 Joe Morrell), Joe Allen, Jonathan Williams (68 Harry Wilson), Daniel James, Connor Roberts, Gareth Bale, Kieffer Moore (86 Tyler Roberts).   Manager: Ryan Giggs
CROATIA: Dominik Livakovic, Domagoj Vida, Dejan Lovren, Tin Jedvaj, Ivan Perisic, Borna Barisic, Luka Modric (90 Milan Badelj), Mateo Kovacic (46 Ivan Rakitic), Nikola Vlasic, Josip Brekalo, Bruno Petkovic (64 Ante Rebic).   Manager: Zlatko Dalic
Goals: Gareth Bale (45+3) / Nikola Vlasic (9)

660. 16.11.2019   16th European Champs Qualifiers
AZERBAIJAN v WALES 0-2 (0-2)
Bakcell Arena, Baku
Referee: Deniz Aytekin (Germany)   Attendance: 8,622
AZERBAIJAN: Emil Balayev, Pavel Pasayev, Qara Qarayev, Badavi Hüseynov, Bahlul Mustafazade, Anton Krivotsyuk (46 Tamkin Khalilzade), Shahriyar Rahimov, Araz Abdullayev (64 Agabala Ramazanov), Dima Nazarov (82 Cavid Hüseynov), Ramil Seydayev, Richard ALMEYDA de Oliveira. Manager: Nikola Jurcevic
WALES: Wayne Hennessey, Ben Davies, Tom Lockyer, Ethan Ampadu (88 Will Vaulks), Chris Mepham, Daniel James (82 Rabbi Matondo), Joe Morrell, Harry Wilson, Connor Roberts, Gareth Bale (60 Aaron Ramsey), Kieffer Moore.   Manager: Ryan Giggs
Goals: Kieffer Moore (10), Harry Wilson (34)

661. 19.11.2019   16th European Champs Qualifiers
WALES v HUNGARY 2-0 (1-0)
Cardiff City Stadium, Cardiff
Referee: Ovidiu Hategan (Romania)   Attendance: 31,762
WALES: Wayne Hennessey, Ben Davies, Tom Lockyer, Chris Mepham, Joe Allen, Aaron Ramsey, Daniel James, Joe Morrell (50 Ethan Ampadu), Connor Roberts, Gareth Bale (88 Harry Wilson), Kieffer Moore.   Manager: Ryan Giggs
HUNGARY: Péter Gulácsi, Botond Baráth, Ádám Lang, Zsolt Nagy, Máté Pátkai, Gergö Lovrencsics, Ádám Nagy (60 István Kovács), Dominik Szoboszlai, Balász Dzsudzsák (72 Roland Varga), Ádám Szalai, Roland Sallai (83 Filip Holender).   Manager: Marco Rossi
Goals: Aaron Ramsey (15, 47)

662. 03.09.2020   UEFA Nations League – Group B4
FINLAND v WALES 0-1 (0-0)
Helsingin Olympiastadion, Helsinki
Referee: Daniel Siebert (Germany)   Attendance: 0
FINLAND: Lukás Hradecký, Juhani Ojala, Jere Uronen, Daniel O'Shaughnessy, Leo Väisänen, Tim Sparv (76 Thomas Lam), Joni Kauko (71 Fredrik Jensen), Glen Kamara, Ilmari Niskanen (86 Pyry Soiri), Teemu Pukki, Joel Pohjanpalo. Manager: Markku Kanerva
WALES: Wayne Hennessey, Ben Davies, Tom Lockyer, Connor Roberts, Ethan Ampadu, Jonathan Williams (60 Neco Williams), Daniel James (90+2 Ben Cabango), Dylan Levitt, Gareth Bale (46 Harry Wilson), Kieffer Moore, Joe Morrell. Manager: Ryan Giggs
Goal: Kieffer Moore (80)

663. 06.09.2020   UEFA Nations League – Group B4
WALES v BULGARIA 1-0 (0-0)
Cardiff City Stadium, Cardiff
Referee: Fábio José Costa Veríssimo (Portugal)
Attendance: 0
WALES: Wayne Hennessey, Ben Davies, Tom Lockyer, Connor Roberts (65 Neco Williams), Ethan Ampadu, Daniel James, Joe Morrell, David Brooks (76 Jonathan Williams), Matthew Smith, Gareth Bale, Kieffer Moore (61 Hal Robson-Kanu).   Manager: Ryan Giggs
BULGARIA: Georgi Georgiev, Cicinho, Ivan Goranov, Anton Nedyalkov, Kristian Dimitrov, Galin Ivanov (70 Spas Delev), Georgi Kostadinov, Todor Nedelev (82 Filip Krastev), Yanis Karabelyov, Bozhidar Kraev (61 Dimitar Iliev), Bircent Karagaren.   Manager: Georgi Dermendzhiev
Goal: Neco Williams (90+4)

664. 08.10.2020
ENGLAND v WALES 3-0 (1-0)
Wembley Stadium, London
Referee: Robert Madden (Scotland)   Attendance: 0

ENGLAND: Nick Pope, Kieran Trippier (58 Reece James), Conor Coady, Michael Keane, Joe Gomez (58 Tyrone Mings), Jack Grealish (76 Harvey Barnes), Harry Winks (75 James Ward-Prowse), Bukayo Saka (76 Ainsley Maitland-Niles), Danny Ings, Dominic Calvert-Lewin (58 Mason Mount), Kalvin Phillips.   Manager: Gareth Southgate

WALES: Wayne Hennessey, Connor Roberts (73 Chris Gunter), Ben Davies, Joe Rodon (46 Ben Cabango), Ethan Ampadu (62 Will Vaulks), Chris Mepham, Joe Morrell (46 Dylan Levitt), Kieffer Moore (40 Neco Williams), Tyler Roberts, Rabbi Matondo, Jonathan Williams (73 Matthew Smith).   Manager: Ryan Giggs

Goals: Dominic Calvert-Lewin (26), Conor Coady (53), Danny Ings (63)

665.   11.10.2020   UEFA Nations League – Group B4
REPUBLIC OF IRELAND v WALES 0-0
Aviva Stadium, Dublin
Referee: Anasthasios Sidiropoulos (Greece)   Attendance: 0

REPUBLIC OF IRELAND: Darren Randolph, Enda Stevens, Kevin Long (25 Cyrus Christie), Shane Duffy, Matt Doherty, Conor Hourihane, James McClean, Robbie Brady (73 Daryl Horgan), Jeff Hendrick, Jayson Molumby (89 Josh Cullen), Shane Long (74 Seán Maguire).   Manager: Stephen Kenny

WALES: Wayne Hennessey, Ben Davies, Connor Roberts, Joe Rodon, Ethan Ampadu, Aaron Ramsey, Daniel James (77 David Brooks), Joe Morrell, Harry Wilson (67 Neco Williams), Matthew Smith (67 Dylan Levitt), Kieffer Moore. Manager: Ryan Giggs

Sent off: James McClean (84)

666.   14.10.2020   UEFA Nations League – Group B4
BULGARIA v WALES 0-1 (0-0)
National Stadium Vasil Levski, Sofia
Referee: Aliyar Agayev (Azerbaijan)   Attendance: 500

BULGARIA: Nikolay Mihaylov, Cicinho, Georgi Terziev, Anton Nedyalkov, Kristian Dimitrov, Kristiyan Malinov (46 Aleksandar Tsvetkov), Todor Nedelev, Yanis Karabelyov, Bozhidar Kraev (75 Ismail Isa), Georgi Yomov, Kiril Despodov (84 Bircent Karagaren).   Manager: Georgi Dermendzhiev

WALES: Wayne Hennessey (79 Adam Davies), Ben Davies, Joe Rodon, Ethan Ampadu, Neco Williams, Chris Mepham, Rhys Norrington-Davies, Daniel James (54 Rabbi Matondo), Matthew Smith (72 Dylan Levitt), Tyler Roberts, Harry Wilson (72 Jonathan Williams).   Manager: Ryan Giggs

Goal: Jonathan Williams (85)

667.   12.11.2020
WALES v UNITED STATES 0-0
Liberty Stadium, Swansea
Referee: Nicholas Walsh (Scotland)   Attendance: 0

WALES: Danny Ward, Chris Gunter, James Lawrence (69 Joe Rodon), Tom Lockyer, Connor Roberts, Tom Lawrence, Harry Wilson, Matthew Smith (46 Josh Sheehan), Kieffer Moore (62 Brennan Johnson), Rabbi Matondo (62 Daniel James), Dylan Levitt (80 Joe Morrell).   Manager: Ryan Giggs

UNITED STATES: Zack Steffen, Antonee Robinson, Matt Miazga, Sergiño Gianni Dest (87 Reggie Jacob Cannon), John Anthony Brooks, Giovanni Alejandro Reyna (79 Timothy Weah), Yunus Dimoara Musah (80 Nicholas Gioacchini), Weston McKennie, Sebastian Lletget (87 Ebeguowen Otasowie), Tyler Adams (71 João "Johnny" Lucas de Souza Cardoso), Konrad de la Fuente (71 Ulysses Llanez). Manager: Gregg Berhalter

668.   15.11.2020   UEFA Nations League – Group B4
WALES v REPUBLIC OF IRELAND 1-0 (0-0)
Cardiff City Stadium, Cardiff
Referee: Petr Ardeleánu (Czech Republic)   Attendance: 0

WALES: Danny Ward, Ben Davies, Joe Rodon, Ethan Ampadu, Neco Williams, Chris Mepham, Rhys Norrington-Davies (62 Kieffer Moore), Daniel James, Joe Morrell, David Brooks (88 Tyler Roberts), Gareth Bale.   Manager: R. Giggs

REPUBLIC OF IRELAND: Darren Randolph, Kevin Long, Shane Duffy, Matt Doherty, Dara O'Shea (81 Callum O'Dowda), James McClean, Daryl Horgan (59 Jason Knight), Robbie Brady (82 Jack Byrne), Jeff Hendrick, Jayson Molumby (76 Conor Hourihane), Adam Idah (76 James Collins).   Manager: Stephen Kenny

Goal: David Brooks (67)

Sent off: Jeff Hendrick (90+4)

669.   18.11.2020   UEFA Nations League – Group B4
WALES v FINLAND 3-1 (1-0)
Cardiff City Stadium, Cardiff
Referee: Jesús Gil Manzano (Spain)   Attendance: 0

WALES: Danny Ward, James Lawrence (46 Kieffer Moore), Connor Roberts, Joe Rodon, Ethan Ampadu, Chris Mepham, Rhys Norrington-Davies (90+3 Chris Gunter), Joe Morrell, Harry Wilson (89 Tyler Roberts), Gareth Bale (61 Tom Lawrence), Daniel James (89 David Brooks). Manager: Ryan Giggs

FINLAND: Lukás Hradecký, Paulus Arajuuri, Joona Toivio, Nikolai Alho, Jere Uronen, Daniel O'Shaughnessy (61 Niko Hämäläinen), Robert Taylor (61 Pyry Soiri), Robin Lod, Glen Kamara, Rasmus Schüller (73 Onni Valakari), Teemu Pukki (89 Marcus Forss).   Manager: Markku Kanerva

Goals: Harry Wilson (29), Daniel James (46), K. Moore (84) / Teemu Pukki (63)

Sent off: Jere Uronen (12)